Learn more about Fonthill Media. Join our mailing list to
find out about our latest titles and special offers at:
www.fonthillmedia.com

Fonthill Media Limited
Fonthill Media LLC
www.fonthillmedia.com
office@fonthillmedia.com

First published in the United Kingdom 2014

British Library Cataloguing in Publication Data:
A catalogue record for this book is available from the British Library

ISBN 978-1-78155-356-5

Printed and bound by CPI Group (UK) Ltd, Croydon, CR0 4YY

Contents

Introduction

My father was a carpenter from the East End of London, and in 1939, aged twenty, was conscripted into the military, being instructed to attend training at Peninsula Barracks, Winchester, where he became a rifleman of the prestigious Rifle Brigade (Prince Consort's Own).

Dad – Walter Frederick William Harding – did not talk much about the war; most of those who lived through those times didn't. However, when questioned he did say that he was involved in the Battle of Kidney Ridge and that he had served in Egypt and Italy. Before his death in 2001, I contacted Colonel I. H. McCausland of the Regimental Museum Archive who was kind enough to give me an idea of the activities of the 2nd Battalion during the war, against which I was able to match Dad's war record.

Later, and unfortunately after my father's death, I was invited to attend the passing of Sergeant Swann's medals into the care of the Rifle Brigade Museum at Winchester. To my surprise, I met Mrs Ann Bayley who had been stationed in Egypt during the North African campaign and whose brother had been my father's officer during 1942. After inviting me to her home, Ann kindly lent me her photos of that period, and contained within these was the picture of the officers of the 2nd Battalion Rifle Brigade taken on 17 March 1942, as well as a letter written by my father.

Lieutenant General Sir Christopher Wallace and Major Ron Cassidy of the Green Jackets Museum and Rifle Brigade Association had assisted me greatly in researching Dad's life in the war, so I decided to research and document the 2nd Battalion's story from the date of the picture to the end of the North African campaign – 422 days in all.

This has been an exercise in finding, collating and documenting information from a variety of sources, including books written by those with far more experience in this topic. I am not a history professional and do not rank myself among those who are. However, with the assistance of people like Ann Bayley, Eddie Blacker, Ken Gray, Vic Gregg, Ian Patterson and Christine Pullen as well as Christopher Wallace and Ron Cassidy, I have been able to produce a manuscript that details the lives of the men shown in the picture, as well as the men they commanded.

I have endeavoured to tell their story from a personal perspective, set within the bigger picture of the war, attempting therefore to show the cause and effect of the needs of Prime Minister Churchill and how this affected the riflemen in the desert, recording the activities of those in the picture both whilst actually fighting and when they were involved in the big chess game played out on a board that was the North African desert. As Diane Lees, Director-General of the Imperial War Museum has said: 'Witnesses from those times are now rare and it is left to us to preserve their memories, their experiences.'

All in all, this book is about and for those officers and men who took part in that campaign. I unashamedly copy the words of Sir William Cope in his book *The History of the Rifle Brigade*

(Formerly the 95th) written in 1877 and found in the Rifle Brigade Journal of 2008, and hope in some way to have replicated this sentiment:

> I write for Riflemen, at the desire of Riflemen and to preserve the memory of the deeds of Riflemen […] Nothing will be considered trivial, nothing out of place in a history of the Regiment which records the valour, the acts, the sufferings or preserves an anecdote of any (of whatever rank) of the members of that brotherhood.

Lastly, I again thank Ann Bayley, as without her trust in letting me borrow her photos, this project would not have been possible, added to the fact that it was her brother who, by saving my father's life at supreme cost to himself, enabled me to be in this position.

Dad was proud of being a rifleman, and I am proud to be his son. I hope that you enjoy reading this!

CHAPTER 1

Day Zero – Setting the Scene

The Picture

On 17 March 1942, the Colonel Commandant[1] of the 2nd Battalion The Rifle Brigade (Prince Consort's Own), 'Jumbo' Wilson[2] visited the riflemen in Egypt, travelling from his headquarters in Jerusalem to Beni Yusef Camp just outside Cairo, where the battalion was stationed to watch a demonstration of the new 2-pounder anti-tank guns issued to the battalion on 2 February 1942, as well as camouflage and company schemes. After the demonstrations, Wilson had lunch with the officers and NCOs, taking part in the traditional photo of the officers in the afternoon taken by S. Sarkis.[3]

This is the story of these officers and the exploits of the 2nd Battalion over the next 422 days.

The officers pictured, some of whom had arrived in the Middle East as early as 1940,[4] had been involved in some of the hardest fighting of the North African campaign, and the men that they commanded were now nearing the end of a well-earned period of recuperation, training and refitting. Lucas Phillips wrote:

> Officers were young men, who over the preceding eighteen months had become desert veterans, used to supporting the armoured regiments in the fast moving North African Campaign. They were accustomed to living hard, to getting a move on and to fending for themselves in the most trying of circumstances.[5]

Godfrey Talbot recalled:

> 'They were the same colour as their surroundings, their faces the same khaki as their shirts and shorts.'[6]

The job of officers was explained by Viscount Montgomery of Alamein KG, GCB, DSO, PC as 'the capacity and the will to rally men and women to a common purpose and the character which will inspire confidence, that leadership must be based on a moral authority and it must be based on the truth',[7] or, as more simply put by US President Harry Truman, 'A leader is a man who has the ability to get other people to do what they don't want to do, and like it.'[8] Relationships between the officers and men had for centuries been frowned upon, the men being far more dependent on officer leadership than in some other Commonwealth countries, a result of doctrine and training as much as social distinctions. However, in the desert these restrictions were often diluted due to comradeship and living in small tight units often separated from others in the same platoon, let alone the same company or battalion. Bellowing parade ground discipline disappeared and in its place came a form of companionship, with officers no longer issuing orders but rather all parties acting together as a team to get the job done.

The Second World War shaped the world in which we now live, fought by our parents and grandparents many of whom at the time were still in their twenties and had been thrown into a conflict not of their choosing. It was a clash of ideologies in order to defeat Fascism; in their mind, a clear-cut case of right versus wrong. [9] Hitler, 'the Great Builder of a new Europe', [10] was portrayed as fighting the Capitalist-Jewish England. [11] The men shown in the picture were therefore fighting to preserve their way of life, not only in the British Isles but throughout Europe. During their time in the desert they had learnt to command, and after a period of recuperation were now ready to rejoin the battle against the Axis forces. We may never see their like again.

The Rifle Brigade

Who and what were the The Rifle Brigade (Prince Consort's Own)?

Their story begins in January 1800, when an Experimental Rifle Corps of officers and men was raised from several foot regiments by Col. Coote Manningham, the first person to use the term 'riflemen' to describe these men, and were issued with the still experimental Baker rifle. A letter of instruction was written stating:

> A corps to be termed the Rifle Corps was to be formed, the whole of the arms are rifled, and a short Roman sword is worn and fixed as a Bayonet. The whole accoutrements are of Black Leather. The colour of the Dress is dark bottle-green. Pantaloons or loose trowsers are worn, and of the same cloth as the Jacket. [12]

The *raison d'être* of the new corps was in many ways a contradiction to the manner in which battles were fought at that time, traditionally calling for lines of disciplined infantry men to advance against an opposing force to a position from where concentrated volleys of musket fire could be delivered, whereas the new riflemen were to be trained to be self-contained small units of ten, to operate independently from the massed infantry. Manningham described his riflemen's role as:

Providing a skirmishing force;
Providing a reconnaissance screen;
Leading the advance;
Covering movements of the Foot Regiments; and
Guarding the withdrawal of the Foot Regiments. [13]

The new Rifle Corps gained its first battle honour in 1801, when serving with Admiral Horatio Nelson at the Battle of Copenhagen, laying down accurate fire from the 'fighting tops', platforms situated close to the top of the mast of fighting ships, [14] under command of Lt Col. The Honourable William Stewart. Despite this, The Rifle Corps along with the 49th (which was to become the 1st Battalion The Royal Berkshire) served not as marines but as a possible landing force. The experiment proved a success and the Corps was brought 'into the line' of the British Army, given the title of

The 95th Regiment of Foot and known as The 95th Rifles. The 2nd Battalion of the 95th was raised at Canterbury, Kent, in 1805, initially fighting in South America as part of Brig.-Gen. Sir Samuel Auchmuty's force, and in 1808 becoming part of Arthur Wellesley's[15] expedition to Portugal, firing the first shots of the Peninsular War, before fighting in most of Wellington's future battles. In 1816, and in recognition of its services, the regiment was removed from the 'numbered regiments of the line' and became known as The Rifle Brigade.

On 29 July 1828, HRH The Duke of Clarence, later King William IV, concluded his address to the Depot Companies of both battalions: 'And what more can I say to you, Riflemen, than that wherever there has been fighting you have been employed, and wherever you have been employed you have distinguished yourselves.'[16]

HRH Prince Albert [17] became Colonel-in-Chief on 23 September 1852 [18] and in his honour the regiment was renamed The Prince Consort's Own Rifle Brigade. Despite his death in 1861, the name was to remain unchanged until 1921 when it became The Rifle Brigade (Prince Consort's Own). In 1880, HRH Prince Arthur, Duke of Connaught became the Colonel-in-Chief after commanding the 1st Battalion since 1876, remaining in this role until his death in January 1942.[19]

The Rifle Brigade first established solid links with the City of London in 1859 when 'The Lord Mayor decided that the establishment of a comprehensive and efficient volunteer Rifle Brigade would be a judicious measure', and this relationship continued through to the Second World War when the majority of the conscripts came from London. The Sounding of Retreat is still held at the Guildhall in London and on specific anniversaries can still be heard to this day.[20] The Caldwell Reforms of the 1870s linked regiments to fixed depots, and so the Rifle Brigade's relationship with Winchester and subsequently the Peninsula Barracks began.

Battle Honours

The colours or regimental flags represent the allegiance of every British regiment to King/Queen and country, but more than that they embody the tradition and past glories of the regimental family for which successive generations have fought and died. They are in effect the manifestation of a regiment's soul.[21] However, due to their independent role as skirmishers the Rifle Brigade did not have the need of a rallying point in battle, as Arthur Bryant states:

> In the hour of crisis its Riflemen could not rally, like others, round a Colour [flag], for they fought in extended order, every man depending for courage on the invisible colours in his heart: 'the black and the green, the finest colours ever seen'.[22]

For the same reason, communication via the drum was also not effective; therefore the brigade turned to the bugle for the receiving and giving of orders during battle, as well as the instruction for the riflemen to return to billets after leave, still known as Sounding the Retreat instead of the usual Beating the Retreat.

Operational Differences

Differences between the brigade and regiments of the line continued, with the uniform remaining bottle green with black buttons and accoutrements as opposed to the more traditional brightly coloured uniforms and polished buttons. In addition, there were other differences:

The Bayonet

The Baker rifle was 12 inches shorter than the standard infantry musket of the time. To remedy the disadvantage in close quarter fighting, the riflemen were issued with a 24-inch sword bayonet, the term 'sword' replacing 'bayonet' in the vocabulary of the regiment from then on.[23]

Firing

Ezekiel Baker [24] wrote that the riflemen should train to fire the weapon from various positions – standing, kneeling, lying down on the face, and on the back – instead of the more traditional firing manner of the men of the line.[25]

Marching

'The rifleman marches at a very quick light infantry pace, being set at a standard rate of 140 steps a minute and at double time of 180 steps per minute,'[26] a pace necessary to advance ahead of regular troops (for example, the French Light Infantry advanced at 76 paces a minute in their *pas de charge* at Waterloo).[27] Rifleman Waller, serving during the Second World War, explained that after doing a thirty-mile route march, they were expected to march the last half a mile to the parade ground at quick light infantry pace: 'This hurt the calves very badly, until after three or four weeks' practice your calves got used to it.'[28] The Rifle Brigade Association Journal states;

> 'Not so very many years ago, to march at more than three miles an hour was looked upon as a "crime" and riflemen have often been reproved for marching, when opportunity afforded and it was desirable, at four miles an hour.'[29]

Another difference as a result of the absence of colours was that the regiment had nowhere to list its achievements in battle, so was given dispensation to show these honours on cap badges (shown below), which also included the Royal Naval Crown at the top in honour of the regiment's action at Copenhagen.[30]

> Copenhagen – 1801
> The Light Brigade – 1803
> The Peninsular War – 1808 to 1809
> The Walcheren Expedition – 1809
> The Peninsular War – 1809 to 1814
> Waterloo – 1815
> The Kaffir Wars – 1846 to 1856
> Boer War – 1848
> Crimea War – 1854 to 1856
> Indian Mutiny – 1857 to 1859

Gold Coast/Ashanti War – 1895
South African War – 1899 to 1902
Egypt – 1902
Sudan Campaign (including the Battle of Omdurman)
First World War
Second World War

The distinguished service history of the regiment was taught to all new recruits. Waller recalled that in 1940 they had weekly two-hour lectures on the regiment, the purpose of which was to instil a feeling that 'they must not let the Regiment down!'[31] further reinforced by the obligation that 'you must not let your chums down', ensuring that the riflemen became fiercely proud of the regiment, creating a *corps d'élite*, or extended family if you will, whose ideal was 'to do everything that was necessary and nothing that was not'.[32] Paddy Ashdown explains further, 'It is not courage that sees a soldier through this critical moment [before battle], it is the shame of letting down his mates.'[33] Lt Gen. Sir Brian Horrocks, under whom The Rifle Brigade served during the Second World War, wrote that he had:

'come to the conclusion that 'Black Buttons', and the Rifle Brigade in particular, are probably the best Infantry Regiment serving in any Army in the world'.[34]

The Riflemen of 1939

Various diplomatic missions and negotiations took place during the last years of the 1930s to prevent war breaking out with Germany, but by early 1939, with the dark clouds of war on the horizon, measures were put in place to reinforce the professional army. Parliament passed the Military Training Act on 27 April, introducing conscription for men aged 20 and 21. Those affected were to attend a military establishment to undertake six months' training, but before this could be completed Britain was at war. The Rifle Brigade received conscripts mostly from London's East End, who went through basic training at Peninsula Barracks in Winchester before moving on to Tidworth to perform their role as a motor battalion. Officers were invited to join the regiment, many already having family or military connections.

Army Military Structure

The British Army at the start of the war was structured as follows:
- An infantry section comprised ten men, led by an NCO;
- Three sections formed a platoon, which included an HQ detachment under command of a Lieutenant;
- Three platoons made up a company led by a Major, with a Captain as second-in-command;
- Four companies plus an HQ company completed the battalion, which was a self-contained unit with liaison officers covering medical, signals, religion, etc.;
- Three battalions would form a brigade; and
- Three brigades would form a division.

A full complement of a battalion numbering 825 was as follows:[35]

Officers	**Non Commissioned Officers**
Lieutenant Colonel	Regimental sergeant major
Officer Commanding	
5 majors	Regimental quartermaster sergeant
Adjutant of the rank of captain	Company sergeant major
5 captains	
Technical officer of the rank of captain	6 company quartermaster sergeants
Quartermaster	Intelligence sergeant
23 subalterns of	Provost sergeant
2nd lieutenant or lieutenant rank	
	Pioneer sergeant
Ordinary ranks	Medical sergeant
643 ordinary ranks	Transport sergeant
	40 sergeants
	79 corporals

Attached to the battalion from other units were:
- A medical officer from the Royal Army Medical Corps;
- An officer from the Royal Army Ordnance Corps; and
- An officer from the Royal Army Chaplain's Department.

Armaments

The standard weapons were the rifle, Bren gun and Vickers heavy machine gun, all riflemen being trained to operate, clean, dismantle and reassemble them. The specifications of each weapon are as follows:

Weapon	Calibre	Weight (lb)	Length (in)	Magazine Rounds	Muzzle velocity (ft/sec)
Short Lee Enfield Mk 4 Rifle (SMLE)	.303	9.19	44.5	10	2,440
Bren Light Machine Gun Mk 1	.303	22.30	42.25	30	2,400
Vickers Mk 7 Heavy Machine Gun	.303	40.00	45.5	250	2,450

The Short Magazine Lee Enfield Mk 4 rifles (SMLE),[36] originally coming into service in 1902 as the 'Number 1' version, were produced until 1957, to version 'Number 5', but there were three experimental versions later. The Number 4 rifle was developed in the early 1930s and was generally introduced in November 1939, becoming the infantryman's standard weapon of the Second World

War. The construction design was simplified with respect to the sights, with a more exposed barrel and the provision of fittings for a 'spike' bayonet. Approximately four million units of the weapon were created. Rifleman Eddie Blacker recalled how the gun worked:

> The sequence of firing a Lee-Enfield was simple – bolt back, forward, fire. The sight was just a titbit at the front of the rifle and then you had a clip which came up and this was marked 200 to 2,000 yards and you just put it to whatever you reckoned it was and sighted up and started shooting.[37]

The normal fire was 15 rounds per minute, although this increased to 25 rounds per minute in rapid fire. However, in the desert the bolt action had to be covered by material after being cleaned to prevent sand from fouling the firing mechanism.

Motor Battalion

In the 1930s, The Rifle Brigade was again charged with taking on an experimental role, becoming part of a 'motor brigade' – a support unit originally intended to be formed from cavalry regiments but ultimately taken by The Rifle Brigade and The King's Royal Rifle Corps, calling for them to provide support to the armoured divisions.[38]

Despite its armour, weight and armament, a tank is vulnerable to infantry and anti-tank gun attack. Tanks were designed to attack other tanks, or as General Lumsden put it, 'It is not for the tanks to take on the guns!'[39] Therefore, to be effective they needed the eyes, ears and agility of infantrymen. This new form of infantry would also be motorised in order to keep up with the tanks, much in the same manner in which knights of old gave horses to ground soldiers and bowmen in order to provide them with protection against enemy pikemen,[40] and would see a motor brigade attached to an armoured division and each Rifle Brigade battalion attached to a regiment of tanks.

The first motor battalion training manual, written by Lt Col. Jack Reeve, set out its purpose as:
- to constitute a pivot from which armour could operate;
- to overcome, with its rifles, Bren guns, mortars and tactical expertise, any obstacles impeding an armoured advance;
- to clear, when necessary, villages, woods and enclosed country;
- to force the passage of rivers and deny them to the enemy;
- to protect the tank laagers at night;
- to hold captured positions and ground;
- to round up and take charge of prisoners after a break-through;
- to carry out patrols and reconnaissance; and
- to do for tanks whatever tanks could not do for themselves.[41]

The motor battalion was to be highly mobile, was able to operate in a semi-independent manner and was very strong in firepower but low in numbers. Its strength originally lay in its use of the Bren gun carriers equipped with the Vickers heavy machine gun, mortar platoons, and highly efficient use of radio telephony and later by the inclusion of an anti-tank company.

Once in the desert, it was decided that joining with two other battalions, 7th RB and 2nd KRRC, the 2nd RB would form the 7th Motor Brigade and be attached to the 7th Armoured Division, who themselves had been formed from the 'Mobile Division' and trained by Maj.-Gen. Percy Hobart in modern armoured warfare.[42] To complement their mobile role they would be using:

Bren Gun Carrier
Crew: 3 including the driver
Speed: 30 mph
Armour thickness: 0.4 to 2.78 inches
Weight: 3.75 tons
Height: 5 feet 2 inches
Power plant: Ford V8 85 bhp
In a manner similar to that of the Long Range Desert Group, crashed aircraft were cannibalised for their heavy machine guns and used unofficially in the carriers.[43]

Fordson WOT 2D 15-cwt trucks
A 15-cwt truck was assigned to each motor platoon section of eight riflemen, including the driver, as transport, designed normally to carry twelve men – this was considered 'roomy'.[44] Tenders for these new 15-cwt GS class vehicles had been sought by the War Office in 1933 and were answered by five manufacturers: Commer, Ford, Guy, Vauxhall and Morris Commercial. It was the Fordson WOT 2D, (War Office Type) that appeared in 1940 and was shipped out to Egypt, powered by the 3.6-litre V8 engine for use by, among others, the motor battalions.

Daimler Scout Car (Dingo)
The Dingo, as it was called, was a new class of small, turret-less, armoured vehicle built by Daimler, although Humber built a similar machine, of which a total of 6,626 were constructed.

Type	Daimler
Weight (tons)	Mk I – 2.8
	Mk III – 3.15
Length	10 ft 5 in
Width	5 ft 7.5 in
Height	4 ft 11 in
Armament	1 x LMG
Speed (mph)	55-60
Range (miles)	200
Crew	2

2nd Battalion

Prior to war being declared, the 2nd Battalion had been serving in India before moving in June 1939 to Palestine to control civil disturbances between the Arab and Jewish populaces, a position that was being exacerbated by the growing influx of Jews fleeing Nazi persecution.[45] As Montgomery[46] commented, 'The Jew murders the Arab and the Arab murders the Jew and it will go on for the next 50 years in all probability'.[47]

Moving to Egypt, they marched from the railway station to the Citadel in Cairo on 18 January 1940 to the band of the King's Royal Rifle Corps, In April, Wilson attended the battalion to tell them that they would be moving at extremely short notice to the Western Desert.[48]

Meanwhile, in the UK those riflemen who had not been part of the heroic Calais operation were told that, along with much needed supplies, they were to join the 2nd Battalion in Egypt as part of Field Marshal Archibald Wavell's force.[49] Later Churchill would write, 'The decision to give this blood transfusion while we braced ourselves to meet a mortal danger was at once awful and right. No one faltered!'[50] They sailed in Convoy WS2[51] from New Brighton on the Wirral for the Suez Canal via the Cape of Good Hope aboard the vessels *Empress of Britain*, *Strathaird*, *Otranto*, *Clan Macaulay* and *Waiwera*,[52] travelling some 14,000 miles, a huge distance but much less perilous than using the Mediterranean route, and arrived in Egypt on 21 September 1940.[53] And so was to begin the 543 days of fighting by the troops initially known as 'Wavell's 30,000' and the Western Desert Force later to become known as the Eighth Army or the Desert Rats that led us to the date of the photo.

Anti-Tank Gun and 'S' Company

After the battle of Sidi Rezegh in November 1941 it was decided that the motor battalion role would be augmented by the addition of an anti-tank function, with the battalion being equipped on 2 February 1942[54] with sixteen 2-pounder guns, being initially assigned to 'S' Company, under the command of Captain Tom Bird. The 2-pounder gun performed well against the thinly armoured Italian tanks, but it was soon found that the same could not be said against the heavier armoured panzers, which along with the absence of a suitable high-explosive shell made it also ineffective against infantry or enemy anti-tank guns. Work had begun on the larger calibre gun in 1938, but production was slow due to the loss of equipment at Dunkirk.[55] Field Marshal Alan Brooke had first seen a demonstration of the new 6-pounder anti-tank gun in April 1941; at that time he stated that he would 'press hard' for it to replace the 2-pounder[56, 57] and so the battalion's 2-pounders were soon replaced with the new Ordnance Quick-Firing (QF) 6-pounder (57 mm) gun, providing it with a gun that did not just 'knock on the door[58] but would blast it open, being able to penetrate the frontal armour of both the Mk III and IV panzers, at 1,000 yards plus.[59]

6-Pounder Anti-Tank Gun

In ideal circumstances the gun would be manned by five men, fulfilling the following roles:
- No. 1 – The commander of the gun;
- No. 2 – Held the rammer and operated the breech lever;
- No. 3 – The layer adjusted the sights and fired the gun;
- No. 4 – Loaded the gun;
- No. 5 – Passed ammunition, and checked fuses and charges.

The commander of the gun would kneel off to one side to see how the shell performed, to give the layer corrective instructions onto the target and to direct the firing of the gun. This role incurred a high incidence of injury as they were outside the line of the shield and had very little protection from enemy shell or machine-gun fire. Rifleman Martin wrote after attending a course on the gun:

To traverse you simply shoved or pulled the barrel via a leather padded hoop that went over your shoulder and through your armpit. To elevate or depress the barrel you turned the cogged wheel with your left hand, the right hand clasping the linked firing bar.[60]

The gun also lacked an adequate sight, there was no magnification and the hair line was too thick so that at 1,200 yards it almost obliterated the target,[61] but scavenging was an art quickly learnt in the desert and in a short time some telescopic gun sights made by Jena-Zeiss[62] and acquired from enemy 88-mm guns, had been found and adapted to enable them to take on targets up to 2,000 yards.[63] Rifleman Martin recalled that it was 'on the whole so simple and basic, but that gun was devastating. It proved its value over and over again.'

Anti-tank guns could often be damaged when being towed, especially in the rough terrain of North Africa. Faced with a similar problem, the French had taken to loading guns on the back of a truck, that is to say *en portée*, and this practice was adopted for the new gun and the truck in question became known as the anti-tank portee.[64] The rear of the truck was fitted with ramps and a winch, enabling the troop to bring the gun down to ground level very quickly, although it was often very tempting to fire the gun whilst still on top of the truck. This however made the high positioning of the gun a good target for the enemy, and Eighth Army instructions made it clear that 'anti-tank guns will never be fired from their portees except when there is literally no time to bring them into action on the ground'.[65]

Patrolling

Since their creation, the RBs had undertaken patrolling as part of their normal duties, this was to continue, although the desert would bring its own hardships:

> Creeping wretchedly across a bare desert [Major Hastings wrote], waiting for some Italian to shoot off or groping by compass with no landmark and perhaps no stars to help, or bumping over stony wastes on the return journey, the riflemen asleep in the back of the truck, the driver fighting to keep his eyes open, the subaltern's eyes glued to his compass, expecting a volley of rounds to whistle at any moment past his ears, proclaiming either that the guard on his company laager were taking no chances or that he had navigated into the German lines.[66]

Rifleman Waller recalled:

> [...] patrols objectives included gaining intelligence, getting close to the enemy and listening to their conversations, the taking of prisoners for interrogation or as a fighting patrol, to attack a weak spot, destroy supplies or just to cause panic amongst the enemy.[67]

It was then considered that the fighting patrol role would be extended by linking the riflemen to other military units to create columns that could operate behind enemy lines and also to protect reconnaissance units.

'Jock Columns'

The armoured cars of the 11th Hussars had been the first British units to cross the Egyptian/Libyan border in 1940, being the only truly experienced reconnaissance unit available to the British forces and having great success against the largely unmotorised Italian forces. With the advent of the more mobile German forces it was found that the Humber Mk III armoured cars were being hammered by the enemy, and it was decided to create a combined force that allowed the 11th Hussars to continue their reconnaissance role but be protected against enemy attack. The result was the 'flying column' which was put under the command of Lt Col. 'Jock' Campbell and was soon to be known as 'Jock Columns' comprising:

- A unit of 11th Hussars (Prince Albert's Own);
- A troop of 25-pounder guns to take on tanks and anti-tank units;
- A company of motorised infantry to protect against infantry attack;
- A signals unit to supply high-level communication; and
- Sappers for laying and raising minefields.

These columns were then able to expand their role to one of roving behind enemy lines, attacking supply trains, enemy laagers, etc., as well as reconnaissance, but although relatively successful they were never big enough or strong enough to make a difference, as Heinz Schmidt of the 15th Panzer Division remarked:

> The desert was alive with small columns of the enemy – 'Jock Columns' they were called – which were a nuisance, as mosquitoes are, but in the end no more violent in their sting. They were never really strong enough to do irreparable damage.[68]

General Montgomery later came to this conclusion when he took command of the Eighth Army, and in August 1942 they were informed that they had to fight on a divisional basis and not go 'swanning about in the blue'.[69]

Ultra

A further element of the war was the understanding and predicting of the enemy's intentions. This could be helped by the interception of coded radio traffic, one side always endeavouring to create the unbreakable code, with the other side working to break it. In order to produce the former, Arthur Scherbius invented the Enigma machine which was able to encipher and decipher automatically,[70] although a more automated, upgraded machine was made by the Lorenz company which was used extensively from mid-1942 onwards. Whilst Ultra was the collective designation given by the British for the enemy wartime cipher keys – which would reach more than 200 by 1945[71] – and related signals traffic decoded at Station X, the information and even the fact that the ciphers had been broken was given only to a very limited number of people. Ronald Lewis has written:

> The name arose because the intelligence thus obtained was considered more important than that designated by the highest British security classification then used (Most Secret) and so was regarded as Ultra Secret.[72]

In the preamble to an interview, Asa Briggs stated:

> The German Enigma machine was an attempt to find a technical solution to the central weakness of all codes: to communicate at all, there must be a pattern which corresponds in some way with a language known to the recipient. This being so, all codes are theoretically breakable. The critical issue is repetition and frequency: herein lies the pattern.[73]

The Germans believed that hundreds or even thousands of mathematicians could labour for generations without success in breaking the codes.[74] In fact from 1942 onwards it was some 6,000 staff working at the Government Code and Cypher School (GCCS) at Bletchley Park who decoded the information. The information received by the Allies became so accurate that Rommel thought that the senior Italian command were betraying him. This was further reinforced by captured British officers who told of an Italian officer who had passed on the details of his operations.[75] Ralph Bennett, an Intelligence Officer at Bletchley Park, recalled:

> Until Alam el Halfa, we had always been hoping for proper recognition of our product … Now the recognition was a fact and we had to go on deserving it. I had left as one of a group of enthusiastic amateurs. I returned to a professional organisation with standards and an acknowledged reputation to maintain.[76]

There is little doubt that the resulting intelligence was to make a considerable, even decisive, contribution to the war effort.[77] It armed the Prime Minister in his decision-making progress in a fashion unknown to any other national leader in history.[78] It was so important that Roosevelt did not inform his Vice-President Harry Truman, who only heard of the existence of Ultra upon the death of the President.[79] Peter Jarvis and Danny Johnson, historians of the intelligence war, state that 'never in a major war has one combatant had his intentions betrayed so comprehensively to his opponent'.[80]

How and Why Egypt

In order to appreciate why the battleground was in Egypt, situated approximately 2,000 miles from the Battle for Britain, we must look to why North Africa was so important to the war effort, especially bearing in mind that much of Europe was occupied by Germany and that Hitler was threatening to invade Britain, a country 'that the defeats in Norway and France had convinced the Axis powers was a rotten hulk, a bankrupt corporation, just waiting for the receivers to move in'.[81] It was the North African shore that provided Britain with the only theatre in which it could fight the Axis forces on land, as well as in addition to being the locked gate to the Middle East with its vast oil reserves. But why were the Axis forces there?

Both Germany and Italy had supported the Fascist General Franco in the Spanish Civil War, signing a secret protocol in 1936, with Mussolini stating on 1 November that 'it formed an axis around which all other European powers which desired peace and collaboration could work together'[82] thus they became known as the 'Axis Powers'. To further cement this relationship, on 22 May 1939, the two countries signed the 'Pact of Steel', each agreeing to come to the other's aid if they became embroiled in a war.

As the war progressed in Europe, Mussolini chose to play a waiting game in order to establish which side would benefit Italy the most, but seeing the lightning German advance through Europe he became concerned that if he did not choose soon there would be no spoils left for him to share. With Britain fighting for its very life, Mussolini declared war on 'the sterile and declining nations of Britain and France'[83] on 10 June 1940, after speaking to his people from the *Palazzo Venezia* that evening and immediately looked towards the British colonies in order to expand the Italian empire. In his view, the British would be too busy repelling the Germans in England to worry about Egypt. He discussed with Hitler in October his plans for an Italian empire spanning the Mediterranean and including parts of French North Africa, but more importantly allowing him to overrun Egypt, conquer the Nile delta and then sweep on through the Middle East to take the Persian Gulf.

The Italians had taken possession of Tripolitania and Cyrenaica[84] from the Ottoman Empire in 1912, merging them with their own colony of Libya in 1934, in which 150,000 native Italians had settled mainly around Tripoli and the coastal towns, whereas Britain had protected Egypt during the First World War to protect it from invasion from Turkey,[85] as reported in *The Illustrated London News*, their involvement continued:

> Britain's treaty with Egypt had been concluded in 1936, but since 1883, when Britain established a virtual protectorate over the country, the relations between the two countries had been particularly close. On 26th August 1936, Egypt and Britain signed a treaty of mutual alliance, and Egyptian independence was fully recognized. British troops withdrew from Cairo and Egypt as a whole, with the exception of the Suez Canal. Alexandria and Port Said were permitted to be used as naval bases, while certain infrastructure works were undertaken to make communication easier from the canal zone. Britain undertook to defend Egypt, whilst Egypt undertook to give Britain all the help needed in the event of war.[86]

Admiral Raeder wrote:

> The Mediterranean question must be cleared up … [after] the seizure of Gibraltar … Germany would then support the Italians in a campaign to capture the Suez Canal and advance through Palestine and Syria. If we reach that point, Turkey will be in our power. The Russian problem will then appear in a different light.[87]

The supply of oil from the Middle East had to be protected or at the very least denied to the Axis forces, the War Cabinet receiving the following report on 4 September 1940:

> Disregarding the effect of any action we may take to curtail them, Germany's oil reserves from her present source of oil and existing stocks are sufficient to meet her minimal requirements and those of the territories under her control till about June 1941. After this date, however, her shortage of oil will become so serious that it seems inevitable that she must before then attempt to end the war or at least make some move to improve her oil position. Apart from ending the war by the defeat of Great Britain, Germany can only improve her oil position to any material extent by driving our fleet from the Eastern Mediterranean, thus ensuring seaborne supplies from Romania and Russia. The capture of Alexandria would deprive the fleet of its base and so secure the desired result [...] Courses of Action open to the Enemy … an attack on Egypt from Libya with a view to driving the

British fleet from the Eastern Mediterranean, obtaining the cotton of Egypt, ensuring tranquil trade for the transport of oil from the Black Sea and eventually relieving Abyssinia.[88]

The successful conclusion of such an operation could also provide Hitler with access to the Indian subcontinent and even a future link with Japanese forces, who were already blockade running from Bordeaux, trading gold for various military equipment they needed to wage war.[89] It was therefore concluded that the elimination of Italy and the consequent removal of the threat to British control of the Eastern Mediterranean would be a strategic success of the first importance.

The Desert War

Italy invaded Egypt on 13 September 1940, with five divisions of the X Army commanded by *Maresciallo d'Italia* Rodolfo Graziani, 1st Marquis of Neghelli, against Wavell's 30,000 Western Desert Force, under the command of Lt Gen. Richard O'Connor. Graziani advanced at a snail's pace, probably due to the lack of mechanised transport and tanks, with Mussolini constantly commanding him to increase the speed of his advance and to attack, attack!

It was an old British joke in the desert war in North Africa that Italian soldiers were issued with running shoes because they never hung around long enough to fight, unlike their allies the Germans. This was just propaganda; the real problem the Italians faced was lack of good equipment and mechanisation, and a leadership structure that gave promotion based on social standing or loyalty to the Fascist cause.

In December, having received reinforcements, O'Connor launched Operation Compass, pushing the Italians back to El Agheila in Libya and taking over 135,000 prisoners, including twenty-two generals, an admiral and the official Italian army brothel.[90] The 2nd RB had excelled themselves at Beda Fomm – a quote of the day puts their action in perfect context: 'Never have so many surrendered to so few!'[91] O'Connor wanted to continue the advance through to Benghazi, but Wavell had been instructed by Churchill to 'halt, change and send his best troops across the Mediterranean to assist the beleaguered Greeks'.[92]

Rommel and Auchinleck

Italy's failure to take Egypt, especially after losing the battle for Bardia on 5 January 1941, forced Hitler to abandon his approach of uncoordinated military actions between Germany and Italy. Under Directive 22 that stated '... where England is employing superior forces against our allies, requires that Germany should assist for reasons of strategy, politics and psychology',[93] he sent the newly formed *Deutsches Afrikakorps* comprising the 5th Light and 15th Armoured divisions[94] under the command of the charismatic, innovative and impulsive risk taker[95] *Generalleutnant* Erwin Johannes Eugen Rommel,[96] who Churchill would later call a 'daring and skilful opponent',[97] to Tripoli in March 1941, under Operation *Sonnenblume* (Sunflower).

At this inopportune moment men and machines were redistributed to the Greek and Balkan theatres, a decision that was always more political than it was military.[98] Rommel immediately took the initiative against the weakened British, pushing them back to Halfaya Pass, at which point the Axis supply line became over-extended and they were pushed out of Cyrenaica, with Tobruk remaining besieged. After two unsuccessful attempts to relieve Tobruk, during which the British armour was badly mauled, Wavell was relieved of the desert command, Churchill citing his tiredness before transferring him to the Indian theatre, stating:

I have come to the conclusion that public interest will best be served by the appointment of General Auchinleck to relieve you in command of Armies of the Middle East,[99] with the Western Desert Force being renamed the Eighth Army on 26 September 1941.

In Operation Crusader, Gen. Sir Claude John Eyre Auchinleck GCIE, CB, CSI, DSO, OBE planned to destroy the Axis armour, but the plan came apart and the 7th Armoured Division, with the 2nd RB under command, were badly mauled at Sidi Rezegh. Rommel advanced to the border with Egypt to attack the main body of Allied infantry, which unbeknown to him had got around his flank and headed for Tobruk, prompting Rommel to withdraw his army to a defensive line at Gazala and then all the way back to El Agheila.

Egypt and Libya – the Terrain of a Battlefield

Egypt has two distinctive and opposing regions:
- the Nile and its delta (often called the black regions because of the fertile soil), which has rich vegetation, settlements and water; and
- the so-called 'red' desert a landscape which is featurelessness – thousands of square miles of nothing.[100]

The desert of both Egypt and Libya has limited vegetation – mostly a scrub known as camel thorn and tamarisk bush – beyond which there is little for the eye and mind to focus on, except possibly the different types of sand (actually dust):[101]
- gritty sand which is good for travelling on;
- finer sand, which gets into everything and in which trucks get bogged down in; and
- the seemingly firm surface of dark gravel, that hides the soft sand below.[102]

Keith Douglas, traversing the rear areas of Eighth Army to join an armoured regiment, was fascinated by the spectacle of men and machines massing in the sands for battle:

Lorries appeared like ships, plunging their bows into drifts of dust and rearing up suddenly over crests like waves. Their wheels were continually hidden in dust-clouds; the ordinary sand being pulverised by so much traffic into a substance almost liquid, sticky to the touch, into which the feet of men sank almost to the knees. Every man had a white mask of dust in which, if he wore no goggles, his eyes showed like a clown's eyes.[103]

Movement over the terrain was recorded in terms of 'going', identifying the degree of opposition which the surface of the ground would offer to the movement over it by various types of mechanical vehicle:

Very Good Going;   Over firm flat gravel, dried mud and undisturbed flat sand, would be suitable for very fast trucks and the landing of aircraft.

Good Going;   Over firm uneven gravel and loose sand, required the vehicles to reduce their speed and was passable with non-desert tyres.

Fair Going;   Allowed for travel over a variety of grounds, including stony, gravel over soft ground and broken country. Low hummocks of less than 12 inches were also passable. In all cases the speed was greatly reduced, the terrain bad for the springs and extra care had to be taken at night.

Bad Going;   Was determined as two types of terrain. The problems caused by broken country, boulders, high hummocks and soft sand, meant that vehicles had to proceed very slowly and that travel at night was impossible. Whereas travel over continuous and steep dunes or very rocky areas was impassable for all vehicles.

Chris Ellis and George Forty provide an excellent description of the area in which the North African campaign was fought:

It consisted of a level inland desert plateau stepping down in steep escarpments to a narrow coastal plain approximately 30 miles in width. The endpoints of these escarpments (south of Sidi Barrani and west of Tobruk), and their main gaps (Alamein, Halfaya near Sollum and Sidi Rezegh just south of Tobruk), along with the (only metalled[104]) vital coast road connecting the two opposing capitals (Cairo and Tripoli), were to become the main focus of the actions that took place.[105]

The campaign would be fought over this strip of land just over 1,400 miles long between Tripoli in the west and Alexandria in the east. This coastal plain is largely flat rocky scrubland interspersed with occasional hills and sand dunes, offering long clear fields of fire for guns and ideal going for tanks. With the exception of the coast roads, maps often bore no similarity to the actual terrain, grandly describing features as 'ridges' which anywhere else would be almost imperceptible rises and dips. Reference was made to the long-forgotten tombs of holy men, Bedouin tracks and underground cisterns now empty and dangerous to the unwary traveller. Bir Hacheim was one such place, a desert watering hole and a crossroads of ancient tracks where Arab traders and their caravans met, It was nothing but a spot on a map, a dusty pinprick in the vast openness of the desert.[106] It was to test Rommel's patience to its utmost limits.

Winds and dust-storms drove through the desert, the worst of which was the khamsin, known by Libyans as qibli,[107] a hot wind from the south which whipped the sand, dragged down tents, and filled everything with hot dust, reducing visibility to almost zero and causing enormous problems for the troops:

In some areas sandstorms are blowing and the desert is obscured in pallid, sunlit wooliness. We close the wooden compartment shutters, but the driving dust seeps through, and the atmosphere is like a fog.[108]

The Arabs have a saying: 'When the khamsin blows, even murder is justified!'[109]

Living in the Blue

Leaving the delta behind and driving through the 'red' desert you were 'in the Blue', where in general (apart from actual combat, which was estimated to take up only approximately 5 per cent of the time)[110] life was healthy albeit primitive, revolving around your unit and truck, leading to an intimate and rewarding comradeship. Water, which was laboriously brought up by the supply columns, was always a problem, but men learned to live on one gallon or sometimes half a gallon a day for all purposes: washing, shaving, drinking, cooking, and keeping truck radiators filled. The water was chlorinated, tasted of petrol or had salt in it,[111] and was usually too foul to drink, so was turned into tea, the stronger the better, and mixed with tinned condensed milk which gave it a 'cappuccino brown' colour.[112] After allowing for tea-making, the remainder was put through a complex cycle. First it was used to wash the teeth; it was then spat into a mug and was used to shave; then, in what can only be described as a wash equivalent of a 'cat's lick', the water was used to wash armpits, genitals and face, although not necessary in that order,[113] the remainder going into the radiator. A liberal application of AL63 anti-louse powder was also recommended to keep up hygiene standards.[114]

Food during the first years was plentiful, but almost invariably consisted of M&V (meat and vegetable) stew and bully beef and biscuits. It had to be shipped in, especially as you could not 'live off the land', with those cooking for the platoon finding more and more inventive ways to prepare it. The British biscuits[115] measuring 4 inches square and half an inch thick were inedible unless soaked overnight, in which time they would swell to twice their size,[116] but when mixed with condensed milk, sugar or jam, they made a palatable porridge called 'biscuit burgoo'.[117] Harry Byrne of the Lancashire Yeomanry recalled:

> The cook wagon, when it could provide a hot meal, did wonders with bully stew, bully fritters, cold bully (which melted in the tin), biscuit porridge, biscuit date pudding and good old cocoa. [118]

There were some animals, but these were few and far between and very shy in nature; herds of small gazelle were sometimes hunted, although not easily caught. Small desert foxes (*Vulpes zerda*) roamed at night, disappearing in the sand if disturbed, and then there was the famous desert rat (*Rodentia dipodidae*), known as the jerboa, which was to become the emblem of the 7th Armoured Division, with its long legs reminiscent of a kangaroo's and furry feet to better grip the sand. On the lower end of the scale there were spiders, scorpions and other arachnids that made desert life uncomfortable and necessitated checking clothing, bedding and especially boots before putting them on.

Rations included fifty cigarettes per week, but bringing the popular brands from the UK and America was not an option, so they were usually of Indian manufacture under the 'V' trade mark. This included an amazing range of goods but which were unfortunately also synonymous with the lowest and cheapest quality: 'V' matches were in the proportion of two good ones to about eighteen bad ones in a packet; 'V' ink was a foul greenish-grey colour with lumps; and 'V' cigarettes were especially bad. 'It was alleged that the manufacturers were annoyed that the troops believed the cigarettes were made from sawdust and camel dung, and officially denied that there was any sawdust in their product!'[119]

When the troops first arrived in Egypt after the long sailing round the Cape and across the Indian Ocean, they were transferred to Geneifi (Geneifa) Camp, a city of tents spread over a fifteen-mile area, approximately seventeen miles from Suez and sixty-eight miles from Cairo, where they were met with a poster stating that there were four basic rules for life in the desert:

- Camp cleanliness!
- Don't murder your mates;
- Purify drinking water;
- Protect food from flies.

Flies were more than an annoyance and became a never-ending battle. H. Metcalfe recalled:

> Eating and drinking became a work of art, one hand waving back and forth over the food, the other hand waiting, then a quick rush to the mouth before they pounced again. They were around mouth, eyes, face, anywhere there was moisture. They settled on the rims of hot cups of tea in their dozens.[120]

The desert flies (*Musca sorbens*) a more aggressive species than that found in Europe, grew fat and bloated. Frederick Jones of 7th RB recalled that 'they moved promiscuously from food to sweat to faeces to rotting flesh and back again, spreading disease',[121] coming in vast swarms just after sunrise. Men entering the Canal Zone were warned that they were entering a war zone with the fly as the principal enemy, and at one point were issued with orders for each man to kill at least fifty flies per day.[122] However, it made no appreciable difference to the fly population and in the end the flies just had to be tolerated. Sanitation was also a major consideration for the Eighth Army, the staff providing rules regarding 'where you go, how you go and how you clean up afterwards'.

Antony Beevor writes of a rifleman declaring that 'when he made it home he was going to spend his time eating chocolate ice cream while sitting on the toilet and enjoying the luxury of pulling the chain'.[123]

Latrines were constructed and managed to reduce the spread of infection. By contrast, the Afrika Korps relied on speed and mobility and had little time for the niceties such as latrines. Men would defecate in the desert, and flies would land on the waste and then on food, wounds, etc., resulting in a high level of dysentery, a problem that would result in a large number of non-combatant casualties in the *Panzerarmee* throughout the campaign.[124]

The most worrying problems, and the ones that lost the Army an enormous amount of man-hours, were sand fly fever and desert sores. The sand flies were tiny creatures that bit you and were gone in a moment, resulting in a fever that could kill, whereas the desert sores, a type of ulcer that proved to be a staphylococcal impetigo caused by the lack of vitamins in the diet, arose from even the smallest cut and took a long time to heal. The men were issued with a kind of blue ointment which had little effect, the sores only being effectively treated by hospitalisation, where the wound was debrided, dressed and the patient fed a high concentrate of vitamin rich foods.[125] Most pictures of the men on both sides of the conflict show them with a variety of plasters covering these sores. John Luxford of the 1st KRRC recalled:

> One only had to bang an arm or a leg against the tank, or gun, or something and break the skin and within 24 hours one would have a very unpleasant, suppurating sore – rather like a boil. The only treatment available was to smother it with a cream or ointment which was a sort of purplish, gentian blue in colour, and it was quite normal to see a man in old, faded shorts and dirty shirt, with his beret on the back of his head, with both his hands bandaged and bandages on one or both knees and spots of purple, blue patches. I even had a sticking plaster on my classic nose where I had

cracked it on the edge of the turret. These boils were damn sore and they certainly helped to pull one down in spirit and feel pretty miserable.[126]

Uniform

The standard British Army uniform was meant for much colder climates, being made of rough wool serge, and as such was unsuitable for the North African campaign, although the hob-nailed leather ammunition boots continued to be used. Accordingly, the khaki drill uniform was worn, comprising lightweight sand-coloured khaki tunics or shirts, long/short trousers worn with boots or shoes, long stockings and hose-tops (with shorts). The unpopular tropical solar topi, issued as part of the tropical uniform, was soon 'accidentally' damaged beyond repair, the most popular method being to drop it in front of a truck or tank, and replaced by berets or caps. The officers especially added various items of unofficial clothing such as suede desert boots with crepe rubber soles, coloured silk scarves, sheepskin or Hebron coats.

The rest of the equipment carried by the rifleman was held by the 1937 pattern canvas webbing designed to secure ammunition pouches, water bottle, entrenching tool and pack for personal items and mess gear. The Bren operator would also carry three Bren gun magazines in pouches and three bandoliers holding 100 rounds for his own rifle.

In general the climate was almost perfect, the days hot but seldom unbearably so; in summer (May to October) it was between 20° and 24°, with the highest temperature during the afternoon. However, the nights turned cold and the temperature dropped very quickly; surprisingly during winter the regulation two blankets were less than adequate, and the night was often so dark that it was easy to get lost without moonlight.

There was a difference between those who were part of the 'fighting force' and those who served in a support role, the total being known as 'on ration' – that is to say, those for whom food, water, pay, etc. had to be supplied. Of these, approximately 66 per cent supported those fighting on the front line in roles such as mechanics, supply echelon, army staff, etc. It was therefore only the balance of some 34 per cent that actually fought.[127] This difference between those turning up for their pay and rations and those who actually fought often caused disagreements between Winston Churchill[128] and Field Marshal Alan Brooke,[129] who almost constantly had to explain that the Middle East was a vast base that required many non-combatants to make it run properly.[130]

One of the most important lessons in the desert was that in order to survive you had to dig trenches, this usually being the first thing that was done when you stopped, especially when creating defensive positions or consolidating captured areas:

To dig down into the sand was not difficult but where the surface had been whittled away by wind and the limestone exposed, powered tools were necessary to gouge out shallow trenches and foxholes, supported by a rough parapet of stones or sangers.[131]

The North African campaign was fought over an area that was almost devoid of civilian life, resulting in few non-military casualties and therefore often referred to as the 'War without Hate' or '*Krieg Ohne Hass*', the name that Rommel chose for his account of the North African campaign: 'If wars must be fought, it is just as well that deserts should be the battlegrounds,'[132] but:

Its significance grew out of all proportion to its scale. On both sides, reporters flocked out to witness it. They were captivated by the haunting landscape and the fighting men of the desert, who flouted military conventions in their attitudes and their dress.[133]

The Gazala Line

Now to return to the battlefield where history seemed to repeat itself.[134] As the Japanese attack in the Far East called for reinforcements, Auchinleck lost two Australian divisions and a sizeable number of aircraft at precisely the time that Rommel was being reinforced.[135] However, Auchinleck knew that he had to progress the campaign and accordingly planned Operation Acrobat, an attack upon the remaining Axis hold on Tripolitania. He assembled stores and equipment for the attack scheduled for the spring, whilst at the same time building the 'Gazala Line', which was designed to prevent Rommel advancing east to Egypt. This was a line of seven defensive boxes, each defended by an infantry brigade group, with artillery, barbed wire and minefields, anchored at the northern end at Ain el Gazala, situated approximately thirty miles west from Tobruk, and reaching down in a south-easterly direction approximately fifty miles into the desert.

This was the first time that an attempt had been made to build a line of this kind so far into the desert, with some 500,000 mines laid in the area of these defences alone.[136] Each box was a fortified area large enough to contain a brigade of men, behind barbed wire and minefields, with the area between each patrolled by armoured or motorised units, and with the main armour located behind the line in readiness for any counter-attack. Rommel considered that the whole line had been laid with great skill, but wrote in his daily letter home:

> The situation is developing to our advantage … and I'm full of plans that I daren't say anything about round here. They'd think me crazy. But I'm not; I simply see a bit further than they do.[137]

True to his word, and before Acrobat could be launched, the *Panzerarmee* attacked on 21 January 1942, sweeping up the Via Balbia coastal road through Mersa Brega towards Agedabia and threatening Benghazi. Caught off guard, the dispersed British units fell back eastwards. Gen. Neil Methuen Ritchie,[138] Eighth Army Commander, was at the time far to the rear at Cairo and considered that Rommel's advance was little more than a raid or a reconnaissance in force.[139] Benghazi fell on the 29th, with the Eighth Army falling back to their positions on the Gazala Line, and by 5 February both armies had taken up a static position, making Operation Acrobat a distant memory.

While in this static position, Rommel took the opportunity of going to Germany with the purpose of convincing Hitler of the need to break the Allied Line and, in order to accomplish this, to provide the *Panzerarmee* with a further three divisions. The request was refused, as the extra divisions were needed for the Eastern Front. However, permission was given for a limited offensive aimed at breaching the Gazala Line and recapturing Tobruk. The *Panzerarmee* would then consolidate its gains while Malta was invaded under Operation *Herkules*.[140] Hitler made it very clear that under no circumstances was Rommel to over-extend his supply lines.

Meanwhile, the 2nd RB moved out to the Western Desert from Capuzzo along the Alexandria road during the night of 23/24 March, arriving at El Imayed the next day and at Mersa Matruh the day after. There the riflemen awaited their orders for the next step taking them to Libya and Gazala.

Once there, the battalion was to spend its time operating forward of the enemy line, acting as a mobile antenna to monitor Axis movements and undertaking patrols to gain intelligence on any impending Axis offensive. The battalion under command of Lt Col. Hugo (Hugh) Wilfred John Cairns, Viscount Garmoyle with the individual companies led at this time by Capt. D. W. Basset of 'A' Company, Maj. R. H. W. S. Hastings of 'B' Company, Maj. The Hon. H. D. G. Prittie of 'C' Company, Capt. T. A. Bird of 'S' Company, and Capt. O. R. H. Chichester of HQ Company.

It is at this time that we lose the first of the officers shown in the picture, when Lt Quartermaster C. F. H. Sandell makes his way back to the UK,[141] being replaced by Lt Quartermaster H. W. Newton, with the added advantage of the battalion receiving a number of Fordson 15-cwt trucks as replacements for their existing transport, the War Diary commenting, 'about whose desert worthiness considerable doubt was felt.'[142]

Training proceeded in defensive box strategies, with an exercise at the end of March involving the whole of the 7th Motor Brigade in an approach march in 'box' formation, ending in taking defensive positions in the same formation at a given point. There were some problems due to the location and the amount of dust created by the movement, which restricted visibility, all of which made it difficult to keep station while on the move.[143] It was something that would be worked on and, as always, perfected.

The 'game of chess' around the Gazala Line continued with movement of the Axis and Allied units harassing, blocking or trying to bypass each other in order to get the better position. When Rommel took over a building previously occupied by the British to use as his headquarters he found a sign painted on the door: 'Keep clean, we'll be back soon!'; he later wrote to his wife: 'We'll see about that.'[144]

Under pressure from Churchill, Auchinleck planned an attack to take place around the middle of May, aimed at providing some respite for Malta as much as removing the Axis from Cyrenaica. In an effort to increase this pressure, Churchill sent a telegram stating that 'according to our figures, you have substantial superiority in the air, in armour and in other forces'.[145] However, what the figures did not show was that the Eighth Army had an insufficient number of reliable tanks of equal quality as the panzers. In an effort to balance the situation, Auchinleck made two important organisational changes. First, he consolidated the activities of the artillery, armour and infantry, managing them more closely at all times and in all places; second, he increased the ratio of infantry to armour, similar to that in a panzer division (in the future an armoured division would consist of one armoured brigade group and one motor brigade group – the former consisting of three tank regiments, one motor battalion and a regiment of field and anti-tank guns; the latter three motor battalions and a similar artillery regiment).[146]

In anticipation of an expected enemy attack the Eighth Army plans were put in place for defence of the Gazala Line, with the 7th Armoured Division protecting the area south of Bir Hacheim. The 7th Motor Brigade was to occupy the Retma defensive box[147] upon receiving the codeword 'Mappin', with the 9th KRRC on the right and the 2nd RB on the left. 'Jock Columns' were created to collect information and harass the enemy communication. 'B' Company 2nd RB was assigned to South Column under command of Maj. The Hon. M. G. Edwardes, (although this assignment was to be for just eight days, as 'North' and 'South' columns were replaced by 'July' and 'August' columns) and was instructed to collect information and harass enemy communications. It comprised:[148]

'July' Column	Commanding: Maj. H. Withers Royal Horse Artillery
	'F' Battery 4 Royal Horse Artillery
	One Troop A/TK Battery 4 Royal Horse Artillery
	One Troop 43 Light AA Battery
	'B' Company 2nd RB
	Detachment Royal Engineers
'August' Column	Commanding: Maj. The Hon. M. G. Edwardes 2nd RB
	'C' Battery 4 Royal Horse Artillery
	One Troop A/TK Battery 4 Royal Horse Artillery
	One Troop 43 Light AA Battery
	'A' Company 2nd RB
	Detachment Royal Engineers

On 26 April, 'July' Column went almost immediately into action, as whilst patrolling the area around Asida they found their way blocked by the enemy forces comprising a half-track troop carrier, one 6-pounder gun and a lorry. Capt. Mosely, who had now taken over command of 'B' Company, ordered the 2-pounder guns to be unloaded, with Sgt Sherman firing at 600 yards, blowing up the carrier and then the lorry. The riflemen then had to withdraw when they came under heavier fire from the enemy 6-pounder.[149]

The battalion moved east towards Tobruk on 9 May to take over the Al Adem box protecting the airfield of Tobruk. Its role included the maintenance of the defences and provision of a guard for the food and ammunition dumps, but this also gave the battalion a most welcome break from the strenuous column activities of the last few weeks. The companies were given the following roles:

- Part of 'B' Company would take over the food dump and await resupply from BI(b) Echelon;
- The remainder of 'B' Company would take over the eastern PoW cage;
- 'A' Company would take over Al Adem aerodrome;
- 'S' Company would take over the south-west position to guard the water; and
- 'C' Company would guard the ammunition dump in the box.

Retma Box

From intelligence and intercepted messages Auchinleck considered that Rommel would attack sometime before the beginning of June.[150] Messages were sent to all units, with the battalion receiving the 'Mappin' codeword and moving to the Retma box. Any enemy force that outflanked the southernmost box at Bir Hacheim would be forced to drive through the line of fire of Retma, now under the command of Lt Col. Garmoyle and populated by:

- 'C' Battery 4th Royal Horse Artillery with 1 troop Light Anti-aircraft;
- Rhodesian Battery 4th Royal Horse Artillery;
- 4 Field Squadron Royal Engineers less one troop;
- 2nd KRRC, relieved by 9th KRRC on 26 May; and
- 2nd RB.

It was here that the 2nd RB received the new 6-pounder anti-tank guns, increasing the morale of the riflemen no end. The Rhodesian Battery provided initial training on the new gun, while the construction of the box continued, providing vehicle and weapon pits, although the minelaying schedule lagged behind. The War Diary also records that 'an attempt was also made to reinforce the battalion with a quantity of unwanted, unasked for and very reluctant Welshmen. An attempt which was eventually foiled.'[151]

The other main defensive boxes, despite being largely incomplete, were now populated as follows:

Coastal box	1st South African Division
Sidi Muftah box	50th (Northumbrian) Infantry Division, which was actually three strongpoints
Retma box	7th Motor Brigade
Bir Hacheim box	1st Free French Brigade

To back up the boxes, the tanks of the 1st and 7th Armoured divisions were concentrated behind the line to act as a mobile counter-attacking force against any enemy elements that broke through, the 5th Indian Infantry Division being held in reserve and the 2nd South African Division forming the garrison at Tobruk.

Operation *Venezia*

The plan, codenamed Operation *Venezia*,[152] called for a feint against the middle of line in order to draw the Eighth Army armour to that area and then striking south, bypassing Bir Hacheim, bearing a resemblance to the 'Crusader' operation in reverse.[153] The Afrika Korps and Italian XX Motorised Corps were to push on through Acroma to the coast, isolating the British divisions occupying the line, whilst the 15th and 21st Panzer divisions would destroy the British armour. The 90th Light Division[154] would advance on Tobruk, whilst the Italian 101st Motorised Division would break through the line between Bir Hacheim and Sidi Muftah to form and keep open a supply line in support of the armour concentration. However, not all were in agreement with the plan, *Generalleutnant* Fritz Bayerlein later wrote:

I never liked this plan and, as Chief of Staff of the Afrika Korps, I told Rommel so continually. It seemed to me altogether too risky to go on without first knocking out Bir Hacheim.'[155]

CHAPTER 2

Zero plus 72 days and the Battle of Gazala

During the afternoon of 26 May a strong khamsin arrived, blanketing the area with swirling sand, reducing visibility and effectively cloaking the enemy movement as they proceeded to their start positions. At 1400 hours the afternoon routine of the Eighth Army in the centre sector of the Gazala Line was disturbed as a heavy barrage landed amongst the defenders, followed immediately by the advance units under command of *General der Panzertruppe* Ludwig Crüwell of the Italian X and XXI Corps and sections of the Afrika Korps and XX Korps. A similar attack was taking place in the north of the line – all intended to give the Allies reason for moving their armoured units into the central and northern sections. Operation *Venezia* had begun.

As soon as the evening British air reconnaissance plane had flown over the centre area, and along with the assumption that they had taken note of the advancing forces, the units of the Afrika Korps and XX Korps immediately turned and raced back to join the main attacking force in the south, beginning to advance at 2030 hours with 10,000 vehicles,[1] intent on sweeping around Bir Hacheim and the southern end of the Gazala Line. Rommel was under the impression that their movements were hidden from the Allies, but South African armoured cars were continually in contact with the enemy from the afternoon of the 26th, reporting back at half-hourly intervals to 7th Motor Brigade.[2]

The riflemen occupying the Retma box listened to the advancing armour, knowing that once it had swept round Bir Hacheim box and the smaller Indian-held box approximately four miles away they would come into direct contact. However, feeling that they were about a day away, and riflemen being riflemen, they settled down to grab some well-earned sleep. During the night 'the great swirling cloud of dust and sand containing the Venezia Force thrust onwards,' despite a few problems with unknown minefields, both real and decoys.

The morning of the 27th came and the force stopped for an hour's rest, before the divisions of XX Motorised, 90th Light Afrika and part of 21st Panzer continued their advance, bypassing the Bir Hacheim Box to attack the partially completed box at Bir el Hamarin. It was occupied by the 3rd Indian Motor Brigade, whose commander, Brig. Anthony Aloysius Emmanuel Filose, announced over open airwaves that he had 'a whole bloody German armoured division' in front of him![3] The panzers collided with the 4th Armoured Brigade and the Indians, resulting in a tank battle during which the Germans were for the first time opposed by the newly supplied Grant tank.[4] The battle delayed the enemy for about three hours before the British armour was swept aside and Retma box came into their sights.

At about 0720 hours, the riflemen had just finished brewing their breakfast tea and were beginning to lay the mines that had arrived the previous night when two large columns of tanks and mixed enemy transport (MET) appeared, all moving rapidly north-east and stopping apparently for no one. They immediately fired the three red Verey lights to signal the general alarm.[5] A Royal Horse

Artillery troop of 'C' Battery and the anti-tank guns of the Rhodesians opened fire, adding several tanks, self-propelled guns and troop carriers to their 'bag' as the vehicles passed. However, had the mining and wiring been completed, the score would have been much higher. The enemy infantry and tanks attacked the west and north-west positions of the box, causing a high number of casualties amongst the 9th KRRC, but by 0845 hours the enemy had crossed the minefield and overrun the forward positions, making the box an unsafe proposition. Garmoyle, showing his usual fearless attitude, drove around the position in his staff car, providing the enemy target practice whilst giving instructions to 'Get going!' By 0900 hours the remaining defensive benefits of the Retma box had been eliminated and the 90th Light Division was plunging onwards towards Tobruk, ignoring the riflemen of the position, who made off in an easterly direction towards Bir el Gubi where they met a large crowd of 'B' Echelon supply vehicles.

Meanwhile, the 'July' and 'August' columns that had been operating in forward positions west of Bir Hacheim were cut off by two enemy columns containing approximately 1000 MET and tanks each.[6] 'July' and 'August' split up, moving east and south respectively, before making for Bel Hamed, just south of Tobruk, and joining up with the rest of the brigade in the afternoon.

Following Rommel's swift southern attack, confusion ensued and was made all the worse as

enemy armoured cars began roaming among the supply echelons, destroying the dumps left largely unprotected by the Eighth Army withdrawal and making it necessary to reorganise the 7th Motor Brigade into columns to provide some defence against these attacks. This decision was to prove just too late for one dump containing the NAAFI[7] whisky supply, which was turned into a few blue wisps of smoke in the distance.[8] Garmoyle was placed in command of 'April' Column made up of 2nd RB companies 'HQ', 'A' and 'B' with 'C' Battery of the 4th Royal Horse Artillery, who were given a roving commission to seek out and harass the enemy – a role that Garmoyle excelled in – whilst the remaining 2nd RB companies, 'C' and 'S', joined 'March' Column whose main task was to protect 'B' Echelon who were taking the supply dumps under control.

As the 15th Panzer Division advanced towards El Adem, it came upon the Advance HQ of the 7th Armoured Division near Bir Beuid, capturing the Division Commander Gen. Frank Walter Messervy DSO amongst other officers and then shortly afterwards again meeting the 4th Armoured Brigade.[9] Col. George Philip Bradley 'Pip' Roberts, leading the 3rd Royal Tank Regiment, wrote:

> There they are – more than a hundred. Yes, twenty in the first line, and there are six, no eight lines, and more behind that in the distance; a whole ruddy Panzer Division is quite obviously in front of us. Damn it. This was not the plan at all – where the hell are the rest of the brigade?[10]

Despite Ritchie not consolidating his armour – instead throwing it into battle in a piecemeal fashion – the Germans took significant losses and as a result halted their advance, allowing the 4th Armoured to withdraw first to Bel Hamed and then El Adem by 1000 hours. With the threat of the panzers temporarily removed, order could be restored with a new administrative base created at Sidi Rezegh on the 28th. Hastings received orders that the 2nd RB was to return to the area of past battles, taking up a position on the escarpment two miles east of the mosque and thus adding to the protection of the Tobruk stronghold.[11]

The battle continued the next day, with one of the fiercest tank engagements of the desert campaign, which saw the 75-mm guns of the Grants hitting the panzers. The day ended as the British pulled back eastwards towards Knightsbridge, the defensive position manned by the 201st Guards Brigade situated at the junction of Trigh Capuzzo and the Acroma–Bir Hacheim tracks.

Rommel's daring plan had not succeeded as he had hoped and he was now bottled in an area bounded by the rear of the Gazala Line in the west, Trigh Capuzzo in the north, Trigh el Abd in the south, and the Acroma–Bir Hacheim track to the east. This was to become known as the Cauldron (*Hexenkessel*) or to the Germans the 'Sausage Pot',[12] all names that aptly described the heat and ferocious battles that would take place there.

Crüwell took his reconnaissance Storch plane to visit the X Corps and was captured after being shot down over the area controlled by the 150th Infantry Brigade. His second in command, Maj. von Mellenthin, initially took control, but upon arrival of *Oberbefehlshaber Süd* (Luftwaffe Commander-in-Chief South) *Generalfeldmarschall* Albert Kesselring requested that he take command instead. Kesselring initially refused but acquiesced, taking command for a few days when advised that not to do so would mean an Italian taking command.[13]

The Cauldron

By the evening Rommel had been apprised of the *Panzerarmee* dispositions and was becoming seriously worried that in excess of a third of his tanks had been lost in one day:

> The panzers were being hit harder than ever before, too, and at longer range, and their crews were learning some of the more bitter lessons of armoured warfare; but for them there was at least the comforting crack of their 88 mms, the bark of the newly arrived captured Russian 76 mm and the sight of their anti-tank screens implacably holding off the British attacks.[14]

The new powerfully armed Grant tanks had torn great holes in their ranks. Rommel wrote:

> Looking back on the first day's fighting, it was clear that our plan to overrun the British forces behind the Gazala Line had not succeeded. The advance to the coast had also failed and we had thus been unable to cut off the 50th British and 1st South African divisions from the rest of the Eighth Army.[15]

The original main objectives of Operation *Venezia* now had to be abandoned.

To make the *Panzerarmee*'s position even worse, the Afrika Korps' supply routes from the west running south below Bir Hacheim became a tempting target for the 'March' and 'April' columns who ran amok through the enemy units, causing great confusion and destroying a number of petrol and ammunition lorries. The 15th Panzer was now so short of fuel that it was forced to laager west of Knightsbridge, closing up with the 90th Light and the Italian Ariete divisions by Bir el Harmat to await resupply.

Resolute and concentrated attacks by properly directed British armour with artillery and infantry support now placed the Eighth Army on the verge of an enormous victory. The *Panzerarmee* was locked up in the Cauldron with little access to supplies or reinforcements. Maj.-Gen. H. Lumsden commanding the 1st Armoured Division commented 'that with Rommel penned up against the 150th, the Eighth Army "had him boiled" '.[16]

Rommel instructed the Italian Trieste Division to gap a route through the Gazala defensive minefield specifically between Trigh el Abd and the Free French at Bir Hacheim from the west, whilst a westward attack occurred on 30 May through the rear of the British Line with the intention of creating a bridgehead on the east side of the minefield and linking with the Trieste. On the evening of 31 May, *General der Panzergruppe* Walther Josef Nehring and Bayerlein met with Rommel. Bayerlein later wrote:

> We were in a really desperate position, our backs against the mine-field, no food, no water, no petrol, very little ammunition, no way through the mines for our convoys, Bir Hacheim still holding out and preventing our getting supplies from the south. We were being attacked all the time from the air. In another twenty-four hours we should have to surrender.[17]

Rommel agreed, saying: '... we cannot go on like this. If we don't get a convoy through tonight I shall have to ask General Ritchie for terms.'[18] The Eighth Army did not move, the bridgehead was established and two narrow paths through the minefields were created. Rommel drove out personally to direct the life-bringing supply column to his virtually immobilised tanks and men, who were by then down to half a cup of water a day.[19] The *Panzerarmee* now replenished, attacked and shortly after 1400 hours on 1 June the weary gunners of the 150th, recently reinforced by 1st Army Tank Brigade occupying the Sidi Muftah box, were overrun. After firing off their last shells, they became PoWs. On 2 June, Ritchie wrote to Auchinleck, 'I am much distressed over the loss of 150th Brigade after so gallant a fight, but still consider the situation favourable to us and getting better every day.'[20]

In fact, Rommel had effectively split the Eighth Army in two. The situation had now dramatically changed from one in which the Eighth Army was surrounding a supply-starved enemy, to one in which that same enemy was driving a wedge into the Eighth Army's 'guts'. Auchinleck seemed to understand the situation better, writing to Ritchie the next day:

> I am glad you think the situation is still favourable to us and that it is improving daily. All the same I view the destruction of 150th Brigade and the consolidation by the enemy of a broad and deep wedge in the middle of your position with some misgiving. I am sure, however, there are factors known to you which I do not know … I repeat that in my opinion you must strike hard and at once if we are to avoid a stalemate, that is unless the enemy is foolish enough to fling himself against your armour. I wish he would but I don't think you can count on this at present.[21]

The Columns of the 7th Motor Brigade

Communication problems and constantly countermanded orders exacerbated by the extended command structure and a fast-moving enemy resulted in many misconceived commands, such as when the 7th Motor Brigade moved through very poor visibility of 1,000 yards or less into the triangle formed by the Acroma, Hajaq and El Adem positions above the Cauldron in order to attack a concentration of 1,000 MET which had been reported in the area, but on arrival there was no sign of the enemy. Upon finding an alternative enemy concentration, the riflemen of the battalion however took the opportunity to attack the large group of enemy vehicles and, despite severe fire, a troop under command of 2nd Lt Toms managed to position two 6-pounder guns close to the enemy, directing their fire from the back of an open 15-cwt truck.

The columns of the 7th Motor Brigade roamed behind the enemy lines, attacking communication and supply columns. On one occasion four Panzer IIIs were set alight by 2nd RB 'B' Company carriers, while a petrol-less Panzer Mk IV was captured and destroyed by 'A' Company under the command of Capt. Basset. This was the perfect role for Garmoyle – 'He seemed to have an eye in every direction.'[22] They were always on the move, dodging an enemy thrust or creeping up to attack the track at another point. This role produced many enemy prisoners and vehicles, captured as well as destroyed, in just over the three days that they were behind enemy lines attacking along the tracks between Mteiffel, Syuali and Cherimia, an area used heavily by the enemy, they destroyed over forty lorries, four tanks, six guns and one self-propelled gun, as well as two Stuka dive-bombers on the last day.[23] Rommel commented on the work of the 'British Motorised Group' during these days and especially on 'August' Column, which particularly distinguished itself in this work against the supply columns.[24] As the month ended, Garmoyle's command – then the most westerly troops in the Eighth Army by many miles – were ordered back to assist the defenders of Tobruk.

Meanwhile, the remainder of the motor brigade not involved in the column work undertook a night march round the southern end of Bir Hacheim, arriving at the Rotunda Mtafel to the complete surprise of the enemy and the extreme annoyance of Rommel. The brigade, and especially the 2nd RB, had a very successful time destroying tanks on transporters, over 100 enemy trucks and a number of guns, and capturing some 300 prisoners, not to mention the release of an even larger numbers of Allied PoWs, before laying mines across the supply route and then waiting to see the devastation that they caused. A few days later, on the 8 June, whilst operating between Bir Hacheim and the Cauldron, Sgt Charles Vivian Calistan, commanding a section of anti-tank portees supporting carriers in an attack on an observation post, came under intense direct fire. Despite this enemy fire he remained in position on the back of the portee, observing the fall of the shells from his guns until he hit one of the enemy guns twice.[25]

The almost constant attacks by the British armour were beginning to take a toll on the supply situation, especially bearing in mind that the gaps across the minefields were quite small. Rifleman Martin with 2nd RB recalled, 'Reports state that the enemy is bogged down through lack of supplies. Everyone is in high spirits and very optimistic.'[26] This view went all the way to the top, as Auchinleck strongly urged Ritchie to counter-attack along the coastal road towards Timimi and Mechili. However, cautious Ritchie was more concerned about Tobruk's exposed position and decided to reinforce the El Adem box and create more boxes to block the gaps through the minefields controlling the access to Tobruk, thereby squandering the opportunity.

Operation Aberdeen

Under continued pressure from Auchinleck, Ritchie undertook a compromise based on a scheme worked out by Messervy and Briggs, calling for a wedge to be driven into the Cauldron to establish brigade positions there. On the night of the 4/5 June, Ritchie at last attacked in order to consolidate the Aslagh Ridge situated in the centre of the Cauldron under an operation codenamed Aberdeen, with the 2nd and 22nd Armoured brigades, 10th Indian and 201st Guards brigades against the Ariete. However, the earlier delay had allowed the *Panzerarmee* time to prepare solid defensive positions. A whirling tank and anti-tank battle began, with the Ariete initialling falling back due to superior numbers before the British were stopped by concentrated artillery fire. Rommel immediately counter-attacked, firing on the British forces from three sides. The brigades fought back stubbornly, but with far too little mobility, resulting in more than fifty British tanks lying brewed up on the battlefield, together with some 4,000 British troops, mainly from the 201st Guards and 10th Indian brigades marching into PoW camps, along with the troops of the newly arrived 10th Indian Brigade which had been operationally wiped out.

Desmond Young wrote: 'The Afrika Korps was itself again.'[27] Rommel now considered that the fighting had only another fortnight to run before they would be through the worst of it, writing to his wife in a jubilant mood: 'The battle continues, though we're in such a favourable position that I've got no more serious worries. I think we'll pull it off all right and reach our objectives.'[28] The fiasco that was Operation Aberdeen had turned the tables on the British, despite them having superior forces and an enemy, seriously in need of supplies, corralled in the Cauldron. It was a wasted opportunity. From the perspective of the British, the battle of the Cauldron was a mournful and unmitigated disaster.

The 7th Motor Brigade now requested permission to return to the Mteiffel area behind the Cauldron, the location of previous successes. Only Garmoyle's 'April' Column was given permission, moving about fifty miles to the saltflat area of Baltat before successfully operating there against numerous enemy targets, where they were twice attacked unsuccessfully by panzers. The successes continued as they broke up an enemy column, destroyed two M13 tanks, one Panzer Mk III, a Kamsporter and a Macchi aircraft, and captured four trucks carrying 1,000 gallons of water. Forty-six British PoWs were released and eighteen enemy prisoners were taken. A further twenty-two enemy PoWs, including an officer, were brought in by Hastings, who also advised that during the attack seventeen MET had been destroyed.

During the evening, Capt. Mosely commanded a patrol to lay more mines on the Mteiffel track, but on this occasion they did not wait around to see the effect of their handiwork, only returning the next morning to see that the mines had caught six MET. Owing to the attention given by the column to this area, the enemy supply route was almost brought to a halt – so much so that that a number of eight-wheeled armoured cars were sent to protect the track and attacked the column whenever possible. This was not particularly successful, as shown on 9 June, when twelve armoured cars attacked but were driven off by the 25-pounder which quickly got their range. The *Panzerarmee* switched to an aerial solution, the column being attacked twice by a force made up of Messerschmitt 109s and 110s and a Macchi bomber which came in at 'zero' feet to mitigate the column's protection by the anti-aircraft Bofors guns, resulting in the loss of a 6-pounder gun and portee but otherwise causing no other damage. By way of retaliation, 'A' Company platoon, commanded by Lt J. Verner, shot down the Macchi.

On their penultimate day in the area they saw aircraft returning from bombing Bir Hacheim, the anti-aircraft section taking the opportunity of downing two Stukas. Maj. Hastings later recalled:

The day before we moved back a formation of over fifty Stukas appeared from the south at hedge-hopping height – if such a term can apply in the desert. After a moment of consternation the column suddenly realized that they would certainly be mistaken for Germans in this unlikely position, far behind the orthodox front line. Everyone who possessed a weapon fired it and it is said that two of these sitting birds were seen to fall, while another was brought down by a patrol of armoured cars a little to the north.[29]

As Cyril Mount recalled:

The Stukas were scary because we'd never come across anything like that before. [We were] very, very scared at first, then you realized you'd be very unlucky if you copped it, because they were a terrorizing thing, more than damaging. They only had two bombs and a siren.[30]

Their luck, bolstered by the positive confident manner of their commander, continued. The night before returning to the brigade they sent out a patrol under the command of Lt J. Copeland to lay some mines the track, the next morning, 10 June, they broke laager early, still hidden by the morning mist, and took a position approximately four miles away, where they watched as the mist lifted sufficiently to see their previous position heavily shelled.

Bir Hacheim

The balance of forces at Gazala having now turned in Rommel's favour, he wrote: 'After this British defeat we no longer expected any major relieving attack on our forces around Bir Hacheim, and hoped to get on with our assault undisturbed.'[31] The Bir Hacheim box, bypassed in the original attack, was manned by 3,700 men of the 1st Brigade Free French commanded by Gen. Marie-Pierre Koenig, comprising no fewer than forty-three separate nationalities including some German nationals.

The first attack by seventy Italian tanks had taken place at 0700 hours on the 27th. By the time it had advanced to within 200 yards of the defenders the force had been reduced by thirty-five tanks, the attack being utterly shattered, the remainder lumbering away back across the desert. The success in ending the attack cheered the defenders on and they sent out fighting patrols which played havoc with the enemy's supply columns over the next few days. At midday on 2 June, the 90th attacked from the south-east and the Trieste from the north-east. A skilfully planned system of field positions, slit trenches, small pill-boxes, over 1,200 machine-gun and anti-tank nests, all surrounded by dense minefields, prevented the assault from succeeding. However, the enemy spearheads had managed to get within half a mile of the *ridotta*, a small desert fort, before a hail of fire tore across the rocky and coverless ground into the ranks of the attacking troops, bringing the advance to a halt.

The next day the shelling and bombing began, continuing day and night almost without interruption, whilst regular attacks from the *Panzerarmee* took place with the intent of trying to break through the minefields. Continued attacks steadily reduced the perimeter but at a high cost to the attackers. It was not so much a matter of if the box fell, but when.

'March' Column, which included both 'C' and 'S' companies of 2nd RB, had moved south to attack the enemy lines of communication, although their operation was less effective than that of 'April', they had more importantly been able to make contact with Koenig, to discuss how to get supplies into the position. Rifleman Martin wrote that 'they are desperately in need of supplies, poor devils.'[32] Previous supply runs had not been successful, as driver R. J. Crawford describes:

> [...] they were moving up towards Bir Hakeim when they ran into the tank ambush. The tanks closed in from all sides, blazing away with their guns. The Bren guns of the supply column hardly had a chance to answer before the gunners were mown down. Then carnage was let loose as the tanks drove straight over the column, smashing lorries onto their sides in all directions. Within a few minutes the column was a mass of blazing wreckage with bodies strewn everywhere.[33]

Now that contact had been made and a method of supply arranged, 'S' Company under the command of Bird was instructed to take the supplies in 100 vehicles to Koenig using the cover of darkness, while the remainder of the column continued their actions against the supply lines. Bird later said:

> My own most exciting time was round Bir Hacheim fort. Two days before it was evacuated, I took some food and ammunition in to them, and in order to do so had to go through the middle of the enemy – all this during the night with enormous, unwieldy lorries.[34]

Owing to the darkness, navigation was all but impossible so the help of a French officer was provided, although he said he doubted that the full complement of 100 trucks was likely to get through, and they agreed to try with twenty-five only. They started the trucks up and drove straight though the lines, minefields and defences from the west as fast as possible, losing only one truck, which went head over heels after falling into a gun pit and landing on a German gun, the remaining trucks arriving in the position just as it got light. Bird had also taken two of the new 6-pounder anti-tank guns, which would be put to good use by the defenders, so much so that Rommel later wrote of his regret that they were in the position.

The activities of the 'March' Column in harassing the supply routes made Rommel think that a relieving force would be sent, enabling the French to stage a breakout. Accordingly, the attacks were stepped up. The Germans, who had a ten to one majority, had twice swarmed over the outer garrison defences in the north-west and twice the French had pushed them back out with hand grenades and machine guns, but with limited men and equipment they desperately needed a pause in the action and more importantly some sleep. At least five times the Germans had sent in officers with white flags to demand Koenig's surrender and each time the French had contemptuously refused, the men jeering and the responses becoming ruder as time went on. The Germans even resorted to such tricks as sending out false instructions on the radio ordering Koenig to capitulate. Morale was increased when General de Gaulle sent a message that, 'All France looks to you in her pride.' [35]

By 7 June, Rommel had assembled 10,000 troops around Bir Hacheim, mostly made up of Italians but including a large number of Germans, with a good quantity of tanks and artillery pieces. Gradually the superior numbers began to tell. Koenig advised Bird that he could not hold out much longer and that he was awaiting Ritchie's permission to leave. Therefore he and his riflemen should leave during the night of 9 June. Bird recalled, 'Then I saw General Koenig inside the fort, collected information, and had to get out, which fortunately went OK, though I won't say without mishap.' [36] They left by the same route that they had entered. Bird in the lead truck went through, but the second truck hit a mine and prevented the column from advancing until it had been moved out of the way, the exhausted riflemen in the back of the undamaged trucks remaining asleep throughout. They rejoined 'March' Column, who over the next three days destroyed forty lorries, six guns and a self-propelled gun.

The attacking force was increased when Rommel added a combat group of the Afrika Korps as the Luftwaffe continually sent formations against the position. Upon receiving Ritchie's order to come out, Koenig ordered those who were able to board the trucks to do so, leaving 1,000 men who could not be moved. Hitler gave instructions to execute any captured legionnaires, whether they were French, anti-Fascist Germans or citizens of other Nazi-occupied countries; to Rommel's credit, all were treated as ordinary PoWs.

The trucks began heading west through the thinnest point of the enemy lines between 2200 hours and the early hours of 11 June. As they drove along the narrow paths gapped by their sappers, they were illuminated by German flares and came under intense fire, but Koenig rallied his men and in a desperate charge at around 0300 hours 2,600 men and one woman drove through the remaining enemy lines, where they would meet 'March' Column tasked with helping the evacuation, before circling round to join the rest of the Eighth Army and receiving a well-earned hot meal supplied by the Royal Army Service Corps.

Black Saturday

Rommel wrote, 'Now our forces were free ... On the afternoon of June 11, I put the Bir Hacheim force on the move to the north in order to seek a final decision without further delay.'[37] That evening the 15th Panzer and 90th Light divisions, with 3rd and 33rd Reconnaissance Battalions under command, advanced to an area six to ten miles south-west of El Adem, and in response the 4th, 22nd Armoured and 29th Indian Infantry brigades moved eastwards from Acroma into the area of Bir Lefa. The 21st Panzer followed the next morning (the 12th), and with the 90th attacked the El Adem box and its strongpoints at Batruna and El Hatian, an attack that was initially repulsed by the 29th Indian Infantry, but during the evening Batruna fell with a loss of 800 soldiers and numerous guns and supplies.[38] Meanwhile, the 4th and 22nd Armoured brigades, with artillery support, had taken up positions on the left of the El Adem box, but the ensuing violent battle around midday saw them pushed four miles further east by the panzers, leaving damaged tanks that could not be recovered on the battlefield that they did not control.

The columns of the 7th Motor watched in the distance, 'a great black cloud rising and covering the horizon, from the east'[39] as the oil tanks and those stores that could not be loaded onto trucks were destroyed by the RAOC and RASC, the columns continuing their move further east as the *Panzerarmee* advanced towards Sidi Rezegh. Initially the panzers were brought to a halt by heavy concentrated fire, but it was not long before the forward elements of the Panzer Reconnaissance Group once again occupied the mosque, although 'July' Column, which included 'S' Company under temporary command of Toms, continued to harass them.

On 13 June, the 21st Panzer Division continued their advance from the west, engaging with the 22nd Armoured, a battle that did not go well for them, and who at the end of the engagement had lost two-thirds of their tanks. This constant loss could not be sustained. On the 11th, Ritchie had been able to field some 300 tanks, a two to one numerical advantage, whereas after the last two days there were now only ninety-five in operating condition. Rommel now planned his attacks using intercepted wireless communications to indentify those areas that were in need of and had called for support, at the same time moving his panzers away from areas that the British armour had been told to attack. To make matters worse, the *Panzerarmee* had by now turned the wedge, splitting the Eighth Army in half into a dominating strategic line and posing a threat not only to Tobruk but more importantly to those units still on the Gazala Line, whose evacuation route, the Via Balbia, was now within range of the enemy artillery. Rommel wrote:

> One after the other of the 120 or so [tanks] which they probably now had left remained lying on the battlefield. A murderous fire struck from several sides into the tightly packed British formations, whose formations, whose strength gradually diminished. Their counter-attacks steadily decreased in momentum.[40]

The Knightsbridge box was abandoned that night after being virtually surrounded and pounded by concentrated artillery barrages all day from all the massed Axis guns that could be brought to bear, the Guards withdrawing to Acroma. Rommel wrote that this brigade 'was almost the living embodiment of the virtues and faults of the British soldier – tremendous courage and tenacity combined with a rigid lack of mobility.'[41] As a result of the losses in both armour and territory over the last two days, culminating on the 13th, the day was to become known as 'Black Saturday' throughout the Eighth

Army. Ritchie now requested permission to fall back to the frontier with Egypt, and with the Italian infantry advancing from the east, Tobruk was surrounded and isolated. Auchinleck, however, was not ready to throw in the towel, insisting that counter-attacks be launched to deny the investment of Tobruk.[42] The next morning, with the Eighth Army streaming east, the German panzer divisions moved off at full speed northwards to attack Tobruk. Rommel wrote:

> Suddenly we ran into a wide belt of mines. Ritchie had attempted to form a new defence front and had put in every tank he had. The advance was halted and our vehicles were showered with British armour-piercing shells.[43]

By evening the barrier had been pierced, and after violent and successful fighting measured by the forty-five British tanks that were now hulks, the panzers continued their advance through the Acroma box, which became untenable, and the garrison including the 1st RB were instructed to evacuate. The way to the Via Balbia was now open, Rommel writing in his diary that 'the 1st British Armoured Division was no longer in a fit state for action and left the battlefield during the night'.[44] British fortunes were at their lowest ebb, Churchill stating, 'The conduct of our large army … does not seem to have been in harmony with the past or present spirit of our forces.'

Auchinleck wrote on the 14th to Ritchie:

> I hope El Adem has successfully resisted attacks today. If El Adem still holds, its area should be reinforced without delay so as to ensure that Tobruk is defended without being invested.[45]

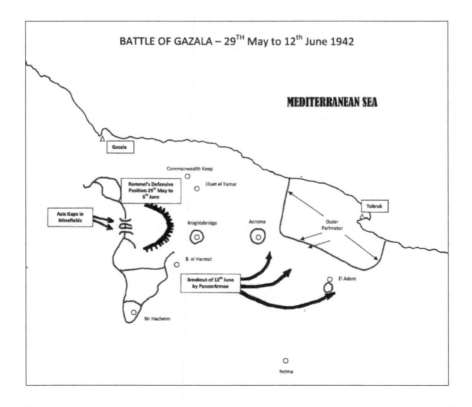

Ritchie replied:

> El Adem supported by 7th Motor Brigade and Mobile Group of 11th Indian Brigade beat off three
> attacks today and drove enemy back inflicting considerable losses … Order for Tobruk to be closed
> as port issued today.[46]

The El Adem box remained in Allied hands, protecting the withdrawal of the units on the Gazala
Line. The 1st South African and 50th (Northumbrian) divisions immediately moved east along the
coastal road, which turned out to be too small to allow two divisions to travel at the same time,
resulting in the 50th being forced to find an alternative route. They attacked south-west against a
position held by the Brescia and Pavia divisions, breaking through with a force of about brigade
strength and heading south through the enemy supply lines, causing serious damage, before turning
east and racing to join the other withdrawing units. However, by the time they reached the Egyptian
border they could not be regarded as battleworthy in any way, shape or form.

7th Motor Brigade Columns

In support of the withdrawal, the 7th Motor Brigade moved with the Gloucester Hussars to engage
the enemy south of El Adem, but the enemy had already moved away by the time they had arrived.[48]
The brigade stayed in position to protect the southern flank, to be joined by 'August' Column, who
returned to their ranks after engaging 300 MET moving east along the Trigh Capuzzo, as well as a
small party led by at least thirty-five tanks moving south-east which they heavily engaged for several
hours. Meanwhile, the 4th Armoured Brigade, reduced to twenty-four Honey tanks and twelve
Grants, followed the South Africans east away from the battlefield.[49] As a battleworthy formation,
XXX Corps had ceased to exist.[50]

With the Allied forces continuing their withdrawal, the 7th Motor columns harassed the enemy,
forcing them to slow down and thus providing vital time for the retreat. The strength of all three
columns was often combined on a single objective, such as on 17 June when 'March', 'August' and
the troops of 'July' Column attacked an enemy column of twenty tanks, guns and MET moving
south down the track to El Gubi, continuing the engagement through the evening, when the enemy
retreated. Since March, Messervy had commanded the 7th Armoured Division through the trials and
losses at Gazala, but on 23 June, at Ritchie's request, he was relieved of his command and replaced by
Brig. J. M. L. 'Wingy' Renton, who as a rifleman commanding the 2nd RB when they first arrived in
Africa had enormous experience of Western Desert fighting.[51] The next day, as they were mopping
up stray enemy parties, the riflemen were advised that Garmoyle had been promoted to command
the 7th Motor Brigade, replacing Renton, the War Diary stating, 'Riflemen had again shown their
worth and accordingly been promoted.'[52] Maj. Hastings wrote:

> To say that the battalion owed its survival to Hugo Garmoyle would be less than the truth; for it was
> the faith and confidence of every rifleman in the judgement and leadership of the Colonel that had
> made it possible to operate continuously, offensively and successfully for so long and often at such
> great distances from the rest of the Army.[54]

Pending a replacement, Edwardes took command of the 2nd Battalion and Maj. Lomers of the 4th Royal Horse Artillery took over command of 'March' Column.

'July' Column and the newly formed 'SQ' Column took up positions preventing the enemy from securing El Gubi, with the result that enemy troops had to be diverted from other activities to protect the *Panzerarmee*'s southern flank, whilst 'March' Column was held in reserve, where they were attacked by twelve Stukas resulting in the Adjutant's truck being hit, although one Stuka was brought down by anti-aircraft fire.

There are many acts of bravery as well as numerous stories related to the activities of the 7th Motor Brigade Columns and specifically the 2nd RB during this time. As an example, I have included the following from Maj. Hastings' book:

'March' column then started operating around El Gubi with 2nd Lieutenant Peter Innes's carrier platoon of 'B' Company out on patrol watching to the north of the rest of the column.

In the distance they saw a half-tracked towing a Panzer Mk III approaching their position through the desert mirage, the crew sitting on top of the tank, taking very little interest in the surrounding area, feeling quite safe in being some fifty miles behind the main battle. Innes gave the order and the whole platoon advanced towards the tank as fast as possible. Seeing the carriers the Germans fired recognition Verey light and upon receiving no response, manned their guns. Innes's carrier was in the front and the distance was soon reduced to the point that the tank had to depress its gun to its lowest setting. Seeing Innes's carrier was about to hit at point-blank range, Sergeant Pevalin drove his carrier onto the back of the tank and with Rifleman Rowett fired their guns through the turret hatch into the confines of the tank.

Another example began with the gunner observation post indentifying a party of German 'Soft-Skins' vehicles, apparently unescorted, moving along a track. An operation was planned using 2nd Lieutenant John Henniker-Major's carriers supported by 2nd Lieutenant Jack Toms' 6-pounder anti-tank guns and advanced towards the enemy. Before they had gone too far they discovered that the vehicles were accompanied by anti-tank guns. The carriers continued their attack, with Henniker-Major ordering his driver to take the carrier to within grenade range of the guns! The carrier just overshot the mark and the carrier was blown up at point-blank range, with Henniker-Major and the crew wounded. Toms' 6-pounders opened fire, the wounded extricated, and the platoon retired, leaving a number of German lorries in flames and the whole column in confusion.[55]

Hastings wrote that 'such local successes made it harder to understand why the Army's withdrawal persisted',[56] but nevertheless the columns now received orders at 2100 hours to move north, crossing the Trigh Capuzzo west of El Gubi.

El Adem was vacated during the night, thus making Ritchie's defensive line from Acroma through El Adem and on to Bir el Gubi untenable. With the enemy cutting the Via Balbia just east of Tobruk, they were now within fifteen minutes of the coast. The El Hatian position held out until the 16th, under constant attacks by the 90th Light Division, when part of the garrison broke out, leaving 500 troops to become prisoners along with considerable quantities of war matériel to fall into enemy hands. Fighting at Gazala had finally ceased. Evidence could be seen of the British defeat all along the roads and verges in the burnt-out vehicles standing black and empty in the sand, among the vast quantities of food, water and fuel, British uniforms to replace the German worn-out ones, new boots for the enemy troops and soft-soled suede desert boots for the officers, and whole convoys of undamaged British lorries to supplement the enemy's transport.[57] Von Mellenthin wrote:

> All British troops in the area were in full flight to the east; some efforts had been made to demolish the supply dumps but we captured enormous quantities of petrol and rations, and a good deal of transport.[58]

The airfields of Tobruk and Gambut were taken, with the bonus of finding some ammunition and weapon dumps that had been abandoned during the 1941 offensive. These would be put to good use.[59] A positively jubilant Rommel wrote to his wife:

> The battle has been won and the enemy is breaking up. We're now mopping up encircled remnants of their army. I needn't tell you how delighted I am. We've made a pretty clean sweep this time.[60]

Tobruk

Operational Instruction 110 detailed the intention that Auchinleck had to continue his offensive through Libya and beyond. However, it also dealt with the possibility that Rommel might undertake a large-scale and ultimately successful offensive, which could result, among other things, in the investment and capture of Tobruk. During the drafting of the instruction the other services had been consulted. Air Marshal Tedder felt that his aircraft would be better served over a battlefield instead of a besieged port; Admiral Cunningham advised that another siege could prove an embarrassment to his greatly reduced force in that he would be unable to keep it supplied as he had done previously.[61] Based on these comments, the instruction included two paragraphs that were about to become very relevant:

> (6) It is not my intention to try and hold permanently Tobruk or any other locality west of the Frontier;
> (10) Work will continue in accordance with the original plans on the El Alamein position as opportunity offers, until it is completed.[62]

Despite the plans generated to provide alternative instructions for use in case of a successful enemy offensive, Auchinleck had no intention of allowing Tobruk to fall, as confirmed in Churchill's letter of the 15 June:

> We are glad to have your assurance that you have no intention of giving up Tobruk. War Cabinet interpret your telegram to mean that, if the need arises, General Ritchie would leave as many troops in Tobruk as are necessary to hold the place for certain.[63]

Auchinleck was fully aware that Rommel had been successful in defeating the armour of the Eighth Army with limited forces of one German motor and two German armoured divisions, helped to some extent by one Italian motor division, and felt that he was not in a position to undertake a large-scale operation for some time. He had written to Ritchie on this basis on 14 June:

This being so, Tobruk must be held and the enemy must not be allowed to invest it. This means that Eighth Army must hold the line Acroma–El Adem and southwards and all enemy attempts to pass it. Having reduced your front by evacuating Gazala and reorganized your forces, this should be feasible and I order you to do it.[64]

These orders were repeated a few days later:

a) The general line Acroma–El Adem–El Guba is to be denied to the enemy;
b) Our forces will NOT be invested in Tobruk and your army is to remain a mobile field army;
c) The enemy's forces are to be attacked and destroyed as soon as we have collected adequate forces for an offensive.[65]

In most people's mind, including that of Churchill, Tobruk was of significant symbolic value.[66] Barr elaborated, 'Tobruk's fame after 1941 ranked with that of Troy, Gibraltar, the Peking Delegation and Mafeking in the past',[67] and I. M. Baxter has written:

[…] this grubby little port in North Africa had become so important it became a fixation. Rommel was well aware he had a reputation at home and the public liked to measure his greatness in terms of triumph on the battlefield. The Battle of Tobruk had become so important to the morale of the German people.[68]

By the 19th, the 7th Motor Brigade were the only part of the Eighth Army still operating outside Tobruk.[69] They continued harassing the newly arrived Littorio Armoured Division that had been tasked with protecting the backs of the forces surrounding Tobruk. Meanwhile, Rommel was preparing for the assault on Tobruk, writing, 'To every man of us, Tobruk was a symbol of British resistance and we were now going to finish with it for good.'[70]

Tobruk was manned by some 35,000 troops comprising Guardsmen, Gurkhas, Indians and South Africans, five regiments of artillery, sixty tanks[71] of the 2nd South African Division under the command of Maj.-Gen. Hendrik Balthazar Klopper DSO. However, the 2nd Division were inexperienced, the tanks were of obsolete design, and many of the defensive mines had been removed for use on the Gazala Line.[72]

On the morning of the 18th, Rommel radioed Kesselring and the general staff announcing, 'Fortress encircled'.[73] Rommel was eager to start – his diary contained twenty pages of the descriptions of the forthcoming attacks. He retired to his bed but could not sleep.[74] At 0520 hours on 20 June, Kesselring's Stukas flew over to begin aerial bombardment of the first strongpoint, announcing the start of the assault, along the same route that O'Connor had used the previous year.[75] Less than an hour later, this strongpoint had fallen and by 0630 hours the defensive points on either side had followed suit, enemy tanks penetrating approximately two miles into the perimeter by 1000 hours. The defensive lines of Tobruk were crumbling, but the defenders were not going to make it easy and continued denying the *Panzerarmee* for the rest of the day.

Auchinleck reported to London:

Enemy attacked south-east face of Tobruk perimeter early morning after air bombardment and penetrated defences. By evening all our tanks reported knocked out and half our guns lost …

Major-General Klopper commanding troops in Tobruk last night asked authority to fight his way out feeling apparently could not repeat not hold out. Ritchie agreed ... Do not repeat not know how he proposes to do this and consider chances of success doubtful.[76]

Ritchie advised that he would endeavour to hold open a gap between El Adem and Knightsbridge, and instructed the 7th Armoured Division to advance on Tobruk, but with a lack of transport the breakout ceased to become viable, leaving Klopper with only one option – capitulation:

Ritchie: '... every day and hour of resistance materially assists our cause. I cannot tell your tactical situation and must therefore leave you to act on your own judgement regarding capitulation ...'

Klopper: 'Situation shambles. Terrible casualties would result. Am doing the worst. Petrol destroyed.'

Ritchie: 'Whole of Eighth Army has watched with admiration your gallant fight. You are an example to us all and I know South Africa will be proud of you. God bless you and may fortune favour your efforts wherever you be ...'[77]

By morning Tobruk was a pile of rubble, emissaries were dispatched to the German forces with an offer to surrender. Upon receipt of their acceptance, a huge white flag was hoisted above the 6th Brigade Headquarters by some native drivers. 'As it opened in the early morning breeze, a great moan of disappointment, anguish and misery welled up from all over the western half of the garrison area.'[78]

The 35,000 troops who made up the garrison of Tobruk Fortress surrendered to Gen. Navarrini's 30,000 troops. On hearing that Tobruk had fallen, Hitler promoted Rommel to the rank of *Generalfeldmarschall*; at 50 years of age, he became the youngest Field Marshal in the German Army. Writing to his wife he conveyed his feelings. 'In being made Field Marshal is like a dream; in fact all this business in the last weeks is lying behind me like a dream,' signing the letter 'Your Field Marshal'.[79]

Leutnant Fritz Starke of the German Tank Grenadier Regiment recalled, 'A few stray Arabs appeared and led us into hiding holes and camps. In winter they had led the Tommies to our hideouts,[80] and *The Daily Telegraph* printed:

While some boatloads may have got away safely by sea, units which held the fortress must henceforth be written off ... There have been grave errors in this campaign. Let us face it![81]

The supplies – 4,000 tons of oil, stores including chocolate, tinned milk, canned vegetables and biscuits by the crate and even mines at Tobruk – would be used to great advantage by Rommel, but the only real solution to his supply problem lay 435 miles away in Alexandria.

The report drafted by the US military attaché Col. Bonner F. Fellers sent to Washington was not complimentary to the British forces:

With numerically superior forces, with tanks, planes, artillery, means of transport and reserves of every kind, the British army has twice failed to defeat the Axis Forces in Libya. Under the present command and with the measures taken in a hit or miss fashion the granting of 'Lend-Lease' alone cannot ensure a victory. The Eighth Army has failed to maintain the morale of its troops; its tactical conceptions were always wrong, it neglected completely cooperation between the various arms; its reactions to the lightning changes of the battlefield were always slow.[82]

Sadler commented, 'At the time it would have required a particular shade of optimism to disagree.'[83]

Having taken Tobruk, Rommel was faced with either consolidating his gains, as instructed by Hitler, watching as all available aircraft and shipping were transferred to Operation *Herkules* (the invasion of Malta), or to take advantage of the situation and continue his advance into Egypt and beyond. From the perspective of the Luftwaffe it was an either/or decision, as there were insufficient aircraft to adequately support both operations. It also had to be taken into account that as long as Malta remained in Allied hands, Rommel's line of communication and supply from Italy was in jeopardy. Rommel decided to convince Hitler to allow him to strike for the delta. In his support was Bonner Fellers' intelligence, stating:

> The British had been decisively beaten and the time was ripe for Rommel to take Cairo and the Nile Delta; the Italians agreed that Rommel had a good chance of success.[84]

Added to this was Hitler's scepticism of the Italians' ability to invade Malta successfully.[85] In opposition was Kesselring, who maintained that the only sensible move was to consolidate the Tobruk position and invade Malta. Rommel succeeded in convincing Hitler to allow him to continue the advance, cabling Mussolini that it would be foolish to break off contact while the 'Goddess of Victory' smiles, and that along with the confirmation that the supplies provided by the Italians could be guaranteed if the ports of Tobruk and Mersa Matruh were in Axis hands, gave his authority to take the delta.[86] Gen. Enno von Rintelen (military attaché in Rome) signalled Rommel just after midnight on 23/24 June:

> Duce approves intention of Panzer Army to pursue enemy into Egypt. Cavallero will arrive in Africa on June 25 on behalf of Duce for discussion and issuing of new instruction …[87]

Marshal Ugo Cavallero, Chief of Italian Supreme Command (*Comando Supremo*), arrived in Sidi Barrani to find Rommel glowing with self-confidence: 'I count on being in occupation of Cairo and Alexandria by June 30.'[88] Mussolini, his sense of the dramatic thoroughly stirred issued a directive on 27 June ordering the seizure of Suez and the closure of the canal. Piloting his own private aircraft, he flew to North Africa complete with a white charger (and, it was said, with cases full of new uniforms) in expectation of a triumphant entry into Alexandria and ready to parade himself down the conquered streets of Cairo.[89]

Rommel now needed to motivate his troops to dig deep into their pot of stamina to continue the advance, and decided to do so by first congratulating them in the Order of the Day:

> Soldiers!
> The great battle in the Marmarica has been crowned by your quick conquest of Tobruk.[90] We have taken in all over 45,000 prisoners and destroyed or captured more than 1,000 armoured fighting vehicles and nearly 400 guns. During the long hard struggle of the last four weeks, you have, through your incomparable courage and tenacity, dealt the enemy blow upon blow. Your spirit of attack has cost him the core of his field army, which was standing poised for an offensive. Above all, he has lost his powerful armour. My special congratulations to officers and men for this superb achievement.

Soldiers of the Panzer Army Afrika! Now for the complete destruction of the enemy. We will not rest until we have shattered the last remnants of the British Eighth Army. During the days to come, I shall call on you for one more great effort to bring us to this final goal – Rommel[91]

Churchill and Roosevelt

Meanwhile, approximately 5,400 miles away in Washington DC, Churchill and Brooke were having a post-lunch meeting in the Oval Office with President Franklin D. Roosevelt. Gen. George Catlett Marshall, USArmy Chief of Staff, came in and handed a pink slip of telegraph paper to the President, who read it and without saying a word gave it to the Prime Minister. It announced that the Mediterranean port of Tobruk had surrendered without warning to the 21st Panzer Division. Gen. Hastings Lionel 'Pug' Ismay recalled, 'This was a hideous and totally unexpected shock, and for the first time in my life I saw the Prime Minister wince!'[92] The American response to the news was instinctive, recalled Ismay. 'For a moment or two no one spoke,' then Roosevelt communicated his sympathy and utmost determination to sustain Churchill, in recognition that 'we are all in the same boat,' by simply saying, 'What can we do to help?[93] Marshall suggested that the armour of an American armoured division be sent to the Middle East immediately, which was approved without delay by the President, and 300 Sherman tanks and 100 105-mm self-propelled guns were released and made ready for transporting, much to the annoyance of the US armoured division that had only just received them. Despite the setback of Tobruk, Churchill had been successful in persuading Roosevelt to agree to the invasion of French North Africa, putting the African campaign before the European and Pacific theatres.

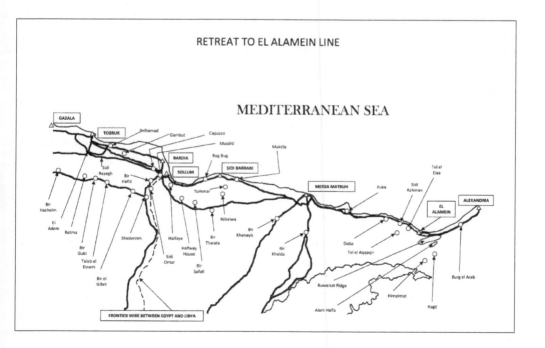

With the fall of Tobruk the remainder of the Eighth Army continued eastwards through the 'wire' into Egypt. Maj. Hastings recalled the impressive sight of the 4th Armoured Brigade in battle formation on the Egyptian side of the wire, facing west. 'B' Company 2nd RB, commanded by Hastings, together with the Light Squadron of the 5th Royal Tanks were probably the last 'formed' Eighth Army body to cross the frontier, withdrawing through the ranks of the 4th Armoured Brigade at about 1800 hours. The change in circumstances required the 7th Motor Brigade Columns to move from harassing the enemy to monitoring their movement and supporting the Eighth Army withdrawal to Sollum, just across the Egyptian border. Rifleman Martin wrote:

> We crossed the wire this morning and are now fighting on Egyptian soil. All our armour seems to have fallen back, leaving just our columns up here. Our main problem now is lack of sleep. Just a couple of hours each day is all we can get and everyone is extremely tired.[94]

Unfortunately during a night patrol with 'July' Column, 2nd Lt John Reeve was killed.[95] The enemy momentum continued, seemingly unstoppable, forcing Ritchie to review his plans, giving as much space as possible between his forces and the *Panzerarmee*, abandoning Sollum, passing Buqbuq and Sidi Barrani, and onto the defensive positions at Mersa Matruh.

Col. Bonner F. Fellers

Rommel had been receiving reports on aspects of the Allied war machine in North Africa since 1941 from his *gute quelle* (good source), otherwise known as Col. Bonner F. Fellers, the American military attaché in Cairo, who as one of the most important Americans in the Mediterranean could travel just about anywhere he liked, being informed of every aspect of the Allied military equipment, tactics and performance. This information was relayed back to Washington two or three times a week using the 'The Black Code', the cipher of which had been stolen from the American Embassy in Rome and sold to the Italians in August 1941.[96] The detailed reports were praised by the Americans for their content and valuable information on the conduct of both the Axis and Allied forces, but were in Rommel's hands within hours of them being sent. This situation could not continue and after the security lapse was discovered in June, Churchill was advised on the 23rd, 'Cyphers now changed.'[97] Within a month Fellers was back in Washington, to something of a hero's welcome.[98]

Egypt

The Afrika Korps spearheads entered Egypt forty-five miles south of Sidi Omar during the evening of the 23rd, with the triumphant main forces surging forward almost unopposed. An astonishing advance of well over 100 miles had been made, although at a cost of reducing his armoured complement to just forty-four tanks. In Rommel's eyes the Eighth Army was extremely weak, but if he could succeed in destroying the tattered remnants there would be nothing left in Egypt capable of opposing his advance to Alexandria and the Suez Canal. He wrote to his wife, 'We're on the move and hope to land the next big punch very soon. Speed is the main thing now.'[99]

On 25 June, Auchinleck accompanied by Acting Maj.-Gen. Eric Edward 'Chink' Dorman-Smith flew from Cairo to the front, using the floor of the otherwise empty Boston bomber to make their plans for stopping the *Panzerarmee* advance, before arriving at the Eighth Army HQ at Maaten Bagush and curtly relieving Ritchie of his post. Auchinleck had now assumed direct tactical command of Eighth Army. Ritchie was shocked by the suddenness of his sacking and returned to the UK. He would be blamed for turning success into a failure. However, the ultimate responsibility for the disasters of Gazala and the loss of Cyrenaica had to lie with the Commander-in-Chief, Auchinleck himself. As felt by Churchill, his main mistake was to have appointed Ritchie in the first place.[100]

The airborne review of the Eighth Army's situation proved that Mersa Matruh could not be held and accordingly Auchinleck ordered the Army to withdraw an additional 150 miles to El Alamein, where they would make a stand. Lt Gen. William 'Strafer' Gott moved the XIII Corps and what remained of his artillery away to the east, Maj.-Gen. Sir Howard Kippenberger, commanding the New Zealand Division newly arrived from Syria, wrote:

> Eighth Army poured back through us, not looking at all demoralized except for the black South African drivers but thoroughly mixed up and disorganized. I did not see a single formal fighting unit, infantry, armour or artillery.[101]

The fact that the Eighth Army had not lost their morale was a credit to the individual officers and men, but the fact cannot be ignored that in these confused, climactic days the system of command had to all intents and purposes broken down.[102] Advising Brooke that he had taken command of the Eighth Army, Auchinleck received a reply from the Deputy Prime Minister:

> War Cabinet are glad to know that you have gone forward to take command of Eighth Army. They have every confidence in you and in your gallant troops, and in your ability to stop the enemy at Matruh and in due course to drive him back.[103]

Auchinleck now took forty-eight hours to determine his next move. 'If he faltered now, he could lose Egypt and the whole Middle East – perhaps lose the war itself, but without doubt put off victory for years.'[104] His next decision therefore was to keep the Eighth Army fully mobile, not making a firm stand at Matruh but bringing Rommel to a halt between El Alamein and the Qattara Depression, as stated in his dispatch: 'In no circumstances was any part of the Eighth Army to be allowed to be shut up in Matruh, even if this involved abandoning the position entirely.'[105] Slowing Rommel down to give the Eighth Army time to retreat was now the order of the day.

The night of 25 June saw the battalion's 'S' Company guarding a minefield gap approximately thirty-one miles down the Siwa Track from Mersa Matruh, through which the enemy intended to pass and attack the rear parties of the withdrawing Eighth Army.[106] Rifleman Martin continued:

> Had a rotten time last night. We were detailed to hold 'until the end' a gap in the minefield through which the enemy must pass. What a ridiculous order! One company expected to hold up the might of the German armour![107]

Their guns facing across the minefield, the riflemen watched the enemy sappers lifting mines in front of them, taking pot shots at them when the opportunity arose. But as dawn broke they received the attention of a few Messerschmitt 109s which shot up the positions, missing the riflemen by as little as 20 feet, and were then treated to a barrage of enemy artillery shells which began falling amongst them. Martin wrote in his diary:

> We contacted the enemy this morning and had a few hours lead slinging. When dawn broke there was about 500 vehicles and guns a couple of hundred yards away from us. We fired the first shot and all hell broke loose for a while. I think we came off best in that sortie, knocking out some guns and tanks.[108]

Holding this position allowed the retreating Eighth Army units to gain some distance between them and the *Panzerarmee*, reducing the chance of an attack on their rear. Accordingly, the riflemen were now given permission to vacate their position to join the withdrawal. In a similar fashion, a concentration of recently arrived British tanks collided with the Afrika Korps and XX Italian Corps in the area of Khalda, launching attack after attack on the enemy formations until late evening by which time eighteen of the new tanks had been sacrificed on the battlefield. Battles continued as on the night of 27/28 June when the 90th Light Division's advance was stalled by the artillery fire of the 50th (Northumbrian) Infantry Division, while the attack of the 15th Panzer Division was stopped by the 4th Armoured and the 7th Motor brigades. This left the 21st Panzer Division to attack the New Zealanders occupying Minqar Qaim Ridge, which resulted in an exchange of artillery fire during which a shell splinter tore a serious deep and ragged gash in Lt Gen. Sir Bernard Freyberg's neck – his thirteenth war wound scar according to Churchill, though of course, as Freyberg explained, 'You always get two scars for every bullet or splinter, because mostly they have to come out as well as go in!'[109]

The New Zealanders withdrawal east was now blocked by the 21st Panzer Division and they needed to move south to break out, with Rommel ordering units of the Brescia and Pavia to seal up the gaps in his line. However, due to poor transport, they did not get into position quickly enough, and during the night the 4th New Zealand Brigade broke through with bayonets fixed, the remainder following them out in transports or escaping via a more southerly route. To Gott it seemed as if the whole division was being overrun and, based on this assumption, instructed the troops under his command to withdraw to prepared positions at Fuka. The *Panzerarmee* was now spread over the battlefield as follows:

- The Afrika Korps were strung out between the coast, ten miles east of Gerwala and a point on the Siwa Track sixty miles east of Matruh;
- The 90th was east of Matruh;
- The 21st was fifteen miles south, with two brigades of New Zealanders to the west cutting them off from the 15th;
- The 15th further south were intent on chasing the 1st Armoured Division, but were being harassed by 7th Motor Brigade.

Faced with this position, Mersa Matruh could not be defended and Auchinleck sent the codeword 'Pike', signalling a general co-ordinated withdrawal to Fuka, but was unaware that Gott had already instructed the New Zealanders to withdraw.[110] The withdrawal now became uncoordinated, as units from corps to division to internal formations all acted independently of each other. The brigades of the 1st Armoured Division left the 7th Motor Brigade to fend for itself, a distinct attitude of 'I'm alright Jack!'[111]

The southern flank was left open, X Corps only discovering the absence of Gott's XIII Corps at 0430 hours the next day at about the same time as finding that their line of retreat was blocked. That evening they broke the division up into brigade-sized units, with vehicles and guns forming up nose to tail in the dark ten yards apart and driving south. As they proceeded they came across several enemy laagers, resulting in pitched battles, the 5th Indian Division sustaining heavy casualties including the destruction of the 29th Indian Infantry Brigade.

Overall, more than 6,000 Allied prisoners and forty tanks with an enormous quantity of supplies were lost to the enemy, providing alternative food rations to the monotonous diet of cheese and the 'AM' brand of canned beef of the Italian forces, known as *Arabo Morto* (Dead Arab) and to the Germans as *Alter Mann* (Old Man) or *Asinus Mussolini* (Musso's Donkey).[112]

Douglas Waller of the 1st RB recalled:

> One dump we went past, we had time for a breather and we stopped. I said to one of our chaps, 'Nip over, see if you can get anything out of there.' The Red Caps stopped him and said, 'You can't come in here, we're going to blow it up.' So he said, 'Well, can't I take something?' but they wouldn't let us. They just blew the lot up. They were blowing up the dumps of food, petrol, on the way back. We were just flapping back until we got to Alamein.[113]

However, without the Military Police on guard, it was often a different story, as told by RB Cpl Peter Taylor:

> We got to a place called Fuqa, where there was a huge NAAFI, which had been abandoned that morning. Such was the rapid advance of the German forces, that they'd had to just down tools and take off. But there was a terrific cauldron of hard-boiled eggs still bubbling merrily on the fire. There were cases and cases of stuff all over the place. We got into the NAAFI, picked up one or two nice bottles of drink and a few of these boiled eggs and took off down the road.[114]

By the evening of the 28th, the 21st Panzer had reached the Matruh escarpment, and were again helping themselves to British stores and equipment. The next day, the 90th Light Division, *Kampfstaffel Kiehl* (Kiehl Battle Squadron) and 580th Reconnaissance Regiment sped through Mersa Matruh as the Eighth Army fire gradually died away and finally ceased. They did not even stop to swim in the blue sea, slowing their advance only to drop off Allied prisoners collected at Fuka, before taking a southern detour of some five miles across the desert towards Bir el Quseir in order to stop stray British units reaching the Alamein Line. Rifleman Martin wrote:

> Still more bad news. Matruh reported evacuated. Enemy at Fuka. Could it be worse? Can you wonder at our state of depression when our small band seems to be the only one doing anything? Our position now is south-west of Daba.[115]

Rommel wrote to his wife:

> Now the battle of Mersa Matruh has been won and our leading units are only 125 miles from Alexandria. There'll be a few more battles to fight before we reach our goal, but I think the worst is well behind us ... We're already 300 miles east of Tobruk.[116]

During the 29th, the desert between Matruh and El Alamein was covered with small columns of Eighth Army and *Panzerarmee* vehicles all moving eastwards, trying to avoid each other, but often not accomplishing this. The 7th Motor Brigade continued harassing the enemy in order to give straggling Allied units time to get back to Alamein, and by last light on 30 June they were completely cut off behind enemy lines.[117] Lt Gen. Sir Brian Horrocks later stated that 'it was largely due to the skill and tenacity with which they carried out a phased withdrawal against the Germans equipped with their superior armaments that Rommel was defeated' in gaining access to the delta.[118]

With Axis forces advancing non-stop, the remaining Allied contingents withdrew to the last defensive line before Cairo, the delta and the Middle East – the El Alamein Line – the breaching of which would have had a psychological effect of incalculable negativity to the war effort. But to do this Rommel had to extend his supply lines, while those of the Eighth Army were shortened or, as one journalist simply put it, the idea was to 'stretch Rommel and break him on ground of our own choosing, bring him on to our anvil and use the sledgehammer'.[119] Rommel wrote:

> [...] this series of engagements had brought the strength of my Army to the point of exhaustion. With our reserves – including the immediately usable booty – beginning to run out, it was only the men's amazing spirit and will to victory that kept them going at all. Not only had no replacement material arrived, but, with an almost unbelievable lack of appreciation of the situation, the supply authorities had actually sent only three thousand tons to Africa during June, as compared with our real requirement of sixty thousand tons, a figure which was never in fact attained.[120]

The 2nd RB, as well as the 1st and 9th RB battalions, was isolated well behind enemy lines, harassing and attacking communications and supply columns, often travelling along the same route as the enemy in an effort to reach the rest of the army. Rifleman Martin wrote:

> Now the fun had started. Here we are about 60 miles on the wrong side of Jerry's lines and we have somehow to get back to our own. We had a small shoot-out and knocked out a few vehicles. Then the tanks were sent after us and, boy, did we nip off smartly![121]

Small conflicts continued as opposing forces found themselves facing each other. Identification was made all the more difficult due to the *Panzerarmee*'s use of British transport and uniforms. At dawn on the 30th, the 7th Motor Brigade unexpectedly attacked the rear of the Italian XX Corps, proceeding to overrun the headquarters and most of one division, then promptly turning 180 degrees and digging in to prevent the rest of the Italians advancing. The Italians called for assistance, with Rommel replying, 'I demand that your corps should carry out the attack, destroy the enemy and reach its objective. The enemy is under orders to withdraw.'[122] Having held up the Italians for sufficient time to provide more breathing space for their withdrawing colleagues, the 7th Motor withdrew, Rommel sarcastically signalling the Italians an hour later, 'Trust your corps will now find itself able to cope with so contemptible an enemy.'[123]

El Alamein Line

Like most of the soldiers of the Eighth Army, the battalion's riflemen were suffering badly from lack of sleep, and fatigue had been steadily accumulating after four weeks of battle with too many night-time raids. To make matters worse, as they pushed on across the desert they were harassed by enemy aircraft, which bombed and strafed their columns with what felt like uncomfortable and alarming regularity. Maj. Hastings wrote of the 2nd RB:

> The Regiment who had been among the first to meet the enemy on 26 May, had been the last to withdraw, the last through the wire; and, in a collection of vehicles which would have disgraced a circus, were among the last to reach Alamein.[124]

The Alamein Defensive Line obtained its name from the small village and railway station of El Alamein, located between Mersa Matruh and Alexandria, about 150 miles west of Cairo. The line was made up of several defensive boxes anchored by the Mediterranean Sea in the north, where the ridge of Tel el Alamein (hill of twin cairns) between the station and the sea was to be found, and progressing southwards to Qaret el Himeimat situated on the border of the dried up salt-lake known as the Qattara Depression. It was this depression that anchored the southern end of the line and prevented the flank from being turned. The Qattara Depression was an almost lunar landscape, proving an impenetrable barrier to most wheeled and tracked vehicles. With a height at its edges of 237 m above sea level, down to its lowest point of 74 m below sea level, it ran diagonally south-west to north-east in the shape of a funnel, starting in the west with its narrowest point some forty miles from the sea at Alamein. Auchinleck had chosen the relatively narrow line well. Both flanks were secured against natural obstacles and the available high ground afforded good visibility.

The most thoroughly developed of the boxes was around Alamein's railway station, where to the north ran the coastal road. Lucas Phillips recalled that the station:

> [...] was a sort of goods yard and a compound surrounded by barbed wire on a line of crazy poles. Behind the station buildings stood a row of shattered shacks with their doors hanging open ... Where the road crosses the metals stood a signal, its arm inappropriately set at 'safety'. The entire neighbourhood seemed to be completely deserted and, as I mounted the platform, I read on the front of the building the name of the place, ALAMEIN.[125]

The railway track was situated approximately two miles inland from the sea, between which was the coastal sand resembling a brackish marsh and on the other side of the track the land spread into an almost totally featureless waste, broken only by the two ridges: Miteirya and Ruweisat. Ruweisat Ridge was ten miles long, running east to west, bare and narrow with an average height of 180 feet above the desert floor, providing good observation facilities, the eastern end flattening out to merge with the surrounding desert.

The next main position was some fifteen miles inland and included the peak at Qaret el Abd, close to the Bab el Qattara defensive box approximately twenty miles from the coast and eight miles from the Ruweisat Ridge. The line had a westerly convexity and provided excellent visibility especially to the north, though the intervening ground, named Deir el Shein, was a depression.

Further south still the desert became more ragged, broken by sharp-edged escarpments and flat-topped hills, the most significant of which was Qaret el Himeimat providing excellent visibility in all directions. The furthest forward position in the south was Naqb Abu Dweis, thirty-four miles from the coast and protecting the pass through the Qattara Depression at the end of the Rahman Track.

The terrain therefore forced an enemy reliant on armour to channel his advance into three avenues of 'good going':

- North between the coast and Ruweisat Ridge;
- Centre between Qaret el Abd and south of Ruweisat Ridge; and
- South between Jebel Kalakh and Himeimat.

The end point of each of these avenues was protected by a defensive box, and the area between would be covered by mobile elements of the now artillery-heavy 'Jock Columns'.

Work had started in August 1941, shortly after Auchinleck's appointment as Commander-in-Chief Middle East, with engineers, civilian labour and varying degrees of enthusiasm[126] set by the varied levels of success or failure in the desert war. Unfortunately, they were not complete. Tom Bird recalled 'that they had been told about the line, but were quite disappointed when they got there as it was just another piece of desert'.[127] When reaching the line the riflemen heard the suave voice of the BBC announcer reporting that the Eighth Army had reached the Alamein 'Line', and looking around at the empty desert on either side indistinguishable from the miles of sand to east and west, made ungentlemanly comments. Albert Martin was more forthright. 'Line? What line? I see no flaming line!'[128]

The Alamein Line as an impenetrable fortress was a figment of public imagination. There were no fortifications, underground headquarters, great guns or tons of ammunition, although astride the coastal road a strong position was almost ready for occupation albeit only partially mined and wired. Other defences had progressed to varying degrees, ending in the position at Naqb Abu Dweis where very little work had been done. As a last precaution in the event that the line could not be held, further defensive positions were constructed in the rear positions, and measures were taken to flood the Nile if needed. The suggested reliance on these positions by Auchinleck would be used against him in later political battles, even though it had actually being proposed by the War Office in 1940, but despite these plans being in place, Auchinleck had no intention of retreating from the Alamein Line and giving up Egypt to Rommel. His notes for a counter-offensive showed that he intended to 'defeat the enemy and destroy him',[129] by using XXX Corps to stop the advance, with XIII Corps, 1st Armoured and New Zealand Division to attack northwards against the enemy's right flank and rear, inflicting as much damage as possible and preventing the occupation from taking place. XIII Corps took over the southern half of the line, with what was left of the New Zealand and 5th Indian divisions, while XXX Corps, with the 50th and 1st South African divisions, concentrated in the northern sector and especially around the El Alamein fortifications. X Corps was placed further east as part of the force to defend Alexandria and the western edge of the delta.

The retreat had been a combination of poor communication, missed opportunities, and well-intentioned actions based on misinterpreted situations by senior staff who were not aware of or could not see the 'big picture'. An RB officer wrote to Ann Crowder, saying that 'in general the fighting has been skilful & successful, but the manoeuvre & coordination bad. We are very angry, bitter and shamed about it all.'[130]

The fall of Tobruk brought to a head the problems of the North African campaign from the perspective of Parliament and the press. At Westminster, Churchill was fighting for his ministerial life, as the disquiet produced by the battle failures and loss of Tobruk increased to almost distrust of the War Cabinet and in particular Churchill's direction of the war as a whole. Churchill had for the last two years exercised almost undisputed authority; he was still the powerful war Prime Minster that Britain needed to defeat the Axis, but was currently extremely vulnerable. When he entered the House for the start of the two-day debate; 'his face was white and set. There was no hint of chubbiness. The lines around his mouth were grim.'[131] On the second day a motion was raised by the right-wing Sir John Wardlaw-Milne, Conservative MP for Kidderminster, aiming to curb Churchill's power:

> That this House, while paying tribute to the heroism and endurance of the Armed Forces of the Crown in circumstances of exceptional difficulty, has no confidence in the central direction of the war.[132]

The Labour MP Aneurin Bevan gave one of his most 'memorably destructive wartime speeches' including, 'The Prime Minister wins debate after debate and loses battle after battle – The country is beginning to say that he fights debates like a war and the war like a debate.'[133]

In his memoirs Lord Winterton clarified the intention behind the attack:

> The gist of the remarks was that if there were a series of disasters such as we had undergone, the Prime Minister must be held constitutionally responsible.[134]

Churchill spoke for forty-five minutes before the vote was taken, resulting in twenty-five adverse votes against 477 in Churchill's favour.[135] Roosevelt cabled Churchill with just three words: 'Good for you.'[136]

Churchill spent the afternoon in discussions with Brooke and several other generals reviewing the Alamein situation and the forthcoming battle. The immediate crisis in London had been averted, but the military situation in North Africa was not settled and Churchill was losing confidence in Auchinleck – something that would have to be resolved sooner rather than later.

CHAPTER 3

Zero plus 107 days and the First Battle of El Alamein

The First Battle of El Alamein was not one continuous battle but a group of engagements extending over most of the month of July,[1] as the exhausted *Panzerarmee* tried to break through the Alamein Line to secure the significant prize of the delta and beyond, whilst the Eighth Army sought to wear down their opponents, depriving Rommel of this goal.

> Some great, decisive battles have been fought at a campaign's beginning, and in history's light there is about them a strange morning freshness, an air of innocence and youthful ardour … But there are other battles, even more far-reaching in their consequence, which are fought at the latter end of long campaigns, in a wintery, grey Arthurian dusk, or in some stony pass beneath a torrid, unsparing sun that knows no romance and no illusion. The soldiers in such battles are trained fighters, lean and sinewy men, toughened by many hardships, disappointments and losses … The first Battle of Alamein was of this latter kind.[2]

However, as Lt Col. Pymann wrote, 'History will establish that one of the greatest hours of the 8th Army was when it stood at bay under AUCHINLECK, NORRIE and GOTT at ALAMEIN.[3] On the morning of 1 July, Auchinleck said, 'These damn British have been taught too long to be good losers. I've never been a good loser, I am going to win.[4]

'The Flap'

At the port of Alexandria, the Mediterranean Fleet now under command of Vice-Admiral Sir Henry Harwood[5] was ordered to disperse between Haifa, Beirut and Port Said, with the damaged RMS *Queen Elizabeth* floated off the harbour bed before sailing to Port Sudan and onwards to the United States.[6] The departure of the fleet was seen by the Egyptians as Britain preparing to 'give up' Egypt, causing a panic among high society as military staff were instructed to burn confidential papers to ensure they could not fall into enemy hands. So many documents were being torched in Cairo that you could buy peanuts in twists of paper marked 'Most Secret', the day becoming known as 'Ash Wednesday' or simply 'The Flap'. Men were rushed from rear areas to reinforce the line, whilst at the same time others were moving back, seeking to replace damaged or missing equipment or seeking medical treatment, with troops everywhere milling around railway stations and main road junctions. The resultant confusion caused Britain's faltering credibility to slide further, with the anti-colonial sentiment already looking at an Axis victory further impacting the morale, spread by correspondents sitting in their hotel lounges trading their ill-informed stories.[7]

The men at the front were amused by stories of panic involving the general staff, with Tuker, commander of 4th Indian Division, expressing his thoughts: 'After all, up front all a man has to lose is his life, while way behind a man can easily lose his luggage. That prospect can be most worrying.'[8] Antony Beevor wrote:

> For the Jewish community the prospect was terrifying, but although the British authorities in Cairo offered them priority on the trains to Palestine, the Palestine administration refused them visas. Jewish fears were not misplaced. An SS *Einsatzkommando* unit[9] was waiting in Athens to begin work in Egypt, and then Palestine if Rommel's string of victories continued.[10]

Meanwhile, a German radio broadcast addressed the women of Alexandria, warning them to 'Get out your party frocks, we're on the way!'[11]

RAF Officer Ann Crowder buried decoding machines in the desert, placing tents on top to disguise the location, whilst continuing the daily routines above. Rommel later wrote:

> The British no longer seemed to trust their luck and were preparing for a retreat. I was convinced that a breakthrough over a wide front by my forces would result in complete panic.[12]

Although battered, ground down and in no small part bemused, the Eighth Army was still far from beaten. The Desert Rats were down but not out, and their morale, despite such repeated pummellings, did not collapse. On the other hand, Rommel was acutely aware that the longer the battle went on, the stronger the Eighth Army defences were likely to become, while with an over-extended supply line, his forces would only weaken.

Rommel Attacks

After chasing the Eighth Army across the desert from Gazala, Rommel was now faced with the last obstacle between him, the delta and the 'riches' beyond, held by a tired and some said demoralised Eighth Army.[13] Lt. Pietro Ostellino wrote to his wife:

> Things here get better and better. As you will have heard from the radio and newspapers, the English and their allies are taking such a beating that they will find it difficult to raise their heads again. They deserve it! Our soldiers are simply marvellous. We cannot fail to be victorious now.[14]

Rommel's plan was to split the Eighth Army at the inter-corps line between XXX Corps and XIII Corps before wreaking havoc among the rear communication and supply lines, hoping that, as at Gazala, the British would then collapse. The attack began in the late afternoon of 30 June, as a single panzer division moved south from El Quseir, making as much noise and dust as possible and alerting the British of their presence and likely intention of outflanking the line in the far south. In similar fashion as the opening sequences of Gazala, once the *Panzerarmee* felt that the 'bait had been swallowed' the panzers turned northwards to rejoin their colleagues in the central part of the line advancing towards the real target. Auchinleck, however, was fully aware of the feint due to his reading of the Ultra transcripts. He therefore did not reinforce the 7th Armoured Division in the south, but as a precaution ordered the 7th Motor Brigade to remain well ahead of the line in the south-western area of Jebel Kalakh to act as an antenna just in case the south was the real target.

The *Panzerarmee* advance continued in the early hours of 1 July, as the 90th Light Division made smooth progress towards the Miteirya Ridge straight into the defences of the 1st South African Division, where they faced gun positions in the shape of a crescent that proceeded to lay down a fierce two-hour artillery barrage. Hearing the noise of the guns, Rommel rushed up in an armoured car, later writing:

> Furious fire again struck into our ranks. British shells came screaming in from three directions, north, east and south; anti-aircraft tracer streaked through our force. Under this tremendous weight of fire, our attack came to a standstill.[15]

Their luck did not change, as when they had extricated themselves from the 1st South Africans they immediately came under the fire of the 3rd South African Brigade, who poured such a tremendous weight of fire on the enemy that they were forced to dig in, only being able to move north again during an appalling khamsin that struck at noon.

The 15th and 21st Panzer divisions were instructed to move up, but were delayed by the sandstorm that had been so beneficial to their colleagues. Then, their luck seemingly having changed, they found their first objective of Deir el Abyad empty, but on swinging south to their next target they discovered that the 18th Indian Infantry Brigade, fresh from Iraq, had occupied Deir el Shein at the end of the Ruweisat Ridge. The extensive minefields of the Deir el Shein box forced the panzers to stop whilst the area was reconnoitred, allowing the Desert Air Force to attack the parked tanks.[16] The 21st Panzer stormed the strongpoint at 1600 hours, the position falling that evening, with 2,000 Indians being taken prisoner and thirty guns destroyed or captured, along with some 1,500 rounds of artillery ammunition which were added to the *Panzerarmee* stores to be fired by the captured British 25-pounders. The Indians defence provided sufficient time for the positions at the western end of Ruweisat Ridge to be reorganised, giving the 22nd Armoured Brigade the opportunity to force the 15th Panzer back.

Rommel now changed his plan, instructing the panzers to form up abreast of the Ruweisat Ridge, with the 21st on the northern slope, the 15th on the southern ridge and the Italians replacing the panzers of the 90th in the attack against XIII Corps. The 15th Panzers advanced in the afternoon along the southern ridge, coming under heavy concentrated artillery fire as well as bombing by the Desert Air Force. An *ad hoc* column was created, called 'Robcol', who held the position east of the ridge, giving the 4th Armoured Brigade sufficient time to come up to take on the 15th Panzer. The 21st Panzer Division were also stopped when they received brigade strength 75-mm fire from the 22nd Armoured Division, firing at their extreme effective range but co-ordinating that fire with at least four batteries of artillery situated south of Alam Nayil.

Named after its commander, Brig. Robert Waller, 'Robcol' linked the 6-pounder anti-tank guns of the 1st RB with heavier 25-pounder guns. Rifleman Laurie Philips recalled:

> Because of the shortage of tanks they decided to use us as 'armour'; with the guns up 'on portee' [*sic*]. We reversed into action alongside the tanks. Because there was a lot of soft sand in the area where we were operating, south of Ruweisat, we had Honey tanks standing by to tow us out if we got stuck and Crusaders to bring us up ammunition and petrol.[17] We put in an attack in the afternoon

and met the 21st Panzer Division head on as it advanced to attack us; we fired over 100 rounds with our gun (we had to pull back for more after we had used the 70 we carried) and it got pretty hot.[18]

Both panzer divisions withdrew just before dusk, harassed by the Desert Air Force who continued their attacks though the night as they returned almost to their start line. Rommel wrote:

> After three days vainly assaulting the Alamein Line, I decided that I would call the offensive off for the moment after the next day's attack. Reasons for my decision were the steadily mounting strength of the enemy, the low fighting strength of my own divisions, which amounted by that time to no more than 1,200 to 1,500 men, and above all the terribly strained supply situation.[19]

He wrote to his wife, 'The struggle for the last position before Alexandria is hard.'[20] Von Mellenthin later wrote:

> Our prospects of victory were hopelessly prejudiced on July 1st. Our one chance was to outmanoeuvre the enemy, but we had been drawn into a battle of attrition. 1st Armoured Division was given an extra day to reorganize, and when the Afrika Korps advanced on July 2nd it found the British armour strongly posted on Ruweisat Ridge, and quite capable of beating off such attacks as we could muster. The South African positions were strong, and 90th Light never had a chance of breaking through them.[21]

Auchinleck, who according to Maj. David Parry of the New Zealand Division, 'had assumed the roles of Corps, Division, Brigade and now even Battalion commander, giving orders on a micro command level direct to the officers and men involved', now drove around in his staff car visiting and cajoling his fighting troops to give him more, calling for them to 'bloody the enemy's nose'.[22] The opportunity arose the very next day, as around 0900 hours the Ariete set off without escort to a position east of Bab el Qattara known as 'Deep Well'. Intending to protect the *Panzerarmee*'s southern flank, they had almost reached Alam Nayil when they came under artillery fire immediately followed by an attack by the 19th Battalion, 4th Brigade of the New Zealand Division, 5th Indian Division and 7th Motor Brigade, who overran them in short order, taking forty-four of their guns and some 350 prisoners. The remaining Italian troops took to their heels in panic,[23] but were then caught in the flank by the 4th Armoured Brigade, reducing their strength down to five M13 tanks and two guns. Rommel later wrote that:

> [...] the reverse [of the Italians] took us completely by surprise, for in the weeks of fighting around Knightsbridge, the Ariete – covered, it is true, by German guns and tanks – had fought well against every onslaught of the British although their casualties had not been light, but now the Italians were no longer equal to the very great demands being made of them.[24]

Rommel instructed the 90th Light to go forward, with the Littorio and his reconnaissance battalions in close support, to cover the gap caused by the Ariete losses, this resulted in them being exposed to fire from all sides. But this time, despite the murderous fire, the Italians did not withdraw, instead taking up defensive positions, their presence remaining an embarrassment to the British, who had their freedom to move around the area severely curtailed. After dusk the Afrika Korps, now consisting of just twenty-six tanks and manned by very tired men, advanced towards the southern slopes of the Ruweisat Ridge only to find the bulk of the 4th and 22nd Armoured brigades waiting for them, again pinning them down with concentric defensive fire.

The initial attacks of the First Battle of El Alamein had been repulsed, the enemy were still fifteen miles short of their objective, and Auchinleck now gave orders to withdraw from the Bab el Qattara and Naqb Abu Dweis positions on the edge of the depression, feeling that the line in these areas was over-extended. The 5th Indian and the New Zealand divisions, including the 7th Motor Brigade, were given a more mobile role.

Rommel was still determined to open the road to Alexandria, regarding the recent impediments as only temporary and convinced that he would break through at which point panic would ensue throughout the British forces. Brooke reported to the War Cabinet at noon on the 3rd, advising them that there was a clear danger that the *Panzerarmee* could break through the Alamein Line and relating the possibilities in the event of this situation becoming a reality:

> If the El Alamein line was pierced, Rommel could either strike east or south but, owing to the fact that the delta was unsuitable for operations by armoured forces, he would have to use infantry, and this would give us an opportunity to meet him on equal terms. If the enemy made his main thrust to the south towards Cairo, he would meet the Army which had been organized in the delta and the 8th Army would be well placed to harass his communications. Similarly, if the enemy kept on towards Alexandria, the Delta Army could attack his flank.[25]

But breaking through was not an option:

> Spirits at home were low. Churchill's people had grown morbidly sensitive about the contrast between the heroic struggle waged by the Russians and their own nation's feeble battlefield showing. A British victory was desperately needed, and only in the desert was this attainable.[26]

Garmoyle Fatally Wounded

The columns of the 7th Motor Brigade continued their operations, with 'March' Column operating to the south of the 2nd Armoured Brigade position, whilst 'April' Column operated further to the west where they encountered an enemy concentration of 2,000 MET along with forty tanks. The enemy force appeared to be attempting to drive through to El Mayid, a town located on the coast railway line approximately twenty-five miles further east from Alamein. They were heavily engaged by 'April' Column, which when supported by heavy artillery fire and bombing from the Desert Air Force brought the force to a halt. During the action Brig. Garmoyle, having rejoined the column after returning from a visit to a neighbouring armoured brigade, received a fatal shrapnel wound to his stomach, dying some twelve hours later.[27] Command of the 7th Motor Brigade was passed to Col. Jimmy Bosville, another rifleman who had previously been in command of the 1st RB, Freddie Stevens replacing him there. While serving in 'March' Column, Tom Bird was also wounded, and evacuated to the rear areas. Rifleman Martin wrote:

> Captain Bird was wounded today, not badly, but enough to put another of our best officers out of combat. Every day now, it seems, one of our men is either killed or wounded to the extent that our

company is down to about half strength. We appear to have brought Jerry to a halt but it remains to be seen whether our efforts have been enough to smash him so that he gives up![28]

The *Panzerarmee* now withdrew, and in expectation of a counter-attack began the construction of their own defensive line, Rommel writing, 'In these circumstances a continuation of the attack next day would have resulted in nothing more than a useless attrition of strength.'[29] He considered this to be no more that breathing space to allow his troops to recoup their strength, explaining further in a letter to his wife, 'Resistance is too great and our strength exhausted. However, I still hope to find a way to achieve our goal.'[30] To Kesselring he wrote, '... the intention [now] is in the first place to hold the front and regroup in such a manner that 2nd New Zealand Division can be encircled and destroyed'.[31] Unbeknown to Rommel, Auchinleck was fully aware of both his strength and the exhausted state of his troops, having received the Ultra transcripts by midnight. However, he had problems of his own, as despite the Eighth Army's withdrawal now coming to a close, he had lost approximately 70,000 of the men who had stood at Gazala.[32] Maj. Hastings was by now working as GSO2 to Gen. 'Wingy' Renton and recalled him saying:

> In the last campaign we won a tactical victory but were strategically defeated because the winning of the victory had left us so weak. This time we had been tactically defeated but had won a strategic victory – because we had given the enemy such a knock that it would take him six months to recuperate, while we should be in a position to have another go in a month or six weeks.[33]

Auchinleck's objective had been to ensure that the Eighth Army remained a fighting force. Although it had lost an enormous amount of stores, men and material, its framework still existed and it was ready to do battle again.

> Auchinleck's distinct and definite intention was to fight to the last at El Alamein, and should this battle go against him to go on fighting every inch of the way in Egypt. This was the intention from the moment he assumed personal command of Eighth Army; by July 3-4 he had fulfilled the first part of it, and had compelled Rommel to face the facts of failure and defeat.[34]

With Rommel's advance to the delta halted and with him now consolidating his positions, Auchinleck had proved that the Eighth Army was not going to be pushed back. The chaos and panic that had reigned in the streets of Alexandria and Cairo over the last few days suddenly stopped on the evening of 3 July. 'Life returned to as it was before the crisis; the packed exits had emptied; the crowds of refugees returned and the somewhat meretricious life of the delta was resumed.'[35] It was just as if nothing had changed.

On 4 July, Auchinleck ordered the New Zealanders to advance north-westwards through the El Mreir position, cutting across Rommel's communication lines, and in so doing the 5th New Zealand Brigade met the Italian X Corps, forcing them to withdraw. Seeing this, Rommel moved the 21st Panzer Division back towards El Mreir, leaving the gap at Ruweisat Ridge protected by the 15th Panzer and 90th Light divisions. These movements gave the impression that the *Panzerarmee* was retreating. Sensing a possible advantage, the British armour attacked, achieving some success against the rifle regiments of the 15th Panzer, until they came across a minefield which halted their advance and providing a lone 88 mm with an excellent range of targets, resulting in the tanks withdrawing.

Auchinleck realised that many of Rommel's successes were achieved when he used the Italian divisions as a fulcrum and the Afrika Korps as a lever against the Allied defences. He now decided to attack wherever the Afrika Korps were not, hitting the Italians and forcing the Afrika Korps to come to their aid, before moving on to the next Italian position. Sun Tzu taught that:

> The enemy must not know where I intend to give battle … For if he prepares to the front his rear will be weak, and if to the rear, his front will be fragile. If he prepares to the left, his right will be vulnerable and if to the right, there will be few on his left. And when he prepares everywhere he will be weak everywhere.[36]

Many such engagements were reported during the day, due mainly to the repositioning of units along the line, providing the Desert Air Force that was supporting the ground troops with the opportunity of making about 900 sorties against the enemy. The 2nd RB saw action throughout the day, with Hugo Salmon being wounded for the third time since arriving in the desert and Jimmy Irwin receiving a slight wound.[37] The worst news came that afternoon when the riflemen were informed that Brig. The Viscount Garmoyle DSO, who had led them through so much, had died of his wounds.

The battalion was by now in serious need of a refit, and it was decided that this should happen on a company basis, with 'S' Company being first to receive this much dreamed of attention. They immediately set off diagonally across the desert for forty miles, where they picked up the coastal road and a short ninety miles later reached their destination where clean water and a cold 'Stella' waited. The next day saw the 7th Motor Brigade withdraw to a reserve area, leaving an observation post in place, armed with one of the anti-tank guns that dispatched a Mk III Panzer, and with the columns continuing operate as before. Skirmishes continued, but the main Axis effort, at least for now, was spent – the attack on Alamein was a failure. Auchinleck had blunted Rommel's aims on the delta, forcing him onto the defensive, but the victory had not been decisive. He now needed to take the initiative.

Auchinleck attacked north-west towards El Mreir on 7 July, the attack soon being brought to a halt. However, a notable success was achieved by the 7th Armoured Division, who, after being reorganised into a light armoured division by adding the armoured car regiments of the 4th Light Armoured Brigade to the 7th Motor Brigade, cut through the Axis lines to reach Fuka by the evening, where they shelled the airfield and fuel dumps before withdrawing. In the south around Qaret el Himeimat, column units of the 2nd RB prevented the incursion of the enemy into the area around the depression at Deir el Ragil, just at the time that the new battalion commander, Lt Col. Victor Buller Turner, arrived.[38] 'B' Company's 3-inch mortars were being used for the first time in an area known locally as 'Lob Bowlers Alley' and Turner immediately helped, firstly spotting for the crew and then loading the bombs 'at a hitherto unprecedented' rate, inflicting heavy damage on the enemy, who withdrew. 'The new Colonel's reputation in the battalion and definitely in 'B' Company was already made!'[39]

Throughout the day the British armour attacked the Axis Line and, as night fell, the artillery of the Eighth Army fired 10,000 rounds into a three-mile sector occupied by the 15th Panzer Division, before the infantry moved forward in the pitch-dark night as far as the enemy outpost line and suddenly flung explosive charges into the defence posts. During the night a fighting reconnaissance group of 21st Panzer Division penetrated into Qaret el Abd, before the advance was held by the New Zealanders. The enemy attacked again the next morning, finally taking occupation of Qaret el Abd.

Based on experience and gathered intelligence during the last battles, Auchinleck now decided to reorganise the army:

1. by grouping the bulk of the artillery together under his sole command. This concentrated control, as opposed to the previous locational concentration, could deliver a truly devastating impact, as explained by Lt Charles Westlake:

His idea was to have a concentration of all artillery that could reach certain targets so that you brought a massive firepower to bear from various directions and by this means you were pretty well sure of destroying the target.[40]

2. by directing his most powerful units against the weakest units of the enemy. This had worked well recently, and he decided to continue hitting these weak spots comprising mostly the 'tired, static, under-equipped and not over-enthusiastic Italian infantry'.[41]

Auchinleck also decided that the 9th Australian Division, with the 44th Royal Tank Regiment under command, was to capture the low ridges at Tel el Eisa,[42] and the 1st South African Division with eight supporting tanks were to take the low ridges at Tel el Makh Khad north of the Miteirya Ridge. The New Zealanders were to pull back from the Bab el Qattara box, with 'March' and 'August' columns assisting them to do so. 'August' took their start positions at first light and from then on protected the south flank of the evacuation, whilst 'March' was to protect the Royal Engineers demolition party, as well as engaging the enemy's forward defence lines on the ridge north of the box, until the demolition was completed. Rommel misunderstood the withdrawal, thinking that the Eighth Army was retreating. He therefore directed the Italian Littorio Division to fill the gap with a force 200 MET, tanks and guns, which were immediately engaged heavily by 'March', 'April', 'July' and 'August' columns, giving the New Zealanders time to withdraw and leaving Bab el Qattara in Axis hands. Turner arrived at 'March' Column just as the above attack materialised, engaging the enemy infantry with 'C' Battery and 'B' Company's machine-gun and mortar platoons, resulting in further heavy enemy casualties.

Those parts of the 2nd RB not operating under the command of the columns remained with the 7th Motor Brigade in the southern sector of the line, experiencing fairly heavy shelling throughout the morning under the direction of the enemy observation posts on Kalakh Himeimat Ridge. The riflemen continued working in the area until 16 July, harassing the enemy by engaging mixed units of infantry and tanks. However, this constant roving operation caused problems of a more personal nature, with kit and personal effects being lost on a regular basis. After losing his kit to a 500-lb bomb, Marten wrote to Ann Crowder:

So far I've twice lost my complete kit in this battle, but have now obtained a third lot. I'm sure to be Stuka-ed soon, but who cares. I slept last night comfortable in a sleeping bag with a pillow and pyjamas (cotton, of course, not silk, but pyjamas). Send me Valet razor blades. Would also like fifty cheroots – obtainable at Ammar in Kar-el-Nil street in boxes of 50 – marked 'Clans' (not 'Colorado') and you should ask for 'manila'. They won't be – but a passable Indian imitation which is what they will give you.[43]

On 10 July, Rommel was awoken shortly after 0330 hours by the sound of an artillery barrage fifteen miles away to the north and understood immediately that he had been outmanoeuvred. The 26th

Australian Brigade attacked along the coastal road, capturing the ridge of Tel el Eisa, virtually destroying the newly arrived and inexperienced 60th Infantry Division 'Sabratha' and overrunning the German Signals Intercept Company 621, capturing or killing most of its members, and taking possession of their equipment and code books on the way. The loss of this unit was a great bonus to Auchinleck, as they had been responsible for intercepting most of the Allied radio traffic, which in battle situations was often sent in plain language code with codewords used for places, units and so on, resulting in Rommel now having little intelligence-related information on the Eighth Army's intentions. In less than two weeks, Rommel had lost two of his most important intelligence gathering mediums.[44]

The Australians continued their advance, threatening the *Panzerarmee* headquarters only three miles further west on the coastal road. This had seemed in dire straits until the 164th Division, newly arrived from Crete, together with the HQ staff, formed a defensive guard to halt the attack. Von Mellenthin later wrote:

> When a Headquarters is threatened the first instinct is to move, and safeguard its irreplaceable equipment and documents. It was clear to me, however, that Sabratha was finished – their artillery was already 'in the bag' – and something must be done immediately to close the road to the west. I called on the staff and personnel of Headquarters to form a rough battle line, which I strengthened with our anti-aircraft guns and some infantry reinforcements which happened to arrive; we succeeded in holding the Australians, who had captured the mounds of Tel el Eisa, and were seeking to thrust up the coast road.[45]

Rommel personally led the 15th Panzer Division to the north during the afternoon to attack the Australian flank, running straight into overwhelming artillery fire from the Alamein box together with the Australian anti-tank guns, effectively bringing him to a halt.

The Rifle Brigade complement in North Africa was now increased with the addition of the 7th RB who also joined the 7th Motor Brigade, adding to the presence of the 2nd RB and the 2nd KRRC, whilst the 1st RB remained as the motor battalion for the 22nd Armoured Brigade, part of the 1st Armoured Division. The 7th RB quickly became acclimatised to the high temperatures, moving directly from the transport ship into battle.[46]

The Allied offensive along the coastal road continued the next day, 11 July, overpowering several Trieste units and swelling the PoW cages. Rommel was forced to transfer more units up from the south as well as focusing the entire *Panzerarmee* artillery on the British advance in order to bring it to a halt. He now launched the 21st Panzer Division against the Alamein box, attacking on the 13th and, supported by every gun and every aircraft he could muster, cutting the box area off in a lightning advance. However, an attack to break the 9th Australian Division defences miscarried, with the panzers not even reaching their lines due to the heavy Allied massed artillery fire, bombing by the Desert Air Force, and the extremely well constructed line, which included many dug-in tanks. The panzers had also assembled not in the Italian Line but in an area 2,000-3,000 yards behind it, providing the Allied gunners with the opportunity of hitting them early, knocking out many tanks before they had even passed their own lines.

The attack was repeated the next day and was repulsed in much the same way, ending after 2½ hours with a loss of more than 600 dead and wounded. Rommel wrote:

> I was compelled to order every last German soldier out of his tent or rest camp up to front, for, in face of the virtual defeat of a large proportion of our Italian fighting power, the situation was beginning to take on crisis proportions.[47]

He had now lost the better part of two Italian Divisions, reducing the operating number of his precious armour still further and all for very little, if any, gain. Rommel's plan had been to escape the rigid, static warfare at which the British were masters, and to gain the open desert around Alexandria where he could exploit his tactical mobile superiority. But this was not to be, and he now knew that it was impossible to follow up his success in Marmarica to a final victory in the delta.

Operation Bacon

Auchinleck now planned to exploit the situation further. The Italian forces occupying the ridge had the tactical advantage of both observation and cover, but it was Auchinleck's plan to knock them off their perch before continuing west; firstly to attack the 15th Panzer Division and then the bulk of the *Panzerarmee's* reserve artillery along with several supply dumps, a strong concentration of anti-aircraft guns, the headquarters of the Afrika Korps and, lastly, the Italian X Corps at Deir el Shein.

Codenamed Operation Bacon,[48] the plan called for the 4th and 5th New Zealand Brigade to attack and seize the western end of the ridge, whilst the Indian 5th Infantry Brigade were to capture the eastern end. The 2nd Armoured Brigade would then move through the centre of the infantry positions to attack and exploit Deir el Shein and Miteirya Ridge.

The operation began at 2300 hours on 14 July, and by daybreak on the 15th, after advancing six miles, the 4th and 5th New Zealand Brigade had achieved all their objectives, occupying exposed positions on the ridge. Unfortunately, the telephone cable back to Divisional HQ had been damaged and the reception on the radio telephone used as an alternative became erratic, causing a communication breakdown that prevented them from reporting that they had reached their objective. As a result, the armour did not move forward in support. Despite this, the Brescia and Pavia divisions were under pressure and Rommel rushed elements of the 21st Panzer from the north and 15th Panzer from the south to bolster the Italians.

Meanwhile, the Indian 5th Infantry Brigade had made small gains on the eastern end of the ridge and when the 2nd Armoured Brigade arrived, the Indians renewed their attack, securing their objectives by early afternoon. The 22nd Armoured Brigade, who were to move up to protect the New Zealand flank, were engaged at Alam Nayil by the 90th Light and Ariete armoured divisions, but with the help of mobile infantry and artillery columns of the 7th Armoured Division they were able to push them back, although too late to protect the New Zealanders' flank. The *Panzerarmee* counter-attacked in the afternoon, with the 4th New Zealand Brigade HQ being overrun at 1800 hours, the 4th were all but destroyed and the 5th New Zealand Brigade were forced to withdraw. The 2nd New Zealand Division incurred in total 1,115 killed or missing and 290 wounded.[49]

Instead of punching a hole through the *Panzerarmee's* defences, Auchinleck was now faced with the situation that he had lost a brigade of troops and left the 5th Indian Brigade in a position open to an enemy attack. At 0250 hours on 16 July, the 9th Australian Division Tactical HQ received an urgent message:

Enemy is clearly concentrating his whole strength against two flanks 5 Ind Div and 1 Armd Div with a view of crushing [them]; this must NOT repeat NOT happen. Every possible step will be taken starting tonight by our own forces to the north and south to distract attention from the centre. No reason of fatigue or lack of resources will excuse anything less than the most vigorous and sustained action.[50]

The panzer attack in the morning made little progress. They were pushed back while, during repeated Stuka attacks and heavy artillery fire, new defences were dug to create extra artillery fire plans and to accommodate reinforcements. From intercepted radio traffic it became clear that a further attack was going to be made and accordingly Auchinleck sent the guns of 'Robcol', including the 'July' and 'August' columns of the 7th Motor Brigade, to the front of the Indian Brigade. The 2nd Armoured Brigade on the ridge itself was reinforced by a regiment from the 22nd Armoured Brigade, with the anti-tank guns of its motor battalion of the Royal Northumberland Fusiliers in support.

The anticipated attack began with heavy shelling as two lots of enemy tanks consisting of forty-four and twenty tanks respectively advanced south from the El Mreir Depression at around 1930 hours. The Germans were attacking with the setting sun at their backs to blind the gunners, but this time they were advancing straight into a well-formed anti-tank ambush, which brought the attack to a halt and forced them to withdraw after dark. The next day it was found that twenty-four tanks, six armoured cars, one self-propelled gun, eighteen anti-tank guns and six 88-mm guns had been left in front of the Indian Brigade's front. Rommel wrote to his wife:

> Things are going downright badly for me at the moment, at any rate, in the military sense. The enemy is using his superiority, especially in infantry, to destroy the Italian formations one by one. It's enough to make one weep,[51] [and in his diary] Our forces were now so small in comparison with the steadily growing strength of the British, that we were going to have to count ourselves lucky if we manage to go on holding our line at all.[52]

By the evening of 17 July the Eighth Army's front had been closed up, reinforcements had arrived in the form of the 161st Indian Motor Brigade from Iraq in order to bring the 5th Indian Division back up to strength, and the 1st Armoured Division had been augmented with 156 newly arrived Valentine tanks of the 23rd Armoured Brigade.

The replacement of trucks continued as 'C' Company operating with 'July' Column was replaced by 'A' Company, who had received a few days' rest and a new complement of trucks, while 'March' Column incorporating 'B' Company headed into reserve. 'S' Company who, like 'A' Company, had been rested and received new trucks at Mena, now moved to operate at the south end of the line. Overall, the riflemen had experienced a high level of casualties, especially among those working in an anti-tank role, including Maj. The Hon. H. D. G. Prittie, who was wounded,[53] as well as Lt John Davies-Scourfield, captured for the third time, along with 2nd Lt Henry Forbes.[54]

Rommel was not only forced to give up on his plans for the delta but was also now desperately short of men, guns, tanks, ammunition, food and fuel, as well as being 1,400 miles from the nearest operating port of Tripoli. The stocks of fuel were further reduced by the sinking of the tanker *Avionia*. A captured paper copy of a signal setting out the orders for the capture of Alexandria highlighted the problem, when an Italian colonel added a poignant pencil note: 'Littorio Division had fuel for 20km – [distance] to Alexandria 150 km.'[55] Rommel's supply line was stretched to breaking point. Malta was still a thorn in the Axis side, hampering the transportation of the much needed supplies, and all this while Auchinleck was benefiting from new equipment and reinforcements, and a shortened supply line.

Not having an easily delivered supply route meant that Rommel was therefore not in a position from which he could launch a serious offensive; he had no option but to wait and hold his defensive line. Churchill, on the other hand, needed results and piled pressure on Auchinleck:

The only way in which a sufficient army can be gathered in the northern theatre is by your defeating or destroying General Rommel and driving him at least to a safe distance. If this was accomplished before the middle of September, the Australian and New Zealand Divisions could return to their station in Palestine and Syria and the 41st Division could be sent to the northern theatre direct ...[56]

Fully aware that Rommel had to be eliminated as soon as possible, Auchinleck prepared Operation Splendour. Gott wrote to Freyberg, who was still in hospital, 'We have great hopes of getting a more definite success soon. I don't think the enemy are in very good shape and ours is improving daily.'[57] Mussolini, after spending the last three weeks expectantly awaiting a triumphal march into Cairo, flew back to Rome. It is not recorded whether his horse went with him.[58]

Operation Splendour

The original plan called for 'destroying the enemy's army in his present location [by attacking them] in the centre with subsidiary attacks on each flank directed against the enemy's rear.'[59] XIII Corps with 1st Armoured Division, including the 7th Motor Brigade and Indian 5th Infantry Brigade, were to proceed across Ruweisat Ridge, while the 1st Armoured Division and 69th Infantry Brigade attacked and consolidated Deir el Shein. The 5th and 6th New Zealand Brigade were to attack the El Mreir Depression, creating a gap which at daylight the 2nd and 23rd Armoured brigades would move through. XXX Corps would remain ready to attack Tel el Eisa and Miteirya Ridge when instructed to do so.

The attack began on 22 July with a bombardment of 2,400 rounds of 25-pounder ammunition along the whole front, followed immediately by continuous and very heavy bombing raids. The 15th Panzer War Diary noted: 'All day long enemy bombers and fighters were over our area, particularly 21st and 15th Pz Divs, on a scale hardly ever before seen.'[60] The added advantage of the bombing raids was that much of the sound of the trucks and tanks moving forward was drowned out by the noise. However, the attack was also delayed due to the risk posed by the night bombing.

The 5th Indian Division's advance on Deir el Shein and Point 63 on Ruweisat Ridge reached the gun emplacements of the 15th Panzer Division, but in a counter-attack were driven back in hand-to-hand fighting. Despite the efforts of the 161st Indian Motor Brigade, it was now considered that the taking of Point 63 was not worth the loss in men. The Indian brigades had suffered heavy casualties, including their commanding officer and four senior officers, in what had been a forlorn hope with little chance of success.[61]

By daybreak there was furious fighting with the New Zealanders 2,000 yards east of the El Mreir Depression. They had been attacked within fifteen minutes of their arrival by the 5th and 8th Panzer regiments, preventing their clearance of the minefields and thereby holding back the 23rd Armoured Brigade advance. The armour were instructed by Gott to take a parallel course one mile to the south, to circumvent the minefield, but due to a communication problem they found themselves in the middle of minefields and under intense fire. When, at 1100 hours, the 21st Panzer attacked them they were forced to withdraw, with a loss of forty tanks and a further forty damaged, leaving them with only seven operating tanks. The 23rd Armoured Brigade in respect of fighting strength had now ceased to exist! The New Zealand positions with no armour to support them were quickly overrun, with a very high level of casualties, a rescue attempt by the 2nd Armoured Brigade being beaten back by accurate anti-tank fire, the minefields hampering their manoeuvre.

'The catalogue of disasters that was "Operation Splendour" was now complete.'[62] Von Mellenthin wrote:

> A complete disaster for the British; owing to a complete lack of co-ordination and control they lost well over a hundred tanks and 1,400 prisoners ... Although our losses were heavy, particularly among the German artillery, the battle of July 22 was very favourable to us and encouraged the hope that we could hang on at El Alamein.[63]

Rommel sent a message to all troops:

> I send all ranks my special appreciation of their gallant action during our victorious defence of 22nd July. I am positive that any further enemy attacks will meet with the same reception.[64]

Tim Marten wrote to Ann Crowder:

> A shocking battle – we won it, and have once again contrived to chuck it away, God knows how. He's taken a bad knock though and how far we go back he won't be quite so well off as appears on the face of it. Bitterly disappointing for us, I don't know what to think. I'm well, but desperately tired.[65]

The defensive battle undertaken by Rommel had prevented the Allies from breaking through their lines, but as the daily report of the *Panzerarmee Afrika* testified, '... [they] had lost heavily, especially in infantry. There were no reserves available to carry on the battle, as all the troops were in the front line.'[66] The *Panzerarmee*'s sappers now returned to laying minefields feverishly; British, German and Italian mines were dug into the sand and soon several sectors were protected by these defences of considerable strength.

Auchinleck meanwhile continued his previous modus operandi of left- and right-hand attacks delivered in quick succession, in which co-operation and communication were paramount. He had set up a Special Liaison Unit to process and present him with the relevant Ultra signals as soon as they were received, enabling him to act on the intelligence without delay, keeping Rommel constantly off balance. To capitalise on this, upon receiving intelligence that the 15th Panzer was staying around Deir el Shein, Auchinleck sent the 26th Australian Brigade to attack Tel el Eisa, while the 24th Australian Brigade were sent to attack Tel el Makh Khad. In both cases the fighting was hard and, although costly, was successful, and by the afternoon the 26th controlled Tel el Eisa, whilst the 24th, with close support from the 50th Tank Regiment, were breaking out across the Tel el Makh Khad.

Patrolling with the Battalion

The battalion's 'B' Company was now relieved of its role with 'March' Column by the returning 'S' Company, who continued to patrol the southern Himeimat Ridge, investigating the location and extent of suspected minefields while supporting the tanks assigned to the column and going out on harassing missions against any targets presenting themselves.

Both the Eighth Army and the *Panzerarmee* sent out patrols in order to gain information on each other concerning disposition, strength, etc. As an example of this, on the night of 23/24 July an 'A' Company patrol commanded by Capt. Whigham was ordered to report on the minefields north of Jebel Kalakh. The patrol, comprising three motor sections, one officer and one NCO Royal Engineers, and an officer of the Royal Horse Artillery, proceeded on foot after de-trucking to search for minefields, but they found no mines, explosive wrappings or disturbed earth. They did, however, come across a small laager of seven vehicles. Deciding to bypass the position, they proceeded for a further 300 yards when a rifle shot and Italian voices were heard, augmented by machine-gun fire, all of which did not appear to be aimed at them.[67] An observation post was encountered at about 0250 hours, at which point Whigham fired a white Verey light and aimed tracer fire at the enemy machine-gun posts, to which the enemy replied on fixed lines, with three machine guns, two Bredas and one 50- or 47-mm gun, quickly followed by several shells from a high velocity 75-mm gun, a small artillery piece and mortar, all falling a long way south of the patrol. However, the small arms fire had killed an NCO, so Whigham – feeling that they had fulfilled their purpose and seeing that the enemy attention was becoming more accurate – decided to return to the trucks.[68]

Patrols were not restricted to information gathering; some were fighting patrols such as that undertaken by 'S' Company on the night of 25/26 July. They were tasked with attacking enemy posts at Jebel Kalakh, consisting of two officers and eighteen ordinary ranks, a machine-gun platoon and supported by 'C' Battery 4th Royal Horse Artillery, commanded by Bird.[69]

The enemy post was fortified by wire and, it was thought, mines, so a barrage was provided by the RHA contingent, with the patrol crossing 2,700 yards of open ground in clear moonlight and immediately being subjected to heavy machine-gun fire. Bird made the decision to press on despite the enemy fire and then, encountering and negotiating a 3½ foot wire fence and trip wire at 100 yards from the post,[70] overran the position, taking sixteen prisoners including the entire crew of an anti-tank gun, two Italian officers, and half a dozen Italians of the Trieste Division killed. In his report, Bird stated:

> The enemy infantry threw small hand grenades which were alarming, but the only damage was a slightly cut arm, and leg to a corporal [Watson] who had a grenade land right at his feet.[71]

Maj. Hastings commented, 'Few patrols have ever been carried out more successfully.'[72]

On the same evening the enemy undertook a patrol against a 2nd RB laager being guarded by Cpl J. Russell and Rifleman Payne. At about 0200 hours, Payne reported movement to the left some 300 yards in the distance and on investigation they counted nine men crossing the saddle of a wadi, aiming to move into the bottom of the next gulley. The group was challenged but gave no reply; the riflemen advanced a further 100 yards and challenged again, only to be met by a single shot that was responded to in kind with a dozen or so rounds, supported by a Bren gun from one armoured car. The enemy made a very noisy retreat, leaving several pieces of equipment on top of the wadi.

Operation Manhood

Despite the local activity, and under severe pressure from Churchill, Auchinleck could not allow the situation to continue to stagnate, issuing a special order on 25 July in an attempt to rouse the army for one last effort to break through the Axis lines:

You have done well. You have turned a retreat into a firm stand and stopped the enemy on the threshold of Egypt ... You have borne much but I ask you for more. We must not slacken; if we can stick it we will break him. STICK TO IT![73]

In order to do this, Auchinleck planned Operation Manhood as the way in which the enemy would be broken, ordering an armoured breakout from the Miteirya Ridge using XXX Corps, reinforced with the 1st Armoured Division, 4th Armoured Brigade and the 69th Infantry Brigade. To achieve this:

- the South Africans were to make a gap in the minefields east of Miteirya by one minute past midnight;
- 9th Australian Division would send a brigade supported by Valentine tanks to capture and hold the eastern end of Miteirya Ridge, in order to protect the northern flank of the main attack;
- 69th Infantry Brigade would pass through the minefield gaps to capture and consolidate a three-mile stretch of the Qatarra track by 0430 hours;
- the last phase was for the 1st Armoured Division, with 2nd Armoured Brigade and 4th Light Armoured Brigade to pass through the gap held by the 69th to destroy enemy armoured forces.[74]

The assembly was made under cover of strictest secrecy. The gap having been made in the minefields, the attack launched by the Australian 28th battalion[75] was advancing in the bright moonlight, supported by artillery and violent Desert Air Force bombing, towards an enemy that was laying down intense fire causing heavy Allied casualties. Despite the casualties and absence of support vehicles, the Australians had taken the south-eastern end of the ridge by 0242 hours, wiping out the greater part of a German battalion and sending a wireless success signal calling for the Valentines of the 50th Royal Tank Regiment who then advanced along the ridge, unfortunately straight into an anti-tank ambush, resulting in a loss of twenty-two tanks and forcing the remainder to fall back.

The 69th Infantry Brigade, which by now was no more than two battalions in strength scraped together from the wreckage of the 50th Division, attacked thirty minutes after the Australians, unfortunately not taking into account the fact that the enemy were now fully alerted to the presence of an attack, and so were immediately subjected to a hail of fire. In turn the 1st Armoured Division, concerned that the enemy was fully aware of the attack and that the 69th had not completed their consolidation or gapping of the minefields, postponed their advance until the situation could be determined.

The *Panzerarmee* tanks now moved behind the 69th positions, cutting off their retreat. The Australians, who were without the tanks of the 1st Armoured and had only a few anti-tank guns, and an artillery barrage that came too late, could only fire at the advancing tanks with their rifles as they overran their positions, crushing men still in their weapon 'scrapes' and spraying the positions with machine-gun fire, giving the men of the 69th no alternative but to give up and march westwards into captivity.

Despite the gap not being held open, the tanks of the 2nd Armoured Brigade continued their advance and entered the partially gapped minefields with severely restricted manoeuvrability. At midday they reported that they were still in the minefields and being fired upon by panzers and anti-tank guns, and withdrawing. The Eighth Army had lost 1,000 men and thirty tanks.[76] Rommel's verdict on the battle:

Although the British losses in this Alamein fighting had been higher than ours, yet the price to Auchinleck had not been excessive, for the one thing that mattered to him was to halt our advance and that, unfortunately, he had done.[77] Operation Manhood was definitely emasculated![78]

Meanwhile, 'March', 'July' and 'August' columns continued to protect the minefields, and it was during these operations that Dick Haywarden was killed.[79]

Both Sides Build Up Their Defences

The recent offensives had exhausted both sides, especially when added to the stress of constant battles since May, giving Rommel and Auchinleck no option but to recognise that further gains were impossible before their respective forces had rested and replenished their supplies and equipment. Auchinleck advised London:

We must therefore remain temporarily on the defensive and recruit our strength for a new and decisive effort, which did not seem possible before the middle of September.[80]

Rommel later wrote:

So ended the great campaign of the summer. It had begun with a fantastic victory, But, after the capture of Tobruk, the immense strength of the British Empire had begun to tell again … While we, on our side, had had to fight every new action with the same formations, the British had been able to take their battered divisions out of the line for refitting, and to throw in fresh formations fully equipped and up to full battle strength. My troops had remained in the fight. Their numbers had grown continually smaller, while losses from dead, wounded and sick had steadily increased. Again and again, it had been the same battalions, carried for the most part in captured vehicles, who had driven up to the British line, leapt from their lorries and stormed through the sand up to the enemy. Again and again, it had been the same tank crews who had ridden their tanks into battle and the same gunners who had pushed their guns into position. The deeds performed in these weeks by both officers and men had reached the limit of human endurance.[81]

As Liddell-Hart states, Rommel's account makes it clear how perilously close he was to defeat.[82] Rommel wrote to his wife on 2 August:

All quiet, except for intense air activity against my supply lines. I'm thankful for every day's respite we get. A lot of sickness. Holding on to our Alamein position has given us the severest fighting we've yet seen in Africa.[83]

The level of sickness mentioned in his letter underlines the position that one in every five German soldier was listed as sick, a number three times that of the Eighth Army.[84]

In Auchinleck's eyes the Eighth Army had a number of lessons to learn. Among these, as cited by Hammond, was the fact that the members of the Royal Armoured Corps saw themselves as an 'Army within an Army'.[85]

Auchinleck had already reorganised the armoured divisions, giving to each armoured brigade a group instead of two armoured brigades and a support group … Now he wanted to go further, abolishing distinctions between infantry and armoured divisions and creating a more mobile formation with greater striking power in place of the infantry division.[86]

In addition, it was now fully understood by the Eighth Army that the art of gapping a minefield, which had not been used since the days of O'Connor, had proved unreliable.[87] It would soon be reinvented with a major role for the RB.

Despite stopping the Panzeramee from entering the Delta and gaining access to the black gold of the oilfields in Persia, the Eighth Army was essentially back where they started in 1940. However, Rommel was faced with extended supply lines and no prospect of reinforcement for his tired and exhausted troops, whilst the future prospects of the Deset Rats were brighter with shortened supply lines and reinforcements on the way. The situation was not lost on Brooke who wrote in his diary:

> If the army cannot fight better than it is doing at present, we shall deserve to lose our Empire.[88]

Churchill Loses Confidence in Auchinleck

At the War Cabinet of 1 August, Churchill reported the fact that offensive operations could not be resumed before mid-September as being 'very depressing' and that he would have to arrange 'a more vigorous handling of matters'.[89] On 23 June, Auchinleck had written to Brooke:

> The unfavourable course of the recent battle in Cyrenaica culminating in the disastrous fall of Tobruk impels me to ask you seriously to consider the advisability of retaining me in my command …[90]

Brooke had first approached Churchill for permission to visit Egypt on 15 July writing in his diary:

> […] the situation in the Middle East was not improving; the Auk was suggesting giving the Army to Corbett.[91] It was essential that I should go out to see for myself …[92]

Churchill flooded Brooke with questions concerning Auchinleck's actions during Operation Manhood, Brooke recalling, 'It is very trying having to fight battles to defend the Auk, when I am myself doubtful at times why on earth he does not act differently.'[93] There was no doubt that Auchinleck, the victor of the Defence of Egypt, was tired. He had overseen the retreat from Gazala, ending in the protection of the delta by preventing Rommel from breaking through the Alamein Line, during which he had sacked two army commanders and was now commanding the Eighth Army directly. An official photographer who was asked to take some pictures of him recalled:

> His bush-jacket and shorts had lost the starch of the Cairo launderers. He was capless and his hair was ruffled by the desert wind. It was thus, a man alone in his hour of challenge and resolution.[94]

Lt Col. Charles Richardson of the Eighth Army Headquarters painted a bleaker picture:

When I observed him, day after day, sitting in the sand spending long hours staring through binoculars at the distant void horizon, I asked myself: 'Has he anything left to offer?'[95]

Understanding this, Churchill now decided that Auchinleck should return to his role as Commander-in-Chief Middle East and others should take on the job of day-to-day command of the Eighth Army. However, to do so he had to go to Egypt and to that end requested permission from King George VI whilst at dinner on 28 July.[96]

Churchill and Brooke Arrive in Cairo

Churchill sent a message to Auchinleck notifying him of his arrival, the visit being codenamed Operation Bracelet:

I hope to arrive in Cairo on Monday, August 3. The C.I.G.S. should arrive by a different route same day. I have asked Field Marshal Smuts and General Wavell to try to come there during same week. Let nothing take your eye off the ball.[97]

Flying in a very noisy and vibrating Liberator bomber from England via Gibraltar, Churchill, dressed in an RAF blue overall, with an entourage of five including his doctor, arrived on the morning of 3 August at Cairo West airfield, joining Brooke who had arrived on a plane a few hours earlier from Gibraltar via Malta, all staying at the British Embassy. They then flew on to Borg el Arab, where Churchill visited the troops whilst sheltering under an umbrella, later saying, 'Now for a short time I became the man on the spot. Instead of sitting at home waiting for the news from the front, I could send it myself – this was exhilarating.'[98]

After long discussions with Brooke, Gen. Jan Christiaan Smuts,[99] and Mr Richard Casey,[100] it was decided that a drastic and immediate change should be made in order to impart a new and vigorous impulse to the army and to restore confidence in the High Command. Churchill offered Brooke the command of the Eighth Army, but despite him desperately wanting to command again he declined the offer, citing his ignorance of desert warfare as a reason. However, he privately told his diary that he 'could exercise a limited control over Churchill and at last he was beginning to accept his advice'.[101]

A new Eighth Army commander had to be found, Brooke and Auchinleck favouring Lt Gen. Bernard Law Montgomery, currently the Commander-in-Chief of Southern Command in England who had commanded the 3rd Division of Brooke's Corps in France in 1940. Brooke's protégé was brimming with confidence and capable of instilling that confidence in those under his command. He was a hard trainer of men and a supreme professional, but with an abrasive character and quirky habits. Churchill, however, wanted to make the choice himself, selecting military commanders for their personality and particularly their reputations for bravery. He had his eye on Lt Gen. William Gott, who had earned the DSO and Bar during the desert campaign and possessed a legendary reputation among the officers and men of the Eighth Army. Writing to his wife, he said, 'I had a long drive alone with Gott, and I convinced myself of his high ability and charming personality.'[102] Brooke wrote in his diary that he had the highest opinion of Gott, but that he was tired. Montgomery wrote that Gott had written to a mutual friend:

I am very tired. Also we have tried every club in the bag and have failed. A new brain is wanted out here on this job; it's an odd job but it needs a new brain. If they want me to do it I will try. But they ought to get someone else, a new man from England.[103]

Over breakfast with Brooke, Smuts and Casey on 6 August, Churchill outlined his plan to split the Middle East Command into two: a Near East command stretching along the coast of North Africa to the Suez Canal, and a Middle East command comprising Syria, Palestine, Persia and Iraq.[104] Although Churchill had lost confidence in Auchinleck, he felt that the man had not disgraced himself.[105] Brooke later discussed the necessary changes with Auchinleck, who was in agreement that:

- the new Commander for the Eighth Army should be Montgomery;
- the new Chief of General Staff (CGS) to be selected once a decision had been made about Gen. Corbett; and
- 'Jumbo' Wilson should be replaced by Gott.[106]

Churchill was in favour of Wilson and Gott, telling Brooke that he was 'failing to make use of the two best men, who had been vouched for by Eden.'[107] Brooke responded that 'it was not astonishing that Eden should select "Old Green Jacket Officers!" '[108]

The next day, and after much discussion, Brooke and Churchill agreed that Gen. The Hon. Sir Harold Rupert Leofric George Alexander, after being snatched away from Eisenhower's team for Operation Torch, should succeed Auchinleck as Commander-in-Chief Middle East in Cairo. Montgomery was instructed to return from exercises to take over command of the First Army from Alexander. Lt Gen. Corbett and Brig. Dorman-Smith were to leave their commands all together, and Gott was to lead the Eighth Army. Churchill wrote to Auchinleck on 8 August:

Dear General Auchinleck,

On June 23 you raised in your telegram to the C.I.G.S. the question of your being relieved in this Command, and you mentioned the name of General Alexander as a possible successor. At that time of crisis to the Army His Majesty's Government did not wish to avail themselves of your high-minded offer ... The War Cabinet have now decided, for the reasons which you yourself had used, that the moment has come for a change. It is proposed to detach Iraq and Persia from the present Middle East Command ... and I offer you the Command of Iraq and Persia including the Tenth Army, with Headquarters in Basra or Baghdad.[109]

Auchinleck, however, felt that the reduction in his responsibilities would be viewed by the public as an appointment of an unsuccessful general. He had been Commander-in-Chief India and held the same position in the Middle East, and was now being asked to take a position which was virtually comparable to that of one of his own army commanders. As an alternative, he asked to be given permission to retire – a request that was granted.[110] He wrote to the Eighth Army on the 16th:

To all ranks EIGHTH Army,

It has been a great honour to have held direct command of EIGHTH Army for nearly two years and it is with great personal regret that I now leave you on arrival of your new Army Comd. During these weeks you have stopped the enemy and in spite of your heavy losses and inevitable disorganisation consequent upon rapid withdrawal from frontier have forced him on defensive, taken ten thousand prisoners from him and destroyed or captured many of his guns, vehicles and other equipment. You will, I know, join in acknowledging the great and glorious part our Air Force have played in helping us to achieve these results. Without their aid the story would have been very different. I thank you with all my heart for the magnificent way in which you have responded to heavy calls I have made on you and for your unfailing cheerfulness and tenacity in worst circumstances. I know you will continue in same fine spirit and determination to win under your new Comd. I wish you luck, and speedy and complete victory.[111]

He stayed for a few more days at Mena House Hotel before flying to India to recuperate.

Upon receipt of his appointment, Gott held his last Corps conference before taking a few days' leave, and then boarding a packed Bristol Bombay transport aircraft of 216 Squadron flown by Sgt Hugh 'Jimmy' James destined for Cairo. It flew along the 'safe' route used by Churchill a few days before and along which Dorman-Smith had travelled only a few hours before, when two Messerschmitt Bf 109s of *Jagdgeschwader 27*,[112] recently involved in a dogfight, fired several bursts setting fire to two of the Bombay's engines and wounding the pilots. The pilot instructed that the rear door be removed and proceeded to crash-land, with Gott and two others escaping and then returning to rescue others just as the Messerschmitt flown by *Feldwebel* Bernd Schneider returned to machine-gun the downed aircraft, which exploded, killing Gott and fifteen others. He was buried with the others a short distance from the burnt-out plane, with the grave bounded by pipes and with three tin helmets and four wooden grave crosses.[113]

Montgomery Takes Command of the Eighth Army

Upon receiving the news of the sad death of Gott, the horrified Brooke sent for Montgomery, He was given the command of the Eighth Army, much to the pleasure of Alexander who had been both a military colleague and friend for many years, the appointment being confirmed by Churchill, who described him as 'quick as a ferret and about as likeable',[114] but who also held the opinion that he had the 'killer instinct' on the battlefield, in his message to the Deputy Prime Minister:

C.I.G.S. decisively recommends Montgomery for Eighth Army. Smuts and I feel this post must be filled at once. Pray send him by special plane at earliest moment. Advise me when he will arrive.[115]

The War Office telephoned Montgomery, saying that the orders given to him the previous day regarding the First Army were cancelled and to hold himself ready to proceed to Egypt. As Max Hastings wrote:

The only land war that Britain could fight against the Axis forces was now controlled by the only three generals that had returned from France with their reputations intact: Montgomery, Brooke and Alexander.[116]

Alexander arrived in Cairo on the morning of 9 August. Churchill and Brooke immediately gave him the following instructions:

1. Your prime and main duty will be to take or destroy at the earliest opportunity the German-Italian army commanded by Field Marshal Rommel, together with all its supplies and establishments in Egypt and Libya.
2. You will discharge, or cause to be discharged, such other duties as pertain to your Command without prejudice to the task described in paragraph 1, which must be considered paramount in His Majesty's interests.

In turn, Gen. Alexander issued the following directive to the troops under his command:

The German/Italian Forces are trying to force their way into the delta to capture Cairo and Alexandria and drive us from Egypt.

It is the duty of every officer and soldier to stand firm and fight the enemy wherever he may find him, regardless of the cost.

The results of the whole war may well depend on how we conduct ourselves in this great battle. As brothers in arms we must have confidence in ourselves, in each other, and in our weapons and determination to win or die. This is the fighting spirit which will give us victory.

SOLDIERS! DO YOUR DUTY.

H. R. ALEXANDER General
Commander-in-Chief
Middle East Forces[117]

Montgomery left RAF Lyneham 'with a light heart and great confidence' on the night of 10 August, reaching Gibraltar at dawn the next day and remaining there for the day before flying to Egypt. He arrived there on the 13th, going straight to Mena House Hotel near the Great Pyramid for a meeting with Auchinleck, who had decided not to hand over to Alexander until the 15th. The meeting was brief; the current dispositions and plans were explained to Montgomery, who then went shopping to get some clothes for the desert, and by that evening was standing on the steps of his caravan addressing his new staff, most of whom at first were sceptical – 'He had not got sand in his shoes and his knees were not yet brown'– and also remembered that he was the fourth army commander in the last twelve months. Montgomery went through his plans for the future, outlining the weaknesses of the previous proposals. Chief of Staff Brig. Francis 'Freddie' de Guingand recalled:

That address by Montgomery will remain one of my most vivid recollections … We all felt that a cool and refreshing breeze had come to relieve the oppressive and stagnant atmosphere … He was going to create a new atmosphere … The bad old days were over, and nothing but good was in store for us. A new era had dawned.

Montgomery finished with these words:

Let us have a new atmosphere … what is the use of digging trenches in the delta? It is quite useless; if we must lose this position, we lose Egypt; all the fighting troops now in the delta must come here alive at once; and will. Here we will stand and fight; there will be no further withdrawal. I have ordered that all plans and instructions dealing with further withdrawal are to be burnt, and at once. We will stand and fight here. If we can't stay here, then let us stay here dead …[118]

After two years of see-saw victories and defeats, Montgomery was determined to 'kick Rommel out of Africa for good',[119] using the Eighth Army's fighting spirit or, as Montgomery, called it 'Binge'.[120] Montgomery sought a different relationship with the troops, explaining that 'in the First World War he had never seen the top brass and he was determined that in his army his troops would know him.'[121] Godfrey Talbot of the BBC said:

> If they had confidence in their supreme commander they would fight and win, whatever the circumstances. But in order to have that confidence, they had to know him. So he got around more than any other general had ever done before, stopping to talk to the men, spreading a map to show the state of the battle, throwing cigarettes from his jeep.[122]

Despite most of the plans being based on those proposed by Auchinleck, Dorman-Smith and Gott, the men of the Eighth Army, from the private soldiers to the senior officers, now felt that they could win.[123] Rifleman Longstaff of the 2nd RB recalled:

> Montgomery came to the southern sector of the Alamein front at Alam el Halfa ... He wasn't talking to the officers – he was talking to the riflemen – he was sitting inside little dugouts with the lads.[124]

While undertaking these early visits, Montgomery was given an Australian bush hat to wear as an alternative to his general's hat, primarily because it was an exceedingly good hat for the desert. It soon became full of unit badges, although accordingly to Bird, Montgomery's request for a Rifle Brigade badge was refused by Vic Turner, who said that 'he wasn't entitled to it'.[125] These, together with a pair of 'Bombay Bloomers' (KD Shorts), made him look more flamboyantly idiosyncratic and even less like a general. The Australian hat was soon replaced by a beret of one of the tank regiments, resulting in the famous image of 'Monty'.

True to his word, Montgomery ensured that all available men were brought to the front. Two new divisions, recently arrived from England and being used to dig positions to defend the delta, would be moved to the Alamein Line immediately. RB officer Capt. Crowder had been trying to return to the battalion for the last few months, after being wounded at Sidi Rezegh in November 1941. After being hospitalised and having returning to fitness, he had been stuck at the Infantry Brigade Depot awaiting relief. He was now able to move to the line with his fellow riflemen, including his driver Rifleman Harding. Rifleman Crimp wrote:

> A large draft arrived yesterday from Geneifa to bring the battalion up to full strength. Evidently a purge has been going on lately at the base, combing out surplus personnel, and many faces I haven't seen for months are now re-appearing.[126]

On Crowder's return he was given the command of a platoon from 'C' Company and began patrolling the areas in front of the enemy minefields, writing to his sister:

> Just got back from a rather bogus Fighting Patrol I did last night. The idea was to walk up and down a front of 1,800 yards long, the enemy side of our minefield, and to go 800 yards the other side of it, then if any enemy patrols came out to shoot them up with Tommy Guns, Brens and hand grenades. However, we walked about from 9 p.m. till 8 a.m. and never heard a soul. But that's not

surprising really as the riflemen in my patrol made such a bloody noise themselves – kept coughing, and knocking rocks about. I gave them absolute hell as I know we would all have been killed had we met an enemy patrol.[127]

Longstaff of 2nd RB described the method of patrolling:

We were now going out on patrol, night after night. There was five miles distance between us and the enemy, so we'd go out on strict compass bearings. We'd go out making sure that there were no lights on the vehicles, making sure the milometer was working, that we had proper watches that we could reply on for distances. We would be armed with one thing –a form of incendiary grenade that he would push into his petrol tank if he or his vehicle was going to be captured. So he stayed there while the rest of us went forward to try and hear who the enemy was in front. At that particular position it was the Ariete Division and the Folfore Division of the Italian Army, backed up by heavy machine gunners of Rommel's Afrika Korps.[128]

Having completed the First Moscow Conference, Churchill returned to Egypt on 19 August to visit Montgomery and the troops. Churchill spent the night with Alexander and Montgomery, who 'expounded in exact detail the first stages of the plan'.[129] Churchill bathed in the Mediterranean before dinner in his shirt as there were no bathing costumes. As he looked along the shoreline he became aware of some soldiers bathing in white trunks. Montgomery later wrote:

I had to explain that no one wore any bathing kit in the Eighth Army. The soldiers wore shorts all day and often not even a shirt; their bodies got very brown from the sun. What in the distance looked like white bathing drawers was actually white flesh, which did not brown because of the khaki shorts![130]

Before he left, Churchill wrote in Montgomery's autograph book on 20 August:

May the anniversary of Blenheim which marks the opening of this new command bring to the Commander-in-Chief of the Eighth Army and his troops the fame and fortune they will surely deserve.[131]

Despite this confident and positive statement, the stress of the war, the travelling and the situation in Africa was beginning to tell on the Prime Minister. On the 24th, back in Britain, Maj.-Gen. Davidson and Maj.-Gen. Kennedy were summoned to his private rooms where they found Churchill in bed, lighting and relighting a cigar without making any appreciable progress with it. He told them 'how with the change of commanders a new wind was blowing, how the Army was all in bits and pieces and that would be put right now!' and of 'the terrible wastage the "poor" Army had suffered!'[132] Brooke wrote in his diary, 'I pray God that the decisions we arrived at may be correct, and that they may bear fruit.'[133]

The Regiment

By this time the battalions of the regiment were positioned throughout the battle zone as follows:

- The 1st RB had spent its time with the 2nd Armoured Brigade, bearing the brunt of the action around the Alamein box, and remained in that position;
- The 9th RB (Tower Hamlets) had been used to plug every gap in the line from Alamein to Himeimat, never staying in one place for too long or under one command and suffering because of it. GHQ now decided that they had insufficient reinforcements to return all four battalions to the proper level of fighting strength, and therefore the 9th RB was disbanded and its riflemen spread between the other battalions.
- The 2nd RB were still operating in the columns of the 7th Motor Brigade, who were then given instructions to rejoin the 7th Armoured Division in securing the southern flank of the Eighth Army, with the 7th RB watching the minefields to prevent any minor advances by the enemy and in the case of a major offensive were to withdraw through Deir el Ragil to cover the desert route to the delta.

They were all soon to be brought to the fore of the conflict yet again.

The *Panzerarmee* Supply Situation

Rommel's supply situation was not improving. During early August the supplies received barely covered the army's daily requirements, making a build-up of supplies for future offensive operations impossible. The Italians, who were in charge of supplying the army, made the excuse that they had insufficient fuel for their escort ships, making the crossing of the Mediterranean too risky. Instead of being dispatched, these supplies piled up in Italian ports. The nightmare did not end even when the limited supplies arrived in North Africa, as Tobruk, the nearest port to the front, had a port capacity of only 600 tons per day. Supplies therefore had to be landed further west and then transported by truck, train or coastal vessel to the front, the cost in fuel of this transportation further reducing the amount that was actually delivered.

The vehicle situation was also causing serious problems. Rommel later wrote:

> The bad state of the roads and the continual heavy demands we were having to make on our transport were resulting in a steady 35% of our vehicle strength being in for repair. As some 85% or so of our transport still consisted of vehicles of British or American manufacture, for which we had no great stocks of spares, it is easy to imagine the difficulties our repair shop was having to contend with.[134]

Kesselring's earlier statement as to the danger of leaving Malta in Allied hands seemed now to have been become a prophecy, as Operation Pedestal delivered enough food and supplies to Malta to allow the island to last until December 1942. From the original fourteen merchant ships that left Gibraltar six days before, on 10 August, only five completed the journey, but one of these was the *Ohio* which delivered 11,500 tons of kerosene and diesel fuel oils. As a result, Malta could resume offensive operations against the merchant ships, reducing Rommel's supplies even further.

Rommel was now faced with an enemy that was being supplied at a much higher rate than he could ever have hoped for, as well as receiving almost limitless new equipment and reinforcements. He had only a finite amount of time before Montgomery became too strong to defeat.

Adding to Rommel's woes was the fact that he was once again experiencing a resurgence of his illness in the form of frequent attacks of faintness and having to employ all his strength just to remain upright. A worried Hitler sent Professor Dr Horster, one of the best-known stomach specialists in Germany, to treat him. Horster wrote to the *Oberkommando der Wehrmacht* (OKW)[135] stating:

> Field Marshal Rommel suffering from chronic stomach and intestinal catarrh, nasal diphtheria and considerable circulation trouble. He is not in a fit condition to command the forthcoming offensive.[136]

Rommel had been in Africa for nineteen months, far longer than any other officer over forty years of age, and could only recommend Gen. Guderian as a replacement, but received the OKW reply: 'Guderian unacceptable.'[137] He was obviously still out of favour with Hitler after having been sacked at the end of 1941. Faced with either handing over to a replacement that he did not have confidence in or staying in Africa, he chose the latter, discussing the problem with Horster, who relented and sent a telegram reading: 'C-in-C's condition so far improved that he can command the battle under constant medical attention. Nevertheless, essential to have a replacement on the spot.'[138]

Alam el Halfa

There were three ridges around the Alamein defensive line: Miteirya, Ruweisat and Alam el Halfa. Rommel planned an attack which would replicate the Gazala attack insomuch as it involved a feint strike against the centre while the main party would turn the flank of the line before driving for the coast. Accordingly, Alexander and Montgomery, like Auchinleck and Dorman-Smith before them, saw that the key to any defence from this type of attack had to be the southernmost of these three ridges, Alam el Halfa was therefore to become the target and the answer to the defence of that attack.

If Rommel had undertaken the attack three weeks earlier he would have found the ridge defended by two weak battalions of the 21st Indian Brigade. Now, however, the situation was vastly different. The ridge was fortified with a succession of strongpoints prepared on its slopes and providing excellent observation and calculated firing patterns over a wide area of bare and difficult desert to the south, with minefields, as described by Dorman-Smith, that:

> [...] ran from each [ridge] like the arms of a starfish so that they gave no support to an invader of this spider's-web system; within which the bulk of the defenders were to keep mobile ready to intervene against an attacker from whatever direction he might come.[139]

In order for Montgomery to obtain the greatest benefit, Rommel had to attack first, so allowing Montgomery the opportunity to defeat him. After discussing the situation with de Guingand it became clear that all the indications were that Rommel would make an early attack. Montgomery would later write:

I understood Rommel was expected to attack us shortly. If he came soon it would be tricky, if he came in a week, all right, but give us two weeks and Rommel could do what he liked; he would be seen off and then it would be our turn.[140]

'Going' Map

In order to prepare for his offensive, it was vital for Rommel to understand the terrain that he was to cross, calculating the fuel cost and the dangers contained therein, and like any other army he would have called for a map to be created that contained this accumulated information. Therefore a suggestion made by Guingand – to create a false 'going' map describing the terrain incorrectly, which would 'accidently fall into enemy hands' – was of great interest. The normal 'going' map would bear indentifying descriptive colours denoting the terrain that was reflected by the map, as follows:

- Red – which meant that the ground was firm and clear and it was possible to drive at more than 10 mph;
- Yellow – which meant that it was possible to drive at speeds of between 5 and 12 mph, taking care to avoid rocks or soft sand;
- Green – which meant that a unit had to check the area before driving on it; low gear was essential; and
- Blue – which simply meant impassable.

The suggested false map would, for example, show the red areas as blue; green areas would be shown as red; minefields would be described as 'deep' when they were shallow. Rommel would therefore be provided with, what would appear to be a perfect route bypassing all these problems, but would in fact lead them into the worst terrain and the deepest minefields. The map was then repeatedly folded, tea stained and torn, then forced into the pocket of a haversack, and given to a patrol who drove a scout car towards a German outpost on the southern part of the line and, when fired upon, crashed the scout car, leaving a dead soldier clutching the haversack.[141]

The Defensive Plan

Montgomery's defensive plan was codenamed Pepsodent and was designed to 'allow' Rommel to break through the line before being 'directed' north towards the ridge, whilst constantly harried by the 7th Armoured Division, where he would find the area of strategic importance between Ruweisat Ridge and Alam el Halfa strongly held by well-positioned 6-pounder anti-tank screens. Four hundred tanks were placed just south of its western edge, with orders that they would not be loosed against the panzers, who instead would be allowed to beat themselves up against the defences and hopefully incur heavy casualties. Sun Tzu taught:

He who occupies the field of battle first and awaits his enemy is at ease; he who comes later to the scene and rushes into the fight is weary. And therefore those skilled in war bring the enemy to the field of battle and are not brought there by him.[142]

This was essentially the plan that had been originally drawn up by Dorman-Smith, based on Gott's interpretation of Rommel's course of action and adopted by Auchinleck, before Montgomery had taken command and had 'accepted this plan in principle'.[143]

If Montgomery could hold the ridge, Rommel would not dare to advance further east whilst the whole of his line of communications was dominated by the Eighth Army, and would have no alternative but to withdraw. Montgomery further decided that the armour would not attack during and after Rommel's withdrawal, removing the possibility that the attacking force could be outmanoeuvred, thus turning a British victory into defeat. He told Renton in no uncertain terms that there would be 'no loosing of the armour' after the trap had been sprung. On the 28th, the armour and artillery elements of the 22nd Armoured Brigade moved off their position, taking the anti-tank platoons of the 1st RB with them towards Alam el Halfa.

Rommel was unaware of any of this. Despite the supply situation and his illness, he knew that he had one last opportunity to break the Allied Line before it became too strong. He therefore planned to penetrate the south end of the line at a point between Alam Nayil and Qaret el Himeimat, before driving past the Alam el Halfa Ridge and onwards to El Hammam, threatening Alexandria, Cairo, Montgomery's headquarters and the rear of the Alamein Line and leaving the consolidation of such rear areas to the Italians.

The mood within the Axis high command had reversed. It was now Mussolini and Kesselring who were urging Rommel to launch an attack as soon as possible, whereas Rommel was becoming reluctant and pessimistic, a mood that was not improved by the fact that he was still short of the vital supplies desperately needed for the attack. The ammunition, fuel and supplies promised by *Comando Supremo* had still not arrived, and to make matters worse, the Desert Air Force had been bombing them on a round-the-clock basis. Even the full moon, so necessary for the attack, was already on the wane, ensuring any further delay would severely reduce the possibility of a successful outcome. Marshal Ugo Cavallero sent a message: 'You can begin the battle now, Herr Feldmarschall. The petrol is already under way,'[143] the message continuing that the tankers would arrive under the heaviest escort in the next few hours or at the very latest the next day. To further reduce Rommel's anxiety, Kesselring had assured him that he could transport by air 500 tons of petrol a day. Friedrich Wilhelm von Mellenthin later wrote:

> In the end he [Rommel] accepted Kesselring's assurance that he could fly in 90,000 gallons of gasoline a day, and we relied on a large tanker due in Tobruk at the end of August.[144]

Based on these assurances, Rommel gave the order for the attack to open on the night of 30/31 August. Professor Horster recalled that on the morning of the attack, Rommel wore a very troubled expression:

> Professor, the decision to attack today is the hardest I have taken. Either the army in Russia succeeds in getting through to Grozny [in the Caucasus] and we in Africa manage to reach the Suez Canal or …[145] and made a gesture of defeat.

CHAPTER 4

Zero plus 168 days and the Battle of Alam el Halfa

Rommel's attack began on 30 August, under a bright moon. The engineers and infantry led the way, the armour advancing from their start lines between Qaret el Abd and Jebel Kalakh towards the Allied minefields. The advance was preceded by heavy artillery barrages landing on the gaps in the minefields through which the 7th Armoured Division had been observed accessing and leaving the Allied rear areas.

Almost immediately the high whine of the Albacore[1] aircraft engines could be heard over the rumble of the tanks engines, as first the parachute flares turned night into day, and then shortly afterwards came the heavier drone of the Wellington[2] bombers bringing bombs that fell onto the massed panzers. The cacophony created by the high-explosive bombs, burning panzers and exploding trucks, was a sound that would be heard repeatedly over the next six days.

The minefields of the southern area of the Alamein Line were held lightly by the motor and light brigades of the 7th Armoured Division, the most western of which was known as First, anchored in the north by the New Zealand minefield. A new 500-yard-wide minefield had been laid to the rear of the First, known as Second, and the one behind that situated on the western edge of Deir el Muhafid, known as Muhafid. Two brigades were to be deployed as a screen over the minefields, whose task was to inflict the maximum delay and damage on any enemy advancing from the west as well as making the sector appear more heavily garrisoned than it actually was.[3] Their orders were not to be drawn into battle; they were to slow the enemy but ultimately allow them to break through to continue their advance onto Alam el Halfa, the 7th Armoured Division snapping at their flank and heels.

The brigade positions were as follows:

- 2nd RB under the command of Turner and supported by 'F' Battery 4th Royal Horse Artillery were in the northernmost positions situated to the south of the 3rd New Zealanders, holding the position to the edge of the Deir el Munassib Depression with:
  - o 'C' Company to the north;
  - o 'B' Company taking the centre; and
  - o 'A' Company to the south.
- 2nd KRRC in the Deir el Munassib Depression;
- South of the depression the composite regiment of 10th Hussars, with 'S' Company 2nd RB under command, looked after two parallel minefields down to about halfway between Munassib and Himeimat;
- South of them, the 4th Light Armoured Brigade was responsible with the 1st KRRC backed by the composite regiment of 4th and 8th Hussars.

Rifleman Crimp of the 2nd RB wrote in his diary:

> There's a general 'sweat' on. The moon is full and Jerry has been 'more or less' expected to launch an
> attack during the last three nights, but so far nothing's happened.[4]

That was to change at about 2200 hours when listening posts placed in front of the minefields
guarded by the New Zealanders heard the sound of shelling and enemy movement, confirmed
shortly afterwards by the mining parties of the RB, who took the opportunity to withdraw.

The Rifle Brigade Blocks the Way

It was not long afterwards that the leading *Panzerarmee* units arrived almost opposite the 2nd RB
position, the enemy engineers beginning to lift the mines whilst the riflemen fired their heavy
machine guns and mortars at them, along with the heavier guns of the 3rd and 4th Royal Horse
Artillery. Von Mellenthin wrote:

> To turn the Eighth Army front it was necessary to pierce a thick minebelt, which the British had laid
> almost as far as the Qattara Depression. Right from the start the offensive got into difficulties, for
> the minefields were far more elaborate than we imagined, and the British covering forces inflicted
> heavy losses on the mine-lifting parties. This threw our whole timetable out of gear.[5] Later estimates
> by the Germans put the number of mines in this sector at 150,000.[6]

Parachute flares continued to be dropped from the sky between the engineers of *Panzer-Pioniere-Bataillon
33* and *200* and the armour, illuminating the area to the benefit of the riflemen. Half an hour later, eighteen
enemy tanks appeared in front of the northern edge of the depression to support the mine-lifting operation,
against which the anti-tank guns of 'A' company and 'F' Battery 4th Royal Horse Artillery laid down fire.

Company carriers under command of Lt George Emerson-Baker advanced through the gap, engaging
and forcing the enemy infantry and engineers to withdraw, before engaging them again at 0500 hours.
A concentration of between 200 and 300 closely packed infantry were then reported to have penetrated
the minefield north of 'A' Company, 'attacking and again hitting or wounding practically the whole party',[7]
before being shelled by tanks and a 50-mm gun, forcing the carriers to withdraw through the minefield.

Meanwhile, in the Munassib area the 2nd KRRC were experiencing problems similar to those of
'A' Company, whilst the combined 10th Hussars/'S' Company RB reported no action. Conversely, the
1st KRRC and 4th Light Armoured at the far south were under serious attack.

The tactical situation became clear as dawn broke. A small attack above the 3rd New Zealanders
had been completely held, but fighting was still going on along the front controlled by the 7th Motor
Brigade, with the enemy incurring heavy losses whilst slowly penetrating the minefields. Rommel's
original plan had been to drive through the area with 'only a short halt to pick up a few odd mines'[8]
and for the forward units to have lined up with the ridge on their right by now, being refuelled ready
for the push to the coast. Instead they were still trying to fully breach the first minefield and were
under heavy significant fire. Albert Martin wrote:

> It has come at last! Jerry put his big attack in and his main forces have concentrated on our front.
> All night we were at it, firing at the enemy only a few hundred yards away until 4.30 a.m. when we

couldn't hold any longer. We withdrew but miraculously with few casualties.[9]

Rommel Breaks Through

Shortly afterwards about sixty tanks broke through the first minefield in front of the 4th Light Armoured position, putting enormous pressure on the left flank of the 10th Hussars. The 'S' Company RB position's became untenable and they were forced to withdraw behind their second minefield to prevent being outflanked. This withdrawal caused a domino effect, as the 2nd KRRC in the depression were put under pressure which was immediately increased when the 90th Light Division broke through with thirty tanks on their right flank, shared with the 2nd RB. Six of the thirty tanks were knocked out; the remainder continued east, forcing Bosville to send the codeword 'Carbon'[10] at 0552 hours, instructing the 2nd RB and 2nd KRRC to gradually withdraw to the rear of the second minefield, this being completed by 0725 hours.

At 0710 hours the 10th Hussars had moved off to engage fifty tanks; two hours later, two groups totalling thirty-three enemy tanks and a large column of infantry advanced towards the Hussars' line. The Hussars could not disengage from the original fifty tanks and still keep in contact with the 4th Light Armoured Brigade, thereby leaving the lines of supply of the 2nd KRRC in danger. Consequently, at 0920 hours, they and the 2nd RB received orders via a runner moving from platoon to platoon to commence withdrawal from the second minefield, with their carriers providing cover.

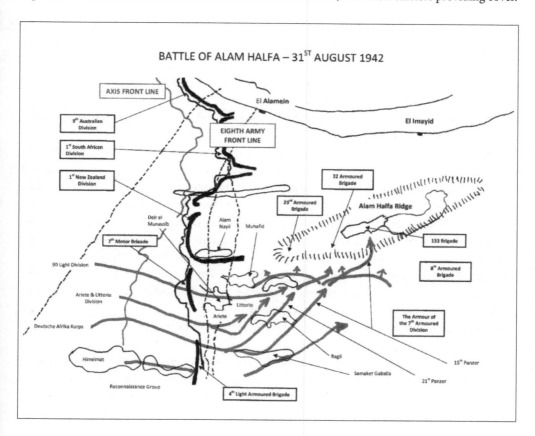

About an hour later, after establishing that the enemy were moving through the minefields in the south, the 4th Light Armoured Brigade including 'S' Company withdrew, whilst ensuring that the enemy incurred considerable casualties.

Rommel returned to his headquarters at 0800 hours to hear the distressing news that Nehring had been badly wounded in an air attack, and Gen. Georg von Bismarck, the commander of the 21st Panzer Division, had been killed when his motorcycle hit a mine.[11] He also had to face the situation that due to the delays at the minefields the original plan was not working, the element of surprise was lost, and he was now considering whether to call the operation off. At this moment Bayerlein, who had taken over from Nehring, advised that he had broken through the minefields and begged to be allowed to advance further.[12] Rommel agreed and instructed the operation to continue, with the amendment that the turn to the north would be taken earlier in order to mitigate the danger to his flanks from the 7th Armoured from the south and the 1st and 10th Armoured divisions from the north. Therefore, instead of passing Alam el Halfa on the east as originally planned, they would now strike towards the sea further west, with the panzers aiming for Point 132 on the line of the ridge, and the Italians for Point 102 at Alam Bueit. A line of telegraph poles leading from Himeimat northwards, turning right and running parallel to Alam el Halfa Ridge would be used as a visual guide for the advance.

The *Panzerarmee* Breaks Out

By midday the minefields were finally breached and over the next hour and a half the enemy advanced through them, before wheeling left directly towards the prepared defences of Alam el Halfa, using Deir el Ragil as a pivot, exactly as Gott had forecast.[13] The 7th RB attacked, inflicting casualties on the enemy MET in Deir el Ragil, whilst the 2nd KRRC and 2nd RB engaged enemy infantry columns until night descended. Meanwhile, the Italian Littorio and Ariete Armoured Divisions moved up onto the left of the Afrika Korps, and the 90th Light Division and Italian X Corps drew up to face the southern flank of the New Zealand box.

Rommel's tanks were now running dangerously low of fuel, unable to refuel due to the attention being given to them by the Desert Air Force, until a thick, yellow choking dust-storm blew up and forced the aircraft to return to base, providing the panzers with an hour in which to fill their fuel tanks unhindered. Setting off again at 1300 hours, the 15th Panzer were followed approximately an hour later by the 21st Panzer, both panzer divisions advancing through the dust-storm but finding themselves in soft sand that caused the petrol gauges to drop alarming, and leaving them 'wondering where the British armour was'.[14] Of the 400 Eighth Army tanks in position on the ridge behind the anti-tank screen, the 22nd Armoured Brigade were massed at the western end, comprising ninety-two Grant tanks and seventy-four Light tanks, supported by the 6-pounder anti-tank guns of the 1st RB and the artillery of the 44th and 2nd New Zealand divisions.

At about 1530 hours, Roberts commanding 22nd Armoured Brigade reported:

Now I see the enemy myself through my glasses. They are coming straight up the line of the telegraph posts which lead in front of our position. On they come, a most impressive array. And now they are swinging east and look like passing us about 1,200 yards from our forward positions. I had given strict instructions that we would not open fire until the enemy were at under a 1,000 yards range.

Here was something of a dilemma … General Gatehouse is with General Horrocks on Alam Halfa itself and a bit further east than we are; it seems that he can see this mass of enemy tanks about to pass our position … at that moment he speaks to me … 'I don't want you to think that we are in a blue funk here or anything like that, but if these fellows continue on as they are doing you will have to come out and hit them in the flank.'[15]

The Guns of the 1st RB Speak

From the foothills below Alam el Halfa Ridge the 22nd Armoured Brigade moved out towards the vanguard of the panzers, consisting of about ninety Mk IIIs, which swung out in three waves to engage the British armour. The German anti-tank screen closed behind them to await the British tanks, which they surmised from past experience would be drawn towards them as the panzers withdrew after making first contact. But the British did not close and suddenly it appeared to the German gunners that the panzers were having to drive further away to engage with the reluctant British armour before they finally exchanged fire at 1628 hours, obscuring the field with smoke and dust.

The battle with the panzers created a gap in the 22nd Armoured line, and the armour of the Scots Greys[16] was ordered to move over the crest of Point 102 to reinforce the position before the Germans became aware of the opening in the line. However, just at this moment the wind dropped and visibility returned to the field, providing the panzers with a clear view of the gap, upon which they advanced immediately. What they did not see were the well-positioned guns of 'B' Company 1st RB, supported by the machine guns of 'I' Company, waiting in dug-in emplacements with a very solid and carefully camouflaged breastwork of sandbags, as well as some in small wadis. The enemy tanks had got to within 300 yards of the guns. The gunners opened fire with concentrated, highly accurate 6-pounder anti-tank fire, 8 Platoon being most involved. It was shortly afterwards joined by the heavy fire of the two divisional artillery units. Douglas Waller recalled:

There were two of us in front and the other two were slightly on our flanks and further behind us. They put us out there and said, 'Mark out something 300 yards away.' Well, we put an empty petrol tin there and they said, 'That's your maximum range. Don't fire above 300 yards.'[…] We were dug in these positions at Alam Halfa and saw an armoured car come whizzing back. 'Tanks are coming!' We sat there and waited. We could see them then. About 70 of them. The first tank started moving and the first commander's tank came up and, very obligingly, almost stopped on top of this petrol tin that we'd put out … Nothing had been fired then so we fired and he was a goner because he was side on. Once we had fired, of course, other tanks started firing at us. One came up and two of the crew baled out of this one to get on the back of this other tank. We fired at it. On the front it just bounced off so we fired at the turret and the track but it still kept going and it started backing away and the machine guns opened up on us which went through the front shield and deflected off the curved shield behind. Also went through and knocked the sights out of our gun. But nobody was hit. If it hadn't been for the shield we'd have all been goners.[17]

Roberts recalled:

Meanwhile the enemy tanks are edging forward again and they have got close to the Rifle Brigade's anti-tank guns, who have held their fire marvellously to a few hundred yards. When they open up they inflict heavy casualties on the enemy, but through sheer weight of numbers some guns are overrun. The SOS artillery is called for; it comes down almost at once right on top of the enemy tanks.[18] We'd disposed our small anti-tank guns behind little hillocks, and as they [panzers] had to tip up to climb – so we could hit them from below as they reached the tops.[19]

Nineteen panzers were estimated to have been destroyed by the RB alone, with Sgt Griffith's gun knocking out five of them. Meanwhile, the Greys had still not appeared, prompting Roberts to signal: 'Come on the Greys, get out your whips!'[20] The panzers overran the positions of 8 Platoon and 14 Machine Gun Platoon of the RB, before seeing the massed armour of the Greys, charging down the slope through the clouds of dust, pennons waving, firing salvos into the panzers, who turned and ran for their anti-tank screen, expecting the Greys to follow. As they reached their screen the only noise they could hear above their engines was the crashing of the 25-pounder shells exploding amongst them and their anti-tank guns. The British had again done the unexpected by not driving into the anti-tank trap, but remaining out of their range to give the artillery free rein over the enemy.

In addition to those of the vanguard, twenty-four panzers[21] advancing behind were reported as moving across the front, but out of range of the guns of the 5th Royal Tank Regiment, before swinging right and parallel with the minefield in front of the 133rd Brigade and 'B' Battery of the 1st Royal Horse Artillery, who started firing armour-piercing shot over open sights into them. They immediately withdrew, breaking off all encounters in order to preserve ammunition and fuel, before turning south, back towards Ragil.

The losses on the day were almost equal. The 22nd Armoured lost twenty-three tanks and the 1st RB had two riflemen killed and eight wounded; twenty were missing, plus Lt Biddell wounded and Lt Ross taken prisoner. The enemy lost twenty-two tanks, although others were lost to non-conflict causes, reducing Rommel's panzer complement to approximately 172. As darkness fell, the *Panzerarmee* received the attention of the British artillery as well as the returning Wellington bombers and Albacores of the Desert Air Force, raining shells and bombs onto their positions, depriving the troops of sleep, wrecking vehicles and causing heavy casualties, especially in the Reconnaissance Group, and as before preventing the supply echelons from getting the much needed petrol to the panzers.

The next day dawned, and before going to church on the Sunday morning, Montgomery reiterated his orders that there was to be no forward movement from the main battle positions except for patrols, which were to concentrate on obtaining information and on the destruction of the enemy's motor transport. Accordingly, the 7th Motor Brigade undertook reconnaissance patrols during the morning, with 'B' Company 2nd RB also setting up listening posts to monitor the enemy activity.

Aerial attacks continued during the morning, preventing the fuel transporters from reaching the panzers and thereby forcing Rommel to limit attacks to the local area only, although he did send the 15th Panzers under temporary command of *Oberst* Crasemann to attack the western end of the ridge, possibly in the hope of outflanking the 22nd Armoured and luring the British tanks into the open. These panzers were almost immediately caught by a devastating artillery barrage followed by an attack by 8th Armoured Brigade, which again refrained from following the withdrawing panzers into an anti-tank trap. By the early hours the 15th Panzers were back where they started and with far less fuel. The 2nd KRRC and 2nd RB continued engaging the enemy as the opportunities arose, as well as providing location information to the Desert Air Force to aid its attacks.

Having no other option, Rommel now instructed his troops to dig defensive positions and await the expected air attacks. They did not have long to wait, the bombers returning from 2300 hours onwards, dropping bombs of all sizes and flying with such impunity that they appeared to be in 'air show formation', prompting Rommel to name them the 'Party Rally Raids'.[22, 23] They caused tremendous casualties and left vast numbers of vehicles burning in the desert. In the bare and coverless country the danger produced by the bomb-bursts was frequently intensified by rock splinters, which increased the casualties exponentially, seven staff officers of the Afrika Korps being killed that night.[24] Rommel was now stranded in enemy territory, with Montgomery fully aware of the conditions of the Axis forces but still not attacking. He later wrote:

> I issued very precise instructions at this stage since it was important to resist any temptation to rush into the attack. The standard of training of the Eighth Army formations was such that I was not prepared to loose them headlong into the enemy; moreover my purpose was to restore the line, and to proceed methodically with my own preparations for the big offensive later on.[25]

At dawn on 2 September the serious air attacks continued relentlessly, and now included the first B-25 Mitchell and B-24 Liberator bombers bearing the white star of the USAAF,[26] as well as the first use of 4,000-lb bombs, which when exploding shook the desert floor. The petrol promised by Cavallero had still not arrived in Africa – tankers shipping 2,600 tons had been sunk and 1,500 tons was still in Italy.[27] Air Chief Marshal Arthur Tedder, AOC RAF Middle East Command, began to bomb Tobruk, reducing further Rommel's last hope of quick resupply. Kesselring did air freight 500 tons, but the transport aircraft used up 280 tons a day in moving the fuel, resulting in only about 100 tons arriving at the most forward airfield at El Daba, with Gen. Westphal stating that it had 'consumed itself'.[28] Once at the front the transport had problems getting through the gaps in the British minefields due to artillery fire, as well as some marauding armoured cars of the 4th Company 8th Hussars.

By now the *Panzerarmee* had just one petrol issue left – enough to travel approximately sixty-two miles over good going. However, the going was far from good. The constant air and ground attacks meant that Rommel had no hope of receiving sufficient supplies and fuel to complete the offensive successfully. Continuing the operation would only result in them being cut off, surrounded and fighting a battle of material attrition. After careful consideration, he reported to the OKW that he was calling off the attack, planning to retire by stages to the line El Taque–Bab el Qattara. The German official version of events would be that the offensive had only been a 'reconnaissance in force'.[29] *Oberleutnant* Heinz Werner Schmidt recalled:

> Reports from forward became steadily more non-committal. We began to feel that the 'final shot' at Alexandria had misfired ... I developed serious doubts as to whether I should ever, as a soldier, set eyes on the Pyramids.[30]

That night the bombers came back, along with the symptoms of Rommel's illness.

Rommel Withdraws His Forces

The RAF reported on the morning of 3 September that Axis vehicles between Himeimat and Alam el Halfa were now pointing towards the west, beginning a slow and deliberate withdrawal of approximately 1,000 vehicles in three columns and moving to the north of Ragil by midday, following the route of their original advance under almost constant artillery and aerial bombardment.

Montgomery reinforced his 'no attack' directive but allowed XIII Corps to close up behind the retreating *Panzerarmee*, restricting offensive efforts to harrying the enemy soft-skinned vehicles and patrol activity, such as that undertaken by a 2nd RB patrol commanded by Capt. Sturt on the night of the 3rd/4th to determine the enemy strength and position at Deir el Ragil, where a circular laager of between thirty and forty enemy MET made up of 15-cwt and 3-ton vehicles was found.[31] Advance units of the 2nd KRRC and 2nd RB also harried the enemy west to the minefield between Ragil and Point 114, actions including blowing up a number of damaged enemy tanks and motor transport after a careful search had provided usable equipment and documents of great interest to the intelligence services.

Seeing an opportunity to isolate the retreating enemy forces, Montgomery instructed the units assigned to Operation Beresford to proceed to drive south, cutting through the Axis supply lines and the route of their withdrawal in the hope of containing them on the eastern side of the line.

Operation Beresford

The Beresford Force, comprising the 6th New Zealand Brigade augmented by the 4th and 5th Royal West Kents of the 132nd Brigade, began their attack at 2230 hours on 3 September against the prepared defences along the withdrawal route around the Muhafid and Munassib depressions. By the morning, despite enemy mortar and machine-gun fire, they had advanced a little over two miles and were occupying exposed positions in front of the newly arrived German Ramcke Brigade and Italian Folgore Division, both parachute units keen on proving that they were better than the ordinary troops. The battle continued throughout the day and by the evening the 132nd Brigade had suffered 700 casualties, with a further 283 being lost from the New Zealanders, and it was becoming evident that the operation had failed. Montgomery instructed that the attack be halted, pulling what was left of the force back and allowing the *Panzerarmee* to continue its withdrawal. The Desert Air Force relentlessly bombed and strafed the enemy as they retreated, littering the desert with abandoned vehicles and the unburied dead of the Afrika Korps.

The 4th Armoured Brigade continued to harass the *Panzerarmee* from the south as it withdrew, with the 2nd RB now moving to the area around Deir el Ragil that Sturt had reconnoitred, engaging the enemy at the western end, which resulted in forty prisoners being taken, with the loss of one of the 6-pounder portees being knocked out by a 50-mm gun. They continued to follow them, passing at least 150 abandoned vehicles on their way, to within 1,000 yards of the last British minefield, watching as the *Panzerarmee* took up residence in the strong positions previously held by the British. The RB created a forward defence line on the Alam Nayil–Himeimat track, with observation posts forward of that line, where they stayed until 12 September before being replaced and withdrawn from the line for rest, recuperation, bathing and inspection by Montgomery at Borg al Arab.

The six-day race was over! This offensive had been Rommel's last chance of gaining the Suez

Canal, and was the furthest point east reached of his whole campaign. He would never be nearer to the delta. More importantly, from the British perspective, the overriding lesson was that, 'Above all, there was hope that Rommel and his Afrika Korps were not, after all, invincible, and that in time Eighth Army could and would beat them.'[32] In 1955, von Mellenthin described Alam el Halfa as 'the turning point of the desert war, and the first of a long series of defeats on every front which foreshadowed the defeat of Germany'.[33]

The next evening, Montgomery issued an Order of the Day, announcing:

The Battle of Alamein [*sic*] has now lasted six days, and the enemy has slowly but surely been driven from 8 Army area. Tonight, 5th September, his rearguards are being driven west, through the minefield area north of Himeimat. All formations and units, both armoured and unarmoured, have contributed towards this striking victory, and have been magnificently supported by the RAF. I congratulate all ranks of 8 Army on the devotion to duty and good fighting qualities which have resulted in such a heavy defeat of the enemy and which will have far-reaching results.[34]

He wrote to a friend in England:

My first encounter with Rommel was of great interest. Luckily I had time to tidy up the mess and to get my plans laid, so there was no difficulty in seeing him off. I feel that I have won the first game, when it was his service. Next time it will be my service, the score being one-love.[35]

The Alam el Halfa battle could be described as having:

[…] more of the characteristics of the 'Grand old Duke of York' than of the Desert Fox. He had marched his tanks right up to the hill he had hoped to pass around; had an ineffectual fire-fight; and then marched them back again.[36]

During the battle Montgomery had chosen to preserve his forces, ensuring that he was able to fight another day when he would be stronger and have better opportunities to deal the blow that would lead to the destruction of the *Panzerarmee*. Exactly as Sun Tzu taught: 'He defends when his strength is inadequate; he attacks when it is abundant.'[37] Roberts recalled:

As soon as Monty joined us, things were entirely different – he saw exactly what the situation was, and went on from there. There was a very clear view in his mind what the situation was, and how it could be handled. The whole atmosphere changed, without any doubt. Alam Halfa went satisfactorily, and so he was thought of as the chap for us – everybody was very impressed after that.[38]

However, there had been disagreements at senior officer level, and one such argument with Horrocks over the 7th Motor Brigade's disengagement from the advancing Afrika Korps resulted in Renton being replaced by Maj.-Gen. John Harding as commander of the 7th Armoured Division.[39] The riflemen of 2nd RB said goodbye to Renton, who flew back to England after commanding them from their first days in the desert.

Devil's Gardens

The two armies now settled down to strengthen their defences, basing these on extensive minefields, just as the opposing forces in the First World War had based theirs on trenches. These mines became a double-edged sword: protecting the owner of the minefield, but also restricting the formation of his attacking forces. Those attacking had first to navigate their own access/egress gaps before attempting to advance into the enemy minefields, which in turn had to be gapped. This compelled them to channel their forces, providing the defenders with time to concentrate their fire, causing delays which further allowed the defending forces to regroup and strengthen their defence capability.

Rommel's engineers began building and expanding their minefields, using mostly mines retrieved from Tobruk and Mersa Matruh. They were to become infamously known as the 'Devil's Gardens' (*Teufelsgarten*) and were based on multiple deep minefields, supported by infantry defences, booby-traps and Rommel's formidable artillery strength of 500 guns located to the rear. The forward minefields would only be lightly held, collapsing before allowing the enemy to move forward onto the deeper more heavily held positions. One battalion would be responsible for a section of the line, say a mile wide and three miles deep, giving Rommel time to create counter-measures, moving the armour to the most advantageous location.

Outer Defences
The outer edges of the minefield were wired and mined to a depth of between 500 and 1,000 yards, depending on the terrain. A continuous minefield was planned to meet the escarpment of the Qattara Depression but was never completed. A second minefield was created, deeper and wider than the first. It was only after this that the main defences were to be found.

Lateral and Flanking Minefields
These minefields were laid to divide the front into sectors that would each accommodate two battalions. These sectors were designed as narrow isosceles triangles whose apexes rested on the front line, with mines along the two long sides but with the bases and centre portions left clear to permit the movement of counter-attacking forces, subject to local conditions.

Weapons Pits
These were created within the outer belt, housing machine guns and light mortars. Each battalion would man the outpost line with one company only, reinforced at night, while the bulk of the infantry and anti-tank gun emplacements would hold the second line. The guns in particular were carefully concealed so that even when firing (with flashless charges) they were practically impossible to spot.[40]

Overall, the entire defensive belt would be some five miles deep, utilising a total of 249,849 anti-tank mines and 14,509 anti-personnel mines, which, when added to the captured British minefields in the south, gave Rommel 445,358 mines of all types in place.[41] Many of the British mines had been created by local engineering companies, known as the Egyptian Pattern Mk I mine (EPI), which were crude and unstable. They used gelignite as their explosive component, which often sweated raw nitro-glycerine. The German equivalent anti-tank mine, or Tellermine (model T.Mi.35), had a circumference similar to that of a dinner plate and was packed with several pounds of explosive, detonated when a tank or truck ran over it. The resulting explosion would break a track or wreck a soft-skinned vehicle, but they would not normally be activated by the weight of a man. Mixed in with the Tellermines were anti-personnel 'S' (Schuh or S.Mi.35) mines, known as 'jumping jacks' or 'bounding mines', which when stepped on or otherwise activated would explode upwards to a height of about 4 feet, trailing a wire that would detonate the main charge and fire 260 pieces of quarter inch by three-eighths-of-an inch rod shrapnel into the air,[42] killing within a range of 50 metres. The engineers also planted captured large-calibre shells and aircraft bombs to be electronically detonated by the men in nearby defence posts, by trip wires or by the explosion of nearby mines. The name 'Devil's Gardens' would be well earned.

Rommel's gains from the 'six-day battle' were the British defences in the south, incorporating the January and February minefields and the excellent observation posts on the top of Himeimat, the loss of which Montgomery played down:

> Moreover, it suited me to have their [Axis] forces in strength on the southern flank since I was considering making my main blow, later on, on the northern part of the front. I remember Horrocks protesting to me that the enemy remained in possession of not only our original minefields but also of some good viewpoints from which to observe his corps area. I replied that he should get busy and make new minefields for his corps. As regards the observation points such as Himeimat, it suited me that Rommel should be able to have a good look at all the preparations for attack we were making on our southern flank: they were a feint.[43]

Rommel, however, was still concerned by the Italians, who made up almost 50 per cent of his force, telling his friend Kurt Hesse that he considered ordinary Italian soldiers good, but that their officers were worthless, their High Command traitors.[44] This opinion was reinforced when captured Allied soldiers said that they had known about his plans to outflank the Alamein Line to take Alam el Halfa and the drive to the coast for some time, considering that he would attack from 25 August onwards. The source of this information? An Italian officer![45] Rommel therefore decided to alternate the German units amongst the Italian ones, thereby stiffening the resolve of the troops as well as the officers.

Montgomery was watching as Rommel made his reorganisations and defences. Patrols – the ears and eyes of the army – were constantly sent out to probe and study the enemy's defences, taking prisoners whenever possible. Meanwhile, the Desert Air Force flew over the lines, taking some 10,650 photographs over the next few months, which the highly skilled Army Air Photograph Interpretation Unit used to produce detailed maps and overlays of the enemy positions.

Brig. Kirkman – who Montgomery regarded as the best artilleryman in the British Army – was transferred from England and a survey was undertaken by the Royal Artillery aimed at spotting the gun flashes of the enemy guns. This produced what no army commander wants: an accurate plot of the order of battle of his complete artillery. Armed with this information, Montgomery began working on the plan for the offensive that was to take place once the Eighth Army had been reinforced, re-equipped and retrained.

Operation Lightfoot Takes Shape

The operational codename[46] given to the offensive bore a sense of macabre flippancy, 'Lightfoot', so called because the operation would be dominated by the proximity of the mines situated throughout the enemy defensive positions. The infantry would have to negotiate these (treading lightly) before sappers would gap the minefield for the armour whose role was to break through to give battle with the panzers. The order, marked 'Most Secret', was sent to corps and divisional commanders and senior staff officers, outlining the basic operation and including the warning that 'The battle for which we are preparing will be a real rough house,'[47] the aim being to trap the enemy in their present area and destroy them there, so as not to allow a battle of movement to take place. Montgomery also considered that the forthcoming battle would be the 'turning point of the war,'[48] the result of which would largely depend on which side could stand up to the buffeting longest. The soldiers would therefore have to be physically and mentally hardened up. 'There will be no tip and run tactics in this battle,' he concluded. 'It will be a killing match, the German soldier is a good soldier and the only way to beat him is to kill him in battle'.[49]

In basic terms, the infantry of XXX Corps would advance through the minefields in the north and secure a bridgehead, codenamed Oxalic, on the outer edge. Eighteen lanes would then be cleared by sappers who followed the infantry, to form two corridors each one mile wide, one for the 1st and a second for the 10th armoured divisions. After travelling one or two miles past the minefields they would regroup at a point codenamed Pierson, collecting any stragglers, and then advance to their objective, Skinflint, to await further orders.

Back in London, the news of Rommel's failure during the battle of Alam el Halfa relieved some of the pressure on Churchill, but it did no more than that. Intending to divert that pressure on to Alexander, he wrote to him on 17 September, saying he understood that the battle would commence in the fourth week of September, i.e. before the Anglo-American landings due in November. Alexander showed the communiqué to Montgomery, who took a pad and wrote a reply for Alexander's comments:

> Firstly Rommel's attack had caused some delay to preparations; secondly the attack needed to have the right moon conditions; thirdly the troops would be insufficiently equipped and trained in September, and fourthly, an attack in September would fail, but an attack in October would result in victory.[50]

The unaltered message was sent by Alexander the same day.

Alexander and Montgomery had also stated that Lightfoot should be launched thirteen days prior to the Torch landings in order to place the maximum amount of pressure on the Axis forces. It had now been decided that the landings should take place on 8 November, thereby setting the Lightfoot start date as 26 October. The last vital element was a full moon, so necessary for mine clearance, meaning that the operation was scheduled to begin on the night of 23 October.

A 'Corps de Chasse' is Created and the Battalion Become Rhinos

Montgomery also planned for the next stage. Those troops involved in the break-in and crumbling part of the attack would be exhausted, and exhausted men are not the best to exploit a breach in the enemy lines or the subsequent breakout. For this he would need a riposte, a 'Corps de Chasse' as he called it, to be held in reserve and which would therefore be fresh when needed to chase the *Panzerarmee*. The riposte would be X Corps, a strong armoured formation augmented with mobile infantry akin to the Afrika Korps:

[They would] bring on an armoured battle where full use could be made of British armour and armament to destroy the enemy and, otherwise, to prevent the enemy's armour from interfering with XXX Corps operations.[51]

In order to create X Corps a complex reorganisation of the Eighth Army had to take place. This included regiments and battalions being placed under new commands – a process that did not always go according to plan, as was the case of the 2nd RB, when they were instructed in a Movement Order of 18 September to move to the divisional training area, some twenty miles west of their present position, and to come under the command of the 10th Armoured Division. After staying there for three days awaiting orders, they were informed that not only were they in the wrong area, they were not to be under the command of the 10th Armoured anyway.

Lt Col. Turner attended a conference on 20 September at X Corps to discuss a training exercise involving the passage of an armoured division through British and enemy minefields by night, at the end of which he was informed that the 7th Motor, and therefore the 2nd RB, would come under the command of the 1st Armoured Division for training and probably for eventual operational purposes. Turner now had to inform the battalion that they were to become part of the new X Corps, but in doing so would be divorced from the 7th Armoured Division and accordingly lose the distinctive desert rat insignia which they had worn since arriving in the desert. They would thereafter wear the charging white rhino on a green background or black oval on their tunics and vehicles, the reverse happening to the 1st RB, who now exchanged their rhino for the desert rat. Albert Martin wrote:

Our pride in and loyalty to the jerboa was total. Many were the times when brawls broke out, usually for no reason, in a Cairo nightclub when the shout went out 'Up the Jerboas!' And believe me, all the 7th Armoured men, from whatever regiment, would form a solid block in mutual defence against all comers.[52]

Turner wrote to his riflemen:

Whilst I fully sympathise with them [the ranks] over this, if the matter is considered it will be seen that the change must take place, as 4 RHA and 2 Rifle Brigade are the only two units of the original 7th Support Group now remaining in the Motor Bde. It would be impossible for two units in the Division to wear different signs to the rest of the Division, while the whole meaning of the sign would be lost if the other units of the Brigade, who have no connection with the 'Jerboa' traditions, were now to adopt them. We are now joining a Division which has proved itself second to none in the recent operations and which is equipped better than any Division in the Middle East. We should all be proud to fight as part of this Division and I am sure we shall soon find that the same spirit de corps will surround the Rhino as has surrounded the Desert Rat.[53]

But this did not stop the disagreements between the riflemen and the Pioneer Corps who were tasked with the repainting of the insignia. Senior officers were shocked for a day or two after the transfer to see pictures of enormous rhinoceroses tossing jerboas to the winds, or gigantic jerboas belabouring rhinoceroses to their deaths, or even hugely pregnant rhinos. Time and discipline soon restored the balance, as 'orders were orders and these were permanent'.[54]

German petrol cans, known as 'jerry cans', were collected from the Allied forces and given to X Corps to hold the fuel that would be so vital for the fast-moving mobile unit. These stout petrol cans with a hinged, air-sealing levered lid, had proved far superior to the four-gallon 'flimsies' then used by the Eighth Army and produced in their millions at a plant near Alexandria, of which a third would leak due to poor construction and the thin metal used, thereby thoroughly deserving their nickname.

Reinforcements were also coming to the Eighth Army. Among these were the 51st (Highland) Division, commanded by Maj.-Gen. Douglas 'Tartan Tan' Wimberley, a battle-hardened soldier who knew his job. For many under his command, Alamein was to be their first taste of battle, but they still had to live up to the past fighting record and deeds of valour attributed to the regiments which, as Brooke recalled, 'stands them in a category of their own'.[55]

The planning, reinforcements and transfers between units were all taking place, but Montgomery needed to concentrate on three essentials: leadership, equipment and training, saying to Churchill that it was vital that the Eighth Army was fit enough for the task, making physical fitness a key element in his plan. Capt. Carol Mather observed:

> The men looked very fit and bronzed and all the rest of it but none of them had walked a mile since they came to the desert. Everybody was riding in vehicles, so they really weren't quite as fit as they looked.[56]

A training film saw Alexander state, 'Physical fitness and hardness in an army is one of the biggest battle winning factors in war,' and that the Eighth Army should be 'fighting fit and fit to fight'.[57] The Official History stated:

> Although it was clear to General Montgomery that Rommel had shot his bolt [at the battle of Alam el Halfa], he resisted the temptation to start a general counter-attack. He judged the 8th Army to be unready, and going off at half-cock would only make it harder to prepare for the decisive blow he had in mind.[58]

The training regime also had to promote the most basic elements of the human psyche, bearing in mind that most of the men in the Eighth Army were Christians and were fully aware of the commandment 'Thou shalt not kill.' The majority had no experience of killing, but now found themselves in the position where it was not only their job but their duty to kill.[59] Montgomery wrote to Brooke:

> The trouble with our British lads is that they are not killers by nature; they have got to be so inspired that they will want to kill, and that is what I have tried to do with this army of mine.[60]

Equipment was now flooding into Suez, moving from there to the main depot at El Amiriya and then the sixty miles to the Alamein front. Added to this, Egypt was becoming a vast workhorse of industry, just as Wavell had predicted:

> An immense variety of work ... notice boards to AA mountings, from meat-safes to carriers for sterilised blood-bottles, from 12,000 crates for Molotov Cocktails to 25,000 trestle tops for tables. Shell and ammunition gauges and extractors of all kinds, fire ladders, open sights for 25-pounders, chairs, covers for machine guns, magnetic detectors of A/T mines, hospital trolleys, jigs, pistons, saddlery, yakdans [the sheepskin jacket beloved of Eighth Army officers], swivel chairs for tanks,

tool chests, steel tent pins, special armouries' instruments etc. were only a few of these varied and special requirements.[61]

All were produced by local workers to supply the Eighth Army ready for the big offensive.

Rommel Leaves for Treatment

Rommel was also planning, deciding that when the attack came it would probably be based on a breakthrough along the coastal road and an outflanking movement further down the line, which the *Panzerarmee* would 'absorb, weakening its impetus before swinging back on the hinge of El Mreir or El Daba'[62] on to the massive Qatani minefield and then breaking through the British lines themselves. However, his personal fitness was causing him a major problem. The stress and lack of rest since Gazala had had a very detrimental effect on him and he was now experiencing regular fainting fits, as well as other health problems, and decided to return to Germany for treatment after passing temporary command over to *General der Kavallerie* Georg Strumme.

With a heavy heart, a worried Rommel left for Germany on 23 September, stopping *en route* at Derna where he met Cavallero to discuss transport problems and obtain his agreement that the Italians would supply 3,000 workmen to repair the roads and improve the railway systems. Ultimately, however, none of Cavallero's promises were kept or improvements made. Resuming his journey, Rommel stopped at Rome to meet Mussolini, who was convinced that the Americans would invade North Africa in 1943 and that it was therefore essential for him to reach the Nile before they arrived. He stated, 'You have done the impossible before, Herr Feldmarschall. We are all sure you can do it again!'[63]

Upon reaching the Wolfsschanze (Wolf's Lair), the first of the Führer's headquarters, he met Hitler, who again promoted an unfounded optimism and sycophantic praise. Göring, President of the Reichstag and Reichsminister of Aviation, dismissed the American threat out of hand: 'Nothing but latrine rumours! All the Americans can make are razor blades and Frigidaires. Rommel replied, 'I wish we had such razor blades.'[64] However, whilst staying with Goebbels, Rommel attended a rally, at which he rather unwisely declared:

> We stand just fifty kilometres from Alexandria and Cairo, and we have the key to all Egypt in our hands. And we mean to do something about it too! We have not gone all that way to be thrown back again. You can take that from me; what we have, we hold![65]

Rommel then left with his wife for the rest and recuperation that he so clearly needed at Semmering in Austria.

Leave and the Delights of Cairo and Alexandria

The Eighth Army troops had been working hard and, in preparation for battle, were given leave. The 2nd RB whilst at Khatatba took this during the week beginning 24 September, each rifleman and officer receiving a four-day pass to Cairo or Alexandria, allowing them to revisit the tourist sites with service clubs, welfare organisations and base camps, all competing to entice the 'tourist' away from the less salubrious aspects of Egyptian civilisation while still enjoying a few precious moments of civilian normality.

The first step was to bathe in clean water, dispose of the torn, sweat- and sand-caked clothing, and dress in new uniforms supplied by the friendly quartermasters, and then to laze around doing nothing, being able to walk without the fear of getting blown sky-high by shells, sleep above ground in a comfortable bed, and sit at a table and eat every kind of delicious food. At the military canteen almost any food could be acquired, but the favourite for the men fresh from the desert was egg and chips. Beer was available, as well as tea – without the taste of chloride or petrol.

A ride in a horse-drawn 'garry' was a must, whilst the Cyprus Bar, an 'in bounds' bar for ordinary ranks, was the place to relax with a beer before going off for one's *de rigueur* photo sitting on a camel with the pyramids in the background, and ice cream and cakes at Groppi's. The officers went to Shepheard's Hotel where they could be reminded of a staid London club, drinking their gin slings served by servants in white galabiyas, in cool musty lounges. All these places drew the men away from the forbidden delights of Burka or Sister Street in Alexandria and similar dens of iniquity in Cairo.

Mine Clearance Task Force

Leave was over far too soon and the delights of Cairo and Alexandria left behind. The riflemen continued their training for their vital role on the Minefield Task Force (MTF), for which Montgomery had called upon the adaptability of the Rifle Brigade, placing them on the forward edge of the armoured battle.

After the July battles, the armoured commanders were concerned that the infantry could not gap quickly enough, resulting in them not getting their tanks through all the minefields in a single night. These problems had to be overcome. According to Brig. Frederick Kisch:

> The MTF would create, manage and protect the gaps through the minefields by way of an intense artillery barrage to smother the enemy gun line; a creeping barrage and establishment of forward positions designed to enable the sappers to approach their task in relative safety and with full fire support to give them protection whilst they are doing their work.[66]

Obviously an added danger to the sappers were enemy positions bypassed by the infantry and still in situ. How could the sapper concentrate on his very dangerous and stressful job and fight as an infantryman at the same time? The answer was for the RB to form a shield, protecting the sappers and simultaneously dealing with the enemy positions still in place. Their orders for this role were:

1. Establish liaison between the Royal Engineers recce parties and 51st (Highland) Division and proceed with them to the first enemy minefield;
2. Clear and maintain 3 gaps 500 yards apart in all enemy minefields up to and including OXALIC. On completion of the original three gaps, a fourth (spare) gap will be made;
3. Mark with the appropriate lights all gaps made in enemy minefields;
4. Mark with lights routes from BEAM line to OXALIC and maintain these lights;

5. Control all traffic WEST of our minefields;

6. Recce and clear for 4th Royal Horse Artillery suitable gun positions in the designated area;

7. Organise as soon as possible a force to take offensive actions against remaining pockets of enemy resistance, or minor enemy counter-attacks; and

8. Be prepared to disband on receipt of orders, and each component to rejoin its parent unit or formation.[67]

The officers and riflemen began training at the Eighth Army School of Mine Clearance set up in Borg al Arab under Royal Engineer Maj. Peter Moore and a New Zealand Engineer, Maj. A. R. Currie, who had worked out that the best mix of skills to complete the job in hand would come from a motor battalion, with attachments of Royal Engineers, Signals, and supporting tanks. As in other military roles, a drill was formed and practised until it became second nature.

The roles of the battalions of the RB differed slightly. The 1st RB, who were to be situated in the south with the gaps being made with the use of flail tanks,[68] a standard tank chassis which had a revolving drum fitted with chains that spun, literally flailing the ground and detonating the mines. Once through the enemy minefields, they would form a bridgehead on the far side of the minefield through which the armour would pass. The 2nd RB, commanded by Turner, was located above the inter-corps line in the area of the 51st (Highland) Division and, following them, the sappers would clear and maintain three lanes plus a reserve, as far as the Oxalic Line, before creating their bridgehead.

Throughout the whole of the line a total of 88,775 improvised hurricane lamps[69] were made from 'flimsies' each with a shape cut into it corresponding to the track that it was to be used on. Those to be used on Moon, Star and Sun routes would be made by the riflemen of the 2nd RB during the days before the battle.

Each gap would have targets set through its route, HQ being advised when each target was reached and consolidated:

Target Code	Sun	Moon	Star
Beam to Rise	2,400 yards on 280°	3,450 yards on 273°	3,200 yards on 278°
Rise to Light	1,500 yards on 259°	550 yards on 254°	1,400 yards on 254°
		750 yards on 272°	
Light to Set	2,750 yards on 268°	2,300 yards on 272°	2,400 yards on 277°
	850 yards on 263°		
Set to Oxalic	950 yards on 270°	1,250 yards on 272°	1,350 yards on 277°
Total distance	8,450 yards	8,300 yards	8,350 yards

A combination of the gap name and target code would provide an accurate position for the MTF in that area. As an example, the signal 'SunRise' would indicate that the unit had completed the mine clearance along the Sun gap for a distance of 2,400 yards along a bearing of 280 degrees.

Capt. Picton and two ambulances would be stationed on Sun route; Capt. Fine and two ambulances would be on stationed on Moon route, and Capt. Jones and one ambulance would be stationed on Star route.

The process would be as follows:[70]

1. The team would advance after the infantry, led by an officer and four men on a compass bearing across the minefield, unrolling a white tape which would mark the middle of

   the gap.

2. Upon reaching the other side of the minefield, a stake would be driven into the ground and a blue light, made out of a water or petrol can, with a shape to identify the particular lane, mounted to shine to the rear.

3. The whole engineering party would then spread out in line abreast and advance in a stooping position, rather like the popular impression of a gorilla on the move, with fingers brushing the ground, backs of hands to the front, feeling for trip wires, eyes anxiously scanning every inch of ground for the treacherous 'S' mine horns. Direction would still be controlled by the man with the compass, who would also unravel the tape.

4. A small utility truck, or sometimes a jeep, would follow with a heavily sand-bagged floor, having a steering wheel extended to avoid impaling the driver if it hit a mine. This vehicle was used to ensure that the forward edge of the minefield had been reached.

5. Behind the vehicle came three teams of nine men, each team to clear a width of eight feet making a 24-foot gap in all:

   a) The first three men of each team unrolled more tapes as guides, and the ones on the outside of each 24-foot gap affixed more guiding lights to guide the heavy vehicles and tanks coming through afterwards;

   b) These three teams of three men working abreast also dealt with the trip wires, booby-traps or 'S' mines found and marked by the first team to go through, if these had not already been defused;

   c) The second trio in each team were the detectors, using electric 'brooms', resembling vacuum cleaners in size and shape, if available, to detect the mines, a role that necessitated standing up in full view of the enemy. If detectors were not available, they prodded the ground with a bayonet held at a 30° angle, dreading the feeling as the bayonet scrapped against the solid exterior of a mine. Each mine found was marked with a white disc, painstakingly exposed, checked for booby-traps, then lifted and stacked, to be defused later.

Timings were planned, and the advance was rigidly practised. Accordingly, it was found that 200 yards could be cleared in an hour using the electronic detectors, but it required the operator to stand amongst the tracer fire and shrapnel whizzing around him, or 100 yards achieved if prodding with bayonets.[71] Once their job was completed, the MTF would be dissolved upon receiving the code phrase 'A hunting we will go'.[72]

The 2nd RB saw men returning from leave and officers being transferred between battalions, as well as receiving reinforcements in the form of seventy-four riflemen arriving from the Infantry Battalion Depot. After Church Parade on the morning of 4 October, Capt. S. W. L. Gibbons and 2nd Lt Fish left the battalion to join 7th RB, while Capt. P. Shepherd-Cross, Capt. J. Ward and Lt Naumann arrived from 7th RB, all of whom would have very important roles in the coming battles. The officers were also, as far as was allowed, brought up to date on how the battle would proceed, attending conferences and working sand models. The battalion as a whole also became involved in Operation Bertram, with the 2nd RB picking up dummy minefields, transporting them to a new location and setting them up over the next two days.

Operation Bertram

The idea behind Operation Bertram was to conceal from the enemy for as long as possible the intention to take the offensive, and, when this could no longer be concealed, to mislead him about both the date and the sector in which the main thrust was to be made. As taught by Sun Tzu:

> It is often possible by adopting all kinds of measures of deception to drive the enemy into the plight of making erroneous judgements and taking erroneous actions, thus depriving him of superiority and initiative.[73]

More specifically, its purpose was to deceive Rommel into believing that the main attack would take place in the south of the line, around the Himeimat area, whilst at the same time camouflaging the troop movements and armour build-up in the northern areas above the inter-corps line. The whole operation, which was broken down into smaller projects, was the brainchild of Lt Col. Dudley Clarke, who had been one of Montgomery's students and had become the acknowledged expert in deception tactics, creating 'A' Force located in Cairo. They were to construct a variety of complicated and flamboyant measures thus creating the most elaborate web of deception. Individual sections of the plan were codenamed Diamond, Brian, Munassib, Treatment, Martello and Murrayfield.

Diamond
This was the scheme to build a 20-mile fake water pipeline to the south of the line in order to supply the large build-up of forces that appeared to be going there:

> The pipe-trench was excavated in the normal way. Five miles of dummy railway track, made from petrol cans, were used for piping. The 'piping' was strung out along the open trench. When each five-mile section of the trench was filled in, the 'piping' was collected and laid out alongside the next section. Dummy pump houses were erected at three points; water points and overhead storage reservoirs were made at two of these points.[74]

The construction of the pipeline was also deliberately prolonged, giving the impression that an attack would not be able to take place for some time.

Brian
All kinds of fake ordnance, munitions, etc. were created from green steel wool, hessian, camouflage nets, old petrol cans and wire, and stored in undisguised dumps in the south. Packing cases containing real stores for the operation were left untended in the north, giving the appearance that they were dummy stores.

Munassib
This involved digging gun pits with dummy guns at the eastern end of the Munassib Depression, to represent three and a half regiments. However, these were then not to be visited, giving the enemy the impression that they were dummy emplacements, but would then be populated with a fighting force and real guns shortly before the attack.

Treatment

Aimed at the Cairo population, this was intended to give the impression that the attack would not come until the first week in November.[75] Senior staff made hotel reservations for late October, Staff College in Halfa extended its term, and Alexander was scheduled to attend a summit arranged to take place in Persia on 26 October.

Martello

This involved making a tank appear to be a soft-skinned lorry by fitting covers on a framework. The empty covers were parked close to the start lines of X Corps whilst the armour was moved around the El Imayed area, and when ready would drive into the tent-like structures, changing their outline to that of a lorry and effectively increasing the number of non-combat vehicles whilst reducing the amount of armour in the area.

Murrayfield

This was the process of appearing to increase the number of armoured units in the southern end of the line. The 10th Armoured Division would drive south during the day and return at night after leaving dummy vehicles, repeating the process on several occasions to appear to populate the southern force. As with Martello, tanks would be hidden beneath the covers to give the appearance of trucks, but in this case dummy tanks would also be erected at the Murrayfield positions located in the south, further appearing to the enemy that the attack would take place in the southern part of the line. The 44th (Home Counties) Division, 7th Armoured Division, including the 1st RB and 4th Armoured Brigade, became very active around the three large (dummy) store dumps in the south, in order to bring all the elements of the operation together.

Montgomery Enlightens the Officers

Montgomery was the master of the carefully prepared battle. Every detail was meticulously thought through in advance, and despite Churchill's pressure on him to attack, he steadfastly prepared the battleground and troops. It was said:

> Before battle he prayed; but in order not to test The Almighty too much, he always ensured that he had twice the number of infantry and three times the number of tanks of his opponent.[76]

The security of the plan continued to be meticulously controlled, with the commanding officers of the units instructed to attend a briefing by Montgomery at the Amariya cinema near Alexandria on 10 October in order to pass over a more detailed version of the plan, again stating that they were to expect a 'dog-fight' that would probably last twelve days. He wrote in a memo:

> This battle will involve hard and prolonged fighting. Our troops must not think that, because we have a good tank and very powerful artillery support, the enemy will all surrender. The enemy will NOT surrender, and there will be bitter fighting. The infantry must be prepared to fight and kill, and to continue doing so over a prolonged period ...[77]

Montgomery later wrote:

> On 6th October, just two weeks before the battle was to begin, I changed the plan. My initial plan had been based on destroying Rommel's armour; the remainder of his army, the un-armoured portion, could then be dealt with at leisure. This was in accordance with the accepted military thinking of the day. I decided to reverse the process and this altered the whole conception of how the battle was to be fought. My modified plan now was to hold off, or contain, the enemy armour while we carried out a methodical destruction of the infantry divisions holding the defensive system. These un-armoured divisions would be destroyed by means of a 'crumbling' process, the enemy being attacked from the flank and rear and cut off from their supplies.[78]

As he put it, 'The days of Balaklavering' were gone![79]

The old desert hands, those with 'sand between their toes', who clung to the old loyalties and who greeted with scepticism the arrival of the new man from home, went to the gathering with not very high expectations. They received that night for the first time a complete assurance that unequivocal victory was at last to be their reward and that never again would they need to 'flog up and down the same piece of desert'.[80] Even as seasoned a hand as Turner declared that the conference was 'absolutely thrilling'.[81] In their minds, they left behind Alexandria and Cairo for ever when leaving the cinema that night.

The five main points of the updated plan were as follows:

1. The main attack by XXX Corps in the north would take place across a front of four divisions. Two corridors were to be cleared through the minefields, and through these lanes X Corps would pass;

2. XIII Corps in the south were to stage two attacks, one directed past the Himeimat Peaks and on to the Taqa Plateau, the other into the area of Jebel Kalakh, both with the object of convincing Rommel that the main attack would take place in the south, thereby forcing him to retain troops in the area;

3. On both fronts the enemy forward positions were to be destroyed, though heavy casualties, especially among the 7th Armoured Division in the south, were to be avoided;

4. Once X Corps were through XXX Corps positions and the main enemy defences, they were to deploy so as to prevent interference with XXX Corps operations against the Axis infantry. Offensive action against the enemy armour would only be undertaken when the infantry battles had been won, drawing the panzers into a mêlée where they would be irretrievably ground down;

5. The battle would commence at night during the full moon period.

The infantry would advance under a rolling barrage, the shells passing overhead and landing a few metres in front, moving forward at regular intervals to enable the infantry to catch up. The enemy would therefore have the minimum amount of time to recover their positions after the barrage before being attacked.

There was always a danger that the infantry advancing in the dark would lose their way and cross into the path of their neighbours. Bofors guns of the anti-aircraft batteries would therefore fire bursts of coloured 40-mm tracer shells along the boundaries between each brigade and each division at the rate of up to 120 rounds per minute, defining the edges in bright coloured lines, and to the rear searchlight beams would lance the sky to intersect above specified orientation points. The soldiers would be heavily laden: each man wore a small pack, a pick or entrenching tool, an extra fifty rounds of ammunition, two grenades and four sandbags. Every battalion was to be capable of fighting for twenty-four hours without relief or resupply, although obviously the hope was that the battalion transport would reach the forward positions before dawn on the 24th.

It was obvious that the attack would produce casualties. Montgomery knew that many brave men – probably the best in the Eighth Army – were going to lose their lives. He informed the Director Medical Services that he expected the battle to result in 10,000 casualties (excluding killed, missing and sick), this estimate would prove remarkably accurate.[82]

In another change to the previous combat methods, the 'Flying' or 'Jock Columns' strategy of the past few years, with divisions split into bits and pieces all over the desert, would be dispensed with. The Eighth Army would now fight by divisions, allowing the artillery to deliver concentrated firepower of devastating effectiveness.

Operations by Front

The operational front would be split on a corps and then divisional basis, tracks through the enemy minefields being marked by cairns of stones with the side facing east painted white.

EL ALAMEIN BATTLEFIELD – October 1942

XXX Corps (9th Australian Division, 51st (Highland) Division, 2nd New Zealand Division, 1st South African Division)

The northern part of the line, above the inter-corps line, was controlled by XXX Corps. Their orders were to attack on a front of four divisions in two bounds, initially to the first line of enemy defences, and secondly to clear the rearmost known enemy defences. Thereafter they were to hold the line gained.

Coastal/Right

Manned by the 9th Australian Division, who were to strongly defend the Tel el Eisa area and carry out a 'Chinese' attack,[83] putting more doubt into Rommel's mind about the actual point of the main attack. The front to begin at the coastal road and extend south to approximately two miles south of Tel el Eisa. Their tracks were called Diamond, Boomerang, Two Bar and Square.

Highland Front/Right Centre

Situated to the south or left of the Australian front, the 51st Highland Division had the widest of all the fronts, extending from a 2,500-yard start line that widened over the distance to the final objective width of two and three-quarter miles. It would be manned by seven battalions and a reconnaissance regiment, with its three lanes named Sun, Moon and Star being gapped by the 2nd RB.

New Zealand Front/Left Centre

On the left of the Highlanders was the 2nd New Zealand Division section, whose front was a similar design to the Scots, but not as wide at the top of the funnel, with a target of the western tip of the Miteirya Ridge. Their front was joined to the 51st by a short branch leading off Star track, and their tracks were named Bottle and Boat, which would be cleared by 133rd Lorried Infantry.

1st South African Division Front/Left

To the left of the New Zealanders, the 1st South African Division section was the southernmost of the central sector, their track being named Hat.

Opposing Forces (164th Division, 15th Panzer Division, Trento Division, Littorio Division, 90th Light Division and Trieste Division – the latter two held in reserve on the coast)

XIII Corps (50th Division, 44th Division and 7th Armoured Division)

Below the inter-corps line the area was controlled by XIII Corps. Their orders were to break through the first two minefields, previously known as January and February, between Munassib and Himeimat.

Southern Front/South

The 7th Armoured Division would follow the flail tanks and create the tracks through the first minefields, after first advancing through the Allied minefields Nuts and May. Upon breaking through January minefield, the 1st RB would form a bridgehead, with 'A' and 'B' companies taking up flanking positions, allowing the armour to pass through and attack the Himeimat Plateau. Tracks through the February minefield would then be cleared. Montgomery instructed Harding:

Your job is to keep 21 Panzer down here by offensive action, but at the same time to keep your division in being so that it can take part in a further offensive, in pursuit or whatever, later on. [84]

Harding termed this, 'Heads you win, tails I lose'.[85]

Opposing Forces (Bologna Division, Brescia Division, Folgore Division, Pavia Division, Remke Division, 33rd Recce Division, Kiel Group, 21st Panzer Division and Ariete Armoured Division)

X Corps (1st Armoured Division, 10th Armoured Division)
Under command of Lumsden, X Corps was to be stationed to the rear of XXX Corps, along the line of Springbok road. Once breakthrough had taken place, the 1st Armoured Division, located on the right, would follow the Sun, Moon and Star tracks created by the 2nd RB, whilst 10th Armoured Division, located on the left, would travel along Bottle, Boat and Hat tracks created by the 133rd Lorried Infantry. These tracks were to be completely swept and marked during the hours of darkness of the first night, allowing the armour divisions to exploit southwards from XXX Corps' final objectives. The 1st Armoured Division was to gain the Oxalic Line before dawn and establish a position about a mile further west; the 10th Armoured Division aimed to cross the Miteirya Ridge, pass through the Oxalic Line under control of the New Zealanders and establish the Pierson Line, anchored about three miles south-west of Miteirya. There they would await enemy armour, prevent 15th and 21st Panzer divisions from joining forces and protect the infantry exploitations.
Once the tracks were in full operation, the 7th Motor Brigade would consolidate a flank guard with their anti-tank and heavy machine guns on the right of the front, while the 133rd Lorried Infantry would consolidate a similar position on the left, protecting the tracks and therefore the armour using them against panzer attack. This stage would see the armour advance to the Skinflint area, lying across the Rahman Track, locating the 15th Panzer Division and engaging them in battle whilst keeping watch for the 21st Panzer Division coming from the south.
    A naval diversion would be undertaken along the coast to make a feint landing at Ras el Kenya, just beyond Fuka, with the intention of ensuring that the 90th Light Division would remain in its coastal defence role, while the Desert Air Force would begin concerted bombing raids on the Axis-held seaports, Tobruk again being heavily targeted, and continuing to cause serious damage to the Luftwaffe.

The Timetable

Montgomery's plan was made up of five phases:

Break in to the enemy defences	23-24 October
Crumbling to break the enemy's local cohesion	24-25 October
Counter	26-28 October
No name was given to the standstill period	29-31 October

| Operation Supercharge | 1-2 November |
| Breakout forcing enemy withdrawal | 3-7 November |

Brooke was advised that the most likely date was to be the 23rd. He wrote in his diary, 'As I had no confidence in Winston's ability to keep anything secret I decided not to tell him about the plan'.[86] But after relenting told Churchill, writing about the result a few days later:

> I discovered that Winston, after giving me a solemn undertaking that he would not tell anybody what I had told him about details of impending ME attack had calmly gone and told Eisenhower and [Bedell] Smith!![87]

Axis Supplies

In the meantime, the supply situation of the *Panzerarmee* was not getting any better,
fuel and supplies had to ferried on lorries from as far away as Tripoli and Benghazi. Driving at a steady 40 mph, this would take a week to reach Alamein, not taking into consideration the wear and tear of the vehicles and the attention given to anything moving along the coast roads by the Desert Air Force.

In the first three weeks of October, sea and air attacks sank no less than 45 per cent of Italian and 59 per cent of German tonnage dispatched. This almost halved the potential endurance of the *Panzerarmee*'s armour and transport from twenty-one to eleven days. On 22 October, *General der Panzertruppe* Georg Stumme commented:

> [The troops were] living from hand to mouth; we fill one gap only to see another open. We cannot build up basic supply which would enable us to overcome critical situations through our own resources and which allows operational freedom of movement, which is an absolutely vital necessity for the army.[88]

Red-faced, almost bursting out of a uniform a size too small for him, with a monocle positively screwed into his eye socket, he hissed the word *plicht* (duty) almost as a threat, making it clear that the testing time was close at hand.[89] Italian soldier Vittorio Vallicella was dejected:

> We are stuck in this desolate plain of El Alamein, tired, hungry, with little water, filthy and full of lice. We know that our Great Leader [Mussolini] is 660 kms from the front, furious because we have been unable to open the gates of Alexandria for him ... For 16 months we have led this life; kept going with a canteen of water (if lucky); at the mercy of fleas and lice. Maybe at this point we can only hope that a bomb takes us out and puts an end to our suffering.[90]

In late October an Italian supply convoy was mauled and the tanker *Panuco* was sent to the seabed by a Wellington Bomber. Westphal demanded a replacement, and was advised that: 'Tanker *Proserpina* ... arriving Tobruk early 26th ... tanker *Luisiana* will set sail with tanker *Portofino* from Taranto evening 27th, put into Tobruk approximately 31st.'[91] This message, designed to relieve some of the pressure from the *Panzerarmee*, was delightfully received and decoded by the Allies, who sat in wait.

Bertram is Activated

Operations Martello and Murrayfield were activated on 20 October under the Bertram plan, and the 1st and 10th Armoured divisions began to move up by stages to their assembly areas behind the XXX Corps front, maintaining wireless silence, with 'S' Company coming under the command of the 2nd KRRC and working in the area of El Imayed under Operation Murrayfield.

On 21 October, in accordance with Montgomery's orders, the commanding officers themselves broke the news to all their own junior officers and men, sitting silent and absorbed in semicircles on the sand, with diagrams of the coming battle before them and with the sun blazing down on their bronzed limbs. General Harding recorded that after the men were advised of the plan, 'the atmosphere of well-designed, objective preparation, lively expectancy and quiet confidence pervaded the division and indeed the whole Army'.[92] Sgt Longstaff of the 2nd RB recalled:

> Before Montgomery, we never knew what our role was – where we were going, what was going to happen, who was on our left flank, right flank – who were our reserves. We didn't even know who the enemy was prior to Montgomery. He gave the order that every soldier will be told who is on his left and who is on his right – who is behind him and who is in front of him, and he will be told what he's going to do. When a man is told those things, he starts getting confidence; he doesn't feel that he's fighting by himself.[93]

But Montgomery made it very clear that despite the superiority in guns and armour and the advantage that training had given the troops, it was not going to be a speedy or easily won victory. Rifleman Gregg recalled:

> A brass hat came round to inspect how we were doing and told us, 'Prepare yourselves for some excitement.' We wondered what he meant by excitement and knew he didn't mean jumping for joy. We went away to make the usual brew and write our letters home.[94]

Martin Crowder wrote to his sister, 'Just a very short note to let you know we start tomorrow night, so you may not see me or hear from me for some time. Don't forget to say a prayer or two for me'.[95] Tom Bird recalled:

> Monty came to give the battalion a talk. I remember him telling the men that they were 'a fine body of men', which was such a cliché; if I'd said it to my company, they would have roared with laughter and they'd have known that I was pulling their leg. However, it seemed to go down quite well. It didn't seem to matter that he was talking in clichés.[96]

23 October

The day before the battle was due to begin was spent in final preparations, and by dawn of the 23rd the Eighth Army was in position all along the front. Soldiers lay in their slit trenches, sweating and roasting in the concentration of heat from which they were forbidden to escape under any circumstances, plagued the whole day by flies. They felt cut off from the world, with a country spreading before them as seemingly empty and barren as it had been for thousands of years, shadowless and motionless, except for the 'Devil's Waters', the dancing mirages of the afternoon. The great effort expended for the provisioning and maintenance of the troops in battle, and for the subsequent operations, was a testament to the echelon and administrative services of the Army. 'The "Quartermaster battle" was won by the British before the fighting soldier rose from his trench for the assault.'[97]

The war correspondents were summoned to Montgomery's Tactical HQ, where in the morning sun they listened intently:

Well, gentlemen, the campaign starts tonight. In the moonlight there will be fought a terrific battle. My object is to remove the Germans from North Africa. It may take some time, but this is what we are going to do. I think this battle may well be the turning point of the war. It has always been my policy that we shall not have any more failures ...[98]

He went on to say that most battles were lost by bad command and staff work. The soldiers rarely let you down. He concluded:

Today every officer and man knows what is wanted. I have addressed all officers down to the level of lieutenant-colonel. They know all about the battle and they have passed it onto the men.[99]

Listeners to both the Home Service and the Forces Programme would later hear Godfrey Talbot's BBC recording of Montgomery's clipped briefing to his commanding officers.[100] Wives, mothers and family members now knew that their relatives would soon be fighting. They hoped and prayed that they would return home uninjured and safe.

That evening the men received a personal message from the Army Commander:

When I assumed command of the Eighth Army I said that the mandate was to destroy ROMMEL and his Army, and that it would be done as soon as we were ready.
We are ready NOW.
The battle which is now about to begin will be one of the decisive battles of history. It will be the turning point of the war. The eyes of the whole world will be on us, watching anxiously which way the battle will swing.
We can give them their answer at once: 'It will swing our way.'
We have first-class equipment, good tanks, good anti-tank guns, plenty of artillery and plenty of ammunition, and we are backed up by the finest air striking force in the world.
All that is necessary is that each one of us, every officer and man, should enter this battle with the determination to see it through – to fight and to kill – and finally, to win.
If we all do this there can be only one result – together we will hit the enemy for 'six', right out of North Africa.
The sooner we win this battle, which will be the turning point of this war, the sooner we shall all get back home to our families.
Therefore, let every officer and man enter the battle with a stout heart, and with the determination to do his duty so long as he has breath in his body.
AND LET NO MAN SURRENDER SO LONG AS HE IS UNWOUNDED AND CAN FIGHT.
Let us all pray that 'the Lord mighty in battle' will give us the victory.
B. L. MONTGOMERY

Lieutenant-General, G.O.C. in C, Eighth Army

MIDDLE EAST FORCES

23-10-42[101]

As the sun set over the desert, the military machine that was the Eighth Army began to stir into life. Throughout the long, hot day, the infantrymen of the assaulting divisions, having moved up the night before and been confined to their narrow slit trenches, now formed up and marched as silently as possible along the dusty tracks past the existing front lines and through the gaps in the protective minefields to their start lines in no man's land. Rifleman Crimp recalled: 'Groups of Jock infantry, in shorts and shirts and tin hats, with bayonets fixed, began filtering forward through the gap. Poor devils – I don't envy them their night's work.'[102]

The 1st Armoured Division established their headquarters with the MTF HQ, which was completed and operational by 2000 hours and contained six telephones, all of which rang simultaneously and continuously until disconnected. Turner returned to the battalion at about 2030 hours, reporting that he had had an uneventful journey except for a bad dust-storm.

'B' Echelon trucks brought up welcome hot meals from the battalion lines in the rear; these were intended to sustain the men for the next twenty-four hours. Officers and NCOs went up and down, checking equipment. Water bottles, a tin of bully beef and a packet of ration biscuits were issued to each man, grenades and ammunition handed out, the men cleaning their rifles and wrapping them in sand covers, acutely aware that a sand-blocked gun could blow up, taking off a finger or hand, all the time ensuring the utmost quiet. An air of quiet confidence in the outcome of the battle was everywhere.

That evening, Stumme radioed his routine evening report to Hitler's headquarters in Germany: 'Enemy situation unchanged.'[103] At 2030 hours, meteorological shells were fired high into the air by the 7th Medium Regiment to test conditions, thereby ensuring accurate shooting. At 2115 hours, the 24th Australian Brigade's Division started their diversion, advancing under a heavy artillery barrage. The 15th Panzer Division reported to their headquarters that they had been under fire for three minutes.[104]

After waiting for the last three nights, Brooke finally received confirmation that the attack would proceed that night. He wrote in his diary:

> There are great possibilities and great dangers! It may be the turning point of the war, leading to further success combined with the North African attack, or it may mean nothing. If it fails I don't know how I shall bear it.[105]

Perhaps the worst of the suspense was over. Maj. Hastings recalled:

> We were now committed: no luck, no accident had transported us to the base. It was no good wishing we had spent more time maintaining the carrier or learning to read a map or had written more punctiliously home or behaved better in Cairo. In a quarter of an hour we would advance through the minefields which we had sat opposite for the best part of two months. It was better to concentrate on what was important at the moment – was there time to have a 'brew'?[106]

CHAPTER 5

Zero plus 221 days. Operation Lightfoot and the Second Battle of El Alamein

At 2140 hours Egyptian time,[1] Montgomery unleashed hell! As the heaviest barrage yet seen in the desert war,[2] created by 882 field and medium guns[3] set to a precise fire-plan based on the BBC time signals, opened fire on the *Panzerarmee* positions. These plans allowed for all the shells to land on the known enemy artillery positions and ammunition dumps at precisely the same time[4] all along the forty-mile front, taking the enemy completely by surprise. Gen. von Thoma, said, 'In one section five out of six of the 88-mm guns were knocked out.'[5]

By the end of the first fifteen minutes, the known German and Italian gun positions opposite XXX Corps' front had received nearly one hundred 4.5 or 5.5-inch shells or their equivalent weight in 25-pounders,[6] the shells passing overhead sounding like an express train roaring through a station. Montgomery wrote:

A wonderful sight, similar to a Great War 1914/18 attack. It was a still moonlit night, and very quiet. Suddenly the whole front burst into fire; it was beautifully timed and the effect was terrific; many large fires broke out in enemy gun areas.[7]

Martin Ranft, a German gunner of 220th Artillery Regiment recalled:

El Alamein was my home for quite a while, because we were stopped. On 23rd October, nine o'clock in the evening, that's when we heard that terrible artillery fire from the British line. I was facing the front line and suddenly the whole sky was red with the gunfire. The shells were howling over you and exploding all around you – it was just horrible. We thought then that the world was coming to an end.[8]

Men were found dead with their mess tins, caught unprepared whilst eating their evening meal.[10] Added to the barrage, but unheard in the general din by their comrades on the ground, forty-eight Wellington bombers were dropping 125 tons of high explosive on the enemy gun positions. When added to the tremendous storm of shelling, and the jamming of the enemy's radio by other specially equipped Wellington aircraft, this completely disrupted the enemy's signal system. Ralph Walling, the Reuters special correspondent, cabled:

Britain's vast new desert army is looking on at an unforgettable sight, beneath a bright moon and across the path of the sun, it is seeing score after score of British and American aircraft of the great air striking force fly over the short 70 mile gap separating the Nile Valley from the El Alamein front, and hearing them pound and strafe the enemy.[11]

At precisely 2155 hours, the guns stopped,[12] as the gunners checked their tables and re-laid their guns, so that when at 2200 hours the barrage resumed, the shells would now land on the enemy forward defence posts and the infantry started advancing across the minefields, treading 'lightly' as suggested by the title of the operation. Every three minutes the creeping barrage lifted forward 100 yards to a new line ahead of the infantry, holding there as the infantry caught up.[13]

At the same time, the first Albacores dropped flares over the target area of Tel el Aqqaqir and for the next six hours the bombs followed the flares. Walling wrote:

> Passing through the British lines while all was yet calm, I drove slowly between columns of men muffled to their ears in greatcoats against the sharp desert winter night. As we came nearer the front we seemed to be driving into a massive arc of fire, spurting against the dim skyline with remarkable clarity. There was no smoke to be seen from this distance, only the flashes running along the horizon to and fro as in a tropical storm of unparalleled frenzy.[14]

Montgomery now went to bed, later writing that he had a very restful sleep, leaving:

1. XXX Corps to secure before dawn a bridgehead beyond the enemy's main defended zone and to provide assistance for X Corps to pass through it;
2. XIII Corps to penetrate the Axis positions near Munassib and for the 7th Armoured Division to pass through Jebel Kalakh and also to secure Qaret el Himeimat and the El Taqa Plateau, supported by French forces;
3. The 24th Australian Infantry Brigade to advance 7,000 yards along the coastal road, promoting the diversion attack and making as much noise as possible. The smoke screen laid by the artillery allowed seventy-five dummy soldiers to rise out of the desert before being lit 'accidentally' by searchlights, drawing considerable fire from the enemy.[15]

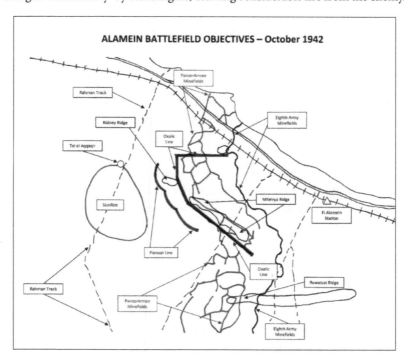

The infantry continued to advance across the minefields in the central sector, the young officers moving carefully to avoid booby-traps and anti-personnel mines, eyes glued to compasses whilst counting their steps towards their target. Enemy defence positions firing small arms and trench mortars at the advancing soldiers were either destroyed or bypassed, to be attended to later. The sounds of the continuous barrage, bombing and small-arms fire were added to by the Bofors anti-aircraft guns, all contributing to the cacophony, dulling the senses, along with swirling artificial dust-storms and cordite smoke produced by the artillery, creating powdery dust which darkened into a spectral gloom.[16]

On reaching the target line, they turned their attention to destroying the bypassed enemy strongpoints, evacuating the wounded and restocking their ammunition. A high proportion of wounds were caused by mortars, including six navigating officers of The Black Watch who were killed or wounded during this first advance.[17] F. G. H. Salusbury of the *Daily Herald* wrote:

> They all walked forward behind their screen of fire under the moon into a wilderness of mines and a venomous welcome of bullets and shells. Some of the mines were touched off by unlucky men; others staggered under the lash of projectiles, fell and rolled over in the sand, spilling their lives and blood. And the artillery rolled on …[18]

However, each of the sections experienced mixed results along the front:

Australian Sector

The 26th Australian Brigade reached their allotted point on the Oxalic Line after some fierce encounters with the enemy, but the 20th Brigade were stopped a kilometre short by stiff resistance. The enemy response had increased as they passed the first minefields and as they pushed on to the main and second defences, the going becoming more difficult.

Highlanders' Sector

The Highlanders, advanced into the strongest part of the defences on their two-brigade front towards a series of strongpoints named after Scottish towns or mountains, 153rd Brigade to the right and 154th Brigade to the left. The task was made more difficult due to the expanding funnel-shaped advance, almost doubling their front by the time they reached the Oxalic Line. Both brigades moved forward to the stirring sound of the regimental pipes, the pipers marching next to each platoon officer, each man with a St Andrew's Cross painted on scrim[19] attached to his back, one battalion forward and the other two ready to follow up, leapfrogging the first to take point position, thereby keeping up the momentum.

Progress began well but slowed as they encountered more and more enemy defence posts that had to be overcome and fewer that could be bypassed. The casualty rate rose, especially among the 1st Gordons, who met concentrated shell and mortar fire when they leapfrogged the 5th Black Watch. By dawn the Highlanders had not penetrated the main defence line and therefore had to dig in, delaying the Minefield Task Force who were waiting to start their clearance duties.[20]

Conversely, progress by the 7th Argyll and Sutherland Highlanders was rapid, as they encountered little opposition but suffered a constant drain of casualties due to the 'S' mines and booby-traps that abounded on their route. Heavy and accurate artillery fire increased the casualty rate, resulting in only one and a half platoons making the final destination and digging in.

New Zealand Sector

The advance on the New Zealand front was undertaken by the 5th and 6th Infantry Brigade, the 5th reaching their objective despite receiving heavy casualties from enemy posts and proceeded to dig in, but having suffered from failed wireless communications. The 6th met heavy concentrated opposition, but despite a slight delay, arrived at their objective and dug in, with other units mopping up the bypassed enemy defensives to ensure that the supporting arms reached the forward troops. They successfully created four corridors right up to Miteirya Ridge, although only one was actually usable at the western end.

Freyberg toasted the Eighth Army with Burgundy, saying, 'If there was ever justice in a cause, this is it. I don't think Itys [Italians] will stick it and I don't think the Boche [Germans] will either – they didn't in the last war.'[21]

The infantry of the 9th Armoured Brigade cleared a gap through the minefield, ensuring that tanks of the 10th Armoured Division were able to gain the crest of the ridge just before dawn, but traffic jams ensued at the eastern end, preventing many tanks from advancing. Those that got through met heavy anti-tank fire from multiple locations and by dawn were forced to withdraw to the reverse slopes of the ridge in hull-down positions.[22]

South African Sector

Owing to the losses incurred in previous battles, the South African Division had been allocated a smaller sector. They advanced in a similar manner to the New Zealanders in that the infantry penetrated the minefields, clearing away the mines to form a corridor for the armour. By 2350 hours they had secured their first objective and their final objective at 0600 hours. Their positions, although dug in, were weakened by the problems that they had in getting support vehicles and heavy weapons up to the front.[23]

XIII Corps and the 7th Armoured Division Attack in the South

In the southern part of the line, the 22nd Armoured Brigade began their ten-mile approach soon after dark. They located the eastern edge of the January minefield at 2300 hours, marking the entrance with red and yellow lights, the northern passage with an amber light and the southern with a green one.

January was thought to be 350 yards in depth, whereas February was estimated to be three times that. Each was to be gapped with four lanes. The clearance teams advanced in four columns, each headed by 44th Reconnaissance Regiment with elements of 4th and 21st Field Squadron Royal

Engineers under command, with half a dozen Scorpion flail tanks causing an awful noise and leaving swirling dust-storms in their wake. A party of engineers swept the lanes, but all the activity attracted the attention of the enemy observers on top of Mount Himeimat, who arranged for heavy fire from artillery, mortars and machine guns to be directed on those waiting for the gapping to be completed. Some of the flail tanks were hit by the enemy fire or just plain broke down, blocking the gaps with 'dead' Scorpions, which slowed the advance.

The 1st RB were through the minefield first, 'A' Company suffering casualties almost immediately, as within minutes the entrance to the gap became 'as crowded as the car park at Cheltenham Races'.[24] Roberts reported that his initial impression was of 'complete chaos, vehicles, tanks and carriers facing in different directions, some still burning, some at curious angles, and enemy shells arriving fairly steadily but not in great quantity'.[25] Number 3 gap was reported as impassable by 'B' Company at 2330 hours due to the soft sand, but twenty minutes later, number 2 gap was reported as clear. However, it was directly in the line of fire of an enemy anti-tank gun emplacement approximately 2,000 yards away, which started firing immediately. The machine gun platoon of 'A' Company attacked the emplacement, killing the crew and turning the gun 180° to fire the remaining shells at the enemy.[26]

The rest of 'A' Company reached the end of the gap, turned south immediately and began to clear the ends of gaps 3 and 4, with the other companies slowly clearing their gaps. The dust dimming the moonlight and reducing the visibility to no more than 10 yards gave the drivers, who were trying to spot the little coloured lights placed every 50 yards or so delineating the edges of the gaps, a most difficult time. It was not until 0130 hours that 'B' Company appeared at the end of gap number 4.

By 0230 hours the southerly lanes had been cleared of mines, and 'A' and 'B' companies now pushed ahead – supported only by their own machine guns, mortars and swords – overrunning three strong Italian posts. This resulted in 'A' Company being reduced from 100 riflemen to just forty and being amalgamated with 'B' Company under the command of Tony Palmer. Some trenches surrendered almost immediately while others fought on. As one group of Italian soldiers came out of a dugout with their hands up, moving towards 'B' Company, shooting started from the rear of the 'surrendering' troops, who dived to the floor, leaving the riflemen exposed to the fire.[27]

A bridgehead had been established by 0400 hours, but it was decided to reduce the number of lanes to two. However, even this proved too ambitious, as intense enemy fire descended as the dawn rose. By 0715 hours, despite breaking through the first minefield, they were still 3,000 yards short of the northern slopes of Himeimat, and being overlooked by the enemy made it impossible to get through the second minefield in daylight hours. There was nothing for it but to dig in as best they could in the flat open ground between the two minefields and resume operations the following night. Casualties mounted, with Tony Palmer being wounded and the 1st RB padre being killed during a burial service.[28]

Minefield Task Force

Back at the Highlanders MTF front area, Edwin Tetlow of the *Daily Mail* reported:

> The desert shook with a succession of cracks and rumblings, and the air echoed to the whistle and whine of scores of shells. Meanwhile, towards the west, our highly trained shock troops – sappers

and lorry-borne specialists – were boring across no man's land and beating out a path for our armour.[29]

The Royal Engineers reconnaissance parties led off as soon as the bombardment began. However, the MTF were not allowed to leave their assembly areas on the Qattara road to approach their start line until after 2300 hours.[30] Then, following the Royal Engineers' route, the marking parties began fixing the white tape. To make matters worse, a last-minute liaison problem between X Corps and XXX Corps resulted in Star track being unusable. The track had been "loaned" to the New Zealanders and not being returned until 0300 hours, forcing those riflemen assigned to Star route to double up with those assigned to Moon route before crossing back into Star route further on. The delay reduced the amount of time that the MTF had to complete their task before daylight, with those responsible for Sun and Star routes locating their first enemy minefield by 0155 hours. Those on Moon route met local resistance, but Turner's request to the 51st Highlanders for infantry support proved unnecessary when a show of force by the armour of 9th Royal Lancers caused the enemy to withdraw. However defective detectors were still to cause a problem. Gen. Briggs (commanding 1st Armoured Division) and Brig. Fisher (commanding 2nd Armoured Brigade) and Brig. Bosville (commanding 7th Motor Brigade) set their Tactical HQ on the track shortly afterwards.

The MTF began to clear the gaps, widening them in the process from the original 8-yard gaps to 16 yards,[31] to be later widened further to the 40-yard gaps needed, as the tanks churned up the sand so badly that those following required space to avoid the worst patches.

The sappers did their best to concentrate on the job in hand and ignore the battle going on around them, while the 2nd and 7th RB protected them and directed the traffic. The bright moonlight enabled them to see and identify the mines, many of which had been uncovered by the wind, the parties lifting them and placing them by the side of the track, always with the prospect of the next mine being booby-trapped or fitted with an anti-lifting device. The riflemen were split between lamp duty and protecting the sappers lifting the mines. Rifleman Horace Suckling recalled being in a three-ton truck, lighting the lamps and handing them to colleagues who fixed them to stakes marking the edges of the safe lanes: 'The noise outside with our terrific barrage meant that we couldn't know what was coming back from the enemy positions,'[32] dulling the men's senses made worse by the dust rising from the artillery barrages and cordite from exploding shells. Some of the riflemen joined in the stacking the mines, as Sgt Swann recalled, in order to speed up the process.

Despite the massive amount of information gathered on the enemy positions, it was found that there were more, thicker and deeper minefields than originally anticipated.[33] By 0430 hours, gaps in the first enemy minefield had been completed on all routes, and work was in progress on the second, as the armour began passing through the last of the Allied minefields towards the first of the enemy ones, but communications were still a problem as the fixed telephone lines were constantly broken by shell fire. On Moon route, defective detectors and enemy resistance completely disrupted the programme, whilst Star route was 'loaned' temporarily to the New Zealanders, it not being returned until 0300 hours, thereby causing further unwanted delay.

Just before first light, the unit, under Capt. D. W. Basset, commanding Sun route, cleared and passed through four enemy minefields and were well on the way to clearing the fifth, six minefields being cleared in all. By now enough gaps had been sufficiently cleared to allow the 2nd Armoured Brigade of the 1st Armoured Division to get forward towards their objective on the Pierson Bound just to the rear of the enemy positions codenamed Snipe and Woodcock. Almost nose-to-tail, the brigade advanced in the accepted desert manner: a scout car of the reconnaissance troop, followed by two tank squadrons, regimental headquarters, the third tank squadron, a battery of Priest self-propelled guns, motorised infantry, a battery each of anti-tank and anti-aircraft guns and finally the supply trucks, in three regimental groups:

- The Bays (Lt Col. Alex Barclay) on Sun route on the right;
- The 9th Lancers (Lt Col. Gerald Grosvenor) on Moon route in the centre;
- The 10th Hussars (Lt Col. Jack Archer-Shee) on Star route on the left.

But even with the gapping complete, their advance was no easy matter, navigating into the dark among endless billowing clouds of dust, with one or two tanks blundering outside the taped gaps and veering off into the minefields with obvious results. Added to this problem was the 16-yard gap. If just one tank broke down there would be a hold-up; the whole area was becoming a huge traffic jam. Maj. Anthony Wingfield recalled the position of the armour as dawn broke:

> To go through the infantry into minefields which had not yet been gapped would certainly end in disaster. To remain where we were in situ, strung out in single file along 'Star' track in daylight, would invite annihilation by 88-mm anti-tank guns and enemy aircraft alike. A third course – that of dispersing in what appeared to be a minefield also seemed uninviting. Jack [Archer-Shee] had just about made up his mind to press on in accordance with the original instructions when the Brigade Commander put him out of his agony by ordering the adoption of the third course.[34]

Luckily it was a dummy minefield and the tanks dispersed accordingly. To add to their problems there were misunderstandings about their positioning, the Bays on Sun route radioing that at 0500 hours they were through the third minefield, whereas they had only just passed the first; the Lancers on Moon route were in a similar position, and X Corps were a long way from where they needed to be.[35]

Progress along Star and Moon routes was still not going well, 'B' Company having gapped three enemy minefields but meeting strong resistance in the fourth where Lt Innis had both his legs broken by shell fire.[36] Sgts Burgess and Brittan and Cpl Findlater were also badly wounded and CSM Noble was killed,[37] whilst very fine work was done by the 7th Field Squadron and the carrier platoon of 'C' Company commanded by Lt Dick Flower. The smooth running of the advance headquarters was down to Capt. Marten, who co-ordinated progress reports and information coming in from all the parties in the enemy minefields. Casualties were also incurred amongst the sappers. Rifleman Moore recalled:

> The cost in sapper casualties was considerable. We had 25 in my squadron on the first night alone out of the deployed strength of about 150. We were, though, wonderfully fortunate, for of these only five were fatal.[38]

The Situation at Dawn on 24 October

As the night dissolved into the dawn of the 24th, the battalion found themselves in a completely overlooked position and coming under fire from artillery controlled by an enemy observation post situated on elevated ground named by the 2nd Armoured Brigade as Kidney Ridge. The name was taken from the fact that its contour was similar to a kidney bean, but was later found to be the Oxalic Ridge.[39]

There was now a degree of optimism at Army HQ, as they had been fairly successful in the first twelve hours of the battle. The four infantry divisions had launched the largest infantry assault of the desert war, and despite incurring heavy casualties from fierce enemy resistance, had not been prevented from advancing. Even the fact that neither the 1st or the 10th Armoured divisions were in a position to exploit this success did not dent Montgomery's optimism. This view was further strengthened when the 133rd Lorried Infantry finally gapped their minefields, allowing the 10th Armoured Division to advance and almost reach their designated position on Miteirya Ridge. Another half an hour of darkness might have been sufficient,[40] but the delay caused by the congestion of two armoured brigades and a lorried infantry brigade trying to get through the narrow passage meant that they could not reach their objective.

Meanwhile, the 1st Armoured Division had not broken out of their minefields and were under the impression that they were 3,000 yards further forward than they actually were,[41] compounded in part by the Highlanders not reaching their objective but being under the impression that they had. This was a symptom of the difference of opinion between the two divisions that would continue throughout the battle, and made more difficult by the rejection by both sides of the offer made by the artillery commander of XXX Corps to undertake a survey to remedy the problem.[42] Meanwhile, in full daylight across the whole front, the soldiers in the most forward positions proceeded to prepare their defences in the newly conquered ground. 'Tired out after the all-night struggle, subjected to sudden bursts of fire, and expecting a counter-attack at any moment, they sat in their pits and scrapes, the temperature rising, tormented by flies and watching the sand beginning to drift over the dead bodies of the enemy as well as their friends and colleagues.'[43]

No matter how optimistic the feelings were at Army HQ, the bridgeheads had to be strengthened before the crumbling attacks designed to break down the local defensive cohesion could take place. The highest priority was therefore now given to ensuring that all the objectives were gained as quickly as possible and that those positions reached overnight were consolidated. Accordingly, Montgomery instructed that without delay:

- corridors through the minefields were to be completed;
- 51st Division was to gain its objective;
- the 1st Armoured Division's gap was to be cleared so they could reach their objective on the Pierson Line;
- New Zealand Division were to invest the Miteirya Ridge and then exploit southwards;
- 10th Armoured were to protect the New Zealand flank, whilst advancing over the ridge with strong artillery support;
- 9th Australian in the north were to start a crumbling operation that night; and
- 7th Armoured in the south were to continue to try and break through the minefield in front of Mount Himeimat.

And so the battalion continued its gapping duties without breaks, Moon route not being cleared until later on the 24th and Star route being cleared the next day, leaving the riflemen physically and emotionally exhausted.

Axis Confusion and Dismay

The feeling at the *Panzerarmee* HQ along the coast near El Daba was anything but optimistic. There was an uneasy atmosphere, approaching dismay. The attack had achieved complete surprise, with communications now almost non-existent, fixed lines cut by the bombing and shell fire, and radio transmission jammed by the Wellingtons of the Desert Air Force. This led to only the scantiest and most uncertain information getting through, often being relayed by messenger to senior commanders, telling a story of simultaneous attacks from the sea to the Qattara Depression but never providing enough information to allow the General Staff any idea of where the main thrust was going to fall. This resulted in decisions being made only in respect of local defence issues and not the big picture. To make matters worse, a couple of battalions of Italian infantry broke and fled completely, unnerved by the barrage and bombing.[44]

Stumme could hear the thunder of the guns and guessed that an attack would take place just south of the centre. However, he needed to assess matters to confirm his suspicion, so decided to set out on a personal reconnaissance of the front to investigate. Driving out with *Oberst* Andreas Büchting,[45] Army Chief Signals Officer, in his staff car driven by Cpl Wolf,[46] to view the 9th Australian's penetration of Minefield 'L',[47] they came under fire, with Büchting dying almost immediately from a shot in the head and Stumme diving from the car to seek shelter. Wolf turned the car round and Stumme ran alongside, holding on, until somewhere along the way back to his lines he had a heart attack and fell off.[48]

By midday, with Stumme still missing and his demise unreported, temporary command was passed to *General der Panzergruppe* Ritter von Thoma, commander of the Afrika Korps. To justify the temporary command the *Fliegerführer* sent a report at 1400 hours that Stumme had been wounded and probably taken prisoner. The report was decoded, and read by Churchill less than twelve hours later. Stumme's body was not found until the next day.

Strategic information regarding the Allied movements was still not being received, so von Thoma decided not to readjust his forces, containing the British attacks locally. Based on this locally driven defence, the daily report to Berlin misrepresented and confused the facts, stating that despite the British having 'succeeded in penetrating the main battle line in several places' that by evening, 'the line was almost all in our hands again'.[49] The report continued that despite ammunition stocks being sufficient for eight to ten days' fighting, 'if the tanker due to arrive on the 26th fails to arrive there will be a serious crisis. The Italian fuel shortage is already very precarious.'[50]

Rommel had been away recuperating for some four weeks in Austria when he was contacted by *Generalfeldmarschall* Wilhelm Keitel of OKW at 1500 hours to ascertain his fitness as well as to advise him that the British had been attacking since the previous evening and that Stumme was missing. A few hours later, Hitler called and Rommel immediately offered to go to Africa, being asked during the conversation whether he was up for it and confirming that he was. However, Hitler was worrying about Russia, where he needed good men, and instructed Rommel to make his way to the airfield at Wiener Neustadt to await his further instructions regarding which theatre he would be sent to.

The Armour Must Get Through

By the afternoon, Montgomery's optimism was waning and he was becoming seriously dissatisfied with the battle situation, telling Briggs in no uncertain terms that if the 1st Armoured were being delayed by the infantry not completing their task then the armour must immediately fight their own way through, regardless of losses. Passing the order forward to Fisher of the 2nd Armoured Brigade, Briggs received the reply, 'Do you mean "at all cost" literally?' Briggs confirmed, 'Yes I do; at all costs!'[51]

The Highlander infantry, supported by the 2nd Armoured Brigade, undertook a reconnaissance attack across the Miteirya Ridge at 1600 hours, with the intention of gathering information on the enemy positions. Advancing along the Moon and Star routes, the armour drove into an unmarked minefield protected by anti-tank guns,[52] which promptly shelled them, resulting in a loss of six Sherman tanks and halting the advance.[53] The reconnaissance attack was resumed later that night, the 2nd Armoured reaching what they thought was their objective but which was actually 1,500 yards further south, as arguments continued between the Highlanders and divisional staff over the exact position.[54]

The New Zealand front saw an attack start with an artillery barrage at 2200 hours, supporting advances of the 5th and 6th New Zealand brigades, whilst the 8th and 24th Armoured brigades advanced over the top of Miteirya Ridge with the 133rd Lorried Infantry Brigade, attracting intense activity and becoming caught up in a minefield running along the crest of the ridge. Sappers began gapping the wrong minefield,[55] but were also hampered by enemy fire and bombing from the Luftwaffe. By the time the attack could be resumed, the supporting barrage had moved beyond the point that the tanks could reach within a reasonable time and Maj.-Gen. Alec Gatehouse, commander of 10th Armoured Division, called off the attack as he was concerned that his tanks would be left exposed on the forward slopes at daybreak.

Commanding the New Zealanders, Freyberg was appalled by the decision, as was Montgomery, who instructed the commanders that they were to break out that night and that if they did not comply with his orders, he would have no hesitation in replacing them. Both Brig. E. C. N. Custance and Maj.-Gen. Gatehouse had no wish to see their tanks destroyed for no purpose, the decision being pragmatic and not driven by feint heart, but Montgomery's orders seemed to have the desired effect and reports were received through the night that the 24th Armoured Brigade had broken through and joined up with the 2nd Armoured Brigade on its right.

XIII Corps Sector

In the southern area, below the inter-corps line, XIII Corps continued to apply pressure on the 21st Panzer around Jebel Kalakh, keeping them occupied and preventing them from moving north. The 1st RB 'I' Company in support of the armour of the 4th County of London Yeomanry (Sharpshooters) tried again to break through the minefields, but coming up against intense enemy artillery and anti-tank fire cost the Sharpshooters fourteen tanks for the benefit of forcing just one squadron through, and although a bridgehead was created in the stony desert, it was under the baleful shadow of Mount Himeimat. The enemy had scattered mines around the outside of the minefields, making any tank movement dangerous, added to which they formed a ring around the exits and were pouring shells and tracer fire into the position throughout the day, knocking out tanks and forcing the remaining Sharpshooters to be recalled during the evening, leaving the 1st RB to defend the bridgehead on their own.[56]

7th Motor Brigade

Back above the inter-corps line, the 7th RB were now brought out of their reserve position just east of Springbok road, Being used to plug a gap between the 9th Australian and 51st Highland divisions. Starting out at 1700 hours, they advanced with the 2nd KRRC along Sun, Moon and Star tracks before arriving at the fourth minefield to find that there was not a gap. One was made by the Australian engineers, and 'D' Company of 7th RB passed through the last minefield at about 0400 hours on the 25th, before overrunning the enemy positions and taking several prisoners, who were handed over to the Australians.

The Australians had set up defensive positions to cover the clearing of four minefield gaps and a lateral track which linked them. The area was very congested, with insufficient room between the 13th Australian Infantry Battalion and the Queen's Bays for both the 7th RB and the 2nd KRRC; therefore the KRRC took up positions behind the 7th RB whilst the carriers fanned out, becoming an 'obvious and vulnerable target'[57] to the 100/17 howitzers and 75/27 guns of *3° Reggimento Artiglieria*, who heavily shelled and machine-gunned the riflemen. The Australians reported:

> The carnage was terrible to watch. The Diggers were sorry for the Tommies, but cursed them for drawing the crabs. Soon there were dozens of shattered burning vehicles, and dead and wounded soldiers littering the desert.[58]

The riflemen responded to the enemy action using machine guns and their 3-inch mortars, with platoon commanders Mike Bird, Peter Lockwood-Wingate and P. E. Flower (before he was killed and the platoon taken over by CSM Jones) directing the fire throughout the day. Nevertheless, the battalion suffered a continuing drain of casualties including Adjt Kyrle Simond. Jones was awarded a Military Cross, his citation reading:

> This Sergeant was directing machine-gun fire on enemy targets, when one of the gunners was hit. He immediately took his place and continued firing. His number two gunner was then hit and was replaced by his platoon officer, who had already been wounded. He had fired about six belts when his officer was killed and was replaced by another Rifleman. He continued firing until this Rifleman was also wounded, when he directed the withdrawal of his section of medium machine guns to a less exposed position. Throughout, he continued steadily firing in the face of heavy enemy opposition.[59]

About 1400 hours, an enemy attack took place on the 2nd Armoured Brigade front by the Littorio Division, during which approximately twenty-five to thirty-five Italian M13/41 tanks and Panzer IIIs turned north and then suddenly attacked the 7th RB position in two waves from behind a ridge. The attack was determined, but only a few tanks reached the RB's position due to their excellent anti-tank fire, whilst the riflemen maintained a continuous and accurate stream of small-arms fire to keep the tanks 'buttoned up'. Cpl Donald Main recalled:

> At the same time a heavy barrage was brought down on our positions, also machine-gun and mortar fire. Since we were in the front with our machine guns, as the tanks drew closer we had to stop firing and take cover in our slit trenches. Our sixteen six-pounders engaged the tanks, several firing at one

particular target, so that the closest was knocked out fifty yards in front. The battalion were credited with fourteen tanks. As some of the enemy tanks were hit, the occupants tried to escape through the turrets. One Italian officer was hoisting himself out when a six-pounder hit him in the chest and he literally disintegrated. In front of the stationary tanks were two Italians sitting on the ground. From the right came cries of 'You rotten Pommie bastards!' The Australians strongly objected to our knocking out the tanks with six-pounders before they came within range of their two-pounders.[60]

The anti-tank crews produced an almost incessant fire, with the guns of Lt Salt and Sgt Allen having particularly good shoots, resulting in at least fifteen enemy tanks being destroyed and forcing the remainder to withdraw. This was the 7th RB's first major success and the first good score of enemy tanks credited to the Eighth Army in this battle.[61]

The position was subjected to enemy artillery fire during the rest of the afternoon and evening, and at 1800 hours 'C' Battery (less 'J' Troop) 73 Anti-Tank Regiment of the Royal Artillery moved up to strengthen the 7th RB against further counter-attacks. Following an attack by the Highlanders, direct assaults on the position were reduced and the 7th RB confined its activities to vigorous patrolling and the destruction of derelict enemy equipment, remaining there for the next few days. Lt Salt transferred to 2nd RB to bring up the officer compliment.

Rommel Returns

Having spent an anxious and uncomfortable night in Austria waiting for Hitler to make a decision, Rommel finally received instructions at 0750 hours on the 25th for him to return to Africa. At 1000 hours he landed in Rome to refuel, having a brief argument with von Rintelen about supplies, and taking off at 1045 hours, before arriving in Crete four hours later. He finally touched down in Qasaba, west of El Daba at 1730 hours, finding an army that had a severe lack of fuel that was restricting its mobility just at the time when it was needed the most. He took back command from von Thoma, who did not seem to be seriously concerned and regarded the situation as purely a matter of ground lost or won, and of minor importance in the grand scheme of things. Rommel immediately ordered that the panzer forces be held back for mobile operations, leaving enemy tanks to be dealt with by anti-tank guns and artillery and not armoured counter-attacks. By 2325 hours on his day of arrival all the men of the *Panzerarmee* received a brief electrifying signal containing the words 'I have taken over the army again. Rommel.'[62] The OKW and Italian Supreme Command decided that the *Panzerarmee* should now be known as the *Deutsch-Italienische Panzerarmee*.[63]

Where Are You?

The heated discussions over the relative positions between the staffs of 51st (Highland) Division and those of the 1st Armoured Division continued. The two lots of staff based their navigational arguments on an artillery grid, but unfortunately those used by the Highlanders differed to that used by the 1st Armoured by 1,000 yards, resulting in the armour believing that the Highlanders' forward units were not on strongpoint Aberdeen but on strongpoint Stirling, and that the enemy localities Snipe and Woodcock were further east than they actually were.[64] The Highlanders paced out their advance on compass bearings and were confident that they were correct, the commander noting that 'in that waste of sand with few features, and a battle raging, it was not easy to be dogmatic'.[65] These differences were to have serious and profound tactical repercussions for the 1st Armoured, as for most of the battle they were 1,000 yards off, as well as for the riflemen of the 2nd RB and 2nd KRRC.[66]

The Night of 25/26 October

The 2nd Armoured Brigade advanced as ordered beyond the forward infantry positions: the Bays on the right, the 9th Lancers in the centre, and the 10th Hussars on the left. On reaching the edge of Kidney Ridge, the Bays and Lancers came under intense 88-mm fire from a well-established anti-tank screen, and in as many minutes the Bays had lost eight Shermans, while the Lancers had lost two crusader tanks. The Hussars advanced through a minefield to outflank the gun positions, but had to call off the attack when it became evident that the enemy were counter-attacking, forcing the 2nd Armoured back behind the Oxalic Line.

Back south of the inter-corps line, the XIII Corps had not been able to penetrate beyond the February minefield, and the 1st RB remained in position at the bridgehead until the early morning when the 132nd Brigade took over, allowing them to withdraw and reorganise before relocating to the northern sector. The 131st Brigade advanced through the 132nd, supported by a creeping brigade against the Folgore Division and Ramcke Brigade occupying Himeimat, but after 2,400 yards they suffered casualties from anti-personnel mines, intense enemy barrage and small-arms fire. Harding called off the attack, leaving the 7th Armoured Division on the southern flank and the tanks of the 22nd Armoured Brigade between the Allied and Axis minefields in support of what was left of the 131st Brigade. Montgomery confirmed Harding's request to withdraw, which was implemented during the night under heavy fire, leaving small groups of the 131st to become PoWs.

Montgomery Changes His Plans

Montgomery's concerns over the progress of the battle increased when he received an update whilst in a meeting with Alexander. The situation was as follows:

- the 7th Armoured Division attack in the south had been called off;[67]
- the 1st Armoured Division were on the Oxalic Line or a little short of it;[68] and
- Fisher, at last accepting that the 2nd Armoured Brigade were not in position at the end of the Pierson Line, was only just sending the Bays, 9th Lancers and the 10th Hussars beyond the front infantry defences.[69]

Despite the successes of the infantry, the armour could not break out of the minefields and therefore the 'crumbling attacks' could not take place, with the further result that the battle's momentum was slowing, becoming static, or 'fizzling out', allowing the enemy to stiffen their defences further and making any future attack all the more onerous.

The original plan was not working. Freyberg urged Montgomery:

[...] to put another timed bombardment with infantry attacking as before to a depth of about 4,000 yards to push him off the guns. They could have had the tanks following behind. We could have been clear of his minefields ... the armour would then have to fight. Thought it was better to face another 500 casualties to each Division and use guns which is our great asset to whack him.[70]

This idea eventually grew into Operation Supercharge, but in the meantime Montgomery changed the plan – with a major reorganisation of the front to be completed by the dawn of 28 October – into an operation more in line with that conceived originally by Auchinleck.[71]

XXX Corps needed a short rest period in which to repair the damage received since they started fighting on the 23rd. Therefore the Australians in the coastal part of the line were to carry the weight of the breakout, with the 1st Armoured Division forming a shield, allowing them to start crumbling operations aimed at taking the coastal road. This would force Rommel to move the panzers to the north where they would be engaged by the British armour. A new reserve would also be created, consisting of the New Zealand Division, 9th Armoured Brigade, 10th Armoured and 7th Armoured divisions, while the 1st South African Division would take over the New Zealand posts on Miteirya Ridge and the 4th Indian would fill the vacated South African positions, XIII Corps moving from the south to take over more of the XXX Corps' front.

The 7th Armoured Division had had a thankless task, but they had succeeded in confining the 21st Panzer Division in the south, as well as keeping their armour largely intact, and were now being released to move north along with other units, eventually leaving just six brigades of infantry to hold a front of twenty-eight miles.[72]

Sinking of the *Proserpina* and *Tergestea*

The individual conflicts were causing mounting losses on both sides. On the Allied side, the valuable Shermans were reducing in number at an alarming rate. However, the rate of this attrition was still in favour of the Eighth Army, as the losses could be made up, whilst Montgomery was fully aware – as confirmed by the Ultra intercepts – that Rommel was not receiving any replacement armour, resulting in a steady reduction in the number of operating tanks. Rommel had deliberated for some time over the decision to move the 21st Panzer Division to the north, being fully aware that he had insufficient fuel for them to return in the event that the south was the main area of attack, but on being advised that the Italian tankers *Proserpina* (4,870 tons) and *Tergestea* (5,809 tons) had sailed with an escort of four destroyers, he instructed the panzers to move on 26 October.[73]

Bletchley Park had intercepted this message and the convoy was being carefully tracked, until the morning of the 26th when an attack eighteen miles from Tobruk set the *Proserpina* alight, the ship sinking the next day, and the *Tergestea* was torpedoed one mile from Tobruk harbour.[74] The *Deutsch-Italienische Panzerarmee* now had only sufficient fuel to bring up supplies for the next two or three days, the daily report stating, 'Unless every possible assistance is given in bringing over fuel, the defensive battle cannot be brought to a successful conclusion.'[75] To make matters even worse, most of the units were under-strength due to casualties, prisoners and sickness, and the men were on half rations.[76]

Point 29

In accordance with Montgomery's new plan, the 26th Australian Brigade, supported by forty Valentine tanks of the 40th Royal Tank Regiment and the guns of five field and two medium regiments of artillery, attacked Point 29 in the coastal area, a raised feature approximately twenty feet higher than the surroundings and providing excellent observation over the surrounding desert. An enemy patrol had been captured, which included a unit commander and maps showing the locations of two of the battalions of the German 125th Regiment of the 164th Division. They advanced towards their first objective, known as the 'Fig Garden', taking the position and immediately calling up ten carriers towing anti-tank guns which crossed the 1,200 yards of sand along lanes identified from the captured documents as clear of mines, before arriving on a high spur of land just one minute after the barrage stopped. The ensuing fire-fight was over quickly, and Point 29 was in Australian hands.

When news arrived of the loss of Point 29, Rommel ordered an immediate counter-attack, being very concerned that the Allied successes would be followed up by an armoured thrust north-west towards the coastal road. He sent the 90th Light Division from El Daba to a position in front of Point 29, attacking after heavy artillery bombardment and air attacks, and reinforced with elements of the 15th Panzer and an Italian division, using smoke to blind the Australian observers, who 'came within an ace' of taking the forward position, but importantly the Australians held on.

The loss of Point 29 forced Rommel to review his strategy of localised piecemeal operations, and he ordered a counter-attack in the area of Kidney Ridge. The 21st Panzer, part of Ariete Division, and 50 per cent of the artillery would laager behind Hill 28, with the 15th Panzer brought to a laager opposite in readiness for the attack.

It was clear to Montgomery that the extremely exposed area around Kidney Ridge had to be taken and held, despite being securely covered by German artillery. To do this, two battalions of motorised infantry would advance during the night, without armoured support, and seize an enemy strongpoint named by the armour as Woodcock. This would be held and used as a 'pivot of manoeuvre' by the armour that would advance through it the next morning to the enemy positions, forcing the panzers into battle.

CHAPTER 6

Zero plus 224 days. Operation Snipe during the Second Battle of El Alamein[1]

The story of Operation Snipe begins at midday on 25 October, when Turner and Lt Col. William Heathcoat-Amory, commanding 2nd KRRC, were summoned to 7th Motor Brigade HQ.[2] They were informed that the 2nd and 24th Armoured brigades were required to break through the Oxalic Ridge and that the riflemen of the two battalions were to advance in the dark through two miles of enemy-held territory to locate and consolidate the enemy strongpoint codenamed Woodcock. Once held, the position was to act as a pivot point for the armour of the two brigades, who would then break out to attack the panzers.

The ridge, within which Kidney Ridge was located, dominating the surrounding area, with the Woodcock position being roughly a mile and a half north-west of the Kidney Ridge feature.

> Beyond the Oxalic Line of ridges, [the terrain] changed suddenly from hard rock to treacherous soft sand and a scattering of low camel-thorn scrub; it became almost entirely featureless and extremely exposed, except for the usual small, anonymous folds in the desert.[3]

The exposed nature of the terrain as well as enemy artillery positions had prevented the 1st Armoured Division from breaking out beyond the Oxalic Line over the last few days.

Turner and Heathcoat-Amory went through the Star track and undertook a hurried and uncomfortable reconnaissance beyond, identifying a start line comprising two cairns of stones, but upon reporting to Lt Col. W. N. Roper-Caldbeck, commanding the 1st Black Watch, where they found themselves being bombarded by 88-mm artillery and continuous machine-gun fire, they were informed that the Scots were attacking two features known as Stirling and Nairn that night. Turner later recalled, 'Well, I wasn't very worried' that two attacks were going on the same night. The conversation with Roper-Caldbeck continued:

> Turner: 'Oh, where are the Black Watch forming up?'
> Roper-Caldbeck: 'See those two cairns of stones back there? They're forming up there.'
> Turner: 'Good God, so are we! What time of day is that?
> Roper-Caldbeck: '2300 hours.'
> Turner: So am I! Well, what bearing are they on?'
> Roper-Caldbeck: '220°'
> Turner: 'How, when STIRLING is almost two thousand yards, can they be attacking 220°? Where do you think you are?' Roper-Caldbeck pointed to a point on the map.
> 'No you are not; you are a thousand yards south of that!'[4]

Two separate operations, with two different objectives using the same start line, was not the best scenario to begin an operation, so Turner and Heathcoat-Amory reported the situation and the navigational difference to Brigade HQ to apprise the Divisional Commander and the Motor Brigade Commander. After hearing their report, Briggs replied:

> Well! If the Highlanders have got all their attack laid on, we can't butt in, so we will call off our attack for tonight and I will get my CRE to survey in the whole of Star route and fix our position before tomorrow.[5]

A Difference of Opinion

The difference of opinion between the Highlanders and the 1st Armoured had been raging since the battle had commenced, the 51st staff recording, 'It has been significant, ever since the morning of the 24th, how difficult it has been for troops to know exactly where they are in this featureless country'.[6] Map-reading in the desert was a far different experience to that in Britain, which was based on the 1-inch Ordnance Survey maps that contained lots of indicators with which to determine your location. In the desert there were very few features, and maps contained few contour lines and names, often only bearing notes of a long-gone place or tomb of some long-forgotten holy man. Moving across this featureless expanse was always interesting: there were Roman water stores that were impossible to see until you almost fell in them, as well as abandoned slit trenches and gun pits all awaiting the unwary. However, even after taking into consideration the general map-reading difficulties, the navigational difference of over 1,000 yards between the two divisions was excessive. As we have seen, this meant that, according to the 1st Armoured, the forward Highland Division troops were not at Aberdeen as they thought, but 1,000 yards nearer to the Stirling locality, placing the strongpoints Woodcock and Snipe further east than they actually were.[7] This was to have major ramifications for the riflemen, and 'the party returned from the recce in considerable doubt and confusion of mind'.[8]

Turner is Recalled for New Orders

The Highlanders had succeeded in their operation of 25/26 October in securing the enemy strongpoints of Stirling and Nairn. As a consequence, at 1600 hours, Turner and Heathcoat-Amory received new orders at Brigade HQ, which was again receiving the attention of the enemy artillery units. Bosville now instructed Heathcoat-Amory to consolidate Woodcock, while Turner was instructed to perform a similar operation at the Snipe position, located roughly a mile and a half south-west of the Kidney Ridge feature, with 7th RB to be held in reserve. Once taken, the positions were to be held overnight and then act as a pivot of manoeuvre the next day for the 2nd Armoured Brigade and 24th Armoured Brigade respectively. The armour of the two brigades would then break out, cutting the enemy's main lateral communications, forcing the Germans to attack them on ground chosen by the British.

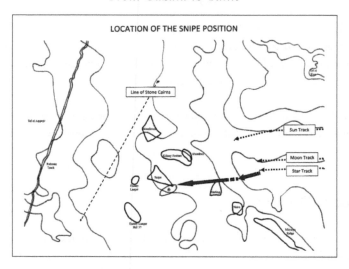

The Number and State of the Riflemen

Having continuously worked with the MTF, taxing their nerve and stamina and resulting in them being able to snatch only a few hours' sleep, the riflemen of the 2nd RB had been through a very trying time during the last three days. Casualties had mounted to the point that the motor platoons were able to field only seventy-six riflemen out of the normal ninety, sixteen anti-tank guns, and the carriers were down to twenty-two from the usual thirty-five.[9]

Turner's command was supplemented to include:

- 239th battery under command of Lt A. F. Baer of the 76th Anti-Tank Regiment Royal Artillery, would increase the anti-tank complement by a further eleven 6-pounder anti-tank guns. The battery had been working with the 2nd RB since the night of 24 October when they had lost contact with the 2nd Armoured Brigade during minefield clearance operations;
- 7th Field Squadron of the Royal Engineers under command of Lt Graham, comprising sixteen sappers; and
- Forward Observation Officer Capt. Noyes of the 2nd Royal Horse Artillery, who would spot for and control the artillery support.

The whole combined force of rifleman, gunners and sappers numbered less than 300, the guns being divided between the companies as follows:

- 'A' Company with 13 and 15 platoons of 'S' Company, fielding eight guns;
- 'B' Company with 239th Battery less one troop, fielding seven guns;
- 'C' Company with 14 and 16 platoons of 'S' Company, fielding eight guns;
- Battalion HQ Company with one troop of 239th Battery, fielding four guns as a central reserve.

Turner sent Lt R. A. Flower, commanding 'C' Company carriers, to identify a suitable start line and liaise with the Black Watch occupying the area at the end of Star track, 'and if possible determine its [Snipe] location'.

1 Officers of the 2nd Battalion The Rifle Brigade 17th March 1942. *Reproduced with the kind permission of Mrs Ann Bayley*

Front Row, Left to Right: David Basset; Desmond Prittie; Tim Marten; Hugo Garmoyle; General Wilson; Mike Edwards; Robin Hastings; Tom Bird; Oscar Chichester.

Second Row, Left to Right:
L. J. Gibbs; Charles Sandells; Dick Flower; Jimmy Irwin; M. Forbes; Philip Flower; J. W. Verner; Eddie Gibbons; P. C. Innes; Hugo Salmon.

Third Row, Left to Right:
Paul Mayer; Martin Crowder; John Copeland; Dick Hayward; Jackie Wintour; Basil Nauman; Revd J. F. B. Keith; Jack Toms; Unknown; Dr Picton.

Fourth Row, Left to Right:
Norman Odgers; Mark Chapman-Walker; John Henniker-Major; Michael Cubitt; John Earle.

2 Riflemen march past officers at Khase el Nil Barracks. *Reproduced with the kind permission of Mrs A. Bayley*

3 Riflemen on Parade in Desert. *Reproduced with the kind permission of Mrs A. Bayley*

4 Platoon of Riflemen at Genifa Barracks in Egypt – Rifleman Harding Rear Line First Left.
Reproduced from Harding Archive

5 Photo of Rifleman Harding (Left) Lt. Paul Mayer (Right) on camels in front of Pyramids.
Reproduced from Harding Archive

6 "Ten Yards Tall" Hugo Garmoyle relaxing in his tent. *Reproduced with the kind permission of Mrs A Bayley*

7 Tim Marten and Charles Liddel with Lunch. *Reproduced with the kind permission of Mrs A Bayley*

Above left: 8 Martin Crowder and John Earle in Cairo. *Reproduced with the kind permission of Mrs A. Bayley*

Above right: 9 Martin Crowder and Girlfriend. *Reproduced with the kind permission of Mrs A. Bayley*

10 Eddie Gibbons relaxing in his tent. *Reproduced with the kind permission of Mrs A. Bayley*

15 Oscar Chichester. *Reproduced with the kind permission of Mrs A. Bayley*

16 A Lee Grant Tank that
fought in and around
Alamein, now situated
outside Alamein Museum.
*Taken by Author and part of
his collection*

17 A Sherman Tank that fought in and around Alamein, now situated outside Alamein Museum. *Taken by Author and part of his collection*

18 Two Anti-Tank Guns that fought in and around Alamein, now situated outside Alamein Museum. *Taken by Author and part of his collection*

19 A German 88 mm Anti-Aircraft / Anti-Tank Gun that fought in and around Alamein, now situated outside Alamein Museum. *Taken by Author and part of his collection*

20 A Postcard Copy of the Snipe Action Painting by Terrence Cuneo. *Reproduced with the kind permission of Carole Cuneo*

21 A British 6-pounder Anti-Tank Gun fought in and around Alamein, now situated outside Alamein Museum.
Taken by Author and part of his collection

22 A Chevrolet Quad of the type used in Egypt to transport the 6-pounder Anti-Tank Gun, now situated at the Royal Artillery Museum "Fire Power". *Taken by Author and part of his collection*

23 Picture of the "Twin Horns" of Djebel Kournine Mountain. *Reproduced from The Rifle Brigade in the Second World War 1939–1945 by Major R. H. W. S. Hastings*

24 The Memorial Inscription at the El Alamein Cemetery. *Taken by Author and part of his collection*

25 El Alamein Cemetery. Photo taken from the top of the Entrance Gate. *Taken by Author and part of his collection*

26 The Rifle Brigade Memorial on Remembrance Sunday. *Taken by Author and part of his collection*

27 Picture of The Rifle Brigade Memorial taken in 1945. *Reproduced with kind permission of The Rifle Brigade Association*

28 Royal British Legion, Loughton Branch. Rifleman Harding marked. *Part of Author's collection*

'Snipe' Gallantry Awards

29 Photo of the Snipe Gallantry Medals held at the Royal Green Jackets Museum. *Taken by and reproduced with kind permission of Christine Pullen Curator of the RGJ Museum*

Above left: 30 Full Statue of Field Marshal Alan Brooke CGIS situated in Whitehall, London. *Taken by Author and part of his collection*

Above right: 31 Full Statue of Field Marshal Viscount Montgomery situated at Whitehall, London. *Taken by Author and part of his collection*

32 Head Statue of Field Marshal The Earl Alexander of Tunis situated at the Guards Museum, London. *Taken by Author and part of his collection*

Meanwhile, the 2nd RB received the MTF disband signal of 'A hunting we will go', bringing the battalion back under command of the 7th Motor Brigade, who issued a warning order to the company commanders to bring together all elements of the battalion, currently stretched out along the miles of minefield gaps. Sgt Swann recalled:

> At about 1700 hours we were told we were going to attack Snipe. Colonel Vic hadn't been very happy because we were all jumbled up and nobody was sure where anybody was.[10]

Flower returned, having identified a suitable start line, an area of about 300 yards situated between two battalions of Highlanders about a mile from the end of Star track. He further suggested that the route to Snipe should be from the start line to a feature marked on the map as a 'double pimple' and that they should then advance 1,700 yards on a heading of 233°.

Turner called a conference with the company commanders in which he formulated the running order of the force. The carriers would form a screen in front, with the motor platoons on foot: 'A' Company on the right, 'C' Company on the left, and 'B' Company held in reserve. Concluding the conference, he advised that the operation was likely to be a 'last man, last round, sort of job' and that they were going to have 'one hell of a fight on our hands!'[11]

Still concerned, and fearing that a terrible mistake was about to take place due to the navigational difference of opinion, Turner returned to the Brigade HQ and found that the 'whole shooting match' were present:[12]

- X Corps Commander – Lumsden;
- 1st Armoured Divisional Commander – Briggs;
- Marshal of the 51st Highland Division – Wimberley;
- Motor Brigade Commander – Bosville; and
- Commander Royal Artillery (CRA).

Turner raised his concerns, the following discussion ensuing:

> Briggs: 'My CRE [Commander Royal Engineers] has surveyed Star route throughout the whole length of seven miles and he said that this is no more than 200 yards wrong in any part of the whole length.'
>
> Wimberley: 'Well, we've walked on our feet every bloody yard of the eight miles from where we are, from our home minefield, where we are now and we can't be wrong.'
>
> Lumsden: 'Come, gentlemen, we might make a book on this!'
>
> Wimberley: 'I think you forget, sir, I am a canny Scotsman, and what's more, I think you are too!'
>
> Lumsden: 'Well, I think you might risk a bob or two.'
>
> CRA: 'I don't think you need to worry; if anything, my concentration is going to be over the Black Watch.'
>
> Turner: 'Then in that case, sir, it will be no bloody good to me at all! They will be so far ahead of me that the Boche will get their heads up before I come over the ground.'
>
> CRA: 'Well, it is too late to do anything now!'
>
> Turner: 'I quite agree. All I can do is to form up on the 1st Armoured Division [and] just march or attack on the flank/back of your falling shells.'[13]

The 47th Royal Tank Regiment

Shortly afterwards, Col. Parkes of the 47th Royal Tank Regiment 24th Armoured Brigade was given his instructions to provide support to the riflemen and to use the Snipe position to create a pivot of manoeuvre for their Sherman and Grant tanks, whilst a similar operation was planned for the 41st Royal Tank Regiment at Woodcock. It was important that the tankers did not to mistake the riflemen for 'Huns'!

Maj. Alf Flatow of 45th Royal Tank Regiment (Leeds Rifles) recalled:

> At about 1100 hours we were called to RHQ where the Colonel had just returned from Brigade with new orders for a move. The gist of what the Colonel told us was the two Sherman squadrons were to advance to a feature called 'SNIPE' after the area had been recce'd by Squadron and Troop Commanders and the tanks were to be dug in as a sort of pill-boxes.[14]

However, shortly after receiving his orders, Parkes became ill and retired to the rest area without passing the orders onto his replacement, Maj. Ward.[15] Meanwhile, the staff of the 15th Panzer sent an appreciation of the main threat to their position stating that 'the enemy's massed tanks might stream through between the III/382 Infantry and II/115 Panzer Grenadier regiments and penetrate our gun position'. This communiqué confirming that the Germans were aware of the threat of the British armoured units, resulting in further enemy armoured units being positioned in the area around Kidney Ridge.

The tanks had been heavily involved throughout the Lightfoot battle, and in consequence the crews were heavily fatigued. Flatow recalled:

> By now we had taken our second and third doses of 'Pep' [Benzedrine][16] tablets and I was feeling very queer – I suffered in a slight way from hallucinations. I kept seeing things which didn't exist. Giving orders the next day, the Colonel kept thinking 'Willie' Williamson was Bill Watson and at night I suddenly saw a man riding a bicycle coming straight for me – in the middle of the desert! We all wished we hadn't taken the darned things.[17]

The Riflemen Start Out

Despite being given such short notice and being widely scattered, most of the riflemen were brought together by 2100 hours, congregating at the exit of Star track for their advance to the start line. The men stood in the darkness of a moonless Egyptian night without the light pollution so evident in our modern world, cold and wearing their steel helmets, heavy back-packs containing rations, a rifle, grenades, entrenching tool and Bren-gun magazines and two bandoliers crammed with ammunition.

By 2235 hours, the battalion had moved to the start line taped out by the Black Watch and were receiving intermittent shelling, although 'A' Company had not arrived yet. Rifleman Crimp wrote:

> Shells keep whizzing overhead regularly, to crash behind us on the gap exit. They make a murderous noise, and their velocity is so great that my tin-hat is continually being blown on to the side of my face. Although fifty feet above us, they seem much lower and it's impossible to resist the purely instinctive reaction of ducking down as each one whizzes over.[18]

The advance to the start line had been difficult, due mostly to the terrain being covered in fine dust created over the last few days by the armoured activity and almost constant shelling by both sides. The dust was now up to 18 inches thick and rose into the air at the slightest movement, creating a dense night fog forming eerie shadows in the dark.[19] The men stood around in groups, unnerved by the lack of slit trenches to dive into should the need arise, thinking of their loved ones and wondering whether they would see them again, and going through their superstitious routines that had saved them in conflicts in the past, itching to have a 'last quick drag and draw' before they moved off,[20] but prevented from doing so by the no-smoking order which had been in force since the start of the operation.

Their deep thoughts were broken as three Wellington bombers came over. Marten recalled:

[They] dropped bombs over us. Two or three people received minor wounds, I was hit in the shoulder but it did not really penetrate through as I was wearing a leather jerkin, a pullover and a shirt.[21]

Turner arrived at the start line at 2255 hours, a few minutes before the barrage was due,[22] and was almost immediately questioned by a young Black Watch officer (BWO):

BWO: 'Are you attacking over that ridge there, sir?'
Turner: 'Yes.'
BWO: 'Well, I've been here all day [and] if anybody showed at all over that ridge there was an absolute storm of machine-gun fire set up. See those dark shapes in front? Well, those are my vehicles blown up on the ground.'
Turner: 'Oh my God!'[23]

Graham and some Royal Engineers investigated and reported back that the enemy had left the area in some hurry, as there were a lot of anti-tank mines scattered about without being dug in. Satisfied with this answer, Turner waited with his men.

The Barrage Begins

The sound of the firing of at least thirty guns[24] from the artillery of the two corps announced the barrage of shells that flew over the riflemen, landing ahead on a bearing of 270°,[25] as expected further to the right of the line of advance and placing their destination further south than 1st Armoured Division staff had calculated, confirming that their positioning had been wrong all along.

Turner recalculated the heading to 2,000 yards at 270°, instructing the companies to reset their compasses and reposition themselves in line with this new heading, ready to advance on the back of the falling shells, Turner recalled:

This meant forming up again on the new bearing and re-setting our compasses, by no means an easy task by the light of a just-rising moon. However, we accomplished it and were only ten minutes late on the start.[26]

He immediately contacted Brigade HQ to advise them of the delay, requesting that the barrage be extended for a further 'ten wisps',[27] wisp being the agreed codeword for one extra minute of artillery fire before the barrage curtain moved forward.[28]

The Battalion Advances

Now repositioned, the battalion advanced from the start line at 2310 hours, Rifleman Suckling recalling:

> We were on our start line at about 2300 hours: there wasn't much moon, and we stood waiting. As we waited for the word to advance, the thoughts of how and what's going to happen went through my mind: we were all the same, nerves taut, parched lips and throat. Then suddenly we were off, with the artillery giving covering fire and all hell was let loose.[29]

The riflemen advanced very close to the exploding barrage, aware that the 25-pounder blast goes in the direction in which the shell was travelling,[30] with 'C' Company carriers leading, due to the lateness of 'A' Company. Each company commander sat in a wireless carrier, Turner in his distinctive corduroy trousers and a leather jerkin. Bird, in his 'famous Hebron' coat, rode out in the lead wireless jeep,[31] followed by the motor platoons:
- 'C' Company on the left, under command of Maj. Charles Liddell;
- 'A' Company on the right, under command of Capt. David Basset;
- 'B' Company to the rear in reserve, under command of Capt. Mike Mosley; and
- Royal Engineer support.

Main communications was under the control of the Adjutant, Capt. Tim Marten, travelling in a 15-cwt truck known as the 'gin palace', measuring the battalion's progress by way of the truck's odometer. He reported their position to Capt. Wood at the 7th Motor Brigade headquarters in plain language code:[32] 'We have just done the Cambridgeshire distance', then 'Getting on for the Cesarewitch now', and finally 'Just running up to the winning post.'[33]

Bird had driven no more than 100 yards when the jeep suddenly dropped into the end of an enemy truck pit obscured in the dark by the dust. These pits were constructed to conceal and protect vehicles in the desert and allowed a truck to drive down a slope to the far end, resulting in the bonnet being only slightly above the surrounding desert floor. In this way the engine and radiator were protected from shrapnel and weapons fire. It was the deeper end that Bird had driven into, with the jeep now stuck into the sand at an obtuse angle, a carrier having to be used to pull it backwards out of the hole, before shortly afterwards the advance continued once more.[34]

Despite this not very auspicious start, the men were relieved to get going, concentrating now on the job at hand and not dwelling on what might be! Turner recalled:

> There was a certain amount of AP tracer and MG bullets flying about, but nothing serious, though right away we could see a good deal of fire in the north from the Woodcock direction.[35]

Pearson at the Start Line

Under Maj. Pearson, the battalion's second-in-command, the guns, portees, ambulances and soft-skinned trucks with the ammunition and rations now moved up to the start line in preparation for the signal that the destination had been reached. A lone German plane came over the position, dropping a parachute flare, which was quickly followed by two sticks of anti-personnel bombs that damaged two or three vehicles and badly injuring three men.[36] Dr (Capt.) Picton immediately provided medical assistance, the result of which was that neither Picton nor the ambulances were to make it onto the Snipe position.

Turner Continues the Advance

They soon came across a series of dugouts occupied by German sappers who, immediately fled westwards, the riflemen 'helping them along the way' by throwing grenades into the dugouts, although some twenty-five or thirty were also captured. For the next 1,000 yards the advance continued until they came across a low trip wire stretched across their front. On the assumption that this might be the edge of a minefield, they halted the carriers, but not the motor platoons, who continued the advance. The weight of the carriers could have set off the vehicle mines, whereas the riflemen in the motor platoons could walk over them without causing detonation. However, they still had to look out for the anti-personnel mines and booby-traps scattered over the minefield, so they were never entirely safe.

The marking of a minefield by a single strand of wire was a common practice used universally by both sides to delineate the outer edges of the minefields, especially when no fence had been set. Turner could see the retreating enemy sappers in the light of the rising moon, and the frustrated carrier crews, withdrawn from the chase, started blazing away through the ranks of the advancing riflemen at the retreating enemy sappers. Running up and down the line of carriers, Turner instructed them to cease fire 'in the most lurid language'.[37] Graham's sappers were sent forward to establish whether the minefield was real and, if it was, how far it extended. He reported back shortly that it was a dummy, and the carriers, after a very frustrating five-minute wait, drove forward to return to their position in front of the battalion.

As the advance continued, Turner became more concerned that they had passed the Snipe position despite the barrage continuing to move forward, but unbeknown to him the new heading had almost doubled the distance that the battalion would have to march to achieve their objective.[38] About a mile and a quarter in the distance Turner could see a low ridge and decided that he would halt the advance when he reached it. He later recalled:

> It was one of those beastly ridges that in the moonlight seem to get farther away the nearer you get to them! So after going another quarter of a mile, I decided to halt where we were.[39]

They had travelled between 2,600[40] and 3,000 yards.[41, 42] In order to confirm that they were in the right area, or near it, Turner instructed Noyle, to request that a smoke round be fired on the objective. At approximately 0015 hours a smoke round was fired, landing about 300 yards ahead of the forward companies. Turner surveyed the area and selected the most appropriate piece of ground that looked like a defendable position, moving his men into it, entering from the east, with 'C' Company taking occupation of the area furthest to the west. It was later to be found that Turner's position was 900 yards south-south-east of the actual Snipe position.[43]

Marten fired a Verey pistol of green over green into the clear moonlit night to denote that the battalion had reached their objective, thereby alerting Pearson that the guns etc. should now be brought forward.

On examining the location they discovered that it was a recently vacated German sapper depot, although Marten thought it might have been Italian. It was positioned in a shallow depression of folds and ripples of soft sand, approximately 900 yards long and between 300 and 400 yards wide, in the rough shape of a kidney, with a perimeter of about a mile and a half. It was overlooked by a slight elevation, never more than 3 or 4 feet high, with an abundance of camel thorn, tamarisk bushes and old bits of engineering stores scattered about, as well as being foul with excreta and the bodies of some dead Germans.[44] In the forward part of the depression was a dugout some 12 feet long and 6 feet wide with a roof made of railway sleepers[45] and covered in corrugated iron, which Turner took as his headquarters and within which Marten and the wireless team including 'Busty' Francis, were positioned. A few other dugouts and trenches were located around the position. Rifleman Moore, the wireless operator for 'A' Company, recalled:

> I had my wireless set installed in a trench, and was in touch with the other companies. 'A' Company commander was in the trench with me ready to direct the action of the company; we spoke only in whispers and wireless silence was maintained as we were close to the enemy.[46]

The dugouts were all shapes and sizes; another one seemed to be an officer's bedroom within which there was not room to stand upright, but, like the others, the corners had been used as a latrine and the new occupants had to be careful where they trod.

Meanwhile, the riflemen of the motor platoons began to dig into the soft sand, emulating the desert slogan of 'Dig or die!' They created the weapons pits and trenches in their allotted sections from which to use their Bren guns and rifles to protect the anti-tank guns from infantry attack, despite the sand constantly and frustratingly sliding back into the bottom of the hole.

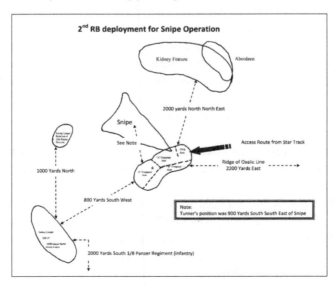

2nd RB deployment for Snipe Operation

Kidney Feature   Aberdeen

2000 yards North North East

Snipe

See Note

Access Route from Star Track

Ridge of Oxalic Line
2200 Yards East

1000 Yards North

800 Yards South West

Note:
Turner's position was 900 Yards South South East of Snipe

2000 Yards South 1/8 Panzer Regiment (Infantry)

Pearson Leaves the Start Line

Back at the start line, Picton continued treating the wounded from the earlier air attack. The soft-skinned vehicles, portees, HQ Company radio set, etc. were made ready to leave, the first convoy of ten vehicles with four or five anti-tank guns leaving at 0020 hours. Sgt Swann recalled, 'We sat around for two or three hours and suddenly we had the command to start up. As soon as the command had worked its way back to me, we were off at a mighty gallop.'[47] After a very rough ride, they arrived at the position at 0145 hours, despite the poor visibility caused by the dust thrown up by the proceeding truck. Swann continued, 'The only way they could keep in line was by heading into the thickest of the dust."[48] Some of the portees became stuck, bogged down in the soft sand, but whilst the 2nd RB trucks had four-wheeled drive, those of the 239th did not. The War Diary suggests:

> If bad going is likely to be encountered it is essential to have efficient towing vehicles for 6-pounder anti-tanks guns. Chev 4-wheeled 3-tonner portees will move a 6-pounder anti-tank gun through soft going. Austins will not stand up to the hard work in soft going.[49]

Pearson returned to the start line and the convoys continued bringing guns, supplies and ammunition to the position, whilst using sand mats, shovels and tow ropes to pull the trucks out of the soft sand, Baer making three or four trips in his M3 half-track to assist.

Flower Seeks Out the Enemy

From the position, Turner could see numerous fires at no great distance towards the west, as well as what appeared to be an enemy tank laager about 1,000 yards north.[50] At about 0100 hours, the carriers of 'A' and 'C' companies were sent out to 'clean the front doorstep!'[51] 'A' Company carriers checked out the area in a north-west direction, which turned out to be elements of the 15th Panzer Division, and returned without incident. However, the experience of 'C' Company carriers sent in a south-west direction was a different story.

Rifleman Martin noted that the carriers were 'slow hot noisy vehicles that would shed a track for no reason, had paper-thin armour, particularly underneath, making [them] highly vulnerable to mines'.[52] They began advancing up and over the edge of the position towards the south-west, making regular situation reports as they reconnoitred the area. After travelling about a mile,[53] they came to the edge of a minefield with a gap in it, where they found some forty or fifty engineers of the 15th Panzer and 164th divisions,[54, 55] a dozen of whom quickly became prisoners, proving to be a slight embarrassment, as Flower had no option but to put them on the back of the vehicles while continuing his advance and waiting for 'B' Company carriers to catch up and take them off his hands.

Under the light of the moon and about 200 or 300 yards away, Flower could see the ominous shape of thirty-two tanks[56, 57] being refuelled by the tenders, with those enemy engineers that had not been taken prisoner running towards them. They had stumbled across the night laager of a mixed force of tanks, self-propelled guns and vehicles, part-German and part-Italian, commanded by *Oberst* Willi Teege of the Stiffelmayer Battle Group,[58] named after *Hauptmann* Otto Stiefelmayer, both of whom held the *Ritterkreuzträger* (Knight's Cross).[59] Instead of withdrawing discreetly, the carriers contemptuously opened fire with their Bren guns and ex-aircraft guns, setting fire to three soft-skinned vehicles. Flower recalled:

They weren't sure where we were or who we were but they managed to locate us and started firing not only high-explosive shells at us but also machine-gun fire from their turrets.[60]

The tanks set fire to some derelict trucks to the rear of the carriers, creating a back-light silhouetting them and making them an easier target for the enemy, resulting in one being hit by a high-explosive shell. The prisoners seeing this as a chance to escape, jumped off the back of the carriers and ran to join their fellow engineers, but unfortunately their colleagues thought they were British infantry attacking their position and promptly opened fire on their own men. The sit-rep[61] back to Company HQ advised candidly: 'There is no need to worry any more about the prisoners!'[62]

Guns Arrive

By 0345 hours, Pearson had made two or three further trips to the position, and the jeeps and 15-cwt trucks had now been unloaded. Unfortunately, not all the anti-tank guns had made it to the position. Of the RB complement of sixteen guns, two had been involved in a collision and a further gun had been stuck in soft sand, despite the Chev portees, and of the complement of eleven guns of the 239th Battery, only six had arrived, mainly due to problems with the Austin portees, producing a total anti-tank gun complement of nineteen. The War diary recorded: '239 Battery are in the circumstances to be congratulated on having got 6 guns to the Snipe position.'[63]

Picton had also remained at the start line, providing medical assistance to the injured there. Fortunately, Rifleman Burnhope, a trained medical orderly, had already moved up to the position to 'temporarily' provide the only medical aid in attendance.

Bird had been put in command of the anti-tank defences around the position, sighting and co-ordinating the guns within the company sectors, as follows:

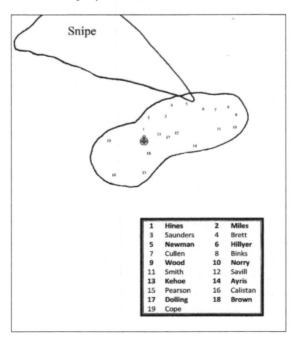

1	Hines	2	Miles
3	Saunders	4	Brett
5	Newman	6	Hillyer
7	Cullen	8	Binks
9	Wood	10	Norry
11	Smith	12	Savill
13	Kehoe	14	Ayris
15	Pearson	16	Calistan
17	Dolling	18	Brown
19	Cope		

- 'A' Company, plus 13 and 15 platoons of 'S' Company, held the north-east sector – 315° to 90°;
- 'B' Company, plus the 239th Battery, less one troop, held the south-east sector – 90° to 225°;
- 'C' Company, plus 14 and 16 platoons of 'S' Company, held the west sector – 225° to 315°; and
- Headquarters Company, plus one troop from the 239th Battery, were held as reserve, with the guns under command of Lt A. B. Holt-Wilson, who was also responsible for the distribution of ammunition around the position.

The soft sand initially helped the gun crews to dig their gun pits to the required level. Turner later recalled that it 'saved us from being either completely blotted out by fire or anyhow over-run because we were so well camouflaged',[64] although the soft sand would cause problems later. The War Diary stated:

> If the 6-pounder anti-tank gun can be placed in good positions (e.g. scattered scrub) in which pits 2 foot deep can be dug they can be employed successfully up to a range of 1,000 yards.[65]

First Action

Back at the enemy laager, some tanks and self-propelled guns moved off, making Flower's situation a little too hot for comfort and forcing him to head back to the position, with some of these armoured vehicles seeming to follow the riflemen in an almost leisurely fashion. On entering the position, the carriers took up hull-down positions around the 'C' Company HQ. By about 0330 hours, one of the self-propelled guns had moved to within 200 yards of Sgt Dolling and Cpl Savill's anti-tank guns, which promptly destroyed the SP. This was the first 'kill' to be attributed to both guns, with the enemy crew being shot by the riflemen but with Savill being wounded in the action.[66]

A Panzer Mk IV also approached the position, unaware that the gunners of 'C' Company were waiting. Holding back until it was within 30 yards, they opened fire, at which point it burst into

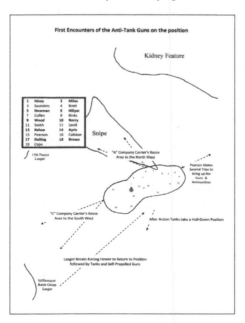

flames. Only one crew member made it out of the tank, immediately jumping into a slit trench and firing at the riflemen until first light when a rifleman crawled out and lobbed a grenade into the trench, settling the problem once and for all.

The guns also suffered a casualty in that Sgt Kehoe's gun of 16 Platoon, commanded by 2nd Lt J. E. B. Toms, fired two rounds and then stopped working. Losing what amounted to 5 per cent of the gun complement in the opening round did not bode well. Crimp recalled that after arriving on the position they were offloading the radio equipment from the truck when:

> […] a chap rushes over from the carriers, who're out in front of the position, to warn the Company Commander that at least four tanks are approaching. So Rusty and I get a move on, and just as we're on the last lap, hauling a battery between us, a sudden metallic spitting of machine-gun fire comes sousing out of the forward darkness in wavering threads. A moment later there's a blinding flash behind us and one of the six-pounders answers with a terrific, punching roar.[67]

The gunners' response shook the nerve of the advancing enemy: they halted, backtracked and took a hull-down position about 400 yards to the south-west, their war diary stating that they had fought against 'single enemy tanks'. Meanwhile, riflemen Crimp and Llewellyn had taken over a deep, commodious ex-German slit trench in which to set up the 'C' Company HQ radio set, with the Company HQ situated in a dugout excavated from the summit of a nearby sand-hillock positioned about 40 yards from the Battalion HQ.   Noyle now moved forward beyond the position perimeter to set up an observation point from which he could call down and direct artillery fire. Unfortunately, he was not heard from again. Turner thought that he had been killed. In fact, Marten recalled that he had 'tried to walk back in daylight, crossing a position strongly held by the Germans, ending up reporting to a 7th RB battalion headquarters at 0747 hours. His signallers remained on the position, but they were of limited use without the observation officer to provide targeting coordinates.[68]

Pearson was unable to leave the position during the first encounter. Swann asked whether they were returning yet and received the reply, 'No, not yet we're not, not while this is going on.'[69] Swann moved over to assist Cpl Cope with his gun, which appeared to be short handed. 'It was an uncomfortable walk because there was tracer whizzing all over the place. Our tracer and their tracer.' There was a short lull and Pearson left, arriving back at the Highland Division lines at about 0545 hours with the soft-skinned transports, other non-fighting vehicles and the captured prisoners. A few jeeps were left on the position, along with Swann, who had not heard them leave, and CSM Aitkins of 'A' Company, who had received permission to stay.

It soon became evident to the riflemen that the desert around the Snipe position, with the exception of the rear, was alive with the enemy. As Swann recalled:

> There's a lot of vehicles here! We had landed right in amongst this leaguer [laager] of German tanks; there were ambulances and everything else. It was an amazing sight, like a giant car park.[70]

To the south-west there was a mound about three-quarters of a mile in length, rising to a height of 37 yards. The map showed it as a 35-yard ring contour, but to the troops it was known as Hill 37, and it provided an ideal observation post for the direction of the artillery fire and as a focal point for the forming-up of attacks. This was the location of the laager of the Stiffelmayer Battle Group that had been attacked by Flower.

Approximately 1,000 yards to the north was a further laager occupied by a regiment of the 15th Panzer Division, and 2,000 yards to the south of the Stiffelmayer was the I/8 Panzer Regiment, which had withdrawn to this position after an earlier encounter with the 24th Armoured Brigade.[71] The area around Hill 37 came alive at about 0400 hours to the sound of the Maybach engines of Teege's armour. Capt. Preve of the armoured *Raggruppamento* was instructed to investigate and attack the enemy forces which had been seen withdrawing north-east, with nineteen M14 tanks under his command, along with nine Semoventi self-propelled guns under the command of Maj. Barone.

The 47th Royal Tank Regiment Advance

Maj. Ward, who took temporary command of the 47th Royal Tank Regiment (24th Armoured Brigade), received his full orders only at 0530 hours,[72] including this update:

> [The] enemy appear to be holding part of Snipe and Woodcock opposite our own troops. Two 88's are reported in this vicinity with 100 German tanks also reported to the south and south-west. The minefields we are to pass are the last in this position and we should face them from now on.[73]

They were again made aware that they should not mistake the British for Huns and further advised: 'We are to hold off enemy counter-attacks by the enemy tanks from the west-south for one day protecting [their] flank.'[74]

Orders, relayed to the individual tank commanders barely five minutes before the "off" required them to leave at 0605 hours,[75] taking the Star track and then heading west to the tip of the Kidney feature, before heading south-east to take up a hull-down position facing south and west, finally stating, 'We are late already so be as quick as you can.'[76] Even these were not fully passed onto 'B' Squadron, who had no alternative but to follow 'A' Squadron as they set off. Flatow recalled:

> During the small hours of the morning the Provost section of Brigade came forward and marked the centre line of the 41st and 47th Battalions, but when first light came there was no sign of them and we got rather worried. However, they approached at last and in my opinion a greater shambles was never before witnessed. Two separate lines of tanks went over the ridge, they lost the centre line, part of the 41st got mixed up with the 47th and I myself was responsible for dashing over to 'Tiger' Slater, a Squadron Leader of the 41st and put him on the right track.[77]

Preve and Barone Attack

At 0545 hours, two enemy armoured groups left their laager: one heading to the laager in the north, exposing their weaker side armour to the British gunners; the second advancing directly towards Snipe, under orders to seek out the enemy but seemingly unaware of the occupied position. The German staff officers reported to Afrika Korps HQ that 'the situation was restored in its whole sector and a few groups of the enemy who had infiltrated were being engaged'.

Leading the second column advancing towards Snipe was a staff car with a Panzer Mark IV Special following directly behind. This was a 25-ton tank with a long, menacing 75-mm cannon and two machine guns with a crew of five, which in turn was followed by an Italian Semoventi self-propelled gun also with a 75-mm howitzer mounted on an M13 tank chassis, together with other SPGs and tanks of different types. The gunners waited until the lead tank was just 200 yards away before opening fire, as the 6-pounder had no night-sight, resulting in two tanks being knocked out by the guns of Brown and Cope. Savills, having been wounded earlier, had his position on the gun taken by Rifleman Chard, who hit one tank and disabled a second in quick succession. The crew managed to bale out of the burning wreck. Bird later remembered:

> When, as anti-tank gunners, we hit an enemy tank and it started to burn the tank crew would (of course) jump out if they could. Our motor platoons would then shoot at them with small-arms fire. It was a pretty mean thing to do, but I don't remember any hesitation. They weren't close enough to be real people perhaps, just little figures in the distance.[78]

The 6-pounders, machine guns and mortars kept up a blanket of fire, Sgt Dolling's gun hitting two panzers. Swann recalled:

> For my first shot I took on a staff car, then I took on a 15-hundredweight truck. By then the gun had bedded down in the soft sand so I took up a Bren gun, firing at a mixture of vehicles.[79]

Marten recalled, 'This was a most encouraging action, as the enemy were unhappily placed in close formation, and all they could do was to scram as quickly as possible.'[80] Sgt Calistan of 'C' Company later wrote:

> We were giving them hell, but we were not by any means getting away with it. Our position was rather exposed, and they let us have everything they had got. When they about-turned and retired we knew that for the moment our guns had won.[81]

Flower recalled:

> Our anti-tank with their 6-pounder guns got their first shoot of the – I was going to say day – of course it was still night – and they let loose at very short range and managed to knock out I think three in that little action, three German tanks which caught fire. The German tank crews dived out of their turrets and, as they dived out of their turrets, the machine-gunners were able to train their guns on these turrets and, in many cases, kill the German crews as they baled out.[82]

Those tanks that had taken cover after the first encounter, lying approximately 600 yards to the south/south-west of the position, now broke cover, but instead of attacking the position proceeded west. The laager to the north also started to move, providing the gunners with more targets, one of which was a Russian self-propelled gun hit by Cope's 6-pounder now commanded by Swann.

> I was just moving the gun into position when a 7.62-mm self-propelled gun came across out front, 200 yards away. There was a road going round the escarpment and this gun was up there firing at us. Colonel Turner said, 'Swann, do you think you could hit it?' I was a good shot, I had good eyes. I said, 'I'll have a go.' I swivelled the gun round and laid it on to a butt in the bank so that the nose of

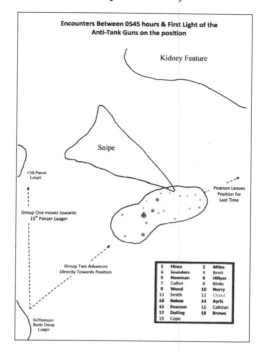

the vehicle, as it came into it, would give me the clue to fire, so I fired at it and I hit it. When it was stationary I put another one into it and the people inside bowled out of it and disappeared.[83]

Turner said, 'I hope to God, Swann, that wasn't one of ours,' to which I replied, 'Well, sir, if it was, I don't think it'll fire another bloody shell.'[84]

The short fire-fight had disclosed the position to the enemy, and they now received heavy shelling from 0630 hours for about thirty minutes. Sgt Saunders' gun of Platoon 15 in the troop commanded by Lt J. B. D. Irwin MC was knocked out and two other guns were damaged, resulting in Saunders being killed; Rifleman Davies was wounded and Bird's second in command and great friend Capt. Hugo N. Salmon, who had been observing and then used his jeep to tow Saunders' gun, received a 'hideous, disfiguring wound in his face, neck and chest' when his vehicle was knocked out by an 88-mm direct hit.[85] Burnhope joined him to administer first aid.[86]

Pearson's gun became deeply entrenched in the soft sand below the height of the depression after firing a few times and had to stop until it could be pulled out and repositioned. This had to be done with the assistance of one of the carriers, which brought down even more fire from the enemy artillery. However, despite being repositioned, the gun was not able to fire properly again. Other guns were now repositioned, a process that involved some being pulled out of the soft sand and others being towed by carriers or manhandled to new locations, to allow as wide a field of fire as possible. The guns also had to be moved to prevent them from toppling over when fired. This was a design fault of the 6-pounder gun, as although it was able to turn on its platform, enabling it to fire at oblique angles, when firing in soft sand it was found that it could topple over if firing in anything other than directly in line with the trail or at most a few degrees to either side. The repositioning activities again exposed the riflemen involved to heavy artillery fire, resulting in further casualties; the indirect enemy artillery fire on the position was to account for far more casualties than the direct fire from the enemy tanks.

It was not only the guns that needed repositioning. Rifleman Gregg, who was in a slit trench, recalled:

The position to our right had gone very quiet. Reggie crawled over to them; they were all goners. They had taken a direct hit from a mortar. 'Dickie' Bird came over and told us to move our position further right to cover the guns. This we did, and any food and water left by the unfortunate lads who had copped it.[87]

The Italians reported back that there was violent fire coming from extremely well dug in and camouflaged anti-tank guns, and as a result, the tanks commanded by officers Camplani, Pomoni, Bucalossi, Zilambo and Buciano had been hit. The remaining armour withdrew out of range of the guns, with some of them taking cover in small, scrub-smudged folds in the ground only a few hundred yards to the west. An enemy spotter plane flew over just as the sun came up, passing over Rifleman Moore who was standing in a slit trench but appeared not to see the occupants of the position despite the previous action. Rifleman Martin was pleased with the result to date:

How often in the past had I seen our armour crucified by well-positioned enemy anti-tank guns [...] Now Rommel had failed to heed the lesson he had taught us and was paying the price.[88]

Blacker and Nelson Arrive

During a short lull there was a loud rifle crack and a man in the next trench to Rifleman Moore was hit. Basset called out that a sniper was firing onto the position, and Turner shouted, 'Keep a look-out lads, we must get that bugger!'[89]

At this time riflemen Blacker[90] and Nelson of 'C' Company, who had got lost during the march from the start line, arrived on the position. Blacker recalled:

We got to where the guns were early in the morning. We walked down and I said to Johnny Nelson, 'We'll have to find the company; I don't know where they've gone!' We went down to one of the guns and found Sergeant Eldo Francise there.
Francise: 'What are you doing?'
Blacker: 'Which way is "C" Company?'
Francise: 'Never mind about "C" Company. See that tank down there?'
Blacker: 'Yeah.'
Francise: 'The two of you, go down there' (as he was saying this there was a pop pop pop, the noise of machine-gun bullets hitting the front of the six-pounder). 'Stop them sods firing at us!'
Blacker: 'Alright, we'll get going there. How do we get down there?'
Francise: 'Use your bloody loaf!'
    So we went down there, staying pretty low as we went. It took four or five minutes to crawl the eighty yards to the tank. It had been hit by a shell and it looked like it had been there for some time. It didn't look like a fresh hit because it had been on fire at some stage.[91]

A tank advanced and one of the anti-tank guns hit it straight away. As three of the crew got out of the tank, Blacker and Nelson shot two of them, the third escaping. He and Nelson now settled down to picking off the enemy snipers who stood up in order to see over a short lip of the position, whilst others were lying on top of the tanks hidden by the equipment, taking pot shots at the riflemen as the tanks advanced. Blacker, an expert shot, referred to his activities during that day as a 'gunfight in a junkyard' as he fired his rifle with impunity. 'They didn't know where we were,' he later recalled. 'It was ducks in a water barrel.' The pair had water and ammunition, although they were using quite a lot of the latter, but no food, and after a while Nelson suggested that he went back to the position to get some. Keeping low so as not to give their position away, he worked his way back to the position during the afternoon; unfortunately for Blacker, he never returned.[92]

First Light

The sun began to rise at about 0600 hours on a day that the weathermen at Eighth Army HQ forecast would be 'Wind light south-east becoming west-north-west. Very little cloud decreasing inland. Slight risk of coastal showers. Visibility ten miles.'[93] As the sun glimmered across the desert, the riflemen could now see the lie of the land. Marten asked Turner, 'Are we in the right place?' to which Turner replied, 'God knows, but here we are and here we damned well stay!'[94]

> The almost flat scene, stretching for a mile and a half all round, shadowed by the faint anonymous folds and ripples of the desert, was overlooked by the slight elevations that formed the horizon on all sides except the south. Patches of low, scrubby camel's thorn stippled and darkened the desert canvas here and there, affording some exiguous cover for those who knew how to use it. Of this scrub the garrison took full advantage and the excellence of their concealment and digging saved them from a great many casualties in what Turner called the 'deluge of fire that poured down on us for the rest of the day'. Turner also identified some strips, small ridges, defiles and zones of dead ground which an experienced enemy could take advantage of when attacking the position.[95]

It was due to this terrain that gunners often waited until the last possible moment to fire in order to be sure that the first shot destroyed the target, but there were also many occasions when due to these features they were unable to see the tank until it was almost on top of them. This was borne out almost immediately after dawn as a German soldier, who had been lying concealed at the centre of the position, was seen to leap up and run at full speed westward towards his own lines. He was unarmed, and the riflemen humanely decided not to shoot him.

The 24th Armoured Arrive

The armour had moved through the Star track at about 0630 hours, a confused irregular formation.[96] As they left the track, they suffered casualties from very heavy enemy shelling of all calibres including 88, 105 and 210 mm.[97] Lt Warwick of 'A' Squadron 47th Royal Tank Regiment wrote:

> On advancing through the enemy minefield, my squadron was held up by heavy shell fire. We replied to this fire until ordered to advance. We then advanced south-west for almost one mile.[98]

At about 0730 hours, the tanks climbed over the ridge on the Oxalic Line approximately 2,000 yards to the east. Rifleman Harding, in 'C' Company sector, recalled, 'There was a deep rumbling sound in the distance behind us and a great cloud of dust as the tanks came over the ridge and surveyed us.'[99] Crimp, in the same sector, wrote:

> Half a dozen Shermans become visible on the ridge behind us to the northeast. The Jerry guns, however, must have the range worked to an inch, for two of the tanks are immediately hit and set on fire.[100]

The tank commanders were also still under the mistaken impression that part of the Snipe position was occupied by the enemy. The fact that the position according to their maps provided by the staff of the 1st Armoured Division showed it to be 1,000 yards away did not help matters. They searched the exposed ground ahead with their field-glasses, seeing a strongpoint ahead comprising guns and weapon pits among the camel thorn, with a sprinkling of burnt-out German tanks nearby, which gave the impression that they were 'live' tanks, and opened fire with their 75-mm high-explosive shells which landed around the sector of 'B' Company and that of the 239th. Marten immediately radioed them, but was unable to make contact. Turner then sent Lt Wintour, the Battalion Intelligence Officer, in a carrier to the ridge, where he found Lt Warwick in his tank *Argenaute*. He later wrote:

> During this advance, I was on the right flank of the squadron, and in touch with a battalion of the Rifle Brigade (2nd Battalion), who were holding a position on the slopes of Kidney Hill.
> Upon arrival, Wintour said to Warwick, 'Look here, you're shooting us up!' Warwick said, 'I'm awfully sorry', with Wintour replying, 'Not half as sorry as we are!'[101]

Warwick continued in his diary, 'Several of our tanks on my left opened fire on these friends, killing several; I screamed over the air to stop this, with little or no effect.'[102] 'A' Squadron subsequently

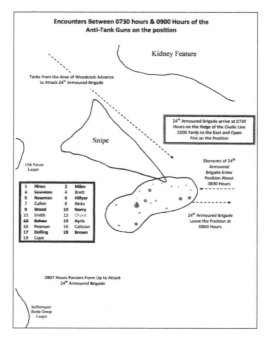

stopped shelling the position, but due to a wireless problem, the rest of the brigade unfortunately continued for some time. Rifleman Moore, manning the wireless set for 'A' Company, recalled, 'What the Colonel said over the air I should not like to repeat.'[103]

The Tanks Move Down

At last the tanks ceased firing on the position, moving down to the location at 0807 hours. The appearance of the British armour was seen by the Germans as a major threat to the III/115 Panzer Grenadier Regiment, which further believed that there were 'enemy tanks behind the unit', presumably the guns of the 2nd RB. Twenty-five to thirty German tanks and some self-propelled guns, along with an anti-tank platoon from the 15th Panzer Division, formed up in the area to the front of Hill 37 with the obvious intent of attacking the British armour, while a further group of panzers laagered to the north began to move towards the position from the area around Woodcock.

By about 0830 hours, the tanks arrived in the north-east sector of the garrison, occupied by the 239th Battery and 'B' Company, intent on 'joining hands' with the occupants. This drew the attention of the 115th *Panzergrenadier* and 33rd *Panzerjäger*, as well as the remaining enemy tanks and guns in the immediate area, all of which seemed to pour intense heavy fire onto the position, with added artillery and 88-mm fire from guns located on the Kidney feature. Col. Becker of the German 15th Panzer Division notified his divisional headquarters that thirty-two vehicles, including carriers, tanks and self-propelled guns, were being engaged around Snipe.[104] Both sides put down smoke to protect their armour, but the Germans used theirs to better effect, targeting a tank by firing a smoke round onto it, then using the smoke as a pointer for the 88-mm armour-piercing rounds which quickly followed.[105] The armour-piercing shell (AP) was a solid shot used against tanks. Burning white hot, it would penetrate the armour plate, sending white-hot fragments through the cramped interior, killing the operators and igniting stored shells, resulting in the 'brewing up' of the tank – the deepest fear of any tank crew.

It is doubtful whether the British tanks ever saw an enemy on which to set their sights, but they presented themselves as excellent targets on a piece of ground that by now the enemy was very familiar with, and within fifteen minutes seven Sherman tanks were hit and set ablaze, together with two anti-tank guns of the 239th.[106] Sgt Bob Smith's gun, close to one of the Shermans that had been hit, was itself knocked out, having never fired, with the added result that Smith was blinded for several hours. Bdr Barnes and Gunner Mercer were killed, and Gunner Kane became shell-shocked. Sgt Norry's gun was knocked out in a similar manner to that of Smith, having never fired, but with no serious casualties.

> Sergeant Smith, in spite of his blindness, moved over to join his friend, Sergeant Ronald Wood, taking Kane with him and nursing him until he recovered. Sergeant Norry's gun, similarly placed close to a Sherman, manned by Voce, Baer's driver, and Gunner Fred Beeson, his soldier-servant [was knocked out]. They saw a man screaming with agony of burns, trying to escape from the turret. They leapt from their trench, clambered onto the burning tank and bore him to their trench. There, some time afterwards, he died.[107]

However, Baer was convinced that at least one of the guns was knocked out by the previous deluge of 'friendly fire'.

It had become clear that the Rifle Brigade and friends were now being subjected to a major trial of strength. Shells were screaming down unceasingly on the position, with their own 6-pounder guns and small-arms fire responding. Burning hulks of tanks, often with their mangled and charred crew still inside or nearby, already littered the ground, and billowing black acrid smoke, mixed with choking dust and cordite stench, burning oil and rubber, filled the air, making it hard to breathe. Rifleman Martin recalled that 'the scene was one of utter confusion and mayhem,'[108] the riflemen having little idea of what was going on, but it seemed as if every tank and gun of the *Panzerarmee* was being directed towards them.[109] Crimp wrote:

> For the next half an hour we get a concentrated dose. It's most unpleasant crouching in the bottom of the pit, packed tight with even more chaps now whose single object is to keep their 'nuts' down as low as possible, silently braced and wondering whether the next one's coming our way. The shells scream down in inexorable succession, and all around us is the driving, rendering crash of high explosive. Several times my tin hat is crushed on my head by the impact of nearby detonations, and once my lungs are filled by a rush of sand. Everybody lies still. You can't do a thing – it just has to happen.[110]

The tank casualties rose with those of 'A' Squadron – *Albion, Defiant, Arran, Adonism, Argonaut* and *Adaptable III* being hit, whilst those casualties within the ranks of 'B' squadron included *Bacchus, Boanwerges, Cadiz, Buffalo Bill, Badger, Blighty, Boar* and *Bruiser*.[111, 112] A direct hit was not the only cause of casualties to tank crews, as even a glancing blow could cause concussion problems and/or release flakes of metal to fly about inside. Sherman tanks later acquired the collective nickname of 'Ronsons' because, macabre as it sounds, they lit first time. Even the Germans were to notice this defect, naming them 'Tommy Boilers'. The major flaw was that the ammunition locker located in the turret was only lightly armoured and a direct hit often exposed the unused shells, which invariably exploded with fatal consequences.[113] In these circumstances the shell was like a devil let loose – 'the demented ricochet within the steel trap'[114] – with the crew trying to dodge the white-hot shards of metal. Added to this danger was that in the event of the tank catching fire, the flames would be fed by the high-powered aircraft fuel from the engine,[115] giving the crew about 90 seconds to scramble through the hatch. It would take half this time to open the doors.[116]

> A tank that is mortally hit belches forth long searing tongues of orange flame from every hatch. As ammunition explodes in the interior, the hull is racked by violent convulsions and sparks erupt from the spout of the barrel like fireballs of a roman candle. Silver rivulets of molten aluminium pour from the engine like tears … When the inferno subsides, gallons of lubricating oil in the power train and hundreds of pounds of rubber on the tracks and bogey wheels continue to burn, spewing dense clouds of black smoke over the funeral pyre.[117]

From the point of view of all parties, 0900 hours assumed an importance, as several things now took place at this time.

British Armour Leaves Snipe

The Snipe position was quickly becoming a killing field for the British armour, who could not manoeuvre within its environs. The enemy moving from the north and forming up in the south-west presented a danger in forcing them to fight in an area that would not be beneficial to their overall mission, and the tanks therefore decided to withdraw to positions behind the Oxalic Ridge, about a mile and a quarter from the garrison, who were not sorry to see them go. As they moved off, they came under fire from the advancing panzers from the north. However, with smoke no longer being fired on the position and the remainder dispersing, the panzers became clearly visible to the guns of the 239th, but at a range of 1,800 yards were too far away for firing to be a guaranteed positive outcome. The War Diary stated that the 6-pounder:

> [...] can be employed successfully up to a range of 1,000 yards [and] will pierce the armour of Mark III or IV German tanks at greater ranges. The limited factor is not penetration but the efficiency of the sight. The present sight has no magnification and has a hair line which is too thick.[118]

Capt. Mosley, commander of 'A' Company, requested that Sgt Binks of the 239th fire at a Panzer Mk IV 'special' and, after much discussion, Binks fired, his third shot immobilising the tank, which was immediately towed away by another. By now the tanks were arriving at their positions behind the Oxalic Ridge, Flatow recalled their arrival:

> And then the atmosphere changed – something happened that made our bowels cling and our mouths dry up – some Shermans appeared over the ridge in front of us, some reversing, some facing us, some in flames – they were odd tanks of the 41st and 47th Battalions retreating, coming out of it. Some stayed with us, blocking our view, getting in our way, others passed through us and went away. The shelling increased, the Colonel's voice boomed over the air, 'The Regiment will not retire one yard but will stand and fight where it is.' Cheerful words! How I cursed everything. The horrible thing was we couldn't see why it was that the other two regiments had retreated and we expected German tanks to come into view at any moment.[119]

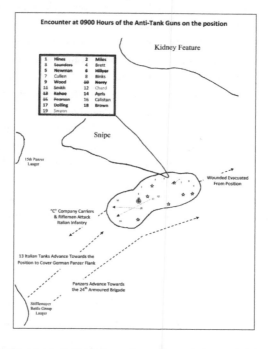

Italian Infantry Attack

Back at the area of the garrison opposite the 'C' Company sector a group of Italian infantry could be seen forming up. Turner told Flowers to 'see them off'.[120] The carriers advanced, supported by the riflemen of the motor platoons, attacking and dispersing the enemy infantry as well as two enemy guns. In doing so, they lost four carriers and had three set on fire, retiring only when they had expended all their ammunition.[121] Gregg recalled:

> Their infantry attacked us with some show of force. Unfortunately for them that five or six metres [*sic*] height advantage (which they had to climb in order to get to grips with us) became their undoing. They were just mown down in front of us, some of them no more than twenty feet away from our guns.[122]

During this engagement two captured British trucks, a 15 cwt and a 33 cwt, were seen towing two field guns into position to fire on the garrison. They were shot up by Bren-gun fire at about 800 yards, one gun being in Swann's hands. These may have been the German engineers of *Panzer-Pioniere-Bataillon 33* who had been ordered to 'take up a defensive position on the right flank of III/115 Panzer Grenadiers Regiment ... Hurry.' The riflemen continued to put their rifles and Bren guns to good use for the next half an hour, shooting at small groups of Italians, whilst the carriers made their way back. Sgt Pearson, whose gun could not be fired, was wounded also during this period and his crew dispersed around the position where they were needed.

Dash to Start Line

The numbers of wounded were mounting and the ammunition stocks getting lower, prompting Capt. Shepherd-Cross, 'B' Company second in command, along with two 'A' Company carriers under command of Sgt Sampher, to leave the position at about 0900 hours in order to take the seriously wounded back to the Highland lines and hoping to return with more ammunition and the doctor. The route back across the long valley was dominated by the enemy, who poured intense fire from anti-tank guns and heavy machine guns on to it, but the convoy was successful in reaching the lines despite the 'B' Company carrier receiving a direct hit from a 75-mm gun. Meanwhile, Marten made radio contact with 7th Motor Brigade HQ, stating, 'Our crying need is a gunner O.P',[123] receiving the reply that one would be sent shortly. Without a Forward Observation Officer (FOO), Turner could not call up and direct artillery strikes on the enemy, or prevent his own artillery from targeting Snipe, which from a distance looked like a good enemy target. Arranging for the trip to the position, Pearson put together a small convoy including Picton, ambulances, the new FOO and more ammunition trucks. However, every time they attempted to get to the position, they encountered such enormous enemy fire that they could not hope to get through.[124]

A Two-Pronged Attack

The last of the events that took place around 0900 hours was the two-pronged attack ordered by Teege: one prong was made up of tanks of the Stiffelmayer Battle Group, namely thirteen tanks and nine Semoventi self-propelled guns of the 12th Battalion, 133rd Tank Regiment, Littorio Division under command of Preve being sent to eliminate the troublesome garrison at Snipe;[125] the second prong involved twenty-five to thirty panzers of the 8th Panzer Regiment, bypassing the southern edge of the Snipe position to attack the tanks of the 24th Armoured Brigade.[126]

The first prong of the attack advanced towards the 'C' Company section, who could initially bring only one gun to bear, but with the guns of Dolling and Brown having been pulled through the soft sand by attaching ropes to the tracks of carriers and repositioned, this number was increased to three. During this manoeuvre the vehicles and men were exposed to both direct and indirect enemy fire, resulting in Lt Salt[127] and three riflemen being killed, but the repositioning allowed four tanks and a 3-ton truck to be destroyed, three of the tanks being hit by Dolling's gun.

The Italian tanks were vulnerable to even the old 2-pounder guns. Against the new 6-pounders they therefore had no chance at all, some of the tanks fixing sandbags on the front to somehow add further protection. The Italian 12th Battalion War Diary embellishes the defensive fire:

The 12th Battalion attacks. In spite of the violent enemy fire and the resultant initial losses of tanks and men, the battalion advances firmly, keeping a certain distance from the anti-tank guns, which are extremely well dug in and camouflaged. Suddenly there is a violent fire from a further eight or ten anti-tank guns hidden on our left and located in depth. Their fire claims a number of victims and the battalion advance then comes to halt. Enemy fire becomes more and more violent.

A further Italian account of the attack read:

Two tanks of 5 Company were hit and immobilized early in the attack and the Semoventi troops opened fire on the forward anti-tank gun. 2nd Lieutenant Stefanelli has his tank hit by an armour-piercing shell, which penetrates and explodes. Lieutenant Pomoni's tank at the head of his company is hit in the engine and the crew miraculously saved. Lieutenant Bucalossi's tank is also hit and set on fire, while Lieutenant Zilambo is wounded in the right leg and saved by Lieutenant Luciano (The Adjutant).

The fire from the three guns brought the attack to a temporary halt. It started again only when:

[…] 2nd Lieutenant Camplani who stands in his turret […] urges his fellow tanks forward once more towards the British anti-tank guns and is only stopped by a belt of mines in front of the position which breaks his tracks. 2nd Lieutenant Delfino continues the attack and is only stopped by the minefields.

The attack was not pressed and the remainder drew back. One junior officer of the Littorio Division watched the terrible happenings, his Catholic eyes glimpsing the hereafter:

Some of the tanks continued to advance even after they had been hit and set on fire, with only dead and dying men inside them, like huge self-propelled funeral pyres, a dead man's foot still pressing down on the accelerator. What a sight! A procession of blazing monsters, shaken by explosions and emitting coloured flashes as the shells inside went off – like something out of a terrifying ghost story. The souls of the dead men must have been trapped in their vehicle; how else could a smashed and blazing tank continue to advance towards the enemy?[128]

The attack having been halted, the remnants withdrew back towards Hill 37.

The main, second prong, attack now started. The aim of the first prong had been to protect the flank of the second group while they moved into position to attack the British armour and to keep the riflemen busy while the twenty-five or thirty Mk IV special panzers from the 8th Panzer Regiment advanced. So intent were they on attacking the retiring British armour, they seemed unaware of the riflemen as they crossed the southern front of the position at about 1,000 yards, presenting their weak side armour to the guns of Brown, Dolling and Calistan, who as soon as the first attack had halted had swung their guns round to bear and begun firing into the enemy ranks. Seeing the effect that the anti-tank guns were having on his force, the commander split it in half, one part attacking the riflemen whilst the remainder continued their advance on the British armour. The result was that those tanks attacking the position presented their weak side armour to the 24th Armoured Brigade, whilst those attacking the 24th presented their side armour to the RB gunners. Those firing from tanks and those from the position proved their bravery as they concentrated not on the panzers attacking them but on those who were attacking their comrades. Turner called this a case of 'cross trumping'.[129] Barrie Pitt has written:

> The range was long but the nerves of the gunners remained steady, neither set switching their fire to the panzers actually attacking them but concentrating instead upon those crossing their sight lines towards the other target.[130]

At least eight tanks were set on fire, with several more being hit.[131] The attack was called off, the remaining panzers again withdrawing to safer positions.

The attacks were not limited to tank *v.* armour/anti-tank guns, as during the assaults the riflemen of the motor platoons were kept busy fighting enemy infantry attacks, the fire generated from machine-gun nests scattered around the area, and dealing with enemy crews of tanks that had been hit.[132] One of the casualties, Cpl Wenman, who had been the number two of Savill's gun in 14 Platoon, was mortally wounded and died six hours later.

No Rescue

Much to the annoyance of Briggs, the constant attempts to move armour forward to support the garrison had been thwarted, as was every attempt to cross the valley by those under the command of Pearson, by the most intense enemy fire. To make matters worse, at about 1030 hours Briggs was made aware from intercepted radio transmissions that the 21st Panzer Division had come up from the south overnight, raising their headquarters only a little west of Kidney Ridge and that the garrison must face this new danger.[133] Rommel had decided days before that any counter-attack would have to advance through the Kidney Ridge area.[134] He had therefore consolidated his panzers and instructed that concentrated heavy artillery barrages be fired along the whole of the XXX Corps front. Having occupied a position further south than originally intended, the riflemen had unwittingly placed themselves directly in the path of Rommel's intended counter-attack.[135] Aware of this, Briggs faced a dilemma: the riflemen needed his protection, but he needed to protect his armour. His decision? The riflemen would have to fight it out alone![136] 'Never was a calculated risk more stoutly justified by those exposed to it.'[137] Calistan later wrote:

The thing that sticks in my memory is our company commander saying we were cut off and there wasn't anything that could get through to us. We could fight it out, and keep on fighting as long as we had a shell or bullet or bayonet. Yes, we understood. There was no rest. When you had time to listen, you realized we had fewer and fewer guns firing.[138]

Swann also reinforced this feeling: 'The thing is the morale of the men, who knew we were fighting to the finish. But we were scoring and this is the thing: we were winning.'[139]

The Position at 1100 Hours

The situation in the position was now becoming increasingly more desperate. Brig. Dunphie described the scene:

The desert sun was at its hottest. The dust, grime, smoke of burning tanks and burning flesh, and hordes of flies, particularly around the dead and wounded, the smell of battle and the smell of death hung over the entire area. Snipe was a most unpleasant and dangerous place that day, and yet the indefatigable spirit seemed to have gripped the riflemen.[140]

Bird, Turner and the other officers went from gun to gun, from slit trench to slit trench – the action of which, despite being no more than 50 yards apart, courted injury and death – giving encouragement, telling them what was going on, cajoling them, moving the wounded to better locations and, where necessary, taking their place. This was what Maj. Hastings called 'Leadership with a capital L',[141] and yet years later, Turner recalled that it was the Cockney humour and sheer steadfastness of the riflemen that really 'kept the show on the road'. The humour was not all one way: Turner said to the occupants of one slit trench who had almost been buried alive by an exploding shell, 'Come on, you're not dead yet!', saying later that Cpl Francis was an inspiration – constantly cheerful and seemingly unconcerned with the danger.[142] Men were moved to locations where they were needed most. Burnhope, still the only medical assistant on the position, treated the wounded along with others who helped when they could and as far as the scant medical supplies would allow, including a few German prisoners who found their way into the position.[143]

There were now only thirteen anti-tank guns remaining that could operate, and ammunition was running low, especially in the south and south-west and north and north-west sectors, where the guns had seen a lot of action. Those remaining were situated and manned as follows:

West/South-west (five guns)
   Sgt Brown
   Sgt Calistan
   Sgt Dolling
   Cpl Savill – manned by Lt Holt-Wilson, Sgt Ayris and Rifleman Chard
   Cpl Cope

North/North-west (four guns)
   Sgt Hine
   Sgt Miles

Sgt Brett
Sgt Newman

North-east (four guns)
Sgt Hillyer (239th)
Sgt Cullen (239th)
Sgt Binks (239th)
Sgt Woods (239th)

The carriers, despite being moved to semi-protective hull-down positions, now received concentrated artillery fire, which was ultimately to last for the next two hours, setting six on fire. The bursting shells that shook the ground and the heavy shot that smashed a gun or carrier caused white-hot jagged shards to whizz across the position, shells passing close to the men could take the breath from their lungs with the vacuum of its passing.[144] Some died from concussive blasts caused by the change in atmospheric pressure as the high-explosive detonation created compression in the surrounding air, killing them without any obvious injury.[145] Crimp wrote, 'Casualties are being brought in, and when Coy H.Q. dug out is full of them, it's decided to park the rest in our trench – so we have to clear out.'[146]

In the quivering heat, the riflemen stood in their slit trenches, sweat running down their backs and dust-covered faces like rivers and watched as on three sides of the island position enemy movements by foot, truck, staff car and armour took place as they prepared their forces for attacks, mostly out of the riflemen's reach but every now and then moving close enough for a shot. Both Hastings and Lucas Phillips later wrote that despite all this, the enemy 'could not shake the spirit of the men in the small garrison.'[147]

'C' Company Sector, 1200-1400 Hours

There was a heavy enemy bombardment around midday, hitting the position hard.[148] Crimp recalled:

> Very soon the barrage starts up again, but most of it falls a short way ahead towards the enemy. The shells, however, are coming from behind us, so they're obviously from our own artillery, a couple of miles back, to keep the enemy off our position and break up his suspected infantry assault. Many of them fall close enough, all the same.[149]

Swann noticed that four lorry loads of Italian infantry were moving forward towards the 'C' Company sector. 'We couldn't move our guns round but we did get the Bren guns at them.'[150] He went down to the commanding officer to inform him of the attack:

> When I came back I lay down with the Bren gun to repel the infantry and they asked the artillery to frighten them. They gave the position of the Italians. Our artillery opened up with shrapnel and the first shell cracked up in the air over the top of us. No casualties at all. The second one landed right smack and I was bowled over. When I picked myself up Eddie Cope was smothered in blood. I was walking around for about a quarter of an hour with my head ringing, after getting Cope back to first aid.[151]

Swann took over the number one position on Cpl Cope's gun in 13 Platoon under command of Lt J.

E. B. Naumann and at other times assisted him in the fire control of the platoon. Even though their flank was exposed to enemy tanks that could not be engaged by their guns, they continued firing on those that they could target.

A shell landed behind the gun, killing the loader and wounding the number four. Swann continued firing until the number three was also wounded, when he crawled over to another gun and brought back its crew and ammunition. Rifleman Flint was the number two on the gun when an air burst from an artillery shell exploded behind it. Swann, acting as number one, was waiting for his number two to slap him on the shoulder as the indication that he could fire – instead Flint's body slammed into his back protecting him from the blast of the explosion.[152] The guns of Dolling and Hine were knocked out at about 1200 hours, Hine taking over Cope's gun at 1300 hours. The gun complement was slowly being reduced by the enemy activity, their numbers going down to eleven: four in the west/south-west sector; three in the north/north-west sector; and four in the north-east sector.

There was a short lull and then the enemy renewed their interest in the position, high-explosive and air burst shells crashing on 'C' Company section. Crowder heard the shells and dived into his platoon's slit trench, pushing Rifleman Harding in front of him. Harding recalled 'seeing Crowder's hand disappear in a red mist'.[153] In fact, he had lost a finger and was badly wounded in the legs.[154] Harding later wrote to Crowder's sister, saying that her brother 'was very unlucky as there were six men in the trench and he was the only one that was wounded'.[155, 156] Crowder remained in the trench, forcing some of his men to find other positions nearby, Harding moving to a position about 10 yards to the rear of Calistan's gun behind some tamarisk bushes.

Around 1230 hours, Salmon, who had been injured earlier in the day, finally and mercifully died,[157] owing to his injuries it had not been possible to move him, and Burnhope had stayed with him in the area of 15 Platoon despite it being in a very dangerously exposed position.[158] Around the same time, the 'friendly fire' finally stopped, but only as a result of Pearson visiting the gun positions of the Regimental HQ of the 4th Royal Horse Artillery and personally requesting that they stop firing.

An intercepted wireless message from the enemy disclosed that they were very concerned at this 'island of resistance', which when added to the other threat of the 24th Armoured Brigade, needed to be dealt with immediately. The situation demanded that Rommel take direct command of the attack against the riflemen.[159]

'C' Company Sector Attacked Again

The ammunition shortage was not going away, particularly in the south-west sector facing Hill 37, and by 1300 hours it was again becoming serious. Bird and Francis returned to the task of transferring by jeep the heavy green ammunition boxes from guns that had not been so heavily engaged, Marten recalling:

> [...] any movement brought down instantaneous machine-gun and shell fire from the enemy and made it difficult, at times impossible, to carry ammunition from guns that didn't need it to those that were dry.[160]

The Italians, noticing that since the last attack the retaliatory gunfire from the riflemen had reduced significantly, probably felt that the defenders were 'on their last legs'. Preve was instructed to attack the south-west corner of the position again with his M14/41 tanks and the 105-mm Semoventi self-

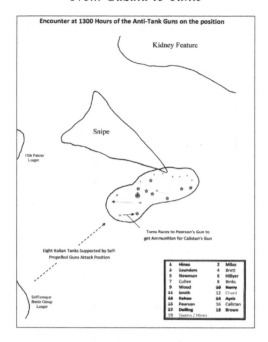

propelled guns under command of Barone in support.[161]

The force advanced towards the 'C' Company sector, which now contained only one gun that could still both fire and be brought to bear, this being Calistan's gun, part of Toms' troop but which did not have a crew. Rifleman Brown was badly shell-shocked and the other two members had been sent away to obtain ammunition,[162] one of whom was Cpl Barnett, who managed to crawl out on his belly to a couple of disabled guns and proceeded to drag two boxes of ammunition over 300 yards back to the gun. However, being under constant fire, his progress was terribly slow.[163]

Seeing the enemy tanks and SP guns, Turner ran to Calistan's gun and took the position of observer,[164] positioning himself off to one side of the gun outside the protection of the shield in order to monitor the progress of the shells. He was quickly joined by Toms who loaded. Turner stopped Calistan from firing until the first tank was within 600 yards.[165] He then hit six tanks in quick succession. The ammunition stock was down to only two or three rounds when Toms darted out from behind the protection of the gun shield and ran 100 yards back to his Bantam jeep near Pearson's gun, loaded four of the precious boxes and, despite intense machine-gun fire streaming down on him, drove back to Calistan's gun. The jeep was riddled with bullet holes and set on fire about 10 yards short of the gun, Calistan recalling, 'God knows how he got to it – they were machine-gunning the whole way.'[166] Toms, Turner and Francis removed the four boxes, forming a human chain to manhandle them to the gun. Artillery barrages continued, with one 88-mm shell exploding close to the gun.[167] Shrapnel from it penetrated Turner's steel helmet and skull,[168] and he keeled over beside the gun, blood pouring down his face from a nasty wound. Despite this, Turner insisted he was OK, refusing first aid and telling them to keep firing.[169] However, he became weaker and finally collapsed, giving his colleagues the opportunity to bind his head and move him to a scrub area about 10 yards behind the gun.[170] Regaining consciousness, Turner asked Rifleman Harding for a knife to cut off the hurried and very tight dressing that was causing him discomfort, settling for its replacement from Harding's emergency field dressing and his assistance to bind the wound.[171] Turner was later to say that if he had not been wearing his helmet, which many of the officers did not at that time, he would have certainly died that day.[172]

Barnett had now got back to rejoin Calistan and Toms, and with the three remaining tanks between 200 and 300 yards away, coolly and with his last three rounds hit and set fire to them, the last being just 150 yards away.[173] On hearing the news, Turner shouted back, 'Good work – a hat trick!'[174]

At about 1330 hours, Teege gave the order for the remaining tanks to withdraw through to their formation line and to disperse in the wadi behind. Those tanks that were not burnt out were recovered, making the losses nine tanks hit and immobilised with three being recovered, and four dead along with eleven wounded soldiers. Teege expressed his admiration in his later report 'for the magnificent courage shown by the battalion and for the way in which Captain Preve commanded the movement of his own tanks and the Semoventi.'[175]

Calistan, seemingly unperturbed by the action, then said, 'Well, we haven't been able to have a brew the whole morning [and] now the enemy have kindly lighted a fire for us, I don't see why we should not have one!' poured enough water for three cups out of his water bottle into a tin and putting it on the flat bonnet of Toms' burning jeep.[176] Turner recalled, 'We soon had as good a cup of tea as I have ever had.'[177] Shortly afterwards Toms was hit in the arm, but continued to command his troop, whilst Barnett left the gun again to look for more ammunition.

Between 1400 and 1600 Hours

Now that the Italian attack had been called off, another lull ensued, although there was almost continuous shell and mortar fire, wounding Dolling and killing Cpl Smith at approximately 1330 hours, made all the more frustrating as without the FOO they could not arrange counter-fire.[178] Enemy infantry made numerous sallies in an effort to make small incursions in the defences but were met with mixed counter-fire from everyone who could fire a weapon.[179] Gregg recalled, 'However much we fired into them, still they came forward. It had now got so bad that it was impossible to touch the bare metal of our weapons.'[180] Crimp wrote:

> The Colonel and Adjutant (Marten) – I can see them from their waists up as they stand in their trench down at Batt. H.Q. – are having grand sport with borrowed rifles, picking off the crews climbing out of the stricken panzers. They vie with each other in choosing their targets, take careful aim, and chalk up their respective 'bags' with mock-emulative gusto.[181]

The carrier platoons continued to fire, but in doing so were targeted more and more by the enemy who hit them one after another. By 1600 hours, the 'C' Company carriers had run out of ammunition, having fired off 45,000 rounds.[182]

Blacker had continued sniping, going through 200 rounds:

> There were at least forty machine-gun nests, at a guess. There were probably more. It wasn't only me at the machine guns because someone else was going round throwing grenades at them but I reckon I must have put out at least some of them because I had a clean shot. They were sitting upright like with our Vickers.[183]

The number of tanks was harder to determine as 'they'd be coming this way and sometimes they'd be going that way. But there were quite a lot out there.' The German snipers would lie on the tanks, taking cover from the various pieces of kit that the tank carried such as tow ropes, shovels, etc., but Blacker 'always knew when I [he] hit the snipers as they rolled off the tanks'.[184]

> The long hot afternoon continued with the desert floor dancing in the rays of the furnace overhead, and was perhaps the hardest part of the day. After the fatigues of the long night, the strain of the gruelling hours under the sun became accentuated by hunger and thirst; there was no chance to eat anything and those who did not have full equipment 'on the man' had nothing to drink either.[185]

Those remaining now suffered from the huge number of flies attracted by the dead bodies, tormenting the men without respite.[186] Having rested for a while under cover, Turner now insisted against all persuasion on visiting his guns once more. The exertion proved too much, resulting in him hallucinating that he was defending a harbour in a naval battle against hostile ships. Seeing a tank, he exclaimed, 'Open fire on that destroyer.'[187] After fainting again, he was taken down into the small headquarters dugout, although even this did not stop him for long, as he soon started moving around the position giving encouragement, and in the end had to be physically restrained.[188]

Bird and Toms continued going from gun to gun, helping to supply ammunition and, where needed, to lift morale, but by 1400 hours both were wounded. Bird recalled:

> I'd gone up to see one of the platoon commanders, Jack Toms, and we were discussing how to re-arrange his remaining men and guns when a shell landed just beside us. He was hit in the hand and I was hit in the head. I kept going for a bit but in due course with the heat and exhaustion I passed out.[189]

Liddell, Flower and Irwin had also been wounded, so there were now no officers in the south/south-west sector putting pressure on the control command functions of the battalion, relying upon the riflemen's ability to act on their own initiative to remedy this lack of structure. Sgt Brown was put in command until Lt Lightly from another area could take over, but while moving across the position, Lightly decided to go forward for better observation and was 'never seen or heard again'.[190] It later transpired that he had been taken prisoner. Each sub-unit, platoon and gun now continued acting independently on its own initiative.[191]

The headquarters dugout was becoming very crowded, what with the men and the flies. Marten recalled:

> My dugout contained two wounded riflemen, a wounded sapper, two signalmen, the colonel (who was by this time quite delirious) Tom Bird (out, groaning quietly), Charles Liddell (very over-excited), Jackie Wintour, our intelligence officer (in excellent and amusing form) and myself. As it was a minute hole, and the flies were quite frightful, settling in hundreds on one's face, clothes and hands, the discomfort and smell were considerable.[192]

Despite the adverse conditions, Marten continued to send clear and concise reports back to headquarters on the operation.

The position once more heard the sounds of tanks from the rear as the American Priest 105-mm self-propelled guns of the 11th (Honourable Artillery Company) Royal Horse Artillery of 2nd

Armoured Brigade came over the ridge to the east on their way to the Woodcock position. A sense of *déjà vu* now came to the position as the crews of the SP guns looked down upon the garrison, again mistaking it for an enemy strongpoint and opening fire. Marten said, 'During an unpleasant day this was the most unpleasant thing that happened,'[193] continuing, 'It seemed to take years before I could get through to Brigade and get them to stop firing at us.'[194]

Rommel's Counter-Attack

When teaching infantry tactics, Rommel stated that a counter-attack had to be a concerted effort; when attacking, you should 'spew' not 'dribble'. In accordance with this hypothesis, he would use all the remaining armour of the 90th Light, 15th and 21st Panzer divisions, amounting to about seventy tanks plus self-propelled guns and as many Panzer Grenadiers as could be mustered in support as possible, setting the attack to begin at 1600 hours.[195] Once through the 'weak' spot situated between the Alamein box and Deir el Abyad, they would advance northwards to cut off the defenders of the Alamein Line and attack the rear of XIII Corps, whilst the Italian Littorio Armoured Division would drive south to the Qattara box. The two principal points of attack were to be Hill 29 and the Kidney feature just north of the garrison's position,[196] but during the afternoon, the 90th Light attack on Hill 29 failed, leaving the only point of attack to be the Kidney feature and by default the Snipe position.

The attack began with thirty German panzers and ten Italian M13s advancing on the axis between

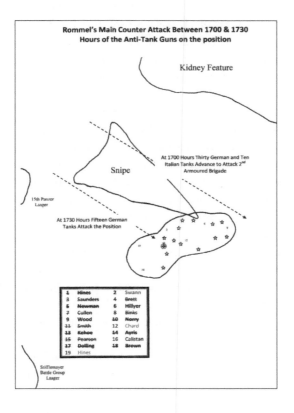

Woodcock and Snipe in tandem with the main force to the north, with a second group of about thirty German panzers following behind. Their War Diary stated that the '21st Panzer Division attacked through the holding element of the 15th', whilst Stuka dive-bombers took off to attack in front of the advancing armour.[197]

The Stukas were met by the Desert Air Force and prevented from reaching the position, the first group of tanks moving rapidly in open phalanx, heading east and then south-east to engage the guns of the 2nd Armoured Brigade.[198] However, in doing so they crossed the east end of the position, seemingly unaware that the British were there. It was later the subject of discussion that these might have been part of the 21st Panzer Division and, being new to the area, were unaware of the garrison. As the enemy passed within 200 yards of the north-east corner of the garrison, the guns of 239th Battery, which had not had an opportunity to engage the enemy since the morning, opened fire and hit at least nine tanks. The 21st Panzer Division noted that 'the attack was halted as a result of strong fire on the flanks from anti-tank guns and dug-in Pilot[199, 200] These tanks moved to within 500 yards of the 239th guns.[201] Being in a shallow dip, and the gunners even lower due to their kneeling position they could not see the guns of Brett and Newman to their left.[202] Their story is best recalled from their War Diary:

They had four guns left in action. Four small guns against forty tanks. Each sergeant took post a trifle to the flank of his gun to observe and correct fire. They were very well concealed, Wood's gun being invisible from fifty paces ahead. Guns loaded, layers following the leaders of the oncoming tanks in their sights, the detachments knelt low behind the small shield, between the widely splayed legs of the split rails. Thrilled and fascinated, the gunners watched the immensely impressive spectacle as the powerful force roared slowly athwart to their front, the sand billowing from the tracks. Baer ordered his guns to hold their fire till he gave the word. They heard Newman's gun bark on the left but still kept silent. 500, 400, 300 yards. Then Hillyer seeing a tank turn to attack Newman fired on his own initiative and scored. Accordingly, at 200 yards, Baer gave the order to open fire. Binks fired immediately. The red tracer darted to the target and a Mark III leapt into flames. On Cullen's gun there was a momentary delay as his layer's hand seized with excitement, froze on the gun. Cullen promptly knocked him aside and took over himself. Extremely cool and resourceful, he immediately clean knocked out two tanks. Wood on the right did not open fire at once. Baer darted over to him and found that the breechblock, fouled by sand, would not close. He knocked it up with an empty cartridge case and Wood fired. For the remainder of the action Baer stayed in the pit, he and Bombardier Percy Walker knocking up the breechblock for every round until it cleared.

All four guns were now scoring. Their shots struck home like hammers on an anvil, glowing red as they drilled through the steel walls. In two minutes a dozen tanks were crippled, half of them in flames. The nearest column then turned to face the guns with their frontal armour and attack them. As they came on, they struck with every weapon in their armoury – with machine guns, high explosive and shrill scream of close-passing armour-piercing shot. The gunners, filled with exaltation at their swift success, stuck to their guns and gave shot for shot. A great long-gunned Mark IV Special bore down straight upon Cullen, approaching to within 100 yards, 'hideously menacing', its machine guns blazing and its bullets penetrating the gunshield. Cullen stood fast and he and Binks hit it together. A minute later Binks's gun, after having knocked out four tanks, was smashed to pieces by a direct hit. Except for himself, all his detachment were killed or mortally wounded, one of them having his head severed from his body. Cullen, a model of steady hand and heart, was also hit, together with his excited layer Gunner Evans. On the gunner's left, some of Irwin's platoon also engaged vigorously. Three tanks and a self-propelled gun fell to Sergeant Pearson, but his own gun and Sergeant Brett's were, in turn, knocked out.[203] Meantime, bursts of fire from the Rifle Brigade machine-gunners streamed out on the enemy tank crews as they sought to escape.[204]

Lt Irwin had ordered the guns to hold fire until the nearest tank was only 100 yards away.[205] Sgt Newman of 15 Platoon claimed four tanks, an SP gun and a Mk II panzer, from which a man wearing a three-quarter-length white jacket baled out, Newman thinking that he might be the commander of the group. The riflemen of 'A' Company also hit these tanks as they were good targets, watching as they were hit, the crews baling out providing the riflemen with targets.[206] Shortly afterwards, Brett's gun, also part of 15 Platoon, was knocked out, while the remaining tanks were effectively engaged by the 2nd Armoured Brigade before withdrawing to hull-down positions some 800-1,000 yards away. They contented themselves with plastering the position with devastating machine-gun fire, further reducing the complement of the garrison, where not only were the majority of the NCOs and officers killed or wounded but several of the gun crews were down to two or three men.

Battalion Overrun and Codes Destroyed

The commander of the second group of tanks saw what was happening to the first and sent fifteen Mk III panzers forward to assist, advancing cautiously onto the north-west sector of the position. The Battalion HQ was now subjected to the most danger that it had faced all day: at 1730 hours, these tanks drove straight at them with machine guns blazing. As they advanced it became more and more likely that the position would be overrun. Marten therefore proceeded to destroy the codes, marked maps and any secret documents.[207] These were soaked in petrol and held outside the dugout to set fire to them between bursts of machine-gun fire, Marten recalling that 'they burnt very satisfactorily'.[208] At that moment they received a message in code from Brigade HQ that now could not be read, so a request was made that it be repeated in plain language.

Three of the fifteen panzers now elected to take up hull-down positions about 500 yards from Battalion HQ. Making excellent use of the desert terrain and ensuring that the gunners could not bring their barrels low enough to hit them, they proceeded to rake the area with 50-mm guns and machine guns continuously until well after dark. The remaining panzers continued their advance, spraying the position with their heavy machine-gun fire. By now there were only three guns that could be brought to bear, and these averaged ten shells each.[209] Newman's gun was almost immediately put out of action, and Cpl Fulton, operating in the number three position, was wounded, but the two remaining guns were ready. Cope's gun, operated by Hine since 1200 hours, and Miles' gun almost immediately came under intense machine-gun fire, resulting in Miles being wounded. The remaining crew – Cpl Driscoll and riflemen de Ros and Solomons – were driven to seek cover in a slit trench. The remaining gun, from Holt-Wilson's 14 Platoon, held in reserve with HQ Company, originally commanded by Savill but now by Chard, was pointing in the wrong direction. Sgt Ayris, whose gun had fired two rounds and then stopped firing earlier in the day, now joined Chard and Holt-Wilson.[210] The three men turned the gun in the soft sand from a bearing to the south-west to that of a north-west direction, attracting concentrated machine-gun fire, with bullets hitting and piercing the gun shield whilst doing so. Chard waited until the tanks were within 200 yards before firing, setting two tanks on fire and damaging a third, but owing to a shortage of ammunition was unable to set it on fire.[211] Those who were able were sent out to obtain more ammunition. Rifleman 'Simmie' Simmons, who had been manning Savill's gun, now left the gun in search of ammunition and was sheltering in a 'C' Company slit trench with Rifleman Harding, who was firing from this position. Harding recalled that 'as he left the trench to continue his search he was hit squarely in the body by a shell – killing him instantly'.[212]

Meanwhile, Hine led his crew to Cope's gun, whose crew had been killed or wounded. With eight Mk III panzers approaching his position, he waited until the first tank was within 200 yards and then knocked out two of them, setting one on fire. Crimp recalled a panzer advancing towards the 'C' Company sector:

> He stops again. His gun veers slightly, till its horizontal. And when he fires the atmosphere seems to sustain a stunning impact. My tin hat hits my head with a hard jolt.[213]

Swann, at this time in the Battalion HQ, saw the tanks advancing at about 100 yards[214] from the unmanned gun of Miles to his right. He later recalled:

> Sergeant Miles had been hit. It was then that I decided that I'd better go across myself, so I stood up and started to run. I had about fifty yards to run and as I did so the German tank opened up with a machine gun. I straight away went to ground and crawled thirty or forty yards on my stomach [...] I hit the tank, over open sights and jammed his turret. I then put another round up the breech and put this one into him, taking careful aim and this time I really hit him. Two chaps baled out of the top and ran, and they left one chap inside badly wounded who was screaming out for help. He screamed for hours on end.[215]

Swann then took on the second tank and set it on fire.[216] 'Another tank came around the side and I got one at him quick.' Rifleman Suckling remembered:

> At about 1700 hours another counter-attack came in. By the sound, there wasn't so much fire coming from our anti-tank guns. Whether they had been knocked out or were just short of ammunition we didn't know. I glanced back behind me, and to the right rear was a Panzer III. This was our lot. We knew that there was a 6-pounder anti-tank gun to our right and facing the front, but there was no firing from it. If any of us were to crawl to it, perhaps we could have a go at the Panzer. We did a John Wayne, raising a tin hat above our slit trench; the tank gave it a burst from his machine gun. It would have been suicide for any of us to get over and have a go. All of a sudden there was an explosion over our position. We all thought that this was the tank firing, then there was a pall of smoke and the smell of burning rubber. The Panzer was burning. It seems this tank was knocked out by Sergeant Swann.[217]

Wintour was in the battalion command post, expressing his own exhilaration and that of the riflemen by leaping up and down, shouting, 'He's got him, he's got him, he's got him!'[218] With the machine-gun fire lessening, Miles' crew, who had sheltered in the slip trench, were now able to return to the gun to assist Swann. The two other panzers were set alight, one after being hit by all three guns and the other by Chard's gun. Hine fired the gun again, putting a shell through a panzer at about 100 yards, that then continued its trajectory, hitting another panzer 10 yards behind the first, which backed away before bursting into flames at about 500 yards.[219] The panzers then withdrew to take up hull-down positions about 800 yards away, but continued to spray the position with their heavy machine guns.

1830 Hours

The enemy, Germans and Italians alike, had now had enough of the small garrison. Their War Diary states that 'the defensive effort of the extremely well dug-in enemy remained undiminished' and that 'the 5th Panzer Regiment task could not be achieved'.[220] This was quite fortuitous, as on average those guns that could still operate were down to their last three shells.

About twenty tanks remained, approximately 1,000 yards away, and Marten ordered a message to be sent to Brigade HQ, reading: 'Twenty tanks lying doggo in valley to the north of us at about 1,000 yards. We are being swept by machine-gun fire from tanks. Expect attack any moment.'[221] He recalled that they could not even raise their arms without drawing fire, but, staggeringly, nearly seventy tanks and self-propelled guns, just seven British, lay destroyed around them. The vehicles:

> [...] lay wrecked or derelict, many still burning, and the black smoke from their fuel trailing forlornly across the desert. To these were added the shattered remains of several tracked and wheeled vehicles [...] Hanging out of the open turrets of the tanks, or concealed within their bowels, were the charred corpses of their crews who had been unable to escape the flames.[222]

Within the perimeter were the wrecks of the seven British tanks, one panzer and the sixteen Bren carriers, several jeeps and ten guns. Five other guns had been damaged, leaving only six guns out of the original nineteen that could be relied upon to engage, manned by Swann, Hillyer, Wood, Chard, Calistan and Hine. Supporting them were a mixture of the original crew and those of other guns that had been knocked out, but the ammunition situation was really desperate. Within this panorama of desolation and death there still remained gallant men, red-eyed, coated with dirt and sweat, hungry and thirsty, but with a spirit that was even higher than when they had first set out.

Bosville Signals the Garrison

Back at Divisional HQ plans were laid for the relief of the Snipe and Woodcock garrisons by the 133rd Infantry Brigade: the 5th Royal Sussex to Snipe; and the 4th Royal Sussex were to relieve Woodcock at 2100 hours that night.[223]

As the Snipe codes had been destroyed, the news that they were to be relieved had to be sent by Bosville in plain language code, but not in easily understood terms as the Germans used English-speaking Polish soldiers in the 'Y-intercept' department who could translate. The message sent read:

> Friends will come and take your place at dinnertime;
> You will have to wait until they are happily settled in your place;
> Your transport will then arrive and bring you home.[224]

Turner, but more probably Marten, understood that they would be relieved, and would be transported out once the men of the 5th had taken their places. However, what they did not know was at what time this would take place! They asked, 'Will it be an early dinner or a late dinner?' and the reply was, 'The fashionable hour!'[225] The fashionable hour for dinner in Cairo was anytime between 2030 and 2230 hours, so it did not help them very much, but Marten decided correctly that they meant 2100 hours.

Between 1930 and 2000 hours the twenty tanks lying doggo now moved away north-west to a night laager. The garrison showed their defiance by firing off their remaining shells at the retreating silhouettes at about 1950 hours and brewing up a tank at approximately 1,200 yards.[226] Turner recalled that this was 'more as a gesture of relief than any hope of hitting them!'[227] As darkness fell over the desert the damaged enemy tanks that could be moved were towed away,[228] with teams collecting their wounded men and the riflemen becoming concerned that the enemy might launch a night attack that the garrison would have little chance of repelling. Marten recalled:

> The Germans were quite active recovering their tanks and collecting wounded. We didn't dare disturb them, even when they came quite close, as we were still getting wounded away, and they were in greater force than we. To start a fight wouldn't help the relief, which anyhow would be a tricky business.[229]

Marten called together the company commanders and those who had temporarily taken their place, stating that the position was still isolated and almost out of ammunition,[230] but that they were to be relieved and gave instructions about how the garrison would pull out:

- The remaining jeeps, carriers and one 13-ton lorry[231] were to remove the seriously wounded to the 51st (Highland) Division advanced dressing station without waiting for relief;
- The battalion should stay on position until about 2100 hours, withdrawing to the area approximately two miles due east of the start line of the previous night, where they would rendezvous with the transport arriving behind the 133rd Lorried Infantry Brigade;
- In the event of an attack, any action to be taken was left to the discretion of company commanders, but in any event it would probably be necessary to destroy all equipment which could not be carried, and get the men away on foot.

The Riflemen Withdraw

The wounded were carefully loaded in the remaining jeeps and carriers, although it was a long business. Two of the jeeps – one carrying the 'wretched' Crowder who was in fearful pain,[232] Naumann and several others – ran into a 'Hawkins' minefield laid by the sappers of the 45th Royal Tank Regiment to the rear of Kidney Ridge,[233] who probably did not even know that the garrison was in front of them. Marten recalled, 'Both blew up. Although nobody received worse injuries than bruises or broken eardrums, it can't have done them any good.'[234] Bird and Turner, who were in the same jeep, fell asleep, only for Bird to be woken and told by the driver that they were in a minefield. Leaving the jeep, he walked in front of it until he thought with incredulity, 'What am I doing?' and got back in, telling the driver that they were in the clear, when in fact they were not![235] Eventually they arrived at the New Zealand dressing station.[236]

The south-west sector received more machine-gun fire from the three hull-down tanks in the area of Hill 37, and with the fear of a night attack by infantry still high, the forward motor platoon and machine-gun platoon of 'C' Company started creeping towards Company HQ as machine-gun tracer bullets passed over their heads. This appeared to the defenders further back as if an attack was taking place, and 'C' Company HQ immediately sent a report to Battalion HQ that they were under attack and withdrew, fortuitously not opening fire. Turner later said, 'This could have had a disastrous outcome, but luckily the returning riflemen were recognised.'[237] Marten recalled, 'The remainder of us waited for the relief.'[238]

It was now 2130 hours and there was still no sign of their 'friends'. The officers commanding 'A' and 'B' companies decided it was time to withdraw on foot. A confirmation was requested from Brigade HQ, who replied that if no relief had arrived by 2230 hours, the guns were to be made unoperational and the battalion was to march out.[239] An hour later, having not seen the 5th Sussex and in accordance with instructions, Marten told the remaining companies to pull out:

> [...] and I waited on with a few people [while] we hastily rendered all the guns useless (of the original nineteen, ten were completely knocked to bits by enemy fire, and five others damaged) and cleared out.[240]

Calistan recalled that he did 'something you may think rather stupid – I went back and kissed my gun'.[241] Holt-Wilson went round every RB gun position and removed the breech-blocks, rendering each one useless to the enemy. Calistan later wrote, 'Some of our troops are back on our position. I hope they have our guns. We still have the breech-blocks, you know!'[242] Baer of the 239th Battery undertook a similar activity, with one gun towed out by Wood. Leaving the position, Marten 'was the last out together with Headquarters at about 2300',[243] shortly before an artillery barrage by our guns started:

> [...] which landed nicely into the German laager to our north. Being old hands the Germans moved towards us, reckoning that the barrage would move towards them. But it didn't, it thickened both backwards and forward and the German tanks were shifted right into the Snipe position.[244]

Unknown to both garrisons, the relieving battalions were new to the desert, having arrived in September 1942 and had moved up as planned, but to the wrong positions, probably based on the 1st Armoured references. Unwittingly, the 2nd RB and the 5th Royal Sussex must have passed each other in the dark.

The riflemen started their walk back. Those with machine guns led, whilst the walking wounded, supported by their comrades, remained in the protected centre, trudging wearily towards the Star route some two and a half miles away from which they had left thirty-six hours earlier. Rifleman Martin recalled, 'Thirty hours! It couldn't be – it felt like at least a week.'[245] Once they had left the soft sand and were walking on the hard ground, they knew that their ordeal was almost over. But they had left behind fourteen dead comrades with another two missing, a miracle really, but the dead lay where they had died, next to the smashed guns and discarded ammunition boxes, the piles of spent shell cases and contorted remnants of Bren carriers.

> Weary in body but not in spirit, the remnant of the gallant company withdrew in good order, leaving behind them the bodies of their comrades who had won the soldier's highest honour.[246]

Calistan set off to walk back, carrying one of the wounded members of his crew called Freddie, who was hit again and died in his arms. He immediately moved back to fetch one of the last remaining wounded men, whom he brought safely back, still under intense fire.[247] Crimp recalled:

About a dozen of us travel together. The sensation of being able to move freely again after being pinned down on our bellies all day is a delicious relief. We march as quietly as possible, but before we've covered a quarter of a mile, machine-gun bullets come spraying after us. Nobody minds, though, as they're obviously being fired at random and most of them fall short.[248]

Maj. A. F. Flatow TD of 'A' Squadron 45th Royal Tank Regiment recalled:

About 2300 hours [*sic*] I heard the sentry's challenge and I walked forward, expecting to meet a volley of shots. Some weird swaying [shadows] approached us. They were dressed in British uniforms but I was frightened of a trick. My mind itself was full of queer tricks and I asked the first wretched man for AB-64. He nearly cried! 'Lord, Sir, we've been out there for twenty-four hours, shot at by both sides and we're all in. Take my rifle!' They were, it transpired, the remnants of a battalion of the Rifle Brigade.[249]

Rifleman Harding walked back, assisting and half-carrying a wounded comrade in the pitch dark. On reaching the British lines he was cautioned by a soldier in a foreign language. Throwing his gun to the floor and swearing at the soldier, he walked past the picket line and onto the first aid post. He had a well-deserved cup of tea shortly afterwards.[250] It had taken him four hours to get back. Marten said, 'Three miles I walked. They were all asleep at brigade when I got there. Reported to the brigadier, who was surprised to see me. I was bloody tired.'[251]

The Service Corps prepared a hot meal for the returning men. Bird recalled his breakfast as being 'watery porridge, with two fatty rashers of bacon on top, followed by bread and marmalade.'[252] Crimp wrote:

The Colour Sergeant, on orders of the Company Commander, throws open his ration-wagon and spends a busy thirty-minutes handing out loaves of bread, oranges, and tins of sausages, bacon, bully, cheese, fruit, jam and cans of water absolutely ad lib.[253]

Some were able to retrieve bedding from their truck, but for many there were only beds for the wounded and the rest, such as Harding, slept on the desert floor. Rifleman Martin wrote:

Is it possible, I wonder, to put into words the emotions of soldiers who have now reached safety after long hours when death or a crippling wound could happen in a second, any second, during those interminable hours? The usual words of pleasure, relief, happiness, thankfulness are totally inappropriate. Substitute bewilderment, incomprehension, drained, numbed or disbelief.[254]

Snipe was not the greatest operation of the war or even the battle; it was simply the brightest and best example of the Eighth Army's now fully developed method of anti-tank defence.[255] It was obvious that they could not be taught anything about effective anti-tank screens.[256] However, from the riflemen's perspective, and to paraphrase Shakespeare in *Henry V*, 'This was their St Crispin's Day.'

CHAPTER 7

Snipe Continued

The 2nd RB, along with the other units under command, equipped only with its own anti-tank guns and without effective 'all arms support', had advanced two miles into enemy territory and held off about seventy enemy tanks plus SPGs attacking in successive waves over a 14-hour period. Ann Crowder received a letter on 27 October from an officer at GOC, saying:

> I thought you'd like to hear that Tim's [Marten] and Martin's [Crowder] party have had a terrific day, and simply covered themselves with glory. Details must obviously be kept dark, but they were right in the thick of it, held their position and ko'ed tank after tank. Just once they sounded worried – we were following the whole thing only ten minutes behind – but they finished in cracking form, and sounded on top of the world and best of all after that, they'll be reinforced and/or relieved pretty soon. Great work. All my friends from Eton were alongside them, and I can't tell you how thrilling it's all been.[1]

But there was a cost!

Snipe Casualties

The official report of British service casualties for 27 October for the Battle of El Alamein as a whole stated that eleven officers and twenty-six ordinary ranks had been killed; thirty-three officers and 286 ordinary ranks wounded; and fourteen officers and 560 ordinary ranks were missing. Included in these the casualties were those incurred during the Snipe operation by the 2nd RB, which amounted to:

- Two officers killed – approximately 18 per cent of the whole;
- Twelve ordinary rank riflemen killed – approximately 46 per cent of the whole;
- Eleven officers wounded (two missing[2]) – approximately 33 per cent (14 per cent) of the whole;
- Thirty-three ordinary rank riflemen wounded – approximately 11.5 per cent of the whole.[3]

Turner considered this number of casualties 'an amazingly small price to pay for the results achieved'.[4] Crimp recalled later that, as at 30 October, 'There's news of our two casualties, whacked four days ago at Star-Set: the condition of the signals lance-jack from H.Q. is still critical, and Les Beale died in dock.[5] Bird said:

> I knew that we had knocked out a lot of enemy tanks and it was regarded as a great victory but at the time it didn't seem to me like much of a victory. All I could think of was that we had lost all our guns and all my officers had been killed or wounded.[6]

Most of the casualties occurred when ammunition was being moved between guns, the majority as a result of artillery fire, although Salmon and Salt were killed when moving the guns into better positions.

The stoic attitude to duty was evident even after the operation had ended, Bird recalled at The Rifles Officers' Mess, that:

My own wound was a bang on the back of the head. I remained with my company for a day or two, during which I was very wobbly, and our M.O. sent me down to the hospital in Cairo which dealt with head wounds. I was there about 3 weeks.[7]

The major innovation in the field of Blood Transfusion made the Second World War the first major conflict in which it was used to save many lives. Glucose-saline solutions were used to replace the fluid part of the lost blood, giving time to get the injured treated and whole blood administered if needed. However, the other major medical innovation of the time, the wonder drug Penicillin, was not used on Allied troops until 1943, despite going into full-scale production in 1942.[8]

Upon taking command, Montgomery had pledged that those wounded would get immediate attention – quite a new thing for desert warfare, where the mobile format of battle, distances and terrain involved made casualty care difficult. After being treated with the emergency field dressings by their comrades or medical orderlies, the wounded were brought in by trucks and jeeps or by their comrades walking across the dark desert to the first step in the evacuation chain, where they were triaged into three types of wounded:

1. Those who had no chance of surviving, who were put in the 'dead tent' with alcohol, morphia and cigarettes;
2. Those with serious or primary wounds, but who could be helped; and
3. The walking wounded.[9]

The walking wounded were instructed to make their way, often with the help of colleagues, to the main dressing station set up around Alamein railway station. Here their wounds were dressed and further treatment plans decided, including being sent to the casualty clearing station and then back to unit or general hospital as necessary.

Those with serious or primary injuries were sent to the advanced dressing station, where they were assessed and essential emergency treatment given, including transfusions and urgent surgery by the Field Surgical Unit, which consisted of a surgeon, anaesthetist and support mounted on a three-ton truck and staff car.[10] Treatment plans were then put into place and they were moved on to the casualty clearing station thirty miles away from the frontline at El Gharhiyah, inland from Alexandria and east of El Hammam, by means of the motor ambulance convoy. Treatment would be given before the wounded were moved further back to a suitable hospital by convoy, train or, among the 'fortunate' 2,000 of the more seriously wounded, by air.

The dead stayed where they fell. Some bodies were never indentified or could not later be found; these have a plaque at the Alamein cemetery, unidentified bodies being buried with the inscription 'Known unto God'. Rifleman Simmons' name can be seen in the section dedicated to the Rifle Brigade.

The KRRC at Woodcock

Heathcoat-Amory of the 2nd KRRC had been instructed to consolidate the Woodcock position in a similar operation to that of the RB's. With guns of the 76th Anti-Tank Regiment, he had decided to motor 2,000 yards with carriers leading, riflemen and machine-gun platoons and anti-tank portees at the rear, setting off at 2130 hours through the Moon track, then debussing under cover of the artillery barrage to march on foot to Woodcock. Unfortunately, motoring forward in the middle of a web of German strongpoints proved to be a mistake. Just as the order was given to debus, the leading carriers were hit by enemy machine-gun and anti-tank fire from a range of only 75 yards.[11] They resumed their march, with clouds of dust raised by the barrage and their own Bren carriers obscuring their view. The stopping of the barrage signified that they had reached their objective and the riflemen began to dig in and position their guns. However, as with the Snipe position, this was further east than the actual Woodcock strongpoint; they nevertheless held the position for the rest of the day against little opposition.[12] The War Diary noted:

> A large number of enemy tanks kept hovering about the position and several times it looked as though they were going to attack. They obviously did not know who or what we were, and after we had knocked out a couple at extreme range they drew off and the threat came to nothing.[13]

The battalion had thus mounted a successful if confused attack, but their presence beyond the forward edge of the Eighth Army's existing positions elicited little response from the enemy,[14] and despite the operation, Point 33 – the true location of Woodcock – remained in the hands of the *Panzerarmee*.[15]

The Next Attempt

The positions of Woodcock and Snipe had to be retained by the Allies, so it was decided that the 5th Battalion Royal Sussex would relieve and consolidate Snipe and the 4th Battalion Royal Sussex would relieve and consolidate Woodcock. They had been informed by Lumsden and Gatehouse that all they had to do in order to take the two positions was to 'walk through', but as with the 2nd RB and the 2nd KRRC, they were to suffer from a similar locational problem. The 5th RS reached what it believed to be the right piece of desert and dug in. However, the story of the 4th RS was a much sadder one.

Pte Eric Laker of the 4th Royal Sussex Regiment, 133rd Lorried Infantry wrote:

> Almost from the start the manoeuvre was a fiasco – unfortunately for us! We arrived at the appointed starting line at approximately 2215 hours, apparently 45 minutes late, for the preliminary barrage by the Corps Artillery had ceased at 2115 hours. Another barrage had started and been cut short again because we were still not there. Absolute chaos reigned. Officers were dashing here, there and all over the place, trying to put their men 'in the picture' but, owing to the rush, instructions were perforce of a very much abridged nature.[16]

They were then obstructed and suffered several casualties by an enemy who turned out to be the 1st Gordon Highlanders, who had recently taken a position on Aberdeen and thought the 4th was the enemy. Then being subjected to heavy fire from the left, the reserve company was sent to investigate and suppress the opposition, and were nearly annihilated in the attempt by the 115th Panzer Grenadier Regiment. Despite their difficulties, they reached Woodcock and dug in on the western edge, their position turning out to be between some German and Italian units. These attacked at dawn, tanks overrunning the defences, with a loss of forty-seven killed and 342 missing. Pte 'Dusty' Ayling of the 4th recalled:

> We were contentedly playing with our automatics when I looked up and saw some of the fellows climbing out of their slit trenches with their hands up! One even had a white handkerchief tied to his rifle. I blinked and then looked around. I saw a tank that had come over the ridge with others on the right of it. A fellow was sitting on the top with a nasty looking LMG which he was waving around in a most unfriendly manner, and walking beside the tank was another chap with a revolver. He was waving his hands around him indicating to our fellows that they were to come to him and surrender. Then to my horror I saw a black cross on the front of the tank.[17]

Lucas Phillips wrote:

> The brigade had been hustled into these assaults with too little forethought. Like those of 7th Motor Brigade on the night before, the operation had been laid on with insufficient opportunity for reconnaissance, with confusion about map locations and with inadequate measures for ensuring that the assaulting troops were correctly guided to their unrecognisable objectives in the dark obscurity of the desert.[18]

Following the operation of the 27/28th:

> Montgomery had for the moment decided to abandon the attempt to break through in the Kidney Ridge area. He held a conference with Leese, Lumsden and their Chiefs of Staff at eight o'clock that morning, October 28th, at which he decided that Woodcock-Snipe was to become a defensive front.[19]

After Snipe

The action at Snipe had forced Rommel to make repeated and costly attacks against the position, helping to 'tip the balance decisively in favour of the Eighth Army at a critical moment' in the battle.[20] The riflemen's stubbornness frustrated his efforts to destroy the armour of the 1st Armoured Division, as well as inflicting losses on both men and machines that he could ill afford.[21] After watching the counter-attack, Rommel wrote in his diary:

> Every artillery and anti-aircraft gun which we had in the northern sector concentrated a violent fire on the point of the intended attack. Then the armour moved forward. A murderous British fire struck into our ranks and our attack was brought to a halt by an immensely powerful anti-tank defence.[22]

Stephen Snelling has written, 'By holding their ground against all odds, they had proven that infantry, resolutely led and armed with effective anti-tank weapons, could withstand armoured attacks.'[23]

When the riflemen and troopers left the position, the Axis forces continued recovering their wounded and the tanks that could be repaired. According to Lucas Phillips, they left behind them seventy damaged and destroyed tanks and self-propelled guns. The war moved on and, with Rommel in retreat, the killing grounds around Snipe were revisited where the remains of thirty-two tanks (twenty-two of which were German) were found. It was decided a month after the battle to investigate the discrepancies in the various reports and personal recollections of the battle. A Committee of Investigation, appointed to note the location of wrecks on the battlefield and analyse the performance of the guns, stated that twenty-one German tanks, eleven Italian tanks and five SPGs had been destroyed, and a further fifteen or twenty tanks had been hit and repaired.[24] Therefore some fifty-seven enemy armoured vehicles had been knocked out. However, based on the wrecks left on the ground, the minimum number of armoured vehicles destroyed was thirty-two against the maximum number claimed of seventy-nine, nineteen of which were claimed by the 239th Battery.[25] The latter number does take into consideration those armoured vehicles that were destroyed by multiple actions aimed at the same targets.

The 1st Armoured Division also undertook an investigation as to the differences of navigational opinion, finding that the Highlanders had been correct in their positioning.[26]

An article in *The Daily Telegraph* by Sgt Calistan, with the headline 'We Knocked Out 37 Axis Tanks in Egypt', reads:

Described by their Corps Commander as 'one of the finest actions of the war', a company of 8th Army riflemen, cut off by the enemy in the Western Desert, fought on for 36 hours and with their 6-pounder guns knocked out 37 Axis tanks.[27]

Awards for Gallantry

It was suggested that several members of the 2nd RB should be awarded gallantry medals for their work on the 27th, and in November 1942, after much discussion had taken place, the following men received notification of their awards:[28]

Col. Victor Buller Turner   Victoria Cross
Maj. Tom Bird   Distinguished Service Order
2nd Lt Toms   A Bar to his Military Cross
Capt. Marten   Military Cross
Capt. Basset   Military Cross
Lt Flower   Military Cross
Lt Irwin   Military Cross
Lt Holt-Wilson   Military Cross
Sgt Calistan   Distinguished Conduct Medal
Sgt Swann   Distinguished Conduct Medal
Rifleman Cope   Distinguished Conduct Medal
Sgt Hine   A Bar to his Military Medal

Sgt Miles   Military Medal
Cpl Barnett   Military Medal
Cpl Francis   Military Medal
Rifleman Burnhope   Military Medal

Turner always said that he had accepted the VC on behalf of his battalion and not for his work alone, Bird stating at The Rifles Officers' Mess:

> He always used to say that it was the battalion's award. Maybe, but Vic certainly earned it over and over again that day. Wherever the fighting was thickest he was there in the middle of it. There were many deeds of valour. Calistan should have had a VC.[29]

However, as Stephen Snelling has written, 'Turner's greatest triumph was also his last … he was still recovering from his injuries when news of the honours showered on his men came through' and would never hold a battlefield command again.[30] Lt Leyland wrote: 'Our Colonel was awarded the V.C. and I gather there was the hell of a "pissy party" in the coy Mess.'[31] A citation was written and recommended by Brigade, Division and Corps commanders for Calistan to be awarded the Victoria Cross.[32] Disappointingly, as he assuredly deserved it, this was not approved by Montgomery,[33] resulting in him being awarded the Distinguished Conduct Medal to add to his Military Medal received for his conduct during the withdrawal of the battalion to the Alamein Line.[34]

Below is a short description[35] of the medals awarded for actions above and beyond the call of duty.

Victoria Cross

The Crimean War was the first major conflict involving British forces during which journalists from *The Times* portrayed the realities of warfare and the acts of heroism that in the past had gone largely unrecognised. In response to public sentiment and in accordance with the proposal of Prince Albert, which included his design, the Victoria Cross was first struck and introduced in 1856.[36]

Since 1920, the ribbon for all VCs awarded has been red. When the ribbon alone is worn, a miniature of the VC is added. The medal itself, created from the bronze of two cannon captured at the Siege of Sevastopol, is crafted by the jewellers Hancocks of London, who have been responsible for production of all VCs since the award's inception.[37]

This medal is still the highest decoration for gallantry that can be received in the UK, and is awarded for 'most conspicuous bravery, or some daring or pre-eminent act of valour or self-sacrifice, or extreme devotion to duty in the presence of the enemy'.[38] King George V's private secretary wrote:

> The King feels so strongly that, no matter the crime committed by anyone on whom the VC has been conferred, the decoration should not be forfeited. Even were a VC to be sentenced to be hanged for murder, he should be allowed to wear his VC on the scaffold.[39]

The warrant states that it was a medal awarded 'to those officers or men who have served us in the presence of the Enemy and shall then have performed some signal act of valour or devotion to their country'.[40] There is a widespread, albeit erroneous, belief that all ranks must salute a VC holder, but there is no official requirement in the Queen's Regulations and Orders. However, the tradition remains, as mentioned in *Defence News* of April 2007, which stated: 'Chiefs of Staff will salute a private soldier awarded a VC.'[41]

Distinguished Service Order

Instituted by Royal Warrant on 6 September 1886, the DSO is an award in recognition of 'individual instances of meritorious or distinguished service in war', intended for commissioned officers below field rank (i.e. Major) for service in war which did not warrant a VC.[42] After the institution of the Military Cross at the end of 1914, it became unusual for a DSO to be awarded below the rank of Major and after 1917 it was more usually awarded for gallantry in action.[43] The medal is the shape of a cross with a raised laurel wreath in the centre, surrounding the Imperial Crown on a red enamelled background. The ribbon is crimson, sometimes called red, with narrow dark blue edges.

Military Cross

The Military Cross, instituted by Royal Warrant on 28 December 1914, is an award for gallant and distinguished services in action by those of the rank of Captain, Lieutenants and Warrant Officers.[44] In 1915, eligibility was extended to include Majors and in 1917 it was awarded for 'act or acts of exemplary gallantry during active operations against the enemy on land'. Cast in silver, the medal has straight arms finishing with ornamented crowns and the Royal Cipher of the reining monarch at the centre. The ribbon is made up of three vertical stripes of white, deep purple and white.[45]

Distinguished Conduct Medal

At the time of the Crimea War, the private or NCO rarely received reward for gallantry. They might have been mentioned in despatches or gained promotion, but it was not until the DCM was instituted by Royal Warrant on 4 December 1854 that non-commissioned ranks in the Army received an award for distinguished service and gallant conduct in the field.[46] The front originally depicted a trophy of arms, but in 1902 this was replaced by an effigy of the reigning monarch. The reverse of the medal bears the inscription 'FOR DISTINGUISHED CONDUCT IN THE FIELD', restricting its award to those who distinguished themselves in action. The medal is circular in shape with a swivelling ornate suspender and ribbon of three equal parts of crimson, dark navy-blue and crimson.[47]

Military Medal

The Military Medal was instituted on 25 March 1916 and generally awarded to NCOs and men, the Royal Warrant stating: 'We are desirous of signifying our appreciation of acts of gallantry and devotion to duty performed by non-commissioned officers and men of our Army in the Field.' The medal is circular in shape with an ornate suspender, both being made of silver, with an effigy of the reigning monarch on the front and a laurel wreath on the reverse, with the words 'FOR BRAVERY IN THE FIELD' surmounted by a crown. The ribbon is dark blue, with five equal centre stripes of white, red and white.[48]

Bar

On occasions a soldier who had received an award went on to perform another act of bravery that was sufficient to be awarded the same medal again. For the second and any subsequent award of the same medal, he would receive a bar to wear across the ribbon of the first gallantry medal, each bar specific to the medal awarded.[49]

Many of the medals awarded for actions during Operation Snipe and other operations, can be seen at the Royal Green Jackets (Rifles) Museum in Winchester, which is among the top holders of VCs in the world, whether owned by the museum or on loan from individuals.

At the Rifle Brigade Dinner held at the Union Jack Club in November 2007, Brig. Dunphie, as guest of honour, spoke about the El Alamein campaign, completing his narrative with the following:

News of the 2nd RB's action at Snipe went round 8th Army like wildfire, and lifted everyone's morale. Rommel and his armour had acquired a formidable, almost invincible, reputation over the past eighteen months. Now a battalion of 300 riflemen, and in particular the anti-tank guns of S Company and 239 Battery RA, had soundly defeated him and destroyed a large slice of his armour. Winston Churchill was later to say, 'Before Alamein we never had a victory; after we never had a defeat.' A bit rich, perhaps, but Alamein was the turning point of the war in the west, and Snipe was the turning point of Alamein. There was still a week of heavy fighting to go before the final break-through, but, with the defeat of Rommel's armour at Snipe, the end was never in doubt. On the regimental front Snipe became an epic of our distinguished history. Like the Peninsular War, Waterloo and Calais, it became the benchmark against which the post-war generation of riflemen had to measure their standards. And this applied not just to those who served in The Rifle Brigade, but also the riflemen of the Royal Green Jackets – and today to the new riflemen of The Rifles. So long as there are riflemen in the British Army, Snipe will always be studied with intense pride and admiration.[50]

CHAPTER 8

Zero plus 225 days.
After Operation Snipe to Operation Supercharge – the Second Battle of El Alamein

Back to the Battle

On the night of 27/28 October, Rommel sent a message to Gen. von Rintelen pressing him again to 'do everything possible to provide the Army with sufficient fuel'.[1] The second need was for ammunition, concluding the message:

> I have to point out that the Army has drawn attention again and again to the need for adequate supplies of fuel and ammunition. It is therefore those responsible for supply who are uniquely to blame for the present grave crisis.[2]

In his mind, he had won all those victories, and then the quartermasters had got him defeated, writing to his wife:

> Very heavy fighting! No one can imagine the fear hanging over me. Once again, everything is at stake. The circumstances we are in could not be worse. I am still hoping we can pull through. I don't need to tell you that I'll give my utmost.[3]

The 90th Light Division continued their attacks to regain Point 29 from the Australians, but despite the strength and resolution shown in these attacks, they were pushed back on each occasion. The day ended with each side battering the other with heavy shelling, but after four days of fighting, despite the success of the Australians and the resistance shown at Snipe, the British had still not broken through Rommel's main defence.

However, things were about to change, as the reorganisations planned by Montgomery on 26 October were beginning to take effect. At the morning conference on the 28th with Leese, Lumsden and their respective staffs, Montgomery intimated that the Kidney area would become a defended zone held by 10th Armoured Division and then to be handed over to XXX Corps while the 1st Armoured Division was withdrawn. He now shifted the weight of the battle northwards, launching an attack along the coastal road and enlarging the ground already in the Australians' possession around Point 29 to sufficient size to accommodate a firm base for the reinforced New Zealand Division's attack. The attack initially progressed well but then slowed due to resistance by the 164th and 90th divisions, who held their positions despite being badly damaged and having to be reinforced by the 15th Panzer.

The German armour then attempted another counter-attack: the 21st Panzer directed against Snipe and Woodcock, while the 15th Panzer was to make ground towards Miteirya Ridge. Rommel rallied his troops: 'The present battle is a life and death struggle. I therefore require that every officer

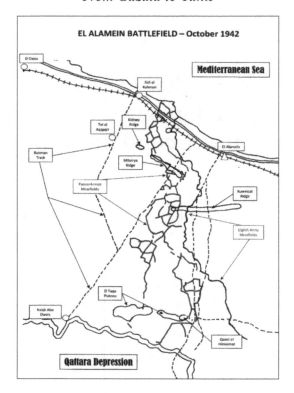

and man will give of his utmost and thereby contribute to its success.'[4] The attacks went forward, but suffered badly from the concentrated fire generated by the artillery and tanks in hull-down positions as well as raids from the Desert Air Force, the attacks first faltering before finally being brought to a stop.

The Australians now continued their advance from Point 29 towards the enemy stronghold known as 'Thompson's Post', a German strongpoint dominating the surrounding desert and formed of multiple trenches and gun pits, with an area of some 1,000 square yards.[5] Rommel wrote:

> I spent the whole of that night [the 28th/29th] with a number of my officers and men on the coast road from where we could see the flash of bursting shells in the darkness and hear the rolling thunder of the battle; no one can conceive the extent of our anxiety during this period.[6]

The 90th Light Division reported in their war diary that 'the northern sector was under a barrage reminiscent of Great War days. The horizon was ablaze with the flashes of enemy guns.'[7]

Churchill's Anxiety

In Britain, Foreign Minister Anthony Eden met Churchill for drinks at 10 Downing Street, saying to him that 'his people' in Cairo had told him that the New Zealanders were being pulled out of the battle and that the Eighth Army was retreating. This seemed to be supported by the daily situation report, which read:

Reorganisation of Corps proceeding according to plan. XXX Corps assumes command of whole

Northern Section. At 2000 hours X Corps (less X Armoured Division) then coming into Army reserve.[8]

However, the enemy intercepts which centred on Rommel's pleading for more petrol, more ammunition and more reinforcements, gave the impression that victory was for the taking. The battle seemed to have stagnated. To Churchill this was most disquieting, and he began to aim outbursts at Brooke: 'What is my Monty doing now, allowing the battle to peter out?' Brooke wrote that it was always 'my Monty' in a crisis. 'Have we not got a single General who can win a battle?'[9] Brooke, supported by Smuts, brought calm to the situation by explaining that Montgomery had:

> [...] advanced the front several thousand yards; did he not remember this entailed a forward move of artillery and the establishment of new stocks of ammunition before another attack could be staged? ... Had he forgotten that the fundamental principle of all strategy and tactics lay in immediately forming new reserves for the next blow? I then went on to say that I was satisfied with the course of the battle up to the present and that everything I saw convinced me that Monty was preparing for his next blow.[10]

These explanations resulted in Churchill sending a telegram to Alexander:

> The Defence Committee congratulate you on the resolute and successful manner in which the decisive battle which is now proceeding has been launched by you and General Montgomery [...] Whatever the cost you will be supported in all the measures which you take to shake the life out of Rommel's army.[11]

As Sadler has written, 'In Montgomery, Churchill had finally discovered a will and egotism to match his own.'[12]

Late that night a much calmer and friendlier Churchill asked Brooke whether he wished he was in Africa directing the battle himself, to which the reply was 'Yes.'[13] The evening ended and they went to their beds, but just before midnight Churchill sent for Brooke again – Bletchley Park had decoded Rommel's daily report in which he described the situation as 'extremely grave'. Thanking Brooke for turning down the offer of the Middle East Command and remaining at his side as CGIS, Churchill said he understood that Brooke could serve his country better by staying in that position than by taking over the Eighth Army.[14] Before finally going to bed, Brooke wrote in his diary:

> This forged one more link between him and me! He is the most difficult man I have ever served with, but thank God for having given me the opportunity of trying to serve such a man in a crisis such as the one this country is going through at present.[15]

Montgomery, however, thought that the BBC was not reporting the full facts and, calling Godfrey Talbot to his command caravan, said:

> 'Talbot, sit down, sit down. The BBC is saying that my men, my soldiers, are having a lull ... Are they using your stuff, Talbot?' I said, 'Well, some of my stuff. And some of it's simply the communiqués issued by your headquarters and your intelligence officers, going through Cairo to London.' 'Well,' he said, 'it won't do. Tell London it won't do. Tell them that the Army Commander has heard them

and they're not giving a true picture.'[16]

Montgomery later wrote:

> It was fairly clear to me that there had been consternation in Whitehall when I began to draw
> divisions into reserve on the 27th and 28th of October, when I was getting ready for the final blow.
> Casey had been sent up to find out what was going on: Whitehall thought I was giving up, when
> in point of fact, I was just about to win … I told him all about my plans and that I was certain of
> success; and de Guingand spoke to him very bluntly and told him to tell Whitehall not to bellyache.
> I never heard what signal was sent to London after the visit and was too busy with Supercharge to
> bother about it. Anyway I was certain the CGIS would know what I was up to.[17]

However, Brooke's own doubts remained:

> On returning to my office I paced up and down, suffering from a desperate feeling of loneliness. I
> had, during that morning's discussion, tried to maintain an exterior of complete confidence. It had
> worked, confidence had been restored. I had then told them what I thought Monty must be doing,
> and I knew Monty well, but there was still just the possibility that I was wrong and that Monty was
> beat. The loneliness of those moments of anxiety, when there is no one one can turn to, have to be
> lived through to realize their intense bitterness.[18]

Meanwhile back in Egypt

The 7th RB were still at El Wishka, in the position between the Australians and Highlanders that they
had occupied on 25 October. During the intervening period they had endured much shelling in the
overcrowded position; accordingly, on the night of the 29th, they were withdrawn twelve miles to the rear
and replaced by the 2nd RB, now under temporary command of Pearson whilst Turner was receiving
treatment. Since Snipe they had been visited and congratulated by all, from senior staff to other soldiers,
and had been paraded on the Qattara road for review by generals. Rifleman Martin recalled:

> […] the top brass came, smiling and friendly and chatty. A war artist perched on a box 10 yards
> away drew the scene. Monty sent a message and we had an extra ration of Victory Vs.[19]

Crimp wrote:

> Battalion parade for a bunch of red-tabs who come to confer the express congratulations of the
> Army Commander. The General who delivers the message lauds our recent exploit as a magnificent
> performance. All through the day, he says, he was in wireless touch with our Batt. H.Q., and was
> always wondering whether we'd get put in the bag. But as reports came through of one enemy tank
> after another being knocked out, excitement at Div. H.Q. had grown terrific.[20]

Their stay at El Wishka was short, as they were soon returned to their role with the MTF supporting
the 1st Armoured in their successful attacks along the coastal road.[21]

The Panzers Attack

It was then that von Thoma convinced Rommel that the attack along the coast was of secondary importance and that the main attack would take place further inland. Based on this it was decided that the 21st Panzer would attack the New Zealanders, whilst the 15th Panzer, Littorio and Trieste divisions would attack from the west along the Rahman Track near to Tel el Aqqaqir. As previously happened, the attacks were hit by the Desert Air Force, concentrations of artillery and the high-explosive shells from the Sherman tanks resulting in a high level of casualties and loss of yet more armour. By midday, Rommel and von Thoma had accepted defeat, and the attack was called off.[22]

The situation from Rommel's point of view was now very serious. The panzer strength had been ravaged over the last five days and despite being augmented by forty-six new or repaired tanks, was still down to half the number that they had started with.[23] The *Panzerarmee* was daily being shattered, captured, crazed and exhausted by the sustained pressure of the British offensive. Interrogation of captured soldiers showed 'a definite weakening of morale and that our Arty concentrations were having a devastating effect both on infantry and tank personnel.'[24] However, they were still holding the Eighth Army, and Montgomery noted in his diary: 'It is essential to break through somewhere.'[25]

During the early hours of 30 October, the 90th Light Division undertook four separate and successive attacks on the Australians' position, and at one point German tanks drove up almost to the muzzles of the Australian anti-tank guns before having to pull back.[26] Ultimately, the enemy withdrew during the day as a sandstorm blew up and 'spread like a great shroud over Egypt, half burying the dead and hid for a brief moment the hate and passion of war!'[27]

In response to the withdrawal a fresh attack by the Australians on the night of the 30th/31st advanced through the 90th Light Division, crossing the railway line and coastal road and forming a salient across both, preventing the withdrawal of the 1st Battalion 125th Panzer Grenadier Regiment. This action convinced Rommel that he had been right all along and that Montgomery's plan was to progress through 'Thompson's Post' and onwards to Sidi el Rahman. Accordingly, he started to consider a general withdrawal to Fuka, moving the 21st Panzer Division to Tel el Aqqaqir to form a mobile reserve to counter any breakthrough in the central sector. Rommel's dilemma was how he might break off and withdraw to safer areas – a difficult operation bearing in mind just how committed his forces were and how much of his force did not have transport, as well as the lack of fuel. As Maj. Hastings recorded:

> The whole army in the northern sector was making progress. There was always a chance that this next minefield would be the last; that if the enemy could be dislodged from this one ridge he would pull out altogether or his main position would be penetrated with the most decisive result.[28]

As a result of their activities since the beginning of the battle, the 2nd RB needed some rest and were withdrawn to a brigade concentration located in the northern sector of the coastal road near El Imayed station. Here the battalion was reorganised, receiving reinforcements of ten officers and forty other ranks and a company from 7th RB, which was used to create a new composite company. Within three days the riflemen of Snipe had been supplied with new kit, clothes and weapons, had enjoyed a bath in the portable bath stations, and were ready and able to re-enter the fray.

Supply and Casualty Problems

The supply problem arose again as more bad news arrived at *Panzerarmee* HQ on the 30th. The tanker *Luisiano*,[29] holding 1,459 tons of petrol,[30] had been sunk off the west coast of Greece, twenty miles from Naverino[31] by a torpedo fired from a Wellington bomber, and that it was expected that little fuel would reach the front in the near future. Two days later, the merchant ship *Tripolino* carrying fuel and ammunition was sunk off Derna, again by Wellington torpedo planes, along with the ship *Ostia*.[32] It was now becoming increasingly more dangerous to ship supplies from Italian ports, resulting in fuel having to be flown in from Crete.

From the perspective of the British, it was not fuel and supplies but the human cost that had to be taken into account, with Churchill and Brooke receiving a report outlining the true human cost to the Allies of the battle as at the end of October:

Officers killed	180
Other ranks killed	1,550
Officers wounded	575
Other ranks wounded	5,885
Officers missing	40
Other ranks missing	2,000
Total casualties:	
Officers	795
Other ranks	9,435[33]

The Highland and Australian divisions suffered the highest level of casualties, approximately 1,950 each, with the 10th Armoured Division incurring the next highest level of 1,350.[34] The issue of available fighting strength was a problem for the *Panzerarmee* also, with the Afrika Korps by now carrying a burden of 9,954 sick men suffering from non-battle-related illnesses out of a complement of 52,000 – just over 19 per cent. Added to this were battlefield infantry losses now running at 50 per cent, with their guns having been reduced by two-thirds, as well as now only being able to muster thirty operating tanks. Despite all this, Rommel was not prepared to give up just yet. If he was going to be forced into a withdrawal, it would have to be undertaken before the British made a breakthrough.

Further Panzer Attacks

Accordingly, Rommel ordered the 90th Light to push forward north of the railway, with elements of the 21st Panzer advancing along a coastal track to attack the Australians. The first attack was repulsed by the defensive positions comprising hull-down Valentine tanks and anti-tank guns, forcing the panzers to withdraw. The following three further attacks were made during the day, some involving hand-to-hand fighting, resulting in the enemy taking no ground, although contact was regained with the 125th Panzer Grenadier Regiment, who were refused permission to withdraw as Rommel was still convinced that the main attack would take place along the coast.

Owing to defensive actions, the 40th Royal Tank Regiment, who had supported the Australians' defence, were withdrawn, while at the same time the brigade was replaced by another, the transfer having been completed by 0300 hours. However, for sometime the road to Alexandra was left undefended. If only Rommel had known about the opportunity and had had the petrol to undertake such a daring move.[35]

Tel el Aqqaqir

Despite being convinced that the main attack would take place in the coastal area, Rommel was fully aware that the 'crumbling' period of Montgomery's overall plan had created a large British salient in the direction of the Aqqaqir Ridge, the dominant German position in the north. Those taking part in the withdrawal had to be protected from this salient, as well as the ridge itself. Accordingly, every available Luftwaffe 88-mm and Russian 75-mm anti-tank gun was sent to create an anti-tank screen, with von Thoma moving his headquarters there to take personal command of the defence. The screen was deployed in depth, with smaller calibre PAK 38 and Italian 47-mm guns sited in the folds in the desert, while the heavier calibre 88-mm guns were dug in further back.

Whilst planning the move, Rommel received a report from the *Comando Supremo* that two British divisions had slipped into the Qattara Depression, advanced through the impassable terrain and scaled the sides, to arrive behind the Axis lines, now reported to be sixty miles south of Mersa Matruh. Luftwaffe patrols were sent out to verify this position and movement of armoured reserves was halted until the attack could be confirmed. It was not until the next morning that the report was found to be false, based on a mistake or fabrication, possibly further supporting Rommel's feeling that Italian intelligence could not be relied upon.[36]

Operation Supercharge

Montgomery had decided that the main attack should take place along the coast, but on receiving Ultra intercepts that the 90th Light Division had arrived fresh from being held in reserve he:

> [...] decided on the night of 30th/31st October the 9th Australian Division would attack strongly northwards to reach the sea; this would keep the enemy looking northwards. Then on the next night, 31st October/1st November, I would blow a deep hole in the enemy front just to the north of the original corridor; this hole would be made by 2nd New Zealand Division which would be reinforced by the 9th Armoured Brigade and two infantry brigades; the operation would be under the command of 30 Corps. Through the gap I would pass 10 Corps with its armoured divisions ... We already had the necessary divisions in reserve and they had been resting and refitting ...What, in fact, I proposed to do was to deliver a hard blow with the right, and follow it the next night with a knock-out blow with the left. The operation was christened Supercharge.[37]

The Supercharge plan was designed to:
  a) destroy the enemy armoured forces;
  b) force the enemy to fight in the open, and thus make him use petrol by constant and continuous movement;

c)   get astride the enemy supply route, and prevent movement of supply services;

d)   force the enemy from his forward landing grounds and aerodromes;

e)   bring about the disintegration of the whole enemy army by a combination of the above.[38]

The hoped-for result of this plan would be to force the panzers to fight on battlefields of Montgomery's choosing, during which they would be hammered, forcing Rommel into a major retreat, ultimately out of Africa. Sun Tzu taught:

> The enemy must not know where I intend to give battle. For if he does not know where I intend to give battle he must prepare in a great many places. And when he prepares in a great many places, those I have to fight in any one place will be few.[39]

Niall Barr put it more simply: 'Rommel had been dragged into a frantic dance "round and round the mulberry bush" so that Supercharge could topple him off his perch.'[40]

The specific plan called for an attack along the front, the infantry advancing first, supported by a powerful artillery barrage, and then the tanks of the 23rd Armoured Brigade. Corridors would be cleared through the minefields to allow the 9th Armoured Brigade to advance and break through the enemy gun line, creating a gap that they would hold open for the 2nd Armoured, 8th Armoured and the 7th Motor brigades. They would pass through into the open space beyond, forcing the enemy armour to use up their precious fuel, preventing resupply and ultimately destroying the remaining panzers. Montgomery was fully aware that an attack against an established anti-tank screen was fraught with danger. Freyberg explained before the attack, 'We all realize that for armour to attack a wall of guns sounds like another Balaclava,' accordingly the plan did not sit well with other officers, especially Brig. John Cecil Currie commanding 9th Armoured Brigade, who was concerned that they would be operating over too wide a front and calculated that they would suffer 50 per cent losses![41] Freyberg's response was that Montgomery:

> [...] was aware of the risk and had accepted the possibility of losing 100% casualties in 9th Armoured Brigade to make this break, but in view of the promise of immediate following through of 1st Armoured Division, the risk was not considered as great as all that.[42]

L/Cpl Mick Collins of the Wiltshire Yeomanry recalled:

> The role of the armour was to push through to just beyond Tel el Aqqaqir and this was fine in view of the fact that we would be travelling in the dark, through our own minefields, through a jerry anti-tank screen, through uncharted Jerry minefields plus anything else they planned to throw at us for good measure. As it later transpired we met all these obstacles and I don't think any of our lads enjoyed it one bit.[43]

However, first they had to get through the minefields placed to the front of the ridge defending the 4,000-yard wide by 6,000-yard deep front. For this the 2nd RB reformed the Minefield Task Force, Crimp recalling:

> A brigade of tanks is going through three more minefield gaps on another sector, one regiment to each gap. Our companies will service the gaps as previously, and one Bren carrier from each

company will tack on to each regiment of tanks and liaise with them while they penetrate a few miles forward into enemy territory, reporting progress back to its Company H.Q. during the course of the night.[44]

The operation was planned to start at 2200 hours on 31 October, but was postponed by Freyberg due to organisational problems, to start at 0105 hours on 2 November, by which time the moon was in its last quarter, reducing the time that the 9th Armoured had to complete the task. This time the 'signature' artillery barrage would be made up of 360 guns, provided by the New Zealand, Highland, 1st Armoured and 10th Armoured divisions, one regiment from the Australian Division and two medium artillery regiments,[45] providing a truly awesome barrage that crashed through the exceptionally cold night. Freyberg commented that it was not as impressive as that of 23 October, the New Zealand divisional observers describing the barrage:

> The ground shuddered as mediums and 25-pounders leapt into action. Flashes like lightning momentarily darted skywards showing up the landscape near the guns. Crash followed crash, relentlessly merging into one tremendous rumble as the gunners behind [the] guns sent off 150,000 rounds along a 4,000-yard front.[46]

The Desert Air Force had bombed the area for seven hours[47] to soften up positions at Tel el Aqqaqir and Ghazal station, with sixty-eight Wellington Bombers led by nineteen flare-dropping Albacores releasing a total of 185 tons of high explosive, destroying the signal system at von Thoma's Afrika Korps headquarters. 'The ruddy glow of their burning could be distantly seen from the British lines, illuminating the palls of smoke that hung over them.'[48] Other divisionary attacks made it appear as if the British were attacking all along the front, while the planned decoy attack along the coast forced Rommel to send the tanks of the 21st Panzer there, until the communications were restored and he finally realised where the main attack was taking place.

After three minutes the medium guns switched to counter-battery fire lasting five minutes before the full barrage landed again for twenty minutes while the infantry moved up. After a difficult march to their start line through powdery sand that 'was like walking through snow',[49] the cold infantry started their advance right on time, behind a barrage that was not a single thin line of exploding shells but a massive carpet of explosions, moving forward at a rate of 100 yards every two and a half minutes.[50] Clouds of dust and smoke rose, blotting out the landscape, as the troops moved forward. Sections and platoons became detached from each other and in some cases the lead units pressed into the tail-end of the barrage. It was the Bofors guns firing tracers along set lines to delineate the boundaries that kept some on line, with two or three smoke shells exploding to give notice that the barrage was moving forward. *Generalleutnant* Adalbert von Taysen recalled:

> A 60-minute barrage rained down in the night on our positions by the telegraph strip. At about 1 o'clock the fire stopped. A few minutes later, British soldiers stormed the 1st and 2nd companies on foot and on carts. Six of these agile little gun carriers managed to destroy the anti-tank guns at point-blank range, then the enemy was on top of us. A battle for the cover holes ensued, with rifle butts, spades, hand-grenades and bare fists. You could just see the silhouettes of the attackers against the night sky. The best way to recognise who was friend or foe was by the flat steel helmets the Tommies wore.[51]

Later, William Munday of the *News Chronicle* would write:

> I had driven at dusk into what had previously been enemy lines. The scenery here was never very much, but now the landscape was ripped and torn as if a million madmen with steam shovels had been let loose there during the night. That is what our guns had done.[52]

Now that the infantry had reached their final objective line, the 9th Armoured could start their attack whilst the clearing up of the multitude of Italian and German defensive posts that had been bypassed could take place.

The 9th Armoured spearhead, comprising three armoured regiments: the 3rd Hussars, the Warwickshire Yeomanry and the Wiltshire Yeomanry, had started their 11-mile approach from Alamein railway station at 2000 hours the night before with about 130 tanks, reaching the Grafton start line with just ninety-four. Currie shook hands with a young tank gunner of his brigade, saying, 'We can't fail!'[53] If his brigade could blow a hole in the line, and if 1st Armoured Division could keep close up to him, then the gates of the enemy citadel would be open at last and the battle won.

The creeping barrage covering the armoured advance, delayed half an hour, started at 0615 hours, the leading squadrons closing up behind it. The occupants of the enemy trenches jumped out and ran before the advance. Some thirty-five of the 50-mm guns were destroyed as the tanks drove over them.[54] While it was still dark they had reached the Rahman Track approximately 2,000 yards from their start point.

> As you know, we should have attacked in the darkness; instead we went in at dawn. That half-hour's delay cost us dear. We were like so many targets in a shooting gallery. At one time during the attack, the dawn wind came up and blew the sand away. It seemed to me that there was a half-circle of guns firing at us, and not just a single line of guns but row after row of them. And they all seemed to be firing at once.[55]

Pitt of the Royal Wiltshires wrote:

> Flash, flash, flash … in a great semi-circle of guns of the enemy wink viciously back at him as great balls of fire seem to leap out of the sand and hurtle towards the oncoming tanks. Some miss their mark and bounce on the sand, to die out gracefully like fireworks in the sky. Others land with a sickening metallic clang on the Crusaders and explosions add dull thuds to the pandemonium of sounds that fills the shattered air.[56]

Armed with only a 2-pounder gun, the tanks could do little against the screen but charge at every flash they saw, driving over the pits, crushing men and guns alike.[57] Currie watched as tank after tank was destroyed, placing the gap opened in the gun line in serious of danger of being closed. As the sun rose behind the British lines at about 0740 hours like an enormous gun-flash above the horizon, pushing away the darkness, the armour was revealed – sitting exposed on the track in full view of the heavy 75- and 88-mm guns positioned in the second line of defence. Major Gibbs of the 9th said, 'The whole world seemed to blow up at once!'[58] One after another of the British tanks were knocked out, resulting in seventy-five tanks being destroyed.[59] Out of 400 men, Currie had lost 230.[60] The mist highlighted by the rising sun and the smoke of the burning tanks continued to obscure the battlefield for some time as close-quarter fighting ensued, with the tanks having to eliminate each anti-tank gun in turn whilst others returned fire at point blank range. But the objective of breaking through the anti-tank line on the Rahman Track had been achieved, giving the 1st Armoured Division the 'door-way' it promised.[61]

The MTF had begun gapping the minefields for the 1st Armoured Division before dawn, the vanguard of which was the 2nd Armoured Brigade comprising the armoured regiments of the 10th Hussars, the 9th Lancers and the Queen's Bays. Rifleman Martin and his colleagues had not been happy to take part in another major operation so soon after Snipe, where:

> They'd all felt they'd had a very lucky escape – to attack again so soon was tempting fate too far. Still, there'd been little they could do about it, and once again Albert had spent the previous day checking, cleaning, and stocking up with rations and water, and wondering what lay in store. You can imagine the reaction. The air was blue with recrimination, the utter disbelief at escaping from the trauma of Snipe now replaced by the grim foreboding of a repeat performance.[62]

They advanced down the Australians lanes Diamond, Boomer and Two-Bar in the dark, leading the tanks of the 2nd Armoured Brigade, who by 0700 hours had deployed west of the minefields approximately 600 yards behind the 9th Armoured Brigade looking for the enemy armour and anti-tanks guns. However, as the historian of the 9th Lancers explained, 'It soon became obvious that the 9th Armoured Brigade had had a disaster: tanks were burning all over the desert in front of us.'[63]

The 9th Armoured had sacrificed itself upon the gun line. Currie met Lt Col. Gerald Grosvenor, the commanding officer of the 9th Lancers, saying angrily, 'Well, we've made a gap in the enemy anti-tank screen, and your brigade has to pass through, and pass through bloody quick!' to which Grosvenor replied, 'I have never seen anything, Sir, that looks less like a gap!'[64] As Bierman and Smith have written, 'If they did not punch a hole in the Axis Line they certainly left a crack that was ripe for exploitation.'[65] Freyberg explained further:

> It was a grim and gallant battle right in the enemy gun-line. Although the 9th Brigade did not reach its objective and had heavy casualties, the action was a success, as the enemy gun-line was smashed.[66]

This advance is recognised as one of the greatest armoured regimental actions of the war. Montgomery would write later, 'If the British armour owed any debt to the infantry of the Eighth Army, the debt was paid on November 2nd by 9th Armoured Brigade in heroism and blood,'[67] but Currie was always bitter about the fact that the 2nd Armoured Brigade had not followed closely behind his brigade. However, had they done so they would probably have suffered the same fate.[68]

After receiving an Ultra intercept, Briggs alerted his brigades that an attack from the German and Italian reserves was due from the north or north-west, ordering the 8th Armoured Brigade to link up with the 2nd and the remains of the 9th Armoured Brigade. The MTF was disbanded and the three battalions of riflemen – the 2nd RB (with the 239th Battery), the 7th RB and the 2nd KRRC – rejoined the 7th Motor Brigade at a central deployment area just north of the ridge between the 2nd and 8th Armoured brigades, with instructions also to deploy against the impending attack.

The whole of the northern and western positions were now being heavily shelled, but with great resolution the 7th Motor Brigade deployed around the Rahman Track just as 'all hell broke loose from all directions.'[69] The armoured brigades advanced, with the 2nd Armoured moving towards the embattled 9th, sappers leading the way through blanketing dust and cloying, oily smoke as the enemy tanks and guns punished them, stopping the 8th Armoured, who had been tasked with breaking through towards the south, by the intense fire. Throughout the day the riflemen of the 7th Motor remained opposite the ridge, watching the tank battle unfold, being fairly heavily shelled, taking their share of the punishment from the guns on the reverse slope. This resulted in a number of casualties, including 2nd RB officers Shepherd-Cross and Holt-Wilson, as well as three anti-tank guns.[70] It was then that the 7th RB rejoined the brigade and immediately came in 'for a heavy dose of shelling', resulting in their own casualties. Knowing that the ridge could not withstand this constant level of attack, Rommel decided to bring up the Ariete Division from the south to support the defence, and to send the tanks of the 15th and 21st Panzers to clear the British tanks from the battlefield. The 7th Motor position was now threatened on all sides, although these attacks were never seriously pressed. The 2nd Armoured Brigade reported these to Briggs:

> 40 enemy tanks to NW, 30 to West, 18 to SW are keeping at long-range behind an anti-tank screen.
> 11 RHA are knocking out anti-tank guns with some considerable success.[71]

Just before midday, about 120 enemy tanks made their attack out of the haze in an endeavour to outflank the British.[72] The two forces met in a grim and exhausting combat, in which tanks, anti-tank guns and artillery would all play major parts, including a 'bus service' of Boston bombers flying over and dropping bombs all day. The *Panzerarmee* during the long and suffocating afternoon continued to deal out the most fearful punishment, receiving punishment in return, the 9th Lancers' historian saying, 'For hours the whack of armour-piercing shot on armour plate was unceasing.'[73]

During the afternoon the battalion was withdrawn only to be attacked by Stukas, which had made two attempts at attacking the tanks but were prevented by the Desert Air Force. Twelve out of the fourteen planes were knocked out of the air, but as the 2nd RB had moved outside of the protection of the Allied aircraft screen, they consequently received the attention of the remainder.

The battle continued during the rest of the day, with the German and Italian tanks being fought to a standstill. The observers in the 90th Light Division commented:

> Smoke and dust covered the battlefield, and visibility became so bad that the general picture was of one immense cloud of smoke and dust. Tanks engaged in single combat; in these few hours the battle of Alamein was decided.[74]

It was the hardest hammering that they had received to date, Rommel seeing his armour reduced by 117 tanks, seventy-seven of which were German.[75] However, just as important was the loss of experienced panzer commanders such as Teege and Stiffelmayer.

> It was a crippling loss. The enemy's chances of saving himself from ruin were now small indeed. First Armoured Division had not succeeded in making capital out of the sacrificial attack of 9th Brigade and it had made no ground at all, but it had fulfilled a substantial part of its prime mission of finding and destroying the enemy armour.[76]

The losses were approximately equal between the two forces, but the British losses represented only a portion of the available armour, whereas the Axis losses were most of their tanks. It was the turning point of Supercharge and became known as the 'Hammering of the Panzers'.[77]

It had been a terrible ordeal. Currie, worn with fatigue and harassed with distress at the agony of his regiments, was found asleep by the commander of the 6th New Zealand Brigade. 'Sorry to wake you, John, but I'd like to know where your tanks are.' Currie waved a tired hand at the little group of tanks around him and replied, 'There they are.' Puzzled at his reply, Brig. Gentry said, 'I don't mean your headquarters tanks. I mean your armoured regiments. Where are they?' Currie waved his arm again and replied, 'They are my armoured regiments, Bill.'[78]

Despite the hammering the panzers had received, the enemy anti-tank screen commanding the approaches to the long, low Aqqaqir Ridge was still in place. Supported by the medium guns, it continued to impede the British breakthrough. The Italians briefly supposed that the British had abandoned their efforts to break through and were heartened by the news of the heavy tank losses which the panzers had imposed on Montgomery's armoured units. Italian officer Lt Vincenzo Formica recorded a surge of exultation in his unit on 1 November:

> Officers and men who had lived through the fighting and suffered for months amid the Egyptian desert through the hottest part of the year saw that all their suffering and sacrifices were to be rewarded with the prize every warrior craves: Victory. We assumed we would be launching a counter-attack. The word was 'Christmas in Alessandria!'[79]

To the Allied High Command such delay was intolerable. Unless the armour could break through the defences that night, they would face exactly the same problem the next morning. To further isolate the anti-tank screen, Skinflint and Snipe strongpoints were attacked and occupied, leaving the gun line along the Rahman Track as the only obstacle blocking the Allied advance. It was for this type of situation that the motor brigade was intended, to push the anti-tank defences aside and restore the momentum to the armoured advance. It was therefore decided that, despite the 7th Motor Brigade having insufficient numbers due to losses over the course of the battle, they would attack that night with the aim of capturing a two-mile stretch of ground north-east of Tel el Aqqaqir. Once the position had been taken, the 2nd and 8th Armoured brigades would advance westwards through the riflemen for three and a half miles before being leapfrogged by the 7th Armoured, who would drive on to Ghazal station.

The 7th Motor Brigade Attack Tel el Aqqaqir

For the attack on the night of 2/3 November the three motor battalions were given separate objectives:
- 2nd KRRC on the left, under the command of Heathcoat-Amory, was tasked with consolidating the Aqqaqir Ridge;
- 7th RB on the right, under the command of Lt Col. G. H. Hunt, was to move forward and consolidate the Rahman Track;
- 2nd RB in the centre, under the command of Pearson, augmented by 'B' Company of 7th RB, along with anti-tank guns of 239th Battery commanded by Capt. Dedger, was to take and consolidate a strongly held position 2,000 yards beyond the Rahman Track.

The 2nd and 7th RB would advance in the same direction. Upon 7th RB reaching their objective, the 2nd RB would continue onto theirs. The 2nd Armoured Brigade would then pass through the positions first thing in the morning to exploit the open ground on the other side of the ridge, on the premise that the enemy immediately in front had pulled out. Then, and only then, could the mobile forces drive off across the open desert in pursuit.

The three battalions moved up to their start lines and dug in for a few hours of restless uneasy sleep in the cold, with the sounds of battle echoing all around them, before advancing at 0115 hours on 3 November, each battalion had very different experiences:

2nd KRRC

Battle casualties over the last few days had reduced the battalion to three companies. They had therefore been augmented by two troops of 6-pounders from 76th Anti-Tank Regiment. The combined force advanced with great spirit into the darkness under the powerful artillery barrage, falling 2,000 yards beyond the enemy line of resistance but soon meeting fierce opposition and incurring heavy casualties. Continuing, they crossed the Rahman Track and advanced onto some high ground, believing that they were on the Tel el Aqqaqir Ridge – in fact, they were not on the ridge but still east of the Rahman Track[80] – but in their eyes the objective had been reached and they confirmed that Point 44 was under their control. However, after starting to dig in they found that their position was too exposed. Despite the terrain allowing only eight of their guns to be brought up, the battalion remained in their position for the rest of the night, before being joined by the 10th Hussars in the morning and seeing the remnants of the Littorio Division coming over the ridge. They proceeded to knock out an Italian tank at 800 yards and forced the other tanks to pull away to hull-down positions from which they shelled the battalion. The riflemen 'gave as good as they got', knocking out a further six enemy tanks before withdrawing and returning to their lines as the sun rose.[81]

7th RB

Whilst the artillery barrage thundered over the 2nd KRRC, the 2nd and 7th RB advanced on 'silent' attacks. Cpl Donald Main recalled:

> In the early evening we were told that [we] would attack at midnight to force a gap for our tanks. It was considered that the area of the Rahman Track was lightly held, although we never found out who was responsible for this view. As we had motored into the line we had heard shouts for stretcher bearers, presumably from the Sherwood Foresters and Green Howards, who were survivors of the previous attack. In view of the barrage, it would have been suicide to attempt to reach them. It was therefore decided that we would make a silent attack, i.e. without a barrage from our guns, although the 2nd KRRC on our left and the 2nd Battalion Rifle Brigade[82] on our right were to receive artillery support.[83]

The 7th RB had advanced to within about 50 yards of the enemy defences when all hell broke loose, as they received heavy fire from the flanks. Main continued:

> Above the noise of the explosions I heard the Company Commander, Major Trappes-Lomax, shout 'Up the Rifle Brigade! Charge!' Major Trappes-Lomax disappeared through a hail of tracer bullets.[84]

They took their objective, taking shelter in enemy trenches before attacking the enemy anti-tank and machine-gun posts, but found that it was impossible to bring up their anti-guns as the enemy had not vacated their positions and had in fact reinforced them. The two opponents entered into a fire-fight, with the enemy advancing, waiting to the last minute before opening up with everything they had, spraying the positions with machine-gun fire. Against these counter-attacks they had no option but to withdraw. Main recalled, 'We met Major Trappes-Lomax and found that only twenty-two of the Company were left. We also met up with the surviving KRRC and our 2nd RB.'[85]

2nd RB

Having had very little time to reconnoitre the target area, the 2nd RB advanced, but with insufficient transport, supplies or guns due to the soft-skinned vehicles and some of the platoon gun portees having remained at the rear positions. Not having any wireless sets, they could not be contacted. To make matters worse, Pearson and the Intelligence Officer had not arrived at the start line until less than an hour before zero.[86]

On reaching the first enemy positions, the battalion attacked with 'A' and 'B' companies in front, supported by the carriers who ranged ahead in line abreast, advancing in a due west direction intending to attack the enemy directly opposite them, whilst 'C' Company to the rear mopped up any bypassed enemy units or those not directly in front of the advancing riflemen.

After advancing 2,000 yards towards the track they came across a position that appeared to be unoccupied. However, it suddenly came alive, laying down some ineffectual small-arms fire, which was soon cleared up by 'B' Company. The battalion now received heavier fire from a 50-mm gun and an 88-mm gun behind them, and it became clear that the enemy had moved round to their rear, pinning down 'A' Company on the right and 'C' Company, who were in reserve, resulting in the destruction of four of 'A' Company carriers. 'B' Company attacked and captured the 88-mm gun position, during which Lt Trollope-Fellows was killed.[87] The leading companies resumed their advance again, despite facing considerable machine-gun fire from the front and still receiving fire from the rear, which was becoming more of a problem than 'C' Company could deal with.

Another position to the front, containing a large number of anti-tank guns, machine guns and infantry small arms, was encountered and consolidated at considerable cost in casualties by the lead companies, who proceeded to dig defensive scrapes in the hard, rocky ground before continuing to clear out other positions. Clearing of a number of smaller positions was then undertaken, with the riflemen taking on the enemy in close-quarter fighting with revolver, rifle and sword, leaping into gun pits to overcome the gun crews. But even these additional positions provided little extra cover. It soon became clear that they faced an enemy that far from vacating their positions had indeed reinforced them, finding themselves in the middle of a strongly held enemy position that prevented the bringing up of the anti-tank guns.

The heavy mortar and machine-gun fire continued, reducing the fighting strength of both the 2nd RB and the twenty or so riflemen from the 7th RB, who were all that remained of a company that had managed to link up with the battalion, to such a level that they had insufficient men to hold their hard-won positions. Expecting an armoured counter-attack at any moment, Pearson now had no more than sixty officers and men in his command.[88] At about 0400 hours, Bosville gave orders for the withdrawal of the 2nd RB. Capt. Mosley and Pearson met to discuss the withdrawal whilst standing in a captured 88-mm gun position, when Mosley and Rifleman Wade were killed by the very accurate sniper fire that had been targeting the position.[89, 90, 91]

The expected enemy counter-attack now took place, with ten tanks firing at the battalion, who called for star shells and Desert Air Force flares to light up the area. However, despite this illumination, the enemy still managed to work themselves around to their rear, making any withdrawal perilous. The riflemen could not remain where they were, so with the wounded piled on the remaining carriers and everyone else hanging on wherever there was room they drove 'bald-headed' through the enemy positions, encountering much fire from enemy machine guns, 20-mm guns and tanks, but making away without further significant casualties. Rifleman Martin recalled:

> As they hurried back across the Rahman Track, shelled and harried all the way, they saw over twenty Stukas approaching. So, too, however, did a dozen Hurricanes, who immediately swooped in to attack. The RAF, as ever, was equal to the task and quickly saw them off.[92]

In the air battle that now took place several of the Stukas were shot down, but more importantly the Stukas jettisoned their bombs not over the riflemen but mistakenly over their own forces.[93]

By first light, most of the riflemen had returned to the previous day's reserve positions, but 'C' Company and two motor platoons of 'A' Company who had been out of touch for most of the action, did not find their way back to the lines until later in the day. Maj. Hastings noted, 'The cost of this unsuccessful trifling, inconsequent, nameless battle, was almost as heavy as that suffered at "Snipe" ',[94] with Cpl Donald Main discovering at roll-call that his company had only fourteen men left and his platoon only three.[95] Rifleman Martin recalled:

> It took some hours for our scattered vehicles to gradually come together and form into a ragged battalion leaguer [laager]. Then came the reckoning. During the night we were oblivious to events occurring more than 100 yards away; now we found we had again suffered many casualties, experienced irreplaceable men whose loss would be felt for a long time to come.[96]

With the unsuccessful attempt and subsequent withdrawal of the 7th Motor Brigade, the scheduled attack for 0530 hours by the 2nd Armoured Brigade was cancelled, as were the further attacks of 2nd and 8th Armoured brigades. However, the continual pressure that Montgomery was applying to Rommel's forces was whittling away the enemy strength to the point of near collapse, and as night came Rommel and von Thoma assessed the situation.

- The battle was now lost and they were outnumbered and outgunned;[97]
- The anti-tank screen had held and the Eighth Army had not broken through, but at a terrible cost in men, with a significantly reduced number of anti-tank guns;[98]
- They now had only thirty-five tanks operating along the entire front,[99] and no tank reserves available;[100]
- With no reserves of men or equipment; the *Panzerarmee's* grip was weakening;[101] and
- Rommel had to save what he could,[102] but it was inevitable that the Eighth Army would at some point, and soon, break through. *It was therefore time to withdraw.*

Rommel noted in the *Panzerarmee's* daily report:

> After ten days of uninterrupted fighting our own losses are exceptionally high, due to the overwhelming superiority of the enemy's infantry, tanks and artillery and the unremitting use he has made of his air force. In the coming night and on 3rd November we expect new attempts to penetrate by strong armoured forces … our forces are no longer sufficient to prevent new breakthroughs. As from 3rd November the army is therefore preparing to fight its way back step by step in face of the enemy pressure.[103]

Not having received a response by 1730 hours, Rommel instructed his troops to begin the withdrawal. In a letter to his wife, dated the 3rd, he wrote:

> The battle is going very heavily against us. We're simply being crushed by the enemy weight. I've made an attempt to salvage part of the army. I wonder if it will succeed.[104]

Rommel sent a further message to the *Comando Supremo*, stating that he was extricating his troops and warning that Italian formations without transport would have to be abandoned.[105] The more mobile units would be swapped during the night for those that would march westwards. Thanks to an Ultra intercept, Brooke had read the message by the next day. Rommel's report was received like a thunderclap by the OKW, now installed at the Wolfsschanze in East Prussia, but was not passed to Hitler until the next day as the officer on duty had been afraid to wake him –he was later reduced in rank. On reading the message, Hitler raved, and reviled Rommel, sending a grandiloquent reply:

> To Field Marshal Rommel. It is with trusting confidence in your leadership and the courage of the German-Italian troops under your command that the German people and I are following the heroic struggle in Egypt. In the situation which you find yourself there can be no other thought but to stand fast, yield not a yard of ground and throw every gun and every man into the battle. Considerable air force reinforcements are being sent to C-in-C South. Il Duce and the *Comando Supremo* are also making the utmost efforts to send you the means to continue the fight. Your enemy, despite his superiority, must also be at the end of his strength. It would not be the first time in history that a strong will has triumphed over stronger enemy forces. You can show your troops no other road than that to victory or death. Adolf Hitler.[106]

Mussolini sent a telegram of similar sentiment via Cavallero.

Rommel, stunned by Hitler's reply, was left wondering what to do. There would be more casualties if his men stayed, but not to obey the order was unthinkable. He telephoned von Thoma, to be told, 'I've just been around the battlefield. 15th Panzer's got ten tanks left, 21st Panzer only fourteen and Littorio seventeen.'[107] Rommel wrote, 'If we stay put here, the army won't last three days … If I obey the Führer's order, then there's the danger that my own troops won't obey me … My men come first!'[108] He came up with a compromise that at least paid lip service to Hitler's orders, appearing to be a readjustment of his forces in order to avoid immediate destruction. Rommel reported back to Hitler on his reduced fighting strength and his level of losses, ending his signal with, 'Every last effort will continue to be made to hold the battlefield.'[109] In order to reinforce his message he sent Lt Berndt to Hitler's headquarters to explain in person that if his orders were upheld, the final destruction of the German-Italian Army would only be a matter of days away,[110] but in the meantime the planned general withdrawal to Fuka was off.

Whilst Rommel's 'readjustment' took place, the British armour had to be held at bay as the *Deutsch-Italienische Panzerarmee* units were pulled back in their ordered sequence, the guns and tanks last, always maintaining a strong rearguard.[111] By daybreak all Axis transport was in full retreat and all foot-bound infantry that had managed to disengage themselves from the fighting were marching westwards, retreating as best they could along the road to El Daba, which soon became solid with Axis traffic presenting very interesting targets to the Desert Air Force. Montgomery received reports of Rommel's withdrawal at 0800 hours, just as explosions were heard in the south as the ammunition dumps were blown up.

Von Thoma is Captured

Rommel refused to believe it when von Thoma advised him that British tanks, armoured cars and a mass of transport were now moving round the southern flank.[112] He surmised that there was nothing to worry about, as the main British forces were committed frontally, with the 7th Armoured Division still in the south and therefore had nothing available with which to undertake this manoeuvre.[113] After trying to convince him of the situation on two further occasions, von Thoma decided to go out on a personal reconnaissance in his private tank to obtain concrete evidence in support of his point.

At 0805 hours, von Thoma reported, 'The situation will become critical if the 150 tanks continue their pressure. Have been engaged.'[114] Shortly afterwards, his ADC returned to Bayerlein, saying that the wireless had been destroyed and accordingly the General had told him to return. A concerned Bayerlein went out in an armoured car to find the General driving straight into the tank battle between the 1st Armoured Division and the remaining panzers.[115] He recalled:

> A hail of armour-piercing shot was whistling about me [from the tanks of the 10th Hussars running towards Tel el Mampsra]. It was a place of death, of burning tanks and smashed flak guns.[116]

The remainder of von Thoma's panzers had attacked and destroyed a Crusader squadron before heavier British tanks came forward, redressing the balance and pushing the panzers back, but not before Briggs' own tank had been knocked out by an 88-mm gun.[117] Unexpectedly, a Mk III panzer crested a dune and was immediately knocked out, the crew pinned down by shell fire from the 11th RHA. About 200 yards from Bayerlein, a man standing next to the burning tank, holding his pistol by the barrel and with a white handkerchief in his other hand, started walking slowly forwards. It was Gen. von Thoma. Capt. Grant-Singer, leading the reconnaissance troop, met him, took his pistol and made him his prisoner, before both officers shook hands.[118] Grant-Singer reported to his commander, 'I've got something here, Sir. I don't know what it is but it looks good!'[119] At the same moment, some 300 Germans who had been sheltering in slit trenches amongst the tanks rose and surrendered.

Von Thoma had dinner that evening with Montgomery, who thought he was a 'very nice chap' and relished the opportunity of discussing a battle with an opponent so soon after it had been fought.[120] Liaison Officer Carol Mather recalled, 'This was a great feather in his cap really. It was just the kind of situation he enjoyed. And it was a very amusing meeting.'[121] When Churchill heard about the dinner he sympathised with the German, saying, 'Poor man; I too have dined with Montgomery.'[122]

During his flight to England, von Thoma relayed to Air Vice Marshal Collier[123] that he considered the Alamein battle to be similar to that of Gen. Nivelle's tactics on the Western Front in 1917, and that the Axis campaigns through Africa had really been tactical and not strategic, having not been able to take Alexandria or Cairo.

The Dam Breaks

Attacks launched on the evening of 3 November initially did not fare well. The Highlanders' advance became bogged under heavy enemy fire, but the attack by the 5th Indian Brigade saw the enemy defence melt away as they withdrew, leaving only stragglers to meet the Indians.

Rommel discussed the situation with Bayerlein, who as a result of von Thoma's capture had now taken over command of what was left of the Afrika Korps, and then met Kesselring who said that, in his opinion, Hitler's message was an appeal based on his experience in Russia and should be ignored.[124] Orders were therefore issued at 1530 hours for the retreat to be restarted. The decision could at least be the means of saving the motorised part of the *Deutsch-Italienische Panzerarmee* from destruction, although the losses in men and units over the twenty-four hour hesitation were immense. As the Official History states, Hitler finally replied that evening: 'I have caused Il Duce to be informed of my views. In the circumstances … I consent to your decision.'[125]

The Highlanders undertook another attack at dawn on 4 November. Maj. Anthony Wingfield recalled:

[We were] directed onto Tel el Aqqaqir, the top of the whole ridge to our front. They found the enemy gone. 2nd Armoured Brigade was ordered to advance immediately, with 10th Hussars leading (always their rightful place!), with The Bays on the right and 9th Lancers on the left.[126]

Montgomery noted in his diary on the morning of the 4th at 0630 hours that 'the armour went through as the dawn was breaking; the dam had broken!'[127] On the one hand he was pleased that the breakthrough had finally been made, but on the other he wished the enemy had stayed and fought, providing him with the opportunity of finally destroying the *Deutsch-Italienische Panzerarmee* in situ.[128] Lt Formica wrote:

As we drove, vehicles of every sort crossed our path, carrying pale and battered men. When I questioned officers and soldiers I realised that our whole line had cracked. It seemed impossible![129]

Rommel wrote in the early afternoon:

[…] powerful enemy armoured forces had burst a 12-mile hole in our front, through which strong bodies of tanks were moving to the west. As a result of this, our forces in the north were threatened with encirclement by enemy formations twenty times their number in tanks. There were no reserves, as every available man and gun had been put into line. So now it had come; the thing we had done everything in our power to avoid – our front broken and the fully motorised enemy streaming into our rear. Superior order could no longer count. We had to save what there was to be saved.[130]

Montgomery, who had been made fully aware of the general retreat, now regrouped his 'Corps de Chasse' made up of the New Zealanders, 1st Armoured and 7th Armoured Divisions, with instructions to break through south of Tel el Aqqaqir and wheel to the right, up to the coast, to cut the enemy's line of retreat.

Good News Sent Home

On the night of 4 November, the BBC radio announcer interrupted the programme to warn listeners not to switch off their radios, his voice shaking with excitement, 'as the best news in years would be given at midnight'. Later, he forgot the usual traditional neutrality: 'Here is some excellent news which has come in the last hour. The Axis forces in the Western Desert are in full retreat.'[131] The news was repeated on the radio in the morning with the jubilant announcement that 'the Eighth Army are advancing and the enemy is in full retreat all along the line', the *Daily Express* headline 'Great News from Egypt' dispelling any fear of false optimism.[132] Churchill advised Roosevelt and Marshall of the victory and received back:

> Having been privileged to witness your courage and resolution on the day of the fall of Tobruk, I am unable to express my full delight over the news of the Middle East and my admiration for the British Army.[133]

Brooke wrote in his diary:

> The Middle East news has the making of the vast victory I have been praying and hoping for! A great deal depends on it as one of the main moves in this winter's campaign in North Africa. Success in Libya should put the Spaniards and French in better frame of mind to make Torch a success. And if Torch succeeds we are beginning to stop losing this war and working towards winning it![134]

Once the Alamein victory was beyond doubt, the church bells of Britain, silent since 1940,[135] were to be rung in celebration of victory, as they had rung after the Battle of Waterloo,[136] from Land's End to John o'Groats and via the radio to all of Europe.[137] Alexander presented a draft statement to Churchill:

The Axis forces in the Western Desert after 12 days and nights of ceaseless attacks by our land and air forces are now in full retreat. Their disordered columns are being relentlessly attacked by our land forces and by the Royal Air Force by day and night.

Churchill replied:

> If the reasonable hopes of your telegram are maintained and wholesale capture of the enemy and a general retreat are apparent I propose to ring the bells all over Britain for the first time this war. Try to give me the moment to do this in the next few days. At least 20,000 prisoners would be necessary.[138]

The very next day, after the Eighth Army had captured more than Churchill's requirement, Alexander was able to signal the Prime Minister 'Ring out the bells!' but Brooke 'implored him to wait a little longer till we were quite certain that we should have no cause for regretting ringing them'.[139] Churchill replied to Alexander that he would wait until he was sure that Operation Torch was a success.

On 9 November, Leopold Amery wrote to Auchinleck:

> I know what you must be feeling now. You always have the satisfaction of knowing that the victory of today was only made possible – and indeed the whole Middle Eastern situation saved – by your getting back to Alamein and holding the position there by your personal intervention. There would have been no champagne today if you hadn't put the cork in the bottle in July. So possess your soul in patience.[140]

Churchill spoke after lunch at Mansion House on the 10th:

I have never promised anything but blood, tears, toil and sweat ... Now, however, we have a new experience – we have victory, a remarkable and definite victory. A bright gleam has caught the helmets of our soldiers and warmed and cheered all our hearts ... [The Germans have received] that measure of fire and steel which they have so often meted out to others ... Now this is not the end. It is not even the beginning of the end. But it is, perhaps, the end of the beginning.[141]

The day after, Buckingham Palace announced that Montgomery had been awarded a knighthood 'for distinguished service in the field' and was promoted to a full general.[142]

It was on 15 November that the church bells throughout Britain were rung to celebrate the victory of the desert army at El Alamein. The sound of the bells from Tobruk were broadcast in Britain.[143] Speaking in a world broadcast, Churchill went on:

But the bells also carried with their clashing joyous peals our thanksgiving that, in spite of all our errors and shortcomings, we have been brought nearer to the frontiers of deliverance.[144]

Frank Gillard of the BBC recalled:

Montgomery became the first general in history who was able to speak to all his troops. Generals used to say that in war you only tell the public when it's beginning and, when it's over, who's won – that's all they need to know. Monty never took that view and increasingly he saw broadcasting as the fourth arm of warfare, after the Services. His Army was his first concern, but he used to say to me, 'I'm also talking to the wives and fathers and mothers and sisters back home, and they'll trust me too. And that will be reflected in the letters they write to their men out here.'[145]

The Armour Breaks Free

The pursuit began in earnest on 5 November. In the words of Montgomery, 'That ended the battle.'[146] The breakout had been accomplished, the hunt was on! The battle now changed from one of grinding attrition to that of fluid mobile warfare. However, Montgomery still had to be wary. The Eighth Army had been in this situation before, one officer reminding him, 'We used to go up to Benghazi for Christmas and return to Egypt early in the New Year.'[147] The further Rommel retreated, the longer and more fragile Montgomery's supply line became. But the swaying of the pendulum had to stop and all hoped that this would be the last swing.

X Corps under Lumsden took the vanguard, while Montgomery left XXX Corps under Leese to reorganise to the west of the breakout area. XIII Corps under Horrocks had the task of cleaning the battle area of Alamein, collecting the discarded war material of the enemy and of the Allied forces, as well as prisoners. At 0400 hours, with a full artillery programme concentrated on a narrow front of 600 yards, the 7th Argylls attacked the positions on Tel el Aqqaqir, which they found largely unoccupied.[148] The 7th Armoured Division, led by the 22nd Armoured Brigade accompanied by the 1st RB as its motor battalion, had broken out by 0830 hours – 'clear out of the maze of minefields and set off at last across the open desert',[149] with a wonderful feeling of release from congestion. They advanced west for ten miles[150] beyond Tel el Aqqaqir before encountering any opposition, in this case the remnants of the Ariete Division. The 6-pounders of the 1st RB slugged it out with the M13s and the Bersaglieri mobile light infantry, famous for their cock-feathered helmets, whilst the 22nd Brigade tanks tried to encircle them,[151] the Italians fighting almost to extinction for the rest of the day until they retreated out of reach.

A line, albeit a weak one, still existed nearer the coast, with the *Deutsches Afrikakorps* and 90th Light Division, the remains of the Italian armour, Trento Division, Ramcke's parachutists and finally the Italian X Corps, the 90th especially fighting doggedly from 0800 hours to midday fending off swarms of British tanks. Meanwhile, the 8th Armoured Brigade drove to Ghazal and found 'enemy tanks and transport streaming westwards along the main road, which was quickly blocked and several tanks knocked out. The enemy there, taken apparently by surprise, fell into the bag.'[152]

The XIII Corps began their role in clearing up those enemy units bypassed by the 'Corps de Chasse', the Italians, who with little food, little hope and no transport, had been abandoned. Both German and Italian stragglers were taken prisoner, some of whom had been captured before by the faster moving armour who had taken their weapons but did not have the facilities to retain them.[153] By the evening any doubt that the enemy had not broken was dispelled. The armoured brigades that Montgomery had hoped would break out at dawn on 24 October were now in the open. Heinz Erdmann recalled:

> The front collapsed and we began to retreat. This was definitely the worst for us; the sand was blowing in our eyes, the air and the fighter-bombers, to say nothing of the artillery and tank fire. At night the coast road and wide strips to the left and right were lit up by flares.[154]

The 2nd RB complement was brought up to strength with a company and an anti-tank company less two platoons from 7th RB,[155] before moving forward about eight miles to laager with the rest of the 7th Motor Brigade. They finally set off in pursuit of the enemy on the 5th, reaching El Daba by about 1030 hours, only to find that it was devoid of the enemy but for some forty-five stragglers who had been bypassed by the advance troops. Rifleman Martin felt that the time had been wasted with changed and contradictory orders. If they had been sent directly to a point west of Mersa Matruh they would have had a better chance of overtaking and cutting off the enemy's line of retreat. That evening they were ordered to drive deep in a long turning movement into the desert,[156] making for Bir Khalida, some forty miles south of Mersa Matruh. They drove twenty-six miles in twelve hours over rough country, to meet up with the 1st Armoured Division, who, running out of fuel, stopped sixteen miles short.[157]

The 7th Armoured Division had been ordered to intersect the coastal road at Sidi Haneish, approximately sixty-five miles west of the Rahman Track, but in similar fashion to the 1st Armoured had finished twenty miles short of their objective after running into a minefield and then running out of fuel. By now the enemy had a massive head start and although there was confidence that they could be caught, this was dissipating with every passing hour.[158]

Battle Casualties

The situation that evening told a depressing story from the perspective of the *Panzerarmee*:

- 15th Panzer Division had eight battleworthy tanks, 200 riflemen, four anti-tank guns and twelve field guns;

- 21st Panzer Division consisted of thirty battleworthy tanks, 400 men in three weak battalions, 16 anti-tank guns and twenty-five field guns;
- 90th Light Division had three weak regiments and one depleted artillery regiment;
- 164th Light Division had 700 men and six anti-tank guns;
- The Italian armoured and motorised formations were comprehensively destroyed on 4 November – one after the other, the Littorio, Trieste and Ariete had sent in their final messages to *Panzerarmee* HQ, informing them that effectively they had ceased to exist on an operational basis;
- The Italian infantry, specifically Bologna and the remainder of Trento divisions, fought out of Alamein and marched into the desert without transport, water or food, not out of choice but actually to seek out units of the Eighth Army to facilitate surrender;
- The Folgore Parachute Division fought to the last round before surrendering.

Rommel had escaped with anything but a recognisable army. From the Ultra intercepts the British were able to determine:

- German casualties were 1,149 killed; 3,886 wounded; 8,050 captured;
- Italian losses amounted to 971 killed; 933 wounded; 15,552 captured.

These numbers would increase as the Axis retreat continued, but it was only when the Allies reached the hospital in Mersa Matruh that they discovered the level of non-combat-related casualties not recorded in the numbers above. The hospital was found to be full to capacity with German and Italian troops suffering mainly from dysentery and typhus, a high level of gastric disorders and a serious epidemic of jaundice and diphtheria.[159]

But a very high price had also been paid by the Eighth Army:

- an estimated 2,350 of its men had been killed;
- another 8,950 servicemen had been wounded;
- some 2,260 were missing in action; and
- at least 332 British tanks had been knocked out during the battle, and 111 guns destroyed.

Wimberley of the Highland Division emphasised the level of casualties with the simple words 'Never again!'

6 November

The next morning the 2nd RB were up early to begin the chase. However, in the back of their minds lay the thought that their trucks had been used and abused over the last few months and were in very poor condition and they hoped that they were still up to the job. Along with the rest of the 7th Motor Brigade, they drove sixty miles across the desert and finally caught up at about 1100 hours[160] with the Special Group 288 who had been given the responsibility for the rearguard action.[161] They attacked with their anti-tank guns and machine guns, while the carriers overran the line. Sixteen lorries full of prisoners were rounded up and sent back, while the 7th RB were sent to the rear to be re-equipped and rest, with the exception of one company under the command of Alastair Dudgeon, which came under command of the 2nd RB in order to bring the battalion up to strength.

Both armies were now suffering from fuel problems, the Axis forces becoming almost immobile for lack of fuel. Their saving graces were that they had reached the hard surface of the coastal road, making the going easier, and the rain, taking Rommel out of immediate danger. In the early evening, the storm and subsequent floods turned the desert into a waterlogged quagmire of cloying mud, resulting in even tracked vehicles being able to move only on the road's hard surface and forcing the Eighth Army advance to a halt. The chase by the 1st Armoured, as well as those of the other two armoured divisions, had now stopped as they waited for the storm to pass and for the supplies arrive. The 2nd RB, down to only twenty miles' worth of fuel, were stuck on the Fuka escarpment, where Maj. P. A. D. Boden MC joined them to take over as second-in-command. It was not until 1100 hours the next day that 'B' Echelon arrived, helping but not curing the problem for both armoured divisions. By 8 November they had still not reached the paved coastal road, unlike the 10th Armoured Division, who now advanced to Mersa Matruh without delay, the port being occupied and fully operational later that day.

The 2nd RB Form Columns

In what almost seemed like an effort to further slow down the advance of the 7th Motor Brigade, it was decided that they would be formed into columns in the afternoon, along with heavy guns from the 2nd Royal Horse Artillery. The attachment to these slow and unwieldy artillery units hampered the fast-moving motorised riflemen, resulting in them not being able to catch up with the enemy and therefore firing no rounds in anger.[162] However, the columns were to have a limited life, being refuelled and resupplied on the 9th with sufficient supplies to restart their advance towards Sidi Husseni, they were disbanded only one day later, the 2nd RB being re-formed as a single unit under the command of Maj. Liddell. The battalion now moved back to the 'I' Aid Concentration Area to be refitted, picking up a couple of American airmen on the way who had baled out the night before. The composite company was disbanded and those originating from 7th RB returned, despite 'B' Company now only having two officers and being effectively non-operational. 'S' Company had sixteen anti-tank guns but were short of portees.

The Axis position deteriorated markedly. On 8 November, the American and British landed on the shores of North Africa at Oran, Casablanca and Algiers. It was the largest amphibian landing in history, entitled Operation Torch. Rommel now faced threats from two directions and wrote in his papers that 'this spelled the end of the Army in Africa'.[163] Hitler ordered that the part of France that had been governed by the Vichy administration was now to be occupied by German troops and gave orders for Operation Brown, the dispatch of a new army to Tunisia, to be implemented immediately.[164] Meanwhile, Rommel chose to undertake a delaying action at Sidi Barrani, approximately eighty miles from Mersa Matruh, so that his retreating forces would have time to get through the bottleneck of small passes at Halfaya and Sollum – 270 miles from Alamein. The exercise had limited success, being able to hold the position only until the evening of the 9th. By the next evening the New Zealanders and 4th Light Armoured Brigade were at the foot of the Halfaya Pass, taking it by the 11th and adding a further 600 Italian PoWs to be taken into captivity. Heinz Erdmann recalled:

Everything blocked up, terrible chaos, screaming, cursing, running about, burning vehicles, rescuing the wounded between them, treating them and carrying them off, and burying the dead. Then at the Halfaya Pass, Sollum, things got more or less back to normal (for us at least).[165]

The Egyptian border was now cleared, the Eighth Army having pushed the Axis forces the 270 miles from Alamein into Libya. Montgomery chose to become cautious, not wishing to be 'pushed back into Egypt, like the others' and restricting further pursuit to smaller formations of armoured cars and artillery. This gave Rommel a further opportunity to control the pace of the retreat, ensuring that it did not become a rout but a well-organised withdrawal. Although the retreat was proving difficult due to the narrow lanes through the minefields of Tobruk and Gazala, as well as the activity of the Desert Air Force, they managed to reach the El Adem–Tobruk line at about midday, using the last of their petrol reserve and intending to stay as long as possible in order to give the retreating troops time to withdraw.

Tobruk is Retaken

Tobruk, 360 miles from Alamein, could not be held. The Sudan Defence Force surrendered on the 13th, the port immediately being opened, enabling the Eighth Army's supply situation to became more stable. In a bid to save face, Rommel declared that in any event 'the little port was only of symbolic value'.[166]

The long trails of prisoners, the tanks and vehicles strewn derelict along the route, the dead bodies of Germans and Italians lying unburied on the sand – all were visible evidence of the Axis defeat. The breakthrough had cut off the Italian divisions without transport and much of what remained was suffering from engine trouble, a large number having to be towed. They had been utterly broken and much of the flower of the Afrika Korps had been killed.[167] On 13 November, Rommel wrote to his wife:

> The battle in [French] North Africa is nearing its end.[168] This will put the odds further against us, Here, too, the end will not be long, for we're being simply crushed by the enemy superiority. The army is in no way to blame. It has fought magnificently.[169]

The Retreat Continues

The British advance continued over the next four days as Rommel retreated. Siwa was captured on the 14th, Rifleman Martin recalling their orders and the result:

> The Motor Brigade will destroy all enemy elements remaining in the neighbourhood of the Siwa Track. That had been done. There wasn't much to destroy anyway – plenty of pockets of demoralised Axis troops who were happy to call it a day.[170]

Derna fell on 16 November, and by the 18th the forward units of Operation Supercharge had taken Benghazi while Rommel reached Agedabia (Ajdabiya), arriving with virtually no petrol.[171] With the rain returning and causing problems to both parties, Rommel wrote to his wife on the 16th November:

> Another good step back. To cap it all it's now raining which makes it all the more difficult to move. Shortage of petrol! It's enough to make one weep. Let's hope the British are having equally bad weather.[172]

His wish was answered when he received a report from the Luftwaffe stating that the British outflanking column at Msus, 560 miles from Alamein, was being badly held up by floods from the torrential rains,[173] nevertheless Rommel had now lost the whole of Cyrenaica.

Meanwhile, the 2nd RB advancing behind the main units had to bypass the Halfaya Pass and Sollum Hill to avoid the congestion by driving south along the Sofafi–Sherferzen Track to Sidi Aziz, arriving at El Daba on the 15th.[174]The battalion now moved to Gazala, the War Diary complaining about the logistical problems:

> This whole move forward from ALAMEIN was attempted by a disorganization of supply not hitherto experienced by 7th Motor Brigade in its numerous long moves in pursuit of the enemy.[175]

But good news followed, as Bird and Flower returned after recuperating from their injuries sustained at Snipe.

This last move to Gazala effectively ended the part taken by the 2nd RB in the chase after Rommel. Along with the rest of the 7th Motor Brigade they made their way to Timimi where they received rest, recuperation and training with X Corps, until it was called forward at the end of February for the Battle of Mareth. The 1st RB in support of the 7th Armoured Division would continue the chase on behalf of the regiment.

After the Battle

The Germans thought that a campaign in Africa, breaking through the delta to the oil fields of the Middle East, would be easy. They changed their mind at El Alamein.[176] However, as Alexander wrote, 'The Germans showed no weakness at El Alamein; their casualties in killed and wounded showed that'.[177] The last phase became a nasty, vicious battle of attrition that heavily favoured the Allies, being lost by Rommel as much due to his squandering of precious resources in unfavourable set-piece operations. The arrival of the new Sherman tanks and the 6-pounder anti-tank guns gave a significant advantage to the Eighth Army, an advantage that was increased by new tactics, such as those exhibited at Snipe.

In August 1942, after the Eighth Army had been pushed back from Gazala, Churchill had looked for a general that could out-fight Rommel and found in Montgomery a man that had the willpower and ruthlessness to do that. Sadler put it very well in his book:

> Monty was not shy in attributing the victory to his own all-consuming genius. In this he may have been prone to overlook that much of the strategic planning had been done previously by others such as Auchinleck, Dorman-Smith, Gott and Ramsden. These are not mentioned. Nonetheless, even his most constant critics must concede that Montgomery brought to 8th Army cohesion, a simplicity and directness of approach that had been lacking.[178]

Casualties

Allied casualties of the 7th Armoured Division, which included those of the 1st RB, showed the cost to the motorised infantry, as compiled by the Army Medical Services in the following chart, showing the distribution of wounds by anatomical region and by arm of service within the division:[179]

Anatomical Region	Armoured	Motorised Infantry	Artillery	Total Wounds
Head	42	80	37	159
Chest	11	40	24	75
Abdomen	17	18	16	51
Back	10	35	21	66
Arms	32	87	53	172
Buttocks	16	41	24	81
Legs	49	165	89	303
Multiple	15	34	19	68
Burns	21	7	11	39
N.Y.D.*	1	34	11	46
Total Wounds	214	541	305	1,060

Not Yet Determined

It should be noted that, similar to the First World War where the main casualties were not caused by bullets, 75 per cent of British battle wounds were as a result of exploding shells, bombs, mortars or grenades, bullets causing only 10 per cent of wounds. The big killer of the war was artillery.[180] But the manner in which those casualties were managed had changed – in triage, transport and treatment.

Montgomery had promised that more positive action would be given to those wounded. 2nd RB Cpl Peter Taylor later wrote:

> The casualty evacuation and withdrawal of people of ours who were killed was incredible. The wounded were got away extremely quickly in jeeps and little armoured cars with stretchers built on to the back of them – strap him down and whoosh – off. They'd have an orderly sitting on the back to see the chap didn't get bounced out. The medical evacuation was heartening because people had been told, 'If you get wounded, you'll be whipped straight away.' We'd never had this sort of thing before.[181]

However, it was not always easy, as Ray Kennedy, a stretcher-bearer from New Zealand taking part in the initial attack on the 23rd, recalled:

> We started collecting the wounded. The enemy made the job very difficult. Streams of incendiary bullets floated by at chest height. Trip wires at instep level glistened in the moonlight, about 12 inches apart. Stretchers bearing the wounded had to be carried by two men, crawling crab-like, counting the wires they stepped between. Any pressure set off a booby-trap, which would cause appalling injuries.[182]

Pte Robert Brady, with the 22nd Field Surgical Medical Team, recalled:

> All the members of the team used to go out and take the wounded back. If you saw a bloke go down you would go and get him. We took the Germans in as well – a casualty is a casualty. He's just a soldier. They picked up ours – we picked up theirs. We had terrible casualties – legs blown off, arms blown off, tummies opened up. We would stop the bleeding if we could, and we tried to stop infections by cleaning the wounds. We gave morphine, if we could get it. We had medical

supplies, but we were in the lines, so you couldn't always replace what you'd used. We had plasma from England, but the soldiers were giving blood for the wounded.[183]

One of the most innovative advantages that the Eighth Army had over the *Panzerarmee* lay in the transfer of blood products to the wounded. Half of those who die on a battlefield bleed to death. A man can lose half a litre of blood without any short-term detrimental effect, but lose two litres and there is a clear danger of bleeding to death within the next thirty minutes. The Germans transfused their wounded on a one-to-one basis: the donor would lie next to the injured man during the whole transfusion process. But this was slow as well as an inefficient use of men, preventing the donor from undertaking other duties. The Allies, however, would decant donated blood and transfer it to where it could be given to the wounded directly, cutting down on the manpower needed, with whole rows of men being transfused by minimal staff levels and on occasion with transfusion taking place at the front itself.[184] The dead, however, still had to be dealt with as Cpl Peter Taylor recalled:

> The dead on our side had all been taken away. They were taken away and buried. I should imagine the engineers had burial details – had graves prepared ready for the possible number of casualties.[185]

The armies had fought along the Alamein Line for about four months, so corpses accumulated, giving the battlefield a smell of its own: a mixture of petrol, excrement and the odour of buried and unburied corpses, described by all who experienced it as 'sickly-sweet'.[186] Stephen Bungay ends his book:

> Around that place in the desert they lie, the young men of Alamein, be they good or bad, better or worse. Nothing beside remains. All around, boundless and bare, the lone and level sands stretch far away.[187]

El Alamein Cemetery

Those who died have been buried in cemeteries situated along the route of the battle, now managed by the Commonwealth War Graves Commission. Its information sheet explains that the battlefield graves of those who died in the desert campaign were moved into the Commonwealth war cemeteries at El Alamein, Sollum, Tobruk, Acroma, Benghazi and Tripoli. The names of soldiers and airmen whose graves are unknown are commemorated, with those of their comrades from the other operations in the Middle East, on the Alamein Memorial, and the names of the missing sailors on the memorials at their home ports. The entrance to the cemetery bears the following plaque:

1939 – 1945

THE LAND ON WHICH THIS

CEMETERY STANDS IS THE GIFT

OF THE EGYPTIAN PEOPLE

FOR THE PERPETUAL RESTING

PLACE OF THE SAILORS, SOLDIERS

AND AIRMEN WHO ARE

HONOURED HERE

There are 7,367 burials in the cemetery at El Alamein, of which 821 are unidentified by name, their headstones bearing the inscription 'Known unto God'. The names of a further 603 men whose remains were cremated are commemorated on the Cremation Memorial within the cemetery. The Alamein Memorial also bears the names of 11,874 soldiers and airmen who have no known grave. The cemetery and memorial were designed by Sir Hubert Worthington, the Commission's principal architect for the cemeteries in North Africa, and the memorial was unveiled by Field Marshal Montgomery on 24 October 1951.

In the marble floor just inside the central archway the following words are set in bronze letters, surrounded by a bronze ring:

TO THE GLORY OF GOD
AND TO THE UNDYING MEMORY OF THE EIGHTH ARMY
23RD OCTOBER–4TH NOVEMBER 1942

Rommel wrote in his notes:

The battle which began at El Alamein on 23 October 1942 turned the tide of war in Africa against us and, in fact, probably represented the turning-point of the whole vast struggle.[188]

After the war, Montgomery spoke at a dinner of Eighth Army officers. Sitting next to and addressing Churchill, he rose to speak, saying:

I believe that when I arrived in Egypt to take command of the Eighth Army, there was a certain amount of speculation on how long some of you might hold your appointment ... [continuing after the applause and laughter died down] and I believe that there was rather more speculation on how long I might hold mine!'[189]

He awoke one morning in February 1976, explaining that he had had a very bad night. 'I can't have very long to go now; I've got to meet God – and explain all those men I killed at Alamein.'[190] Field Marshal Montgomery of Alamein died on 24 March that year.

CHAPTER 9

Zero plus 249 days.
Forward Then to Victory

Author's note: In order to balance the story I have included a brief account of the activities of the First Army, who had landed on the West African coast under Operation Torch, together with that of the Eighth Army and then the 2nd RB, initially under separate headings and then combining these for the final battles.

The Eighth Army

Rommel's only real option was to withdraw to the relative safety of Tunisia, whilst constantly holding the Eighth Army back to allow his troops time to accomplish this. The 7th Motor Brigade War Diary explains this from the Allies' point of view:

Reasons for going to Tunisia:
1. The obvious advantage of consolidating forces;
2. The short crossing to TUNIS (400 miles from NAPLES, not much more than 200 miles from Palermo) is not only quicker but also safer than the crossing to TRIPOLI (400-odd miles from PALERMO) which is within comfortable range of MALTA for aircraft most of the voyage;
3. The FRENCH have left a MAGINOT line on the frontier as a bulwark against invasion from TRIPOLITANIA.

Meanwhile, Montgomery continued the chase. Benghazi was taken on 20 November, with the hope that it would ease the Allied supply problems, but it was then found that many of the harbour facilities had been destroyed, leaving it without electricity, running water or a sewage system. Despite these problems, it immediately became the Eighth Army's rear headquarters, with work beginning without delay to make it operational. Agedabia was reached on the 23rd, the men of the Eighth Army having travelled 778 miles in just twenty days.[1] Rommel deployed onto a front of a little over 100 miles between El Agheila (Al Uqaylah) and Mersa el Brega. Montgomery wrote:

> This was an area of soft sand and salt pans at the southernmost point of the Gulf of Sirte; there were only a few tracks through this sand sea, and so long as Rommel held the area he could hold up our advance.[2]

But there was always the possibility that the German forces may recover and attack, as intimated by the German News Agency, commenting on the silence of the German High Command on

'Cyrenaica':

> Developments are underway which might be pretty unpleasant for the British. What is happening
> in the Aghella positions is an operation undertaken on German-Italian initiative, the end and
> aim of which has naturally not yet been revealed by the Germans. By the sudden movement of
> Rommel, Montgomery's deployments of a few days ago no longer have the same point. Unless we
> are mistaken, the operations of the Afrika Korps are based on the assumption not only of their
> receiving reinforcements, but also on concentrating their forces. – Reuters[3]

Mussolini instructed Rommel that the line was to be held at all costs. However, despite Rommel
feeling that Montgomery was overcautious, he could not risk him 'following up and overrunning us'.
He therefore convinced Cavallero that in the event that he was attacked by a superior force he should
withdraw to Buerat (Bu'ayrat al Hasun) at the western end of the Gulf of Sirte (Surt),[4] effectively
countermanding Mussolini's order and resulting in Rommel being labelled as a pessimist among the
officers at the high command. Brooke wrote of his concerns:

> Operations in Tunisia not going as fast as they should and on the other hand Monty's pursuit of
> Rommel badly delayed by weather. As a result Rommel given more time that I like to re-establish
> himself.[5]

Later, after reading the Ultra intercepts, he wrote more enthusiastically:

> Kesselring states that he has insufficient forces to hold both Tunis and Bizerta and wonders which
> he should hold, since neither of them individually can achieve much. If this is correct there should
> be a chance of pushing him into the sea before long.[6]

Still concerned that the necessary supplies would not be delivered, Rommel flew to the Wolfsschanze
on the 28th, where he met at 1700 hours a decidedly icy Hitler. Rommel opened the meeting with
the statement: 'If the army remained in North Africa, it would be destroyed.'[7] Hitler raged at the
unscheduled appearance of the field marshal: 'How dare you leave your theatre of command without
asking my permission?' he bellowed,[8] further stating that Rommel was a defeatist and his men
cowards. Rommel asked Hitler whether it was better to lose Tripoli or the Afrika Korps, and Hitler
replied that the Afrika Korps didn't matter and that he had been right to order 'no retreat' in Russia
during the first desperate winter; there would be no return to Africa now. After further discussion,
Hitler quietened down and confirmed that his supplies would be made available, Göring would
return to Italy with Rommel to ensure their delivery.[9]

On the journey Göring detailed his plans to ensure that the Luftwaffe took control of North Africa.
Units of his private 'Praetorian Guard', the Hermann Göring Division, were already on their way to
Tunisia, but he wanted more control. His estimate of the personal opportunities offered by the African
theatre was to prove a disastrous fallacy.[10] Hitler's concerns, however, were focused on the activities
of the First Army and operations in Russia. Consequently Rommel's supplies were never received,[11]
leaving him a) without the necessary petrol to fuel his mobile forces, and b) unable to mount a
successful defence against a British outflanking attack, and for the same reason having no other option
but to never accept battle with Montgomery.[12] It now became increasingly evident that the British

would attack soon and from the night of 6 December he instructed the Italians to begin pulling back, despite the move swallowing up practically all the meagre amount of petrol that they had received.

Montgomery Attacks El Agheila

Upon arrival at El Agheila, Montgomery halted to build up the army's supplies to sufficient levels to ensure that the advance to Tripoli could be sustained once it started, not attacking the line until the evening of 12/13 December. He knew his opponent, a man who was at his most dangerous when cornered, and did not intend to provide Rommel with an opportunity to counter-attack, the result of which could start the pendulum swinging again. But by the time that the attack took place, Rommel had evacuated the line, the Long Range Desert Group reporting that 3,500 Axis vehicles were heading west along the Via Balbia, as they began their approximately 300-mile journey to Buerat. Maj.-Gen. Sir Charles Gwynn commented:

> It would have been satisfactory if Rommel had given Montgomery an opportunity of gaining a decisive victory, but his retreat from such a strong position affords convincing proof that his losses at El Alamein were not exaggerated. It is also an indication of the inability of the Axis powers to reinforce him owing to the number and serious nature of their other commitments.[13]

Montgomery chased after the withdrawing *Panzerarmee*, the New Zealanders catching up with the rear units at Merduma on the 15th, but during a sharp engagement on the coastal road at Nofilia (An Nawfaliyah) the enemy fought between the two brigades[14] continuing westwards, with the light elements of the 7th Armoured Division taking up the chase. A Cairo radio broadcast announced that the Axis forces were in a bottle that Montgomery was about to cork, Rommel commenting to his officers that 'the bottle would soon be empty if only we could get our tanks full', a situation that was unlikely to be rectified any time soon, especially as nine petrol tankers had recently been sunk on their way to Tunisia.

The retreat to Buerat continued, with almost constant rearguard actions fought against the pursuers by the 15th Panzer and 90th Light divisions. The Eighth Army entered and consolidated Sirte ten days later, with its forward patrols crossing Wadi Thamitt close to Buerat, behind the defence lines of which the *Deutsch-Italienische Panzerarmee* (soon to be renamed the First Italian Army) had all passed by 29 December.

Faced with the defences of Buerat, which patrols had found were not as strong as they first thought, but which were strongly supported by natural obstacles such as Wadi Zamzam,[15] and fully aware that the next defence line available after this was Tripoli, Montgomery again delayed his attack to build up ten days' worth of petrol, ammunition and equipment, sufficient in his mind for the battle and the breakthrough. On the afternoon of the 19th, Rommel received an order from Mussolini: 'Resist to the uttermost, I repeat, resist to the uttermost with all troops of the German-Italian Army in the Buerat position.'[16] Rommel had repeatedly pointed out to the high command that the British might chose not to make a frontal assault on the Buerat position but instead go round its southern flank. 'I asked for instructions for such an event. On each occasion I received an answer referring me to the Duce's order.'[17] On the last day of 1942, the Italian High Command tempered the instruction somewhat by stating that if destruction of the army was imminent, it could retire to the west. However, the instruction ended with the note that it was essential to maintain resistance in Tripolitania for at least a month or two! Rommel reminded them 'that the length of our stay in Tripolitania would be decided by Montgomery and not by the *Comando Supremo*', instructing the Italian non-motorised troops to fall back to the Tarhunah–Homs line the very next day. Rommel later wrote:

> To add to our worries, we were in continual state of anxiety about Tunisia. We received virtually no comprehensive information on which we might have formed a judgement of the situation on that front. Both armies[17] were supposed to assume that the other could maintain its position and to act accordingly. My main fear was that the British and Americans might take their correct operational decision and attack the Gabes bottleneck from Southern Tunisia, this driving a wedge between the two armies. It was, in fact, partly this that made me in such a hurry to get back to the west and if it had been left to me and I had more petrol, I would probably have moved across into Tunisia far earlier than I actually did.[18]

The understanding of the situation from the Allied perspective can be seen from the intelligence report of the 7th Motor Brigade, which concluded:

> Rommel has still a fair-sized force under his command consisting of what has been saved on the retreat and what arrived in TRIPOLI while the ALAMEIN was going on. The morale of the GERMANS is said to have been in no way impaired and P.W's [Prisoners of War] have been quite confident that TRIPOLI would be held; their confidence, however, appears to be based on blind faith in ROMMEL and ignorance of the news. They have also the advantage of having reached a good defensive position at the WADI ZEMZEM and have their best defensive position of all at HOMS still in reserve. The greatest weakness in ROMMEL's position is that he is short of men and short of supplies, and as NEHRING [commanding the Russian front] is not only easier to supply but also has definite priority, he is almost certain to receive no reinforcements and is likely to continue to be short of supply. Petrol has been a constant problem throughout the retreat (the delay at NOFILIA is said to have been due to shortage of petrol) and the position is not getting any easier despite the shorter lines of communication, owing to the attention his convoys are receiving from the Royal Navy and the R.A.F.[19]

Battle for Buerat

Montgomery started his attack on 15 January with his signature heavy bombardment delivered by the artillery and air force, after which the 51st Highland Division advanced forward along the coastal road, with 450 tanks under command of the 7th Armoured Division, along with the 1st RB as their motor battalion and the 2nd New Zealand Division striking out to the south at the desert flank of an enemy who fielded just fifty panzers of the 15th Panzer Division.[20] The 15th withdrew towards the line Tarhunah–Homs, situated about seventy miles from Tripoli, with the rest of the Axis forces following, their rear protected by the 90th Light Division. There was no respite as Homs fell to the Eighth Army on 19 January, with Rommel heading for Tripoli, although even here his stay was short-lived and he vacated on the 22nd, the armoured cars of the 11th Hussars entering the city streets at dawn the next day, three months to the day after the launch of the attack at Alamein.[21] Before leaving, Rommel tried to raze the city and aimed to destroy the airfield but was largely unsuccessful, the damage being quickly repaired, although eight block ships had been sunk in the harbour to prevent access,[22] thereby ensuring that the first transport ships did not enter the harbour until 3 February. The British military administration was to find Tripoli a bankrupt city in a bankrupt country – a people bankrupt financially, materially and mentally. Public works had been sabotaged, stores looted, food exhausted.[21] It was therefore ordered:

> No member of the British forces in Tripolitania, whether officer or other rank, shall have any food – breakfast, lunch or supper – at hotels or restaurants in Tripoli, with the exception of the tea shops where tea and buns could be purchased.[22]

By late February, Tripoli harbour would be open and discharging well over 3,000 tons of supplies a day,[23] despite regular bombing raids by the Luftwaffe, which were turned away by the new and effective anti-aircraft defences, but in the meantime trucks commandeered from X Corps, including those of the 2nd RB, were to be used to transport supplies from Benghazi to the front.

The taking of Tripoli effectively ended the desert war, as Rommel had now left Libya, crossing the Tunisian border and setting up a new headquarters just west of Ben Gardane in the early hours of the 26th. Mussolini had endeavoured to populate Cyrenaica and Tripolitania with Italian settlers in the hope of making it 'the granary of Rome'. This rebirth now seemed a long way off; Rommel had lost Tripolitania to the Allies.

Tunisia

Tunis, the site of ancient Carthage, is the name of the country and the capital city, the name Tunisia being used as a convenience.[24] It is a very different place to Libya and Egypt, with a more lush terrain and very little desert, the flat landscape being exchanged for mountains and hills known as djebel or jebel, and wadi being the name for a valley. It is also roughly rectangular in shape with the Mediterranean coast on the northern and eastern boundaries, whilst the inland border with Algeria sits astride the Atlas Mountains, its boundary with Libya running through a line of low mountains and the Matmata Hills. The country benefits from two deepwater ports at Tunis and Bizerta, which housed:

> [...] a naval force of destroyers, submarines and other warcraft. It has hidden submarine and seaplane harbours. But below, the French have built an enormous subterranean fort capable of holding big guns, anti-tank guns.[25]

The First Army

The forces that were combined to invade Algeria and northern Tunisia under Operation Torch were designated as The First Army under the command of Lt Gen. Sir Kenneth Anderson. Initially the army consisted of British and American forces, but after the Vichy government joined the Allied cause it was augmented by French troops.

The main force landed in Vichy-controlled North Africa on 8 November in three locations; Western Force landed 35,000 American troops direct from the USA in Morocco; Centre Force landed 39,000 American troops from England on Royal Navy ships in the Oran area of Algeria; and

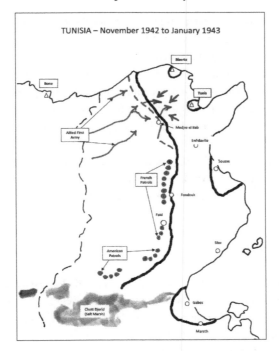

Eastern Force landed a combined contingent of 33,000 British and American troops from England via Royal Navy ships in Algiers.[26] The double agent 'Garbo' notified his German handler that an invasion of French North Africa was to take place imminently. Unfortunately for the Axis forces, the B1A department of MI5 ensured that this was received on the eve of the landings, just as the BBC continuously repeated the phrase 'Attention! Robert arrive', the secret signal that alerted the resistance groups to the invasion.[27]

Despite secret negotiations undertaken by American General Mark Clark in October 1942 after being dropped off by British submarine HMS *Seraph*,[28] the forces were initially opposed by the French with varying levels of enthusiasm. However, as later negotiations proceeded, their attitude to the Axis forces hardened and by the 22nd the North African Agreement had been signed by the commander of the French armed forces, Admiral François,[29] signifying that they had become part of the Allied cause. The First Army now consisted of US II Corps, British V Corps, British IV Corps and French XIX Corps.

Concerned that the whole of the southern French coastline was open to invasion, Hitler instructed German troops to cross the Demarcation Line into the *Zone Libre* under Operation *Anton*.[30] Marshal Pétain's government would still be recognised, but his personal reputation was now in tatters.[31] The presence of the regiment in the North African campaign now included the 10th RB, originally known as the 2nd Battalion Tower Hamlets Rifles, as the motor battalion for the 6th Armoured Division. Four days after the initial American landings, 'B' Company of the 10th RB sailed into the Bay of Algiers, assembling shortly afterwards at Arba just outside Algiers itself. The landings initially caught the German forces by surprise, Anderson, seizing the advantage, rushed east in a bid to capture Tunis and Bizerta before the enemy woke-up to the danger, just as Hitler reinforced the Tunisian army, renaming it the 5th Panzer Army under the command of Col.-Gen. Hans-Jürgen von Arnim.

The First Army advanced in three columns: the northernmost column was halted at Djefna, approximately thirty miles from Bizerta; whilst the two southern columns met near Djedeida, less than twenty miles from Tunis, where they faced heavy German resistance and were also halted. The 5th Panzer Army counter-attacked and forced them back to a new defensive line at Sbeitla, to the east of Kasserine, by the middle of February. The First Army was also experiencing logistical problems in having to contend with the French-built narrow gauge railway from Algiers which constantly broke down and on which American rail trucks would not fit. The short-term solution was to send 5,000 trucks from the US; on arrival these were loaded with supplies and signed over to Arab drivers, who were promptly never seen again.[32]

With the arrival of von Arnim, and with Rommel crossing the Libyan border, there were now two German generals who would have to work together. However, von Arnim thought that Rommel was reckless, while Rommel thought that von Arnim was the opposite.[33] It was not going to be easy.

Casablanca Conference

The conference between 12 and 24 January attended by Churchill, Roosevelt and their respective staffs at the Anfa Hotel in Casablanca set objectives for the Allied war effort, the most important of which was the setting of 30 April as the deadline to end the North African campaign. This would provide sufficient time for the build-up to Operation Husky, the invasion of Sicily, whose objectives were:

1.   to gain the Allies free passage through the Mediterranean;
2.   to open the door to Rome;
3.   to draw German troops from other theatres;
4.   to attack on Europe's soft underbelly; and
5.   to knock a teetering Italy out of the war.[34]

Churchill and Roosevelt ended the conference with the announcement that the unconditional surrender of Germany and Italy was the only acceptable end to the war, Roosevelt qualifying the policy later by stating that it did not entail the destruction of the populations of the Axis powers but rather 'the destruction of the philosophies in those countries which are based on conquest and the subjugation of other people'.[35]

After the conference, Churchill and Brooke visited Tripoli, moving through the palm-lined boulevards and public gardens before Churchill gave a speech at 1330 hours to Montgomery and some 2,000 officers and men of the Joint Headquarters of the Eighth Army in a small natural amphitheatre:

> The last time I saw this army was in the closing days of August on those sandy and rocky bluffs near Alamein and the Ruweisat Ridge, when it was apparent from all the signs that Rommel was about to make his final thrust on Alexandria and Cairo. Then all was to be won or lost. Now I come to you a long way from Alamein, and I find this army and its famous commander with a record of victory behind it which has undoubtedly played a decisive part in altering the whole character of the war ...
>
> Thereafter and since, in these remorseless three months, you have chased this hostile army and driven it from pillar to post over a distance of more than 1,400 miles – in fact, as far as from London to Moscow. You have altered the face of the war in a most remarkable way ... In the words of the old hymn, you have 'nightly pitched your moving tents a day's march nearer home'. Yes, not only in the

march of the army but in the progress of the war you have brought home nearer. I am here to thank you on behalf of His Majesty's Government of the British Isles and of all our friends the world over …

Let me then assure you, soldiers and airmen, that your fellow-countrymen regard your joint work with admiration and gratitude, and that after the war when a man is asked what he did it will be quite sufficient for him to say, 'I marched and fought with the Desert Army.' And when history is written and all the facts are known, our feats will gleam and glow and will be a source of song and story long after we who are gathered here have passed away.[36]

The next day he drove in a white staff car with an Eighth Army insignia on the left wheel arch and an RAF symbol on the bonnet into Tripoli,[37] moving past the assembled forces who were amazed to see the Prime Minister among them, recovering sufficiently to remove their helmets and giving three cheers. A short time later, in Tripoli's main square, surrounded by veterans of the Eighth Army, Churchill took the march past of one of the desert divisions, 'the tears streaming down his face'.[38]

Returning to Britain, he gave a speech to the House of Commons on 11 February, praising Montgomery and Alexander, stating that he had received a communication from Alexander:

Sir,

The Orders that you gave me on August 15, 1942, have been fulfilled.

His Majesty's enemies, together with their impedimenta, have been completely eliminated from Egypt, Cyrenaica, Libya and Tripolitania.

I now await your further instructions.

Signed General Alexander[39]

Rommel is Ordered to Return

It would be an understatement to say that things were not going well for Rommel. His health had deteriorated with the stress of the withdrawal and the continued logistical problems, and he was again instructed by Hitler to return to Germany to seek medical attention. Despite the reason given, it was becoming obvious that the Axis High Command was not prepared to put up with his disobedience and intransigent attitude any longer, insisting that he hand his command over to the Italian *Generale d'Armata* Giovanni Messe. To Rommel this was not acceptable, and using the fact that he had not been given a specific date to leave, remained in situ.[40]

Notwithstanding the shortening of the Axis supply lines as a result of withdrawing to Tunisia, together with its superior port capacity, the Axis armies were still suffering from supply shortages resulting from the almost constant Allied action, as a result of Ultra and photo-reconnaissance directing attacks against shipping by aircraft, submarines, Force K out of Malta and Force Q out of Bône. Consequently, almost a quarter of Axis supplies shipped from Italy failed to arrive during the early months of 1943.[41]

It should be noted that the constant attacks on the Axis fleets had taken a terrible toll: between 1940 and the end of 1942, the Italians had lost 72 per cent of their merchant fleet in the Mediterranean. The Germans added more ships, and even more were built in an effort to make up the difference, but despite these measures the overall tonnage had been reduced in size by 23 per cent.[42] Gen. Warlimont described the Tunisian logistical position as a 'house of cards!'[43] Rommel felt that North Africa was lost and that his only option was to gain as much time as possible in which to evacuate his battle-

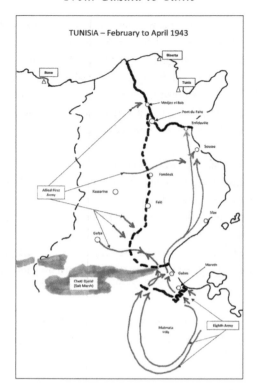

hardened veterans for future use in Europe.[44]

By mid-February, von Arnim's 5th Panzer Army comprised the 10th Panzer Division, *Fallschirm* (1st Paratroop) Panzer Division, Hermann Göring Division, and numerous smaller units amounting to a total of:

- some 110,000 troops, including 20,000 Luftwaffe personnel and 33,000 Italians;
- around two hundred tanks, including some of the new Panzer V Panther[45] and eleven Panzer VI Tigers,[46] as well as
- Nebelwerfer launchers that fired a volley of six 5.9-inch rockets.[47]

The First Army and the Battle of Sidi Bou Zid

Meanwhile, the First Army was still trying to bisect the Axis forces so that they could deal with the smaller divided parts on a piecemeal basis, this time by advancing from Gafsa through to Gabes.[48] In answer, Rommel ordered the 21st Panzer Division and elements of the 10th Panzer Division to attack them at Sidi Bou Zid and Sbeitla. He wrote, 'The Americans had as yet no practical battle experience, and it was now up to us to instil in them from the outset an inferiority complex of no mean order.'[49] On St Valentine's Day, Operation *Frühlingswind* (Spring Wind) saw Stuka dive-bombers attacking the defensive line in the area of Sidi Bou Zid. As the panzers closed in on the outnumbered, inexperienced and outgunned Americans in poorly concentrated positions that did not support each other,[50] the defenders were mauled and the attackers achieved success beyond all expectations, allowing the panzers to continue their advance on Sbeitla without delay.

The next day, under Operation *Morgenluft* (Morning Air), the Germans again attacked the Americans, this time at Gafsa, arriving at dusk to find the town deserted, the result of a shortened Allied defensive line that provided a gap which Rommel lost no time exploiting before continuing his advance to Kasserine, which he occupied on 17 February.

The Battle of Kasserine Pass

Rommel now proceeded on the 19th to advance through the Kasserine and Sbiba passes towards Thala and Le Kef in order to threaten the flank of the First Army, facing a mixed force of ill-prepared Americans and French, whose saving grace was that they had control over artillery positioned in the surrounding heights. The Germans were immediately bombarded, bringing their advance to a halt and forcing Rommel to attack the hills above before sending reinforcements into the pass, attacking the Americans and triggering their collapse during the afternoon of the 20th.

Now through the pass, Rommel split his force: one heading towards Tebessa, while the other advanced slowly towards Thala. They met a unit from the 26th Armoured Brigade, who although outgunned, held the advance long enough for the defenders of Thala to bolster their defences, the artillery of the US 9th Infantry Division giving the Germans a very unpleasant surprise when they got there. Similarly, the advance along the Sbiba Pass towards Tebessa ran straight into the 1st Guards Brigade, 18th Regimental Combat Team and two infantry regiments of the 34th Infantry Division, who halted the attack, forcing the Germans to take up defensive positions.

The success at Kasserine was now wasted as it could not be exploited further. The Germans were just too weak to break the Allied iron grip over the area, despite the US II Corps having suffered 6,600 killed, wounded and missing against enemy losses of 989,[51] they were still faced with the old problem that the Allies could replace their losses, whilst the Axis could not.

Allied Command Structure

It was now time to consolidate the Allied armed forces into a coherent command structure. The Eighth Army joined the First Army under the banner of the 18th Army Group, with overall theatre command given to Alexander as deputy C-in-C to Eisenhower, who retained command of the whole Allied land forces, Tedder being appointed C-in-C of all air forces in the Mediterranean theatre. Individual command of the Eighth and First armies remained in the hands of Montgomery and Anderson respectively.

In accordance with the overall plans laid at Casablanca, Alexander stated that his objectives were to destroy all the enemy forces in Tunisia by 30 April 1943. In order to achieve this:
- Eighth Army was to advance north of GABES;
- First Army was to draw off Axis reserves which could be used against the Eighth.

It seems almost to follow suit that Rommel was promoted in February to the role of commander of the new Army Group Africa (*Heeresgruppe Afrika, Gruppo d'Armata Africa*), consisting of 5th Panzer Army and the 1st Italian Army, and tasked with managing the defence of Tunisia. He wrote to his wife, 'I may have the Army Group now, but the worry is no less. I'm dictated to by Rome in every single thing, yet the full responsibility is mine.'[52]

The Eighth Army and the Mareth Line

During his retreat through Egypt and Libya, Rommel had laid plans to renovate and upgrade the abandoned French fortifications at Mareth, approximately twenty-five miles from Medenine. They comprised three lines of defensive fortifications, twelve miles wide and nineteen miles deep, including concrete pill-boxes hidden deep among the rugged hills and rocks, enhanced further with wire and minefields.[53] The defences, constructed in the inter-war years in order to protect the French occupiers of Tunisia from attack from Italian-held Libya, ran inland from the Gulf of Gabes, through the formidable natural anti-tank ditch of the Wadi Zigzaou, and anchored in the Matmata Hills. It was considered by the original French owners to be defendable from all directions,[54] and after an operation in 1938 had failed to find a route through the 'sand sea' stretching away to the west for many miles of the Matmata Hills,[55] was also considered to be incapable of being outflanked. Rommel, however, thought that the British might be able to achieve such a manoeuvre, and intended to remain alert to the possibility, no matter how remote.[56]

Rommel summarised the Axis position:

> At present the two armies in Tunisia are holding a front about 400 miles long, with centres of gravity at two points, one in the area west and south-west of Tunis and the other in the Mareth Line between the coast and the mountains. Some 350 miles of this line are only very lightly held and, in some places, owing to our lack of troops, not held at all. The greater part of the Fifth Panzer Army's front is mountainous, but even in the mountains an enemy infantry attack could open almost any of the weakly held passes from the rear. Between the two armies there is a large gap on either side of the Shott el Jerid, which, in the dry season, will offer excellent opportunities for operations by the enemy motorised forces.[57]

Owing to Rommel concentrating the majority of his forces on Operation *Morgenluft*, the Eighth Army faced only a holding force at Mareth, giving Montgomery the opportunity to attack and consolidate Tataouine on 18 February, before advancing north to capture Medenine on the 20th. He was now just a few miles from the Mareth Line, with the 7th Armoured, 51st Highland and the 2nd New Zealand divisions amassing almost 500 anti-tank guns between them to support the offensive.[58]

Rommel returned to the bunkers of the Mareth Line, completing the move on 25 February. Von Arnim attacked the Americans under Operation *Ochsenkopf* (Ox Head), which advanced along a sixty-mile front with the intention of consolidating the important junction at Beja. The attack was initially successful but was then pushed back, forcing von Arnim to take up defensive lines – a stalemate that was to last until 19 March, when Rommel instructed the operation to end but resulted in the lost of seven Tigers, four Panzer IVs and eight Panzer IIIs, from his fast dwindling panzer force.[59]

A Message from Montgomery

Montgomery now felt it was time to send a personal message to the troops of the Eighth Army who had fought so hard since Alamein, but were now needed to show that stamina in fighting again:

Personal Message from the Army Commander to be read out to all troops

1. The enemy is now caught in a trap and he is hitting out in every direction trying to gain time and to stave off the day of final defeat in North Africa. He has attacked in central Tunisia, and in northern Tunisia, he is now concentrating in northern Tunisia, and obviously he will attack us next.

2. If he does attack us, that will be the very opportunity we want; we have strong positions, plenty of artillery, plenty of anti-tank guns, and plenty of tanks; the enemy has never yet succeeded in any attack against a co-ordinated defensive layout.

3. Not only are we well equipped with everything we need. But in addition, the soldiers of the Eighth Army have a fighting spirit and a morale which is right on the top line.

4. If the enemy should attack we will stand and fight him in our present positions. There must be NO WITHDRAWAL and of course NO SURRENDER. We have a very great superiority over the enemy in tanks, and provided the defended localities hold firm then we will smash the enemy attack and cause him such casualties that it will cripple him; we will in fact give him a very 'bloody nose'.

5. IT WILL THEN BE OUR TURN TO ATTACK HIM and, having been crippled himself, he will be unable to stand up to our attack and we will smash right through him.

6. Therefore, the quickest way to end the war in North Africa would be for the enemy to attack the Eighth Army and to receive a 'bloody nose'. It would be magnificent.

7. So, if the enemy attacks, let us all show him what the famous Eighth Army can do.

8. Good luck to each one of you, and good hunting.

Tunisia 2-3-43

B L MONTGOMERY

General

G.O.C. in C

Eighth Army[60]

The Battle of Medenine

Rommel did exactly as Montgomery had predicted, undertaking a spoiling attack on the Medenine lines on 6 March under an operation he called *Capri*, but which was later to be known as the Battle of Medenine, intending to disrupt and delay the Eighth Army's suspected offensive on the Mareth Line.

On the day of the attack the sky was cloudy and the whole battleground shrouded in mist, with the 15th, 21st and 10th Panzer divisions totalling 160 tanks, backed by 1,500 infantry and some 200 guns, advancing 'hell for leather' towards the British.[61] The defensive positions were strong and well planned, using the hilly country to the advantage of the British, along with the setting of the most powerful anti-tank screen the Eighth Army had ever assembled consisting mostly of 6-pounders, some 17-pounders, 3.7-inch HAA guns and lastly a troop of captured 88-mms.[62] The enemy made little impression and, with the loss of fifty-five tanks,[63] abandoned the attack as dusk fell. Montgomery had given Rommel the 'bloody nose' that he had promised, and with no British tanks lost and casualties amounting to 130, he had definitely won the day. Churchill later wrote:

Nothing like this example of the power of massed anti-tank artillery had yet been seen against armour. This was probably Rommel's sharpest rebuff in all his African exploit.[64]

Montgomery not so eloquently stated that 'the Marshal had made a balls of it!'[65]

Again Montgomery did not exploit the opportunity of engaging the withdrawing forces and instead went back to his preparations for the attack on the Mareth Line. However, the soldiers of the Eighth Army benefited from the 'repatriated' GI chocolate and cigarettes lost by the Americans at Kasserine. The next day, the British demolition teams cautiously approached the disabled remnants of the panzers that had been unable to return to the Mareth Line, destroying what could not be used and removing what could.

Montgomery wrote to the troops:

On 5th March Rommel addressed his troops in the mountains overlooking our positions and said that if they did not take Medenine, and force the Eighth Army to withdraw, then the days of the Axis forces in North Africa were numbered. The next day, 6th March, he attacked the Eighth Army. He therefore should have known that the Eighth Army NEVER WITHDRAWS; therefore his attack could only end in failure – which it did. The days of the Axis forces in North Africa are indeed numbered.[66]

Learning from the failed attack, Rommel knew that time was running out. Montgomery was obviously planning a major offensive and given a possible breakthrough of the Mareth Line, suggested that a withdrawal take place to the next natural defensive position, the little town of Enfidaville. Hitler refused permission to withdraw, again accusing Rommel of defeatism and giving him irrevocable orders to return to Germany. Passing command to Messe, Rommel flew from Sfax on 9 March at 0750 hours, shortly after giving signed photos to tearful aids, but he still had a few cards up his sleeve. When Messe came to take command of the German troops, he found that they were answerable only to Bayerlein, the situation being further exacerbated by neither von Arnim nor Kesselring paying the slightest attention to their nominal superiors at Italian Supreme Command.[67]

Despite his illness, Rommel flew directly to Hitler's Wehrwolf headquarters in the Ukraine, some 100 miles from Kiev, to try and convince Hitler and Mussolini that a withdrawal was necessary at least to Wadi Akarit, approximately forty miles behind Mareth and above Gabes. On arrival at Hitler's fortress he had a very icy encounter with the Führer, who had intended to present Rommel with the 'Gold Medal for Military Valour', but delayed this due to what he called his defeatist attitude. However, by the next day he had relented and presented him instead with 'diamonds' to his Knight's Cross. Rommel recalled that he instructed him to take some sick leave 'and get myself put right so that I could take command again later for operations against Casablanca. It never occurred to him that things could go wrong in Tunisia.'[68]

Meanwhile, back in Tunisia the planned withdrawal designed to save what was left of the Afrika Korps was initially refused, partially approved and then rejected on the authority of the *Comando Supremo*, and the Mareth Line remained strongly held by four Italian divisions and two German.

The 2nd Battalion The Rifle Brigade

From the perspective of the regiment, it had been the 1st Battalion operating with the 7th Armoured Division that had continued the chase. They had experienced a gradual change in the terrain from the desert of Egypt, through the comparatively fertile country of Tripoli, to the pivotal moment when the Allies had passed El Agheila, advancing further west than ever before,[69] while the 2nd and the 7th Battalions had spent the time recuperating, training and re-equipping in Libya. It was now decided that both battalions, being part of the 7th Motor Brigade, would move forward to continue the fight as Rhinos of the 1st Armoured Division. As Rifleman Martin put it, '[…] we were held in reserve or being fattened up for the big one, as the more cynical observed.'[70]

Since being removed from the chase in November to the brigade area at Bir al Karmusah (Carmusa) they had been in a defensive role against the possibility of a counter-attack, the next ten days were spent patrolling the area as far as the Derna escarpment and along the Giovanni Berta to Karmusah road. The 7th Motor Brigade then moved back further east, to the 1st Armoured Division area at Timimi, near Ras Chechiban, approximately 115 miles from Karmusah, taking part in a ceremonial parade for the Corps Commander Gen. Horrocks.

Ras Chechiban is situated in the area of Jebel Akhdar, meaning 'Green Mountain', lying east of Benghazi and west of Derna, a wooded and fertile highland area rising in some places to an altitude of 1,600 feet and at lower levels cut by several valleys. This area was also known as the Cyrenaica 'bulge' and in previous campaigns had been outflanked. However, if held strongly it could be used to launch attacks southwards, it being prudent to have the 7th Motor Brigade there to be used in the unlikely event that Rommel reversed his withdrawal. It was a terrain that was the complete opposite of what the 2nd RB had been used to since coming to North Africa in 1940, and as such must have lifted their spirits enormously as they trained, and swam in the sea close by.

The experience that the 2nd RB had gained in the desert since 1940 had shown their worth in previous battles. They were therefore put to training for the Tunisian theatre, at the same time giving them a chance to heal their wounds, rebuild their strength and bring their fitness levels up to a high standard, so that when they were needed they would again be ready. Martin wrote:

[…] the CO and his officers had the almost impossible task of keeping an idle battalion busy, sharp and enthusiastic. So training was intensified, this time for a different, more static, more defensive type of warfare over constricting terrain – mountains, hills, defiles and even inhabited built-up areas. We practised new methods movement, line ahead rather than our usual wide dispersal; how to operate on foot without the consoling comfort of our home on wheels; to come to terms with the never-too-popular hand grenade and sticky bomb; how to create an effective roadblock, laying fixed lines, and the process, unknown to us, of clearing the enemy holed-up in buildings in a built-up area. All new stuff in anticipation of a hostile situation away from the desert. A shock for us all. We had known no other battlefield but the desert, so none of us was happy at what might lie in store.[71]

To gain command experience, as well as knowledge of different duties, the officers moved between battalion positions and were occasionally drafted away from the regiment on temporary assignment. In December, reorganisations included many who featured in the photo of just eight months ago, as well as others who had joined since:

- Maj. O. R. H. Chichester left to take up an appointment with the British Military Mission to the Egyptian Government;
- Capt. H. J. F. Wintour returned and took over command of HQ Company;
- Capt. I. H. D. Whigham rejoined from 7th Armoured Division and took over command of 'B' Company;

- Capt. D. W. Basset MC left the battalion on a posting to Middle East Technical College as an instructor;
- RSM Pinnar became Quartermaster, Regimental Quartermaster Sgt White rejoining the battalion as RSM.

And again in February there were further reorganisations:

- Capt. Shepherd-Cross and Capt. Williams rejoined the battalion;
- Lt Copeland left to become an inspector at Middle East Technical College;
- Capt. Ward and Lt Nuttall left the battalion;
- Lt Norman became the Technical Officer;
- Capt. R. A. Flower took command of 'A' Company.

In February, the riflemen were at last given a week's leave; no pyramids this time, but plenty of bars and cafés in Derna to slake their thirst. Upon returning they said goodbye to Maj. Bird, who left the battalion to take up a role as an assistant to Field Marshal Wavell in India. He would be missed, but 'S' Company would remain in the safe hands of Capt. Marten, who relinquished the Adjutant's role to P. T. Flower. Rifleman Martin wrote, 'We of "S" Company were all very sorry to lose a commander we had known for so long and who earned our trust and respect.'[72]

In the same fashion as when they first came to the desert, the riflemen now learnt about the non-combative dangers of Tunisia, amongst them diseases many of which they had not seen before:[73]

Illness	Transfer/Carry Method
Typhus fever	Lice, fleas, ticks
Typhoid and paratyphoid fevers	Milk, vegetables and water
Undulant ('Malta') fever	Goat's milk, cream, cheese, etc.
Leishmaniasis	Sandflies
Relapsing fever	Lice, ticks
Hookworm and other worm diseases	Bathing, drinking water, food, etc.
Plague	Rats and rat flies
Smallpox	Droplet infection
Malaria	Mosquitoes

Motor training was restricted somewhat by the lack of petrol, but the trucks commandeered to transport supplies from Benghazi to the front were returned in mid-February, with an extra 5,000 miles[74] added to the odometers and needing a very urgent overhaul and service. Non-motorised training was supplemented with frequent route marches carrying full kit, PT every day and regular two-mile runs. By the end of the month there were signs that the 2nd RB would soon be called to the fight and, in a similar fashion to that of March 1942, the battalion was visited on 28 February by the Colonel Commandant. A ceremonial parade was put on in the morning and after lunch the obligatory photo was taken of the officers.

The first step to the front took place when battalion orders were received:

The PANZERARMEE AFRIKA, less 21 Armd Div, is now mostly behind the Mareth Line with 164 Div. situated forward in the MATMATA HILLS round BENIKREDDACHE (E46) and Armd Cars

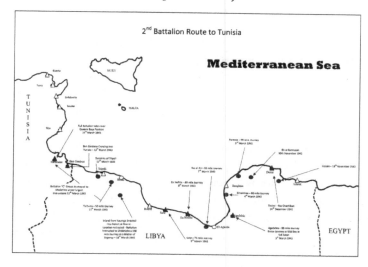

and Tks forward to the line in the plain.[75]

They were instructed to move to Tunisia over the next twelve days in a journey of just over 1,000 miles, from Timimi, around Benghazi to Agedabia, through to Sirte and Buerat, and into Tunisia.

The orders called for them to leave at 0800 hours on 2 March, moving out in company blocks positioned 100 yards apart in the following order:

- Tactical HQ Company and 'A' Company would lead in Block 1;
- 'B' and 'C' companies would be positioned in Block 2;
- 'S' Company and the remainder of HQ Company would bring up the rear in Block 3.

The battalion would travel at a maximum 20 mph, and there would be a twenty-minute break in each even hour and a daily halt between 1200 and 1245 hours, except when any off-road movement was made impossible due to scattered mines. Water ration during the move was to be half a gallon per man per day. Martin recalled on the start of the second day:

A dull cold day with persistent rain fitted our mood perfectly. Greatcoat collars up, mittens, scarf and ground-sheet wrapped round us, we looked anything but an army intent on victory.[76]

On 5 March, they halted at midday during their ninety-eight-mile 'march'[77] exactly, and by sheer coincidence, at the Sidi Saleh position where two years before they had cut off the retreating Italian Army. On the 10th, they suddenly received urgent instructions from brigade to 'march' 148 miles in a single day, the greater part of which was on a dusty desert trail taken after leaving the main road at Buerat. They were not given a reason for this increased activity, but it may have been due to the German spoiling attack which turned into the Battle of Medenine.

On 14 March, 363 days since the photo was taken, and having crossed the border into Tunisia, they reached a position five miles from Medenine. There they were met by an advance party with the news that they were to relieve the 6th Queen's (131st Brigade) in their position on the north-western slopes of Tajira Chir, codenamed Edinburgh Castle, looking across the open terrain at the main road passing through the Matmata Hills before moving on to Gabes. Crimp recalled:

At sunset we move off along the road, with orders for fifty yards space to be strictly preserved between vehicles. I travel in the White with Cpl Trueby, Rusty Llewelyn and a new chap, Allnut. There are several stops, for lengthy periods, and its dark when we pass through Medenine, which looks an attractive town in the half-moonlight ... Later, we leave the road and make our way into some hills – using tracks and open ground – and take up positions in a small valley.[78]

The battalion was brought into the position by Boden after dark, with 'A' Company on the right, 'B' Company on the left and 'C' Company held in reserve. By 2230 hours, the anti-tank guns were divided up between the companies, with one platoon per company, and a listening post established 800 yards forward. The 7th RB took the position on their left, whilst the 1st Sussex relieved 131st Brigade on their right. The 2nd and 7th RB were back in the front line.

The 2nd RB were to spend the next ten days patrolling the area – a period that was broken on the 19th when Montgomery came to visit the battalion, spending two hours talking to both officers and men, and visiting the positions – whilst the 1st RB, along with the 22nd Armoured Brigade, were held in a central reserve.

Operation Pugilist

With the arrival of reinforcements, including the 7th Motor Brigade, Montgomery was now ready to launch Operation Pugilist, the intention of which was to break through the Mareth Line before sweeping up the coast to attack and consolidate Gabes, and then continuing on to Sfax. To achieve this the Eighth Army placed the 50th, 51st (Highland) and the 4th Indian divisions, along with the 201st Guards Brigade, artillery and RAF support, on the narrow front directly in front of the Mareth defences. Montgomery called for:

- The line to be broken at its northern end near the coast by the 50th Division, who would open the defences to allow the tanks of the 22nd Armoured Brigade and anti-tank guns of the 1st RB to cross Wadi Zigzaou, before advancing through to Gabes;
- The New Zealand Corps were to swing around the Matmata Hills in a wide left hook, marching 160 miles to fall on the rear of the enemy before advancing onto Gabes through the Tebaga Gap, a pass between the Matmata Hills to the east and the Djebel Tebaga Hills;
- As a diversion, the US II Corps would attack, under Operation Wop, the town of Gafsa, drawing Axis forces away from the Mareth and Tebaga areas.

Montgomery sent a message to the men: 'If every man did his duty, nothing would stop EIGHTH ARMY,' finishing with the exhortation, 'FORWARD TO TUNIS! DRIVE THE ENEMY INTO THE SEA!'[79]

Operation Wop was the first action that the Americans had seen since Kasserine. Alexander was still not confident as to the performance of his American contingent, but decided that a few modest operations with good prospects of success would build up the experience of these 'green' troops.[80] The 16th and 18th Infantry brigades of General Patton's US II Corps deployed outside Gafsa under cover of darkness during the night of 16/17 March, attacking at midday after a short delay, and finding the defences unmanned and the town undefended, but heavily booby-trapped.[81] The 1st Rangers encountered a similar result from their attack on El Guettar on the 18th, and by the 19th,

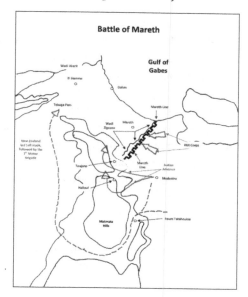

the Sened position was also taken, the operation being further extended to seize a ridge east of the original target of Maknassy and the Mezzouna airfield. The presence of the Americans worried von Arnim, and he instructed his armoured reserve to hold the hills east of Maknassy and to attack the US 1st Infantry in the area of Gafsa. The Americans were repeatedly attacked but the enemy were beaten off each time, resulting in the panzers being badly mauled.

Meanwhile, the 7th Motor Brigade situated in the centre of the Mareth Line, 'A' Company 2nd RB took over the KRRC position on the left and 'B' and 'C' companies took over the remaining 5,000 yards of the front. Patrols continued; those sent out under the command of Whigham and Hawke returned, having not encountered the enemy, but enemy aircraft activity increased as the night progressed.

On 20 March, the opening phase of Operation Pugilist began with the 50th Division struggling after a creeping barrage across the rain-soaked Wadi Zagzaou, penetrating the heavily mined Italian defensive line near Zarat and forming a bridgehead. The tanks and anti-tank guns found the wadi impassable due to the terrain and heavy rain, so when the 15th Panzer counter-attacked on the 22nd, much of the bridgehead was recaptured. Shortly afterwards, Montgomery decided not to persist with this phase of the operation, abandoning what was left of the bridgehead.[82]

New Zealand Attack

The New Zealand Corps, reinforced by the 8th Armoured Brigade and an assortment of Free Frenchmen totalling some 24,000 men, took the wide detour round the Matmata Hills along a route discovered by the Long Range Desert Group and named 'Wilder's Gap', to the Mannerini sector. Advancing towards the Tebaga Gap they found stiff opposition on the hills south of El Hamma from the 21st Panzer and 164th Light divisions, who had been sent there by Messe, resulting in the advance becoming bogged down. Breakthrough had not taken place at either the US front, the Mareth Line or the attack through the Tebaga Gap, resulting in a deadlock on all fronts, with the threat of stagnation and failure of the operation hanging over everybody. A breakthrough had to take place. Montgomery decided that the best place for this to happen was at Tebaga, shifting all his hopes onto the New Zealand position and reorganising the other fronts accordingly. The 1st Armoured and 4th Indian divisions were instructed to join the New Zealanders at Tebaga, while the 1st RB took over part of the line in the area held by the 7th Motor Brigade so that they could join their armour.

The 2nd RB left their position on the Mareth Line at 2100 hours on the 24th, straight into a huge traffic jam at Medenine caused by two divisions trying to get through the town at the same time. Some units of the 2nd and 7th RB had to drive round the town square several times before being able to move out of the town centre, resulting in them not leaving Medenine until after midnight. They then continued across rough and rocky country, the ground of which had been torn up by the preceding vehicles, creating the fine, deep dust several feet thick that seemed to have haunted them since Alamein. All this reduced the speed of the convoy, preventing it from taking advantage of rest stops until after midnight on the 25th/26th when the 2nd RB stopped for a few hours' sleep. The 7th RB, not being so lucky and had to motor on through the night. Arriving at 1400 hours on 26 March, they were told that the attack was due to take place at 1600 hours, and had just enough time for a brew and a quick wash to get rid of the dirt from the journey before going into battle.

The Mareth Line

As the 1st Armoured and 4th Indian divisions, together with the 7th Motor Brigade, made their way through the hills, further attacks now took place along the Mareth Line in order to distract the defenders. The 4th Light Armoured Brigade drove the enemy out of the steep hills astride the main road to Toujane, whilst the 1st RB successfully attacked the Djebel Saikra position under a barrage from 'C' Battery 5th Royal Horse Artillery, supported by a squadron of Sherman tanks of the 4th County of London Yeomanry, but at a high price. The riflemen went straight up the slopes of the hill at 0500 hours in the face of heavy machine-gun fire, before taking possession of the entire feature and capturing a large portion of the Italian Pistola Division by 0900 hours at a cost to the 1st RB of five riflemen dead and seven wounded, and two officers killed and one badly wounded.

The Battle of El Guettar

On the 23rd, the US II Corps had again moved down into the passes on the Gafsa–Gabes road to face the 10th Panzer Division supported by artillery, infantry and Stuka dive-bombers, all of whom proceeded to maul the lead US units. This time, however, as the panzers continued their advance they drove into a US minefield laid as part of an ambush and were immediately bracketed by the US massed artillery, anti-tank guns and tank destroyers from the hills flanking the road. Thirty-two panzers were destroyed and the infantry units suffered a high level of casualties in a very short time, forcing the remainder to withdraw to Gabes in disarray.[83] This became known as the Battle of El Guettar, the first victory of the previously 'green' US troops against the experienced Army Group Africa. Rommel had evidently failed to instil sufficient fear into the Americans to stop them mauling the panzers.

Operation Supercharge II

By 26 March, the units had arrived at the Mannerini sector, providing Montgomery with all the elements needed for the next attack. Operation Supercharge II called for the reinforced New Zealanders to break through the Tebaga Gap before driving towards Gabes, forcing the enemy off the hills on either side of the El Hamma track and creating a safe passage for the 1st Armoured Division to push through to El Hamma, cutting off the Axis retreat from Mareth. After half an hour's aerial bombardment and artillery barrage along a two-brigade front, the New Zealanders, supported by the 8th Armoured Brigade, started their attack at 1600 hours, driving the 21st Panzer Division from their positions. As dusk drew down, the 1st Armoured advanced along the track, 'the flames of burning enemy tanks shone brightly on either side',[84] the 7th Motor Brigade behind them. The enemy had improvised an anti-tank defence that brought the advance to a halt, but by dusk a gap had been made through the defences, which by the light of the moon the 1st Armoured poured through, driving for El Hamma before breaking off within fifteen miles of the town as darkness called a final halt for the day. The 2nd and 7th RB were now deployed south-east of El Hamma to cut off the 21st Panzer Division's retreat from the hills. Unfortunately, they were not to engage the retreating panzers, as the enemy had taken an unmarked track and thus evaded the riflemen. When the 1st Armoured advance resumed the next day they found El Hamma abandoned, and by midday the King's Dragoon Guards had reached Gabes just ahead of the New Zealanders.

With El Hamma taken, the Mareth position became untenable and von Arnim had no option but to withdraw Messe's forces for fear of them being cut off. A concentrated rearguard action against the New Zealand flank by the 164th Light Division, 15th Panzer and 21st Panzer divisions allowed the withdrawal to be completed by 28 March, but despite this, no fewer than 7,000 prisoners were taken by the Allies,[85] with the Axis forces having been driven out of the most formidable defences in North Africa.[86]

The Army Group Africa retreated back to Wadi Akarit, the next natural defensive position situated fifteen miles north of Gabes, which was a line of hills to the south flanked by the sea on one side and impassable rocky hills and the salt marshes of Shott el Fedjadj on the other. With the occupation on 29 March, the Battle of Mareth was over and accordingly Operation Supercharge, having achieved its objective, was terminated on the 31st.

Wadi Akarit

The whole of the Eighth Army was now approaching the Akarit lines, the natural topography and manmade defences of which forced an advancing army to seek out alternative routes through the wadi for wheeled and tracked vehicles. The 7th Motor Brigade were situated on the left of the advance and were instructed to work their way through four tracks that had been identified as possible alternative routes. The 2nd KRRC and the 2nd RB found their allotted tracks either so impossibly rough as to be inaccessible to wheeled vehicles or strongly held by the enemy. The most westerly route was found to be passable between Djebel el Beida and Djebel Haidoudi by 'D' Company of the 7th RB, but in moving along the track Eddie Gibbons, the company commander, was killed by a mine.[87] Further investigation proved that it was lightly held. Accordingly, they attacked during the night with 'swords fixed', taking the pass by 0530 hours. However, as the sun rose they found that their position was overlooked by the enemy in the hills above the pass, who immediately started to rake their positions with machine-gun and artillery fire. The 7th RB called for support from the 2nd Armoured Brigade, who unfortunately did not arrive until 1000 hours. 'By the time the leading armoured regiment came in sight the enemy's forces were stronger, the [7th] Battalion already much weakened.'[88] The tanks and riflemen held on under heavy enemy fire until 2200 hours when they received orders to withdraw, with a loss of three officers killed, nine wounded and two missing, while the riflemen suffered four killed, seventy-five wounded and sixty-two missing, although twenty of these were later found to have been killed and most of the rest wounded.[89] The action came close to being successful and could have been 'a decisive and far reaching success, but without the support of the armour and divisional artillery they were instead badly mauled for no gain.'[90] Maj. Hastings wrote:

> [If it had worked] there would have been every chance of a complete breakthrough, of turning the whole Akarit position, probably cutting off great numbers of the enemy and at any rate making unnecessary the Battle of Akarit and the casualties which that entailed.[91]

The Battle for Akarit

As an alternative route could not be found, Montgomery planned and progressed a set-piece operation, codenamed Scipio, to take Wadi Akarit. It started with the *de rigueur* artillery barrage at 0415 hours on 6 April, the 50th, 51st (Highland) and 4th Indian divisions being assigned the task of breaching the enemy defences. The 4th Indian Division were to make a silent attack in the dark on the dominating hills of Roumana Ridge, whilst the 51st would attack across the wadi. Once a gap had been made, the New Zealand Corps would pass through, followed by the 1st Armoured Division, to surge up the main Tunisian plain through the vast Forest of Olives. The Highlanders recalled, 'The wadi looked almost sinister; not a movement or a shell burst anywhere, these enormous hills overlooking everything.'[92] Despite hard fighting and some problems with anti-tank defences and counter-attacks by the enemy, a gap was made through the defences by the 4th Indian Division, the 1st Armoured Division moving through and out onto the plain behind, with the 1st RB passing through the Highlanders at about 1900 hours. The 7th Motor Brigade had been allocated an area closer to the coast, and their advance had been much less eventful than that of their fellow riflemen, concentrating on collecting PoWs. The 7th RB camped in the village of Bou Thadi where they were welcomed by the French inhabitants and introduced to butterfly bombs dropped on the Battalion HQ during the night.[93]

Now threatened by the Eighth Army and the Americans from the Gafsa area, Army Group Africa decided to withdraw from the southern end of the plain, moving out during the night from a potential bottleneck, although still intending to deny the Allies the use of Sfax and Sousse for as long as possible.

The next phase was to fall on the shoulders of the Americans, supported by artillery and close air support, the 78th Infantry Division advancing down the Beja–Medjez road towards Tunis, through difficult mountain terrain. Over the next ten days they cleared a front ten miles wide, while the 4th Infantry Division on their left punched towards Sidi Nasr, putting enormous pressure on the enemy, which was steadily being squeezed between opposing Allied forces from the north and the south.

On 8 April, the Eighth Army advanced, forcing the enemy to withdraw through Mezzouna in the Sidi Bou Zid area, the town being clear of enemy troops when they entered the town at first light. This slow pace with little enemy contact was frustrating to the 2nd RB riflemen, although this situation suddenly changed when they engaged thirty-three tanks, three of which they destroyed, the remainder moving off westwards in the direction of Djebel Telil towards the 2nd Armoured Brigade, who remained in contact with the withdrawing panzers thought to be from the 10th Panzer Division.[94] On this high note, the riflemen took up a rest position in the recently consolidated Mahares area. However, the 7th Motor HQ was attacked by Junkers Ju 88s that dropped anti-personnel and time-delay bombs, causing several casualties, before the brigade moved to the area of Bou Thadi where they again received numerous butterfly anti-personnel mines from the enemy.

Meanwhile, the Eighth Army was preparing to enter Sfax, the defenders hurling across their last shells from the rearguard positions before leaving the important harbour town. However, the forward units of the Eighth Army discovered a minefield across the road from Mahares which delayed their entry into the town. Clifford Webb of the *Daily Herald* watched as the sappers did their work, prodding the road and verges with bayonets:

I saw the front wheels of a lorry hurtle into the air as one deadly mine exploded with a shattering roar … The sun rose, and soon it was time for the cavalcade of battle to move off. Delighted French people, who had cowered in their battered buildings from the noise of war during the night, came out to greet the conquerors. The ceremonial parade took the main thoroughfare to the harbour, while platoons of shock troops threaded their way through side streets and made for the aerodrome.[95]

Sfax was occupied the next day and the 22nd Armoured Brigade continued moving west through Kairouan. Sousse, some sixty miles further on, was taken on 12 April. Meanwhile, the 1st RB had continued their advance north past Sfax in an attempt to block the Axis forces' line of retreat from the town, but the enemy had passed their destination by the time they got there. They now operated on the left of the army from the area of Sidi Abdul Kader, situated about twenty miles inland from Enfidaville.

After discussing the strategy with Eisenhower, and coming to the conclusion that despite them being undermanned, the First Army were in the best position to attack the enemy in the north,[96] Alexander accordingly gave instructions for them to be reinforced with the 1st Armoured Division and consequently the 7th Motor Brigade. The 10th RB arrived at the concentration area north of Bou Arada on 17 April, soon to be joined by the 2nd and 7th RB, whose move had been a secret of the highest importance, but to everyone's surprise, the Arab townspeople of Le Kef welcomed their arrival by stretching a banner across the street with the words 'Welcome to the 8th Army'.[97] Maj. Hastings wrote:

Certainly the inhabitants of Northern Tunisia, fed presumably by BBC propaganda, had an intense curiosity about the appearance of the Desert Rats. At least one of the riflemen is suspected of having sold to some gullible Arab the dirt from the bottom of his jeep. Guaranteed as the genuine 'Sable d'Egypt'.[98]

Their stay at Le Kef also occasioned a visit by Alexander to the brigade, while for the first time since leaving England the 7th found themselves amidst green fields, red-roofed cottages and the sound of cuckoos. Unfortunately, there was also plenty of rain along with the ubiquitous mosquito, always waiting to strike.

The meeting of the First and Eighth Armies was commented on by Pat Boden:

Here we saw for the first time the British troops of the First Army. It was interesting to compare the difference in outlook, technique and appearance between the members of the two armies. The first and most obvious differences were those of appearance and technique. First Army lorries were all painted dark green and brown, and when in harbour were parked in huddles, making the best use of any available cover. Eighth Army transport was painted the colour of sand and the drivers continued to rely on dispersal as the best protection against air attack. There is little doubt that the best solution would have been a compromise between the two methods, both of which were carried to absurd extremes. The officers and men of the First Army were readily distinguishable from those of the Desert Army by their dress. The former were more or less correctly dressed and, more often than not, wore steel helmets as a matter of routine. In the Eighth Army it was almost unheard of for an officer to wear battledress trousers, and steel helmets were worn only on very rare occasions.[99]

The vehicles of both battalions were painted in a darker colour to coincide with those of the First Army, although the supply of paint did not quite meet the demand, resulting in some strange colour schemes.[100] The battalion's first meeting with the Americans of the First Army was recalled by Martin:

> Then we met our first GIs, or rather they met us. They came thundering across to our truck with their tank and in no time at all we were lifelong buddies, both groups gazing in bewilderment at our respective equipment, dress and the soldier's usual paraphernalia.[101]

In the south, Messe retreated 120 miles from Mezzouna to Enfidaville, about nineteen miles from Sousse and the last natural defensive position before Tunis itself. The Eighth Army, in close pursuit up the coastal road, were supported by the RAF and USAAF, who bombed Enfidaville on 14 April, partially destroying the town. However, Messe created strong defensive positions supported by the natural terrain, preventing the Eighth Army from breaking through and forcing them in turn to dig

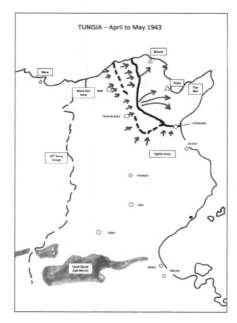

in.

The top north-east corner of Tunisia was now all that was left of the Axis-held territory in North Africa, with approximately 250,000 soldiers protecting the 100-mile perimeter, which was being squeezed between the Eighth Army in the south in front of Enfidaville threatening Tunis, and the US II Corps, now under Bradley, further north threatening Bizerta.[102] But the enemy still controlled the vital northern passes of Longstop Hill, Bald and Green Hills, Pont du Fahs and the hills north of Enfidaville.

The Axis supply and reinforcement chain was breaking down, leaving von Arnim little ammunition to fight with, a problem further exacerbated when two huge ammunition ships were destroyed within sight of Tunis on 6 April by Allied bombers. The seemingly never-ending problem with fuel was also still causing concerns for the German engineers, who began distilling fuel from local wines and liquors to provide fuel for the remaining eighty panzers.[103] The destroyers of Adml Andrew Browne Cunningham imposed a tight blockade, Cunningham issuing orders to 'sink, burn, capture, destroy. Let nothing pass.'[104, 105] As an alternative to marine transport, Kesselring decided to use the huge Messerschmitt Me 323 *Gigant* (Giant) aircraft, powered by six Gnome-Rhone 14-cylinder radial engines[106] and six jettisonable rocket-assisted take-off units, providing a payload of approximately 20 tons of much needed fuel, supplies and reinforcements. Six of the slow-moving aircraft, with a top speed of around 130 mph, were shot down on 22 April[107] by a mixed force of Spitfires and P-40 Tomahawks.[108] The loss of the Me 323s, and of general transport aircraft which had been reduced by half over the last two months,[109] resulted in all further flights of the transport aircraft being suspended by Göring, and Kesselring began to withdraw what was left of his Luftwaffe squadrons. Reinforcements simply ceased to be sent, morale was at rock bottom and the troops began to joke about 'Tunigrad', forcing von Arnim to issue warnings against 'rumour-mongering' and 'defeatist opinions'.[110] Wolfgang Horn, a young German soldier, wrote, 'I express only a weak hope that we can hold out until the end of the war; behind us is the sea, so we face certain capture or death in the battlefield.'[111] Ultra intercepts confirmed that the Axis supply situation was becoming dire, added to which the Allies now had a majority of six to one in infantry and a fifteen to one superiority in tanks. Von Arnim described the Axis supply situation as 'catastrophic'.

However, it was not all going Alexander's way. Churchill wrote to Stalin on the 24th, explaining some of the difficulties:

Since we entered Tunisia we have taken some 40,000 prisoners and killed or wounded some 35,000 German or Italian troops. 1st Army have lost about 23,000 men, 8th Army about 10,000. Two thirds of these casualties have been British. The terrain is mountainous with flat plains surrounded by rugged peaks, every one a fortress.[112]

But in Alexander's eyes the end was in sight and he decided that the two main players at this end would be the augmented First Army and the American II Corps, who would jointly administer the final *coup de grâce* by taking Tunis and Bizerta. He sent a note to all the troops to encourage them on the final drive:

Special Order of the Day

Headquarters
18th Army Group
21st April 1943

SOLDIERS OF THE ALLIES

1. Two months ago, when the Germans and Italians were attacking us, I told you that if you held firm, final victory was assured.
2. You did your duty and now you are about to reap its full reward.
3. We have reached the last phase of this campaign. We have grouped our victorious Armies and are going to drive the enemy into the sea. We have got them just where we want them – with their backs to the wall.
4. This final battle will be fierce, bitter and long, and will demand all the skill, strength and endurance of each one of us. But you have proved yourselves the masters of the battlefield, and therefore you will win this last great battle which will give us the whole of North Africa.
5. The eyes of the world are on you – and the hopes of all at home.

FORWARD THEN, TO VICTORY

H R Alexander

General,

Commander, 18th Army Group[113]

It was time to complete the job. Operation Vulcan was the name given to the main attack against the defences at Medjez el Bab, an area that Rommel had considered ideal for the assembling of motorised forces and therefore an 'Achilles' heel' for the main Axis forces. Whilst the US II Corps were to advance towards and capture Bizerta,[114] other units of the First Army were to capture Tunis, the Eighth Army was to attack northwards from Enfidaville, and the French were to advance towards Pont du Fahs.

Enfidaville

An attack to tidy up the Enfidaville position, overlooked by the imposing Zaghouan Mountain, rising 3,500 feet, with neighbouring hills and ridges running down to the sea on either side of the town, was undertaken extending the front by only three miles against a feature held by three enemy battalions. There was an alternative option to bypass the positions by moving along the coastal road, but this was considered not to be viable and it was therefore decided that the Eighth Army would once again dig in and hold the newly won position.

Operation Vulcan

On 23 April, Operation Vulcan began in earnest as the First Army began their offensive towards Tunis, their flank protected by the US II Corps. Despite their progress being slowed by mines and from being heavily shelled, the attack was sufficiently successful on the northern part of the sector for the 6th Armoured Division to pass through the lines. The 1st Armoured Division were ordered to follow them, with the 1st KRRC in turn following the armour. The 2nd and 7th RB and 2nd KRRC moved off at first light to an area west of Goubellat–Bou Arada, approximately equidistant from Medjez el Bab and El Fahs, just over forty miles from Tunis, across the Goubellat Plain.

On the 25th, the 1st Armoured Division took up the running, but made little progress as the 2nd and 26th Armoured brigades were held up by anti-tank and artillery fire emanating from around Kournine, an area dominated by Djebel Bou Kournine (Horned Mountain), a gaunt, rocky, two-humped mountain of 1,500 feet.[115] On top of this the enemy had installed an observation post, giving good views of the surrounding area and as far as the cornfields of Bou Arada, and reminding the riflemen of Jebel Himeimat in the south of the Alamein Line.

The advance was halted and the 1st Armoured Division were given the role of consolidating the area and containing as much of the German forces as they could. The 2nd RB moved to a position south-east of Goubellat, where 'A' and 'B' companies came under enemy shelling in the evening of the 26th and where Lt J. B. D. Irwin, of 'B' Company, commanding the anti-tank guns, was killed, along with L/Cpl Lintooth, by a direct hit on the slit trench where he was taking shelter, two other riflemen receiving minor wounds. The next day, it was the turn of 'A' Company to be severely shelled.[116] The shelling continued the day after, by which time Rifleman Moore of 'A' Company recalled that the enemy were still holding two hills overlooking the town, the carriers spread out in a valley:

> Our carrier was parked near the edge of a gully that went down the middle of the valley. A young newly arrived officer was chatting to our NCO. I had just remarked to my pal that things were quiet when a volley of reports came from quite close. Next minute, shells were landing around us. I dived with the others down into the valley and as we did so, our carrier went up in flames with a direct hit. 'Bloody tanks,' said our NCO, 'they are using 88-mm guns.' As he spoke a shell landed right on top of us in the gully. The blast hurled me against the side and a cleft in the gully protected me from the flying shrapnel. More shells were landing on the edge and in the gulley. My pals were lying all around, some cut to pieces, others dead. The young officer lay stretched out on the ground. I thought he was unconscious but when I went over to him and tried to bring him round I could see he was he was dead – killed outright by the blast.[117]

Lt J. B. Russell was the young officer who had been killed; Lt C. H. F. Clerihow and L/Cpl Viney were wounded and later died. Sgts Doe and Sampler were wounded. Moore had been wounded in the foot, along with nine other riflemen who were hurt.[118]

Attack on Djebel Bou Kournine

The observation point on top of Djebel Bou Kournine directing the constant artillery fire was preventing the Allied advance from progressing, but a night patrol undertaken by the 1st KRRC discovered an alternative route which was hoped would break the deadlock. On the night of 29 April, they advanced to attack and consolidate the Argoub el Megas feature.

In the meantime, the 2nd RB, supported by two squadrons of Churchill tanks of the 51st Royal Tank Regiment, were ordered to attack and capture the top of the mountain, Rifleman Martin wrote:

> The summit, to our astonishment, was believed to be occupied by approximately 30 men with light machine guns and mortars. The 30 men had inflicted damage and delay to our forces out of all proportion to their meagre number. Their determination and professionalism won our respect.[119]

There was no natural cover round the mountains so a daylight attack was out of the question. The enemy troops were also present in the approaches to the mountain as well as in positions on the two peaks and the connecting narrow pathway between them, and the smooth, steep surface was covered in loose shale.[120] 'Its sides towards the summit were composed of a series of cliffs and ledges, hard rock and loose boulders.'[121] As the objective was so narrow, it was not possible to deploy more than two companies, and Pearson, commanding 2nd RB, ordered that:

- 'C' Company, with 51st Royal Tank Regiment under command, was given the task of the preliminary attack up the south-east slope to secure the eastern peak, and once this had been taken was to move onto the western peak;
- 'A' Company was held in reserve, ready to provide back-up to 'C Company if called upon;
- 'B' Company provided a carrying party to bring rations, ammo, etc. up to the top when secured; and
- 'S' Company remained in the laager area, ready to move up if called upon to do so.

Artillery could not provide a barrage as the top of the mountain was too small, with knife-edge walkways. The riflemen would therefore proceed without their support. In preparation, 'B' Company sent a fighting patrol commanded by Lt J. M. Hawke onto the northern slopes to cut the enemy telephone lines. This was undertaken without the action being detected, while 'C' Company, commanded by Maj. Liddell, moved to their start line at 2130 hours, some 2,000 yards west of Kournine, before advancing as far as the rock wall. They came under sustained light-machine-gun fire, mortar fire and grenades, as well as heavy defensive fire from enemy located around the foot of the hill. Crimp recalled:

> Shooting has already started. Red and white tracer are measuring the 45-degree mountain side from just below one of the peaks to its base, hitting the ground at the bottom or sometimes a spur of the slope and bouncing off in sharp tangents. And as blatant accompaniment comes the clean-cut staccato of the guns firing.[122]

Martin recalled:

> The approach to the top was over loose shale, layers of rock, large stones and stunted trees. Demanding enough in daylight with no resistance. But this attack was at night and would be opposed. The route was strewn with anti-personnel mines and booby-traps. There was no cover from the expected small-arms fire and barring the very summit was a sheer vertical rock wall about 5 feet high – the final obstacle to the assailants already bruised, battered and exhausted by the strenuous climb.[123]

Lucas Phillips wrote:

> On this foundation the Germans had constructed a most ingenious defensive system, where every booby-trap and device known to their sappers were employed. One of the more original of these took the form of mines which could be dangled on lines over the cliff's edge at suitable moments.[124]

Crimp repeats the comments of men who made the climb through the shale that made movement noisy and difficult:

[…] crawling up sheer precipices to find every level expanse swept by machine-gun fire; of wounded rolling all the way to the bottom; of trip wire mines and booby-traps on handgrip ledges; of areas automatically illuminated on approach by flares and bulbs, immediately drawing fire; of premature rifle-shots from stumbling men, supposed to have given the game away; and of walls and caves and all sorts of cunning defensive devices on the summit, piled round with the dead of previous assaults.[125]

Sgts Cunningham and Bull were killed and three ordinary ranks severely wounded, Sgt Brandisham dying towards the top. Crimp reported that 'he fixed his sword and clambered up the defensive wall before being hit in the chest by machine-gun bullets'.[126]

The success signal would be a red over green Verey light repeated three times at one-minute intervals. Unfortunately, this was never sent, as within two hours of starting their advance they were in trouble, Liddell calling for assistance from 'A' Company using the signal three reds repeated at two-minute intervals. Flower was given discretionary orders to undertake the attack based on whether he felt that it was feasible. After weighing up the pros and cons, 'A' Company advanced towards the western peak where they were immediately hit by heavy fire from very secure positions situated along the road. Bypassing the enemy positions, they attacked the western peak, Lt J. W. Verner's platoon almost reaching the top, where they found the final ascent unscalable. While searching for an alternative route, Verner was hit and badly wounded. No other platoons reached the plateau or none were more successful than Verner's, although Lt Mike Leyland got near enough to throw some grenades into the enemy position.[127] Martin wrote:

> That final rock face dashed all hope of capturing the position. The moment an attacker heaved himself to the top of the rock, and before he could get upright, he was assailed by machine-gun fire.[128]

Communication between the two companies was non-existent, and Pearson drove out in a carrier trying to contact Flower and Liddell, neither of whom could be found. It was now becoming quite evident that the 'C' Company attack on the eastern peak could not succeed, even with the supporting attack on the opposite peak by 'A' Company. Liddell returned at 0400 hours to headquarters, stating that 'as far as he could ascertain, all 'C' Company were off the hill',[129] with Flower reporting the same in respect of 'A' Company at dawn. Men were still coming in, and Pearson, Liddell and Flower remained with 51st Royal Tank Regiment and the carriers on the plain, making numerous advances to the lower slopes to recover stragglers while the 4th Royal Horse Artillery fired smoke rounds onto the top. Martin recalled:

> Groups of exhausted men made their way back to us, drawn faces, sagging shoulders and an unnatural shine in their eyes graphically conveying the trauma of the past three hours.[130]

Meanwhile, Verner's condition became worse and repeated attempts to reach him failed, as every movement drew down heavy fire from the enemy. By daylight, when he was seen by Flower, he was undoubtedly thought to have died from his wounds sometime during the night. Rifleman Altfield of 'A' Company was also killed, with four wounded and a further man missing, whilst 'C' Company suffered two ordinary ranks killed, Lt Leyland having been seriously wounded, along with five ordinary ranks and a further two missing. With the riflemen withdrawing, the Churchill tanks took up a position on the lower slopes of Kournine. On 1 May, memorial services were held for those killed, including the death toll from 'C' Company which had risen to five, plus Sgt Cowl of 'B' Company.[131]

Djebel Bou Kournine was never taken but the 1st KRRC had reached their objective, and after suffering a good deal of shelling and mortaring, gained support from the 2nd Armoured Brigade who took up a position on their flank, allowing the Argoub el Megas feature to be consolidated and the deadlock broken.

The area to the north of the feature had been reinforced by panzers and anti-tank guns, preventing any further advance until 5th Corps attacked along the valley from Medjez el Bab, forcing the enemy to withdraw, as confirmed when the 2nd RB occupied the feature. This withdrawal rendered the enemy position on top of the mountain untenable, forcing them to leave. On 8 May, 2nd RB burial parties returned to the mountain to find Verner's body on a ledge very near to the top. On closer examination they came to the conclusion that the position was virtually impregnable due to the natural hazards, made all the more dangerous by the enemy sappers' ingenuity. Whilst on the mountain, one of the riflemen stepped on a trip wire attached to some 'S' mines, which exploded and wounded five ordinary ranks including Sgts Duncomb and Thattam.[132] Crimp recalled a member of the party from 'C' Company saying:

> It was a horrible sight. The slopes and summits were littered with the bodies of men from all units engaged in the successive assaults, and some of the earlier casualties were in an appalling state. The ground, of course, was too rocky for the Jerries to bury them.[133]

The Eighth Army again attacked north of Enfidaville through well-defended and difficult country but again achieved little. Alexander now decided that this would become a holding operation, ensuring that enemy troops would remain within the 130-mile defensive perimeter, thus preventing them from opposing the attacks in the north.

All Four Battalions Under Command of The First Army

The 7th Armoured Division and 1st RB moved up to join the 2nd and 7th RB in IX Corps under the command of Gen. Horrocks.[134] All were to join the 10th RB for Operation Strike, the attack on Tunis, starting out at the end of April. As Maj. Hastings wrote, 'The 18th Army Group now had a single purpose, all fighting the same war.'[135] Montgomery advised Alexander:

> You don't want to attack on the whole front. That suits the Germans fine! They've got no transport, no petrol … the thing is to pick the best place and then overwhelm it and the Air Force'll see they [the Germans] don't move anything – they haven't the petrol to move anything. Then punch home – you'll be through in 48 hours.[136]

In order to keep other enemy elements from interfering with the main operation, the following sub-operations were undertaken:

- The Eighth Army was to contain the Axis forces in the defensive lines around Enfidaville;
- The French were to attack Pont du Fahs; whilst
- The Americans would advance towards Mateur, about thirty miles from Bizerta.

Operation Strike

Under Alexander's direction Operation Strike called for the 4th British Division of the First Army and the 4th Indian Division from the Eighth Army to drive a narrow wedge into the enemy defences for the armour, after first advancing along the main approach road to Tunis under a massive artillery barrage of 442 guns, as well as bombing raids by the Desert Air Force.

The divisions advanced through the Medjerda Valley, with resistance collapsing on both sides of the road, then on to Forna, Massicault and Manouba, cracking and opening a gap in the German Line by noon. The 6th Armoured behind the 4th British Division, the 7th Armoured Division behind the 4th Indian Division, with the 1st Armoured in reserve, were to follow up on the right to exploit the initial breakthrough. The 7th Armoured proceeded through the villages of Sidi Salem, Sidi Abdallah and Peter's Corner on a 3,000-yard front, moving cautiously towards Tunis and hardly hampered by minefields, meeting only isolated tanks, self-propelled guns and small parties of infantry, but always under the threat of a counter-attack that fortuitously never materialised. Although von Arnim had been alerted to the forthcoming battle by the movement of assets between the two armies, he was totally surprised by the timing. He used his meagre resources, most of which had been provided in the last merchant ship to reach Tunis on 4 May,[137] to the best of his ability, but in the end was forced into the conclusion that the end of the North African campaign was in sight.[138]

Maj. Hastings wrote:

It would be nice to record that the regiment, which had played so prominent a part in all the phases of the African war, had a decisive role in the final advance. In the event it was not required to do so, for such was the success of the infantry divisions, following up an air and artillery bombardment on a new scale, that enemy resistance collapsed on both sides of the main road. When the armoured divisions were released the battle was practically won. There remained the pursuit to Tunis, the sealing off of the base of the Cap Bon Peninsula, and the rounding-up of the Axis forces.[139]

Tunis is Taken

The 2nd RB were ordered to move forward and were able to occupy a position on the Srassif el Garaa feature, allowing the 2nd Armoured to advance, meeting no opposition, with 'C' Company occupying an empty farmhouse at Sidi Mahdi, whilst an 'A' Company patrol under Lt J. C. L. Boyes went out to check on enemy positions. The 2nd Armoured Brigade took over the position the next day, after 'B' Company gapped a minefield for the Shermans. The 7th Armoured Division and 1st RB advanced down one side of the main road, whilst the 6th Armoured Division made parallel progress, effectively cutting the Axis forces in half.[140]

By 0900 hours, the 7th Armoured were in the suburbs, and shortly afterwards in the centre of Tunis, firing their 75-mm guns into any building that showed resistance.[141] The 1st RB, who had laagered the night before about twelve miles away at St Cyprien, entered a largely abandoned Tunis in the afternoon around 1600 hours, behind a company of the 1st Royal Tank Regiment led by 'I' Company. A troop of 11th Hussars had driven through to the docks before the enemy realised they were there!

As they entered the town they were besieged by crowds of French and Arabs greeting the riflemen with flowers, fruits, wine and kisses, but at the same time being sniped upon by the remaining

German soldiers who had awoken to find that the British were driving through the town.[142]

Glum groups of enemy soldiers stood among the joyous civilians, their rifles slung on their shoulders, watching the British roll by. A few offered feeble resistance, firing shots or tossing a grenade.[143]

> The confusion was unbelievable – at one moment cheers and laughter, the next rifle fire from the buildings, and tanks firing at point-blank range into houses across the street. German vehicles would drive out of side-streets at high speed into the stream of traffic, firing all their weapons or hoping to slip by unobserved.[144]

Meanwhile, Italian soldiers were busily trading their uniforms for civilian clothes, and amongst all this there were freed British PoWs standing around in the rain.[145]

Bizerta is Taken

Further north, the Americans were fighting some of the most ferocious actions of their campaign,[146] finally taking a major enemy position on Hill 609 before forcing their way through the road to Mateur. In doing so they broke the back of the defences protecting Bizerta, forcing von Arnim to withdraw his forces. The Americans entered the town on 7 May to find it abandoned.

With Tunis and Bizerta taken, the enemy were effectively cut in half. The northern half, squeezed between the US II Corps and other units of the First Army, capitulated and were collected by the 1st RB. They had driven through Tunis before turning north to the River Medjerda to start the sorting out and collecting of approximately 200,000 prisoners. The booty far exceeded anything they had seen before, being made up of whole regiments of artillery, whole parks of vehicles, infantry brigades, workshops and stores, as well as all the equipment needed to administer the Axis forces – many senior officers became PoWs, as only a few of the generals and staff had been able to slip away by air.

The enemy in the southern portion around the base of the peninsula between Hammam Lif and Hammamet were squeezed between the First Army and the Eighth Army, itself split into two large but somewhat disorganised bodies.[147] One, in the east, moved towards the Cap Bon Peninsula; the other, in the west, remained in the area of Hammam Lif, around Grombalia. The 6th Armoured/10th RB and 4th Armoured divisions advanced along the Tunis–Hammamet–Enfidaville road in order to block the enemy retreat and to prevent them from falling on the 8th Army positions at Enfidaville, whilst the 1st Armoured Division cut eastwards across from the Goubellat area to reinforce them. Crimp recalled the drive:

> The valley gradually broadens out, and at Grombalia, a road-junction, the southerly range towards which we now turn is a mile or two off. The wide plain is tall with wheat, and shells are coming over, tearing small craters in it.[148]

When the 6th Armoured column arrived at Hammam Lif, a small town on the shores of the Gulf of Tunis, standing in a narrow gap half a mile between the steep mountains and the sea and commanding the route from the north to the Cap Bon Peninsula, they found it was heavily defended by the enemy armed with anti-tank guns and artillery. The 10th RB advanced towards the town to deal with some anti-tank guns and were met with shelling and heavy machine-gun fire. Quickly realising that the job was too big for one battalion, they were told to hold back while the Guards

Brigade was ordered to clear the town. In the meantime the Lothians and Border Horse forced their way along the sea shore, breaking the anti-tank defences and giving the 10th RB the opportunity to drive into the town. They swept aside the French occupants to take the blue and white painted palace of the Bey of Tunis, whose Ruritanian guards laid down their 1914 rifles without delay.[149]

There was now only one enemy block remaining in this area, that commanded by Gen. Graf von Sponeck and consisting of the German 90th Light Division, Italian Ariete and Young Fascists divisions, who had proclaimed that they would fight to the last, mirroring Hitler's orders to fight to the last round.[150]

The 2nd RB Take Up Positions at Creteville

Although not involved in the main breakout battle, the riflemen of the 7th Motor Brigade were directed to move across the Grombalia plain towards the Cap Bon area. The route, however, was receiving shell fire and was seen to be a difficult crossing, causing their advance to be delayed until the next day and effectively excluding them from the battle along the Medjez road. But once through, they moved with the 1st Armoured Division to an area south of Creteville where the narrow Khanguez el Haujad Pass connected the Enfidaville position with the peninsula. Crimp recalled their orders:

> The idea is for our Division to cut them off from behind. The road goes into the hills from here and our companies will secure the flanking heights, while tanks will move down it.[151]

On arrival, the 2nd and 7th RB climbed up the sides of the pass to establish observation posts on the heights overlooking the road running east from Creteville to Grombalia, directing accurate fire on the gun lines of the Hermann Göring and 10th Panzer divisions, who were holding the area.[152] At first light on 10 May, the 2nd RB 'A' Company saw a German observation post, consisting of the battery commander, another officer and seven other ranks, as well as a number of Italians, moving across the crest of the hill in order to return to their battery situated about 2,000 yards away. They were engaged by the riflemen and promptly surrendered. The battery troops, seeing their commander capitulate, spiked their guns and started to pull out, with 'A' Company engaging them and destroying some of their vehicles. The remnants of both the 10th Panzer and the Hermann Göring divisions now withdrew to a mountainous area in the south of the pass, which was a perfect stronghold and from which the armour made frequent and effective attacks.[153]

From their position the 2nd RB had a magnificent view and could see the 6th Armoured Division and their fellow riflemen of the 10th RB moving around the south from Hammam Lif, the German tanks and guns pulling out, with those guns that had exhausted their ammunition being destroyed by the enemy. In the distance an enemy hospital ship was seen moving away from the port of Cap Bon. The 1st KRRC moved through the 2nd RB position to gain access to the higher positions, but it was not until the 10th that the 2nd Armoured Brigade could advance and join up with the 6th Armoured Division at the village of Grombalia.

The enemy fight was becoming unbalanced. There were some units who when engaged or approached would surrender, whereas others would fight to the last round. Allied officers approaching enemy units expecting to discuss terms would be met by a hail of Spandau bullets.[154] On 10 May, two German officers from the Hermann Göring Division approached the battalion lines, explaining that they had come to discuss arrangements for surrender of their unit. Crimp recalled the company commander ordering:

> [...] the scout car to be made ready for an immediate move forward. Evidently a group of enemy are advertising their willingness to jag in and a formal surrender must be arranged. But he's taking no chances. The steel extension is bolted up on the scout-car door, the visor-plate is fixed across the windscreen and engine-shutters are closed ... Thirty minutes later they come back, somewhat shaken. There's a large hole in the scout car bonnet, torn by shrapnel, and another where the same piece has ricocheted through the driving board inside ... While a parley was in progress between the Jerries and our officers,[155] some enemy guns, either deliberately or not realising the position, opened up. One shell, which landed within twenty yards of the scout-car, killed outright an R.A. officer[156] who had joined the proceedings, and wounded two of the Jerry representatives.[157]

Lt Riddick and Sgts Chipping and Green were also wounded. The shelling continued on and off during the day, but many of these bombardments appeared to have no objective, leading to the conclusion that the enemy were firing off their last rounds.[158]

The Hermann Göring and 10th Panzer Divisions Surrender

On 11 May, the 2nd RB with a squadron of 10th Hussars under command and supported by divisional artillery attacked the enemy-occupied stronghold at the top of the hills through the Khanguez el Haujad Pass. At first they met strong opposition from infantry, and were then shelled fairly heavily until they reached the shelter of the pass, out of view of the enemy. The carriers of 'B' Company climbed Sidi Otsmane Hill, encountering two 88-mm guns that were shelling 'A' Company and whose gun crews took to prepared slit trenches protected by dug-in infantry. The carriers went in, and by last light were among the infantry, who showed no inclination to fight. They began mopping up the position, taking the surrender of the officer commanding. Among the prisoners was a German Major who stated that as they had no more ammunition, most of the Hermann Göring Division would surrender.[159] Crimp received a radio message from the 'C' Company carriers:

> Their officer sounds a trifle nonplussed. He's keeping watch on a bridge, where the road spans a valley, and all's been quiet. Then suddenly had come the sound of heavy traffic approaching, and a stream of vehicles appears on the other side with headlights on. 'What shall we do?' asks the carrier officer. The Company Commander's reply: 'Block the bridge and keep them waiting till first light'.[160]

That night Rifleman Harding recalled:

> Suddenly in the distance a line of white lights could be seen driving nose to tail towards our positions. These turned out to be trucks, ambulances, motor cycles, staff-cars and half-tracks filled with German soldiers all with white flags.[161]

These were approximately 200 soldiers of the Hermann Göring Division, along with their commander *Generalmajor* Franz.[162]

By the morning it was all over. Rifleman Crimp wrote, 'The Hun has jagged in.'[163] An 'A' Company carrier patrol was met by a German officer commanding a 10th Panzer Division Reconnaissance Unit who stated that he and the troops under his command wished to surrender.[164] As the patrol moved further south along a wadi in order to organise the surrender they saw a Volkswagen staff car flying a white flag. It was occupied by *Oberleutnant* Bock of Divisional HQ 10th Panzer Division, who carried with him a letter signed by *Generalmajor* von Brausch,[165] divisional commander, stating that they had come to the end of their ammunition and now wished to surrender.[166] Bock was given the terms of unconditional surrender, stating that no more equipment was to be destroyed. These were accepted and a carrier platoon, along with Pearson's car, was driven through the enemy outer defences to the 10th Panzer headquarters, resulting in Brausch surrendering to him later that morning.[167, 168]

Prisoner-of-war cages were created at Grombalia and Hammam Lif, the 2nd RB being sent there to start processing their enemy PoWs, who were either directed or sent there under guard. A few days later, they were leaving the hills and forming up in a cactus grove with the rest of the 1st Armoured Division nearby for the drive northwards in bright sunshine. Crimp recalled that 'by the afternoon the battalion has "taken up residence" near the sea twenty kilometres from Tunis',[169] but they would soon be back in Tripoli where they received some well-deserved leave.

The fight had continued between von Sponeck and the 6th Armoured Division. The air force dropped bombs, artillery barraged their positions, tank and infantry made attacks, including those of the 10th RB, all trying to force them out of their positions. Maj. Hastings wrote:

> On 12th May, after a heavy bombardment, the hillside suddenly sprouted white flags and Sponeck, who had finally ordered the 'cease fire', dressed immaculately in green uniform and greatcoat with scarlet facings and lining, drove in to surrender to generals Freyberg and Keightley.[170]

The campaign had ended for the 10th RB. Just six months before, they had been in Scotland.

Surrender

Some enemy units continued to fight on, but the end of the road had been reached. The remainder of the Afrika Korps signalled on the night of 12/13 May that its ammunition was exhausted and it could no longer fight. Its chief of staff surrendered to the 4th Indian Division. The Desert Rats of the 7th Armoured continued their advance, wheeling northwards, pursuing the remnants of 15th Panzer Division up the coast as far as Porto Farina, outside Bizerta, where they also surrendered.

> White flags go up; first in small clusters, turning into larger groups as platoons merged with companies. White everywhere, as if butterflies were dancing over the hills.[171]

On 13 May, Mussolini promoted Messe to the rank of Marshal of Italy and on that day he surrendered all the troops under his command to Freyberg.[172] This was followed by an extraordinary collapse of morale at the Führer's headquarters. Rommel wrote that 'it was a complete surprise to them!'[173] As he heard of the fall of Tunisia, Hitler told Goebbels of his total distrust and dislike of his generals. 'All generals lie, he says. All generals are disloyal. All generals are opposed to National Socialism. He just can't stand them!'[174] Rommel had always known this, having written earlier, when given command of the Army Group Africa:

> What will history say in passing its verdict on me? If I am successful here, then everybody else will claim all the glory … but if I fail then everybody will be after my blood.[175]

In his diary, Brooke pondered the last few months:

> At 2.30 p.m. we went on to the White House to attend meeting with the President at which they laid down their conversation of the future strategy. I could not help wandering back to eleven months ago when PM and I were alone with President in that room and Marshall came in with news of the surrender of Tobruk!! I could see us standing there and the effect it had on us. And then I wandered through the last eleven months with all their anxieties, hopes, disappointments and worries. And now! At last the first stage of my proposed strategy accomplished in spite of all the various factors that have been trying to prevent it. I felt rather as if in a dream, to be there planning two stages ahead, with the first stage finished and accomplished.[176]

Maj. Hastings wrote:

> The collapse was complete. Amid scenes far more remarkable than those attending the end of the war in Europe, the Afrika Korps, the German Tunisian Army and the whole of the Italian armies in Africa, with all their equipment, their dumps, their supplies and their administrative base, fell at one dramatic blow into our hands.[177]

Von Arnim stated, 'Even without the Allied offensive I should have had to capitulate by 1st June at the latest because we had no more to eat.'[178]

A message was sent from the headquarters of the Afrika Korps to the *Oberkommando des Heeres* (OKH) stating:

> Ammunition shot off. Arms and equipment destroyed. In accordance with orders received, the Afrikakorps has fought itself into the condition where it can fight no more. The Deutsches Afrikakorps must rise again. Heia Safari! Signed: Cramer, General Commanding[179]

At the end of the day, the German High Command announced that 'the heroic battle of the German and Italian African units had today reached its honourable conclusion'. Alexander, the master of understatement, sent a signal at 1415 hours on 13 May to the Prime Minster: 'Sir, it is my duty to report that the Tunisian Campaign is over. All enemy resistance has ceased. We are masters of the North African shores.'[180]

The battle for North Africa was over.

CHAPTER 10

Zero plus 422 days.
The Photo Updated

Since the picture was taken, 422 days had elapsed and the officers had travelled from the plush delta area of Egypt through to the green lands of the Tunisian countryside – a distance as the crow flies of 1,305 miles. They had experienced sorrows, with colleagues lost and injured, but also triumphs. Some of the officers had transferred to other battalions, whilst others had moved to staff positions, but all would remember their experiences during those 422 days leading up to the end of the battle for North Africa.

Early in June, Churchill wrote the following in Montgomery's autograph books:

The total destruction or capture of all enemy forces in Tunisia, culminating in the surrender of 248,000 men, marks the triumphant end of the great enterprises set on foot at Alamein and by the invasion of N.W. Africa. May the future reap in the utmost fullness the rewards of past achievements and new exertions.[1]

The 2nd RB were amongst the oldest desert warriors, having first entered the theatre in June 1940. The 1st RB came to Egypt in November 1941; the 7th RB arrived in July 1942, coming off the ships and straight into battle; the 10th RB were still training in Scotland six months before the fall of Tunis; and lastly the 9th RB, formerly the Tower Hamlets Rifles, arrived on the last day of 1940, fighting with the 2nd Armoured Division and disbanding due to lack of reinforcements in August 1942.

On 16 May, a dinner was held in Tunis at the instigation of Brig. Bosville, attended by sixty-four officers drawn from the four battalions of the regiment. It was a unique occasion, and with champagne at 2s 6d a bottle,[2,3] one that was celebrated in suitable fashion. Those of the disbanded 9th RB were also included, bringing the regiment's representation up to the full five battalions that had fought in Africa – a sufficient indication of the part played by riflemen defending Egypt, in driving the enemy out of Cyrenaica, Tripolitania and Tunisia, in destroying the Italian armies and defeating the Afrika Korps.

There were losses, of course, as is common in war. A Book of Memory, placed in Winchester Cathedral in 1946, included a list of the regiment officers and other ranks who were killed or died on active service during the Second World War. Details follow of those men included in the picture who were lost:

Brig. Garmoyle DSO and Bar
Hugh (Hugo) Wilfred John Cairns, Viscount Garmoyle was the eldest son of Lt Col. The Earl Cairns CMG, late of The Rifle Brigade, having joined the regiment in 1927 whilst it was in Colchester.

Garmoyle commanded a company throughout Wavell's Libyan campaign, receiving a DSO from Auchinleck in December 1941, before shortly taking over the command of the 2nd RB from Col. Douglas. Six months later, in June 1942, he was promoted to command the 7th Motor Brigade. On 3 July 1942, he was with 'April' Column when it was shelled by the enemy and he received a fatal injury, dying the next day. The then Col. Bosville of the 1st RB took over the command of the 7th Motor Brigade. Capt. Marten wrote to Barbara Crowder:

> [...] the tragedy of Hugo's death. He did brilliantly throughout – never more than in bringing the brigade back 300 miles intact and able to fight as well at the finish as at the beginning, with morale unimpaired – having done rearguard to 8 Army on the southern flank the whole way harried, harassed and delayed him effectively wherever the high-ups permitted and having inflicted considerable casualties on the enemy. He has been awarded (posthumously) which he greatly deserved.[4]

Garmolye's divisional commander said:

> [...] a brilliant and inspiring leader – and completely fearless – he was never happier than when commanding a mixed column operating on the enemy flanks and behind enemy lines. A very fine tactician with a wonderfully quick eye for ground, he was a born desert fighter, and he applied desert guerrilla tactics to motors and modern weapons with striking success.[5]

His death was a great loss to the battalion, Capt. Marten recalling:

> He was always too brave and nonchalant, strolling about under shell fire right in the front – about ten yards tall with his hands in his pockets, but he wouldn't have been Hugo had he been otherwise. We were proud and pleased when he was made Brigadier a fortnight ago, though it was a blow losing him from the battalion. He handled the Brigade marvellously through the withdrawal – which is never an easy business, and we certainly remain an entirely undefeated and undepleted body of men, ready to have a crack any time. He was the most perfect commander ... the last of the great men of the desert, bar one or two.[6]

He was only thirty-five years of age when he was killed, his wife Elizabeth returning to England, having also lost her brother Tony Franklin, another RB man.[7]

Capt. M. K. Crowder

Martin Keith Crowder, the eldest son of Mr and Mrs Crowder, was born in Bombay in November 1918, and was educated at London University. He became a student at the S.E. Agricultural College before joining the regiment on 20 April 1940. Promoted to Lieutenant in October 1941, he became the battalion's intelligence officer and was wounded in the Sidi Rezegh battle, before being promoted to Acting Captain in March 1942.

During Operation Snipe he commanded a platoon of riflemen situated in the south-west sector of the position, protecting the anti-tank guns of 'C' Company and situated close to Sgt Calistan's gun. He was wounded about midday on 26 October 1942, protecting one of his platoon members, Rifleman Harding, by pushing him into a slit trench to evade a shell barrage. Crowder had been hit by shrapnel in his right hand, losing one finger, breaking another and received extensive wounds to his legs, resulting in an open wound of the right one.

Crowder spent a long afternoon and evening in a dirty dugout, during which time his wounds probably became infected,[8] and then had a very uncomfortable journey to the dressing station of the 51st Division, during which he was driven over a mine that promptly exploded. Once at the dressing station he was transferred immediately to an ambulance for the journey to a field hospital,[9] then the next day put onto a hospital ship bound for Haifa in Palestine and the 12th General Hospital at Sarafand. His leg was suspended from numerous pulleys, weighed down with sandbags in order to extend it. He wrote – with his left hand – to his sister, 'Can't tell you how painful it is! The finger I lost is OK – but the broken finger hurts a bit. They think I will be here for six months.'[10]

Unfortunately, the infection increased, necessitating his removal to a hospital in Jerusalem. Upon visiting him, Ann told the doctor to contact her if he got worse, but that if necessary they should amputate the leg, as she would prefer her brother with one leg than not have him at all. Crowder became engaged to his girlfriend and was visited by Turner, who found him 'cheerful'. Crowder requested that Ann came to see him, but the request was refused by her commanding officer. However, a few days later at a dance her CO said, 'What are you doing here? I gave orders for you to fly to Jerusalem immediately as your brother is dying.' Arriving at the hospital operating theatre and waiting for some considerable time, Ann was asked by a nurse what she was doing. She said, 'Waiting for my brother Martin Crowder to come out!' to which the nurse replied that Officer Crowder had died an hour ago and that she should get along.[11] The doctor later told Ann that the infection had worsened and that they had tried to save the leg but had been unsuccessful. Crowder died of his wounds – he was just twenty-four years of age.

On 22 December, Capt. Marten wrote:

> I imagine he was so badly wounded that the doctors could not save him unless he could summon up a little extra energy and determination himself. But the poor old boy was so weakened by loss of blood and so dazed with pain, that he was defeated.[12]

Quintin Hogg[13] wrote:

> I first met Martin Crowder when I was posted to 'S' Company of the 2nd Battalion, while they were stationed at Port Said in March 1941. He had been with the battalion during the first advance in my new company. In a battalion so full of delightful personalities, his vivid charm nevertheless stood out. All who knew him will share the sense of the loss of this gay, vital, brilliant personality who accompanied us so bravely and so worthily on part of our way to victory.[14]

Capt. E. W. L. Gibbons

Edgar 'Eddie' Gibbons was originally a member of the 2nd RB, but transferred along with Paddy Boden and Charles Liddell to the 9th RB when a call was made for experienced officers in the battalion that was being re-formed in the delta. When the 9th RB was disbanded, Gibbons returned to the 2nd RB before transferring on 4 October 1942 to the 7th RB. On 31 March 1943, when commanding 'D' Company, he was killed by a mine whilst searching for a route through the passes near the Wadi Akarit position. It is surmised that he was visiting the battalion on the day that the photo was taken.

Capt. H. N. Salmon

Hugo Noel Salmon had been born into a military family in 1921, the son of Col. and Mrs G. N. Salmon. He attended the Royal Military Academy, Sandhurst, before joining the RB and being promoted to Lieutenant in December 1939. In May 1941, he escorted Italian PoWs to India, before returning to the battalion. He was wounded by shrapnel on 23 November, during the battle of Sidi Rezegh, remaining in hospital and then on leave until February 1942.[15] At the Battle of El Alamein he was second-in-command of Bird's 'S' Company, and during Operation Snipe was mortally wounded, dying a few hours afterwards.[16]

Brig. J. M. L. Renton wrote:

[…] of a quiet, rather shy disposition, Hugo possessed a high standard of leadership which was displayed in countless night patrols during the last two years. His charm, sympathy, and kindness made him much loved by those serving with him and under him, and he could always be relied on to do a difficult job thoroughly well. He was one of the many outstanding young officers who quietly and unassumingly formed the backbone of the Battalion during two years of war in the desert. His death is a sad loss to the Regiment.[17]

Lt J. B. D. Irwin MC

James 'Jimmy' Benjamin Duncan Irwin was the only son of the Ven. and Mrs Irwin, born in February 1916 and marrying Miss P. Graham, before joining the RB as a 2nd Lieutenant in March 1941. He was awarded the Military Cross for his actions during Operation Snipe where he commanded a troop of guns in the northern sector of the position and his cool leadership supported his troop during the action.[18]

On 26 April 1943, he was killed by a direct hit on the slit trench he was occupying whilst in an area south-east of Goubellat in Tunisia. Marten said of him that a company commander could not wish for a better platoon commander:

We all have a special regard for the old 'desert rats' of which Jimmy was certainly one, and the blow and disappointment are all the greater when one of them is killed, especially when victory in Africa is so nearly won. When his turn came Jimmy would have made an absolutely first-class company commander. But even greater than the loss from a purely military point of view is our sense of personal loss. He was the most likeable and honest person I have ever met, and his cheerfulness and good humour, often in unpleasant circumstances, endeared him to everyone.[19]

2nd Lt J. M. W. Reeve

John M. W. Reeve, the only son of Brig. J. T. W. Reeve, was born in 1920 and joined the regiment in March 1941. The following appeared in *The Times* dated 19 September 1942:

Second-Lieutenant John Reeve, The Rifle Brigade, was mortally wounded in the Western Desert while on night patrol, and for the few hours he had to live showed characteristic courage.

Brig. J. M. L. Renton wrote:

John Reeve joined the battalion in the summer of 1941, and was present throughout the fighting that autumn during the advance to Cyrenaica. He was killed while on patrol round El Adem in June 1942. Very much above the average in brains, with a keen sense of humour and good powers of leadership, the regiment loses in him one of the most promising of our young officers, and one who can be ill spared.[20]

2nd Lt J. W. Verner

John Wingfield Verner, the younger son of Sir Edward and Lady Verner, was born in 1910 and served in the Middlesex Yeomanry before being gazetted to The Rifle Brigade on 17 August 1940. His regimental obituary, written by Marten, reads:

When the Battalion was fighting in the Medenine area he carried out a cool and successful daylight reconnaissance of Gabel [Djebel] Saikra which confirmed the impression of ability and imperturbable courage that he so painstakingly concealed beneath an unassuming exterior. He was leading his platoon with great gallantry up the slopes of Gabel Koimine [*sic*] when they almost succeeded in scaling the rock wall at the summit. Officers and men alike will always remember him as a quiet and loveable character, whose humour and imperturbability were typical of much that was good in the Battalion.[21]

What can be said about the losses? Charlie Beckwith, who had commanded a company of the 95th during the Peninsular War, sent a letter to a colleague after hearing about the deaths of their colleagues:

Our friends it is true are fast descending into the tomb and we shall soon follow; but we shall lay down by the side of brothers who loved us during our lives. [They] and a long list down to the rank and file were all united in one common bond of common danger and suffering. God bless us all![22]

With regard to the remainder, officers had come and gone, and their stories continue below:

Lt Gen. Sir Henry Maitland Wilson

Maitland Wilson visited the battalion on several occasions. He was the GOC-in-C Egypt under Wavell and although he exercised no field command, was primarily responsible for overall direction of the war in Egypt. He commanded the British Expeditionary Force first in Greece, then in Palestine, Trans-Jordan and Syria, before taking over as C-in-C Middle-East and Supreme Allied Commander Mediterranean in 1944.[23]

Maj. T. A. Bird MC with Bar, DSO

Bird commanded 'S' Company, the anti-tank gun company, and was wounded during Operation Snipe. In January 1943, he left the battalion for six months as an assistant to Wavell. It must be noted that Bird was twenty-four years of age whilst commanding 'S' Company at Snipe. Rifleman Martin wrote on the occasion of Bird leaving to join Wavell:

A great one for seeking out trouble, he was also adept at getting us out of trouble and we appreciated that. He had been in the desert from the outset, with short breaks needed to recover from wounds, had collected a DSO and two MCs and was probably directly and indirectly responsible for more enemy tanks than any other person. His sabbatical was well deserved.[24]

Capt. D. W. Basset MC
Basset commanded 'A' Company when the photo was taken and fought with the battalion through until December 1942, when he was posted to Middle East Technical College as an instructor.

Captain O. R. H. Chichester
Chichester was a company commander who had been in the desert since 1940, fighting with the battalion throughout, until he left on appointment to the British Mission to Egypt in December 1942.

Capt. (T/Maj.) The Hon. M.G. Edwardes
The second-in-command of the battalion when the photo was taken, Edwardes took over temporary command when Garmoyle was promoted to command 7th Motor Brigade pending Turner taking over. Edwardes then transferred back to the 1st RB as second-in-command before being made a Brigade Major in the 7th Motor Brigade and receiving the MBE in October 1943.[25] He relinquished his commission in 1953, before taking up a position in the Australian military.

Capt. L. J. Gibbs
Gibbs was a member of the Royal Army Ordnance Corp (RAOC), which was the battalion's link for supply and maintenance of weaponry, munitions and other military equipment. Gibbs had joined the battalion in September 1940, continuing to serve with them until November 1942 when the role was taken over by the Royal Electrical and Mechanical Engineers (REME).

Capt. R. H. W. S. Hastings
Hastings was the battalion's Adjutant from 1941 until June 1942, leaving the battalion to take up a position with the 7th Armoured Division and XXX Corps as GSO2, before transferring to the 1st RB as second-in-command in May 1943.[26] In 1950, he wrote *The Rifle Brigade in the Second World War 1939-1945*, the definitive work on the regiment during this period.

Capt. The Revd J. F. B. Keith
A member of the Royal Army Chaplains' Department (RAChD), Capt. Keith served in a religious capacity to the battalion. He had joined the battalion in October 1941, supporting its officers and riflemen until August 1943.

Capt. F. W. Marten
Marten came to the desert in 1940, joining the battalion in January 1941. He was the battalion's Adjutant during the Snipe operation and took command of 'S' Company when Bird left in January 1943. Marten, who spoke fluent German, proved an invaluable asset to the battalion during the surrender of the German forces in 1943. He was twenty-six years of age during Snipe.[27]

Capt. Dr Picton MBE, MC
Picton joined the battalion on assignment from the Royal Army Medical Corps in November 1940,

being promoted to Captain in August 1941. He provided medical services to the battalion until June 1943, when he returned to England.

Capt. (T/Maj.) The Hon. H. D. G. Prittie

Prittie commanded 'C' Company, but was hospitalised in June 1942 and afterwards transferred to the Middle East Tactical School at Gaza as an instructor before returning to command the company during the Italian campaign.[28]

Lt J. P. E. C. Henniker-Major

John Patrick Edward Chandos Henniker-Major was severely wounded in June 1942, when he attacked an 'apparently unsupported' enemy truck column whilst commanding a carrier platoon. His wounds were treated in Cairo, where he made a slow recovery,[29] but it was the last time he would fight with the Rifle Brigade. He resigned his commission and rejoined the Foreign Office, where he directed guerrilla operations on behalf of Tito and the partisans in Yugoslavia. He became the 8th Lord Henniker and was knighted in 1968.[30]

Lt W. A. Chapman-Walker

Chapman-Walker was originally part of the 2nd RB in 1940, becoming ADC to Lt Gen. Sir Henry Maitland Wilson in December 1940, rising to a Major and receiving the MBE in January 1944.

Lt J. R. Copeland

Copeland fought with the battalion, being promoted to Major before being killed in April 1944.

Lt M. F. V. Cubitt

Cubitt arrived in April 1940 and fought with the battalion until June 1942, when he was admitted to hospital. He did not return to the battalion.

Lt P. T. Flower

Flower arrived in August 1941 as a 2nd Lieutenant. In February 1942, he became the Regimental Intelligence Officer and then Adjutant in January 1943.

Lt R. A. Flower

In April 1941, Flower joined the battalion as a 2nd Lieutenant, in the summer of 1942 becoming, in Maj. Hastings' eyes, one of the 'stars' of the column work. During the Snipe operation he was wounded whilst commanding 'C' Company carriers, and was promoted to 'A' Company Commander in March 1943. His medals can be seen at the Royal Green Jackets Museum.

Lt C. N. F. Odgers

Odgers arrived from the Infantry Base Depot in January 1941 and left to join the 7th RB in July 1942, where he became a Company Commander.

Lt Quartermaster C. F. H. Sandell

Shortly after the photo was taken, Sandell left the battalion to return to Britain.

Lt H. J. F. Wintour

Wintour joined the battalion as a Lieutenant straight from England in 1941. At the time the photo was taken, he had only recently returned from hospital. He was the Intelligence Officer during Operation Snipe and was promoted to Captain, commanding a company in January 1943.

2nd Lt J. Earle

Earle joined the battalion in October 1941 and was allocated to 'C' Company, taking command of the platoon in January 1943 before becoming the Regimental Intelligence Officer in December 1943.

2nd Lt M. Forbes

Forbes was new to the desert at the time the photo was taken, remaining with the battalion until June 1942.

2nd Lt Peter C. Innes

Whilst Innes was working with the MTF on the 24 October, 'B' Company's gap was finally completed, Maj. Hastings writing:

> [...] mainly due to the extreme gallantry of the sappers and the fine work of the carrier platoons under Peter Innes and Dick Flower. Just as 'B' Company's task was complete, Peter Innes was badly wounded, having both legs broken by shell fire as he stood beside his carrier.[31]

He did not return to active service with the battalion for the remainder of the war.

2nd Lt P. E. Mayer

Mayer joined the battalion in the desert in July 1941, leaving for Britain on 24 March 1942. He attended the reunion dinner held in London on 27 April 1946.

2nd Lt J. E. B. Naumann

Naumann joined the battalion only one month before the picture was taken. He commanded 13 Platoon of guns during the Snipe operation, which included those of Hine and Cope, and was wounded, not returning to the battalion until January 1943.

2nd Lt J. E. B. Toms

John Edward Bowring Toms arrived in the desert in June 1941, taking command of a troop of anti-tank guns in June 1942, which included Calistan's gun in the Snipe operation. He was wounded, losing two fingers, and was awarded the Military Cross. Owing to his injury, he served the rest of the war as an instructor, being promoted to Captain in January 1943.

Campaign Medal

In August 1943, a campaign medal – the Africa Star – was awarded to all who served at least one day in North Africa between 10 June 1940 and 12 May 1943. In addition, there were bars inscribed '1st Army' and '8th Army' to be worn on the ribbon. Anyone who served with the First Army qualified for the bar, but only those who had served with the Eighth Army after 23 October 1942 were entitled to wear the '8th Army' bar. As Stephen Bungay wrote, 'It looked as if in official eyes they only became the Eighth Army through fighting that third and final battle at El Alamein, Montgomery's battle.'[32] Auchinleck, with Brooke's backing, tried to get the position changed in 1944, and again in 1961, but to no avail.[33]

Remembering the Fallen

At the eleventh hour of the eleventh day of the eleventh month of 1918 the guns fell silent after the Armistice, meaning a state of peace existed between opponents in order to discuss terms.[34] A peace treaty was later signed after four years of the most terrible war the world had known. At the time it was called the Great War, first being referred to as the First World War by the journalist and rifleman Charles à Court Repington in 1920. A two-minute silence is held annually on this day, and, following the Second World War, memorial services began to be held on the second Sunday in November to commemorate both wars.[35]

'The Remembrance Poppy is an emotive and volatile symbol that commemorates millions who died and suffered during the 20th century's many bitter conflicts.'[36] Similar in appearance to the scarlet corn poppy (*Papaver rhoeas*), the Remembrance Poppy started on its journey of becoming the symbol of remembrance in Lt Col. John McCrae's poem 'In Flanders Field', but it was two ladies –one from America, Moina Michael, who campaigned for the symbol to be adopted; the other from France, Anna Guérin, who sold silken red poppies to raise money for veterans and orphans – that established the emblem. 'Today, around 80 million Remembrance Poppies are sold annually around the world, honouring all who have paid the ultimate price of conflict.'[37]

Even before the war had ended, plans were made for a series of memorials to be built around the country, the most important and well known of these being the Cenotaph situated in Whitehall, London. Originally built from wood and plaster for the 1919 victory parade, it was rebuilt to a design of the architect Sir Edwin Lutyens, who said:

> The plain fact emerged and grew stronger every hour, that the Cenotaph was what people wanted and they wanted to have the original replaced by an individual memorial in lasting stone.[38]

Each memorial is different and has its own story to tell to the people of the local area.

In 1920, the Unknown Soldier was buried in Westminster Abbey, an unidentified soldier picked at random to honour the ordinary serviceman and to provide emotional or spiritual relief for survivors. Over a million people visited the tomb in its first week.[39]

The real memorial to those who fell, as well as those who took part, resides in the memory. Therefore it was on the King's initiative that people were asked to remain silent at eleven o'clock, to cease activity, to stand with heads bowed and to think of the fallen, on the morning of 11 November each year. Despite the war footing, and in support of the advances being made in North Africa, Brooke placed a wreath at the Cenotaph on behalf of the Army Council on the day following Churchill's 'End of the beginning' speech at Mansion House.[40] After the Second World War, both conflicts were remembered on the nearest Sunday to 11 November, with many choosing to attend some sort of service, usually in church. As interest in both wars waned, numbers commemorating the day declined, until in 1996 a political decision to restore the two-minute silence was made. Once again it was to become an integral part of national life, albeit once a year.[41]

The Rifle Brigade memorial is located in Lower Grosvenor Gardens on the corner of Hobart Place and Grosvenor Place, with the wall of the gardens of Buckingham Palace opposite. The memorial consists of a large stone plinth in front of a stone curved screen with three bronze figures, two of which stand either side of the stone plinth. The figure on the right is an officer from 1800, while the figure on the left is a rifleman from 1806, both wearing the uniform of the Regiment of the period. The third figure is of a rifleman in First World War uniform, marching with his rifle slung.[42] The memorial was designed by the sculptor John Tweed, born in 1869 and recognised as one of the foremost British sculptors, who was also responsible for the bust of Cecil Rhodes at the National Portrait Gallery,[43] and bears the inscription:

> In memory of 11,575 Officers, Warrant Officers, Non-Commissioned Officers and Riflemen of the
> Rifle Brigade who fell in the Great War 1914 – 1918
> And in memory of 1,329 Officers, Warrant Officers, Non-Commissioned Officers and Riflemen of
> the Corps of the Rifle Brigade who fell in the World War 1939 – 1945

It was unveiled on 25 July 1925 by HRH Prince Arthur, Duke of Connaught and Strathearn, Colonel-in-Chief and third son of Queen Victoria, who served as Governor General of Canada from 1911 to 1916.

Army Restructuring

As part of a Ministry of Defence reorganisation in 1966, The Rifle Brigade was joined with The Ox and Bucks Light Infantry and The King's Royal Rifle Corps to form The Royal Green Jackets, made up as follows:

- 1st RGJ   The Ox and Bucks Light Infantry (43rd and 52nd);
- 2nd RGJ The King's Royal Rifle Corps;
- 3rd RGJ The Rifle Brigade.

In 1992, a further reorganisation took place whereby the 1st RGJ were disbanded, the 2nd RGJ being renamed the 1st RGJ and the 3rd RGJ being renamed the 2nd RGJ.

As a result of the 'Future Army Structure', The Rifles were created in 2007 by the amalgamation of The Devonshire and Dorset Light Infantry, The Light Infantry, The Royal Gloucestershire, Berkshire and Wiltshire Light Infantry and The Royal Green Jackets. The regiment is made up of five regular battalions and two Territorial Army battalions, the regular battalions being made up as follows:

- 1st Battalion   1st Battalions The Devonshire and Dorset Light Infantry and
                             The Royal Gloucestershire, Berkshire and Wiltshire Light Infantry;
- 2nd Battalion   1st Battalion The Royal Green Jackets;
- 3rd Battalion   2nd Battalion The Light Infantry;
- 4th Battalion   2nd Battalion The Royal Green Jackets;
- 5th Battalion   1st Battalion The Light Infantry.

Therefore, for those wishing to follow the 2nd RB through to The Rifles, they can be found in the 4th Battalion.

The Royal British Legion

From an early age, I spent a lot of my time involved with The Royal British Legion, the nation's custodian of Remembrance. My father, Rifleman Walter Frederick William Harding, collected money for charity and helped ex-servicemen, for whom every year we as a family were expected to sell as many poppies as we could, both in Loughton High Street and door to door. The two-minute silence was always observed, and on the second Sunday in November I remember standing with pride, watching my father march past the local dignitaries, until in due course he became the President of the local British Legion branch and took his place on the podium. At the end of the day we would read the exhortation, taken from a poem by Laurence Binyon (1869–1943):

> They shall grow not old, as we that are left grow old:
> Age shall not weary them, nor the years condemn.
> At the going down of the sun and in the morning,
> We will remember them.

Written on the order of service, and spoken at the annual remembrance service at Grosvenor Gardens, is a passage from the Bible – St John 15:13:

> Greater love hath no man than this, that a man lay down his life for his friends.

But for me it is the epitaph on the Kohima Memorial – despite it being from the Burma theatre of war some 5,400 miles from the UK – that encompasses not only those men who died for our country but those who lived and were forever changed by their experiences. It reads:

> When you go home,
> Tell them of us and say,
> For their tomorrow,
> We gave our today.

Endnotes

Chapter 1

1. At the turn of the eighteenth century almost all the regiments of the line had one battalion only, commanded by the Colonel. However, a rifle brigade had four battalions who were often widely spread and may not have even been in the same theatre; it was therefore decided that each battalion would have its own Colonel Commandant who would work under the general supervision of the Colonel-in-Chief.
2. Sir Henry Maitland Wilson GBE, KCB, General Officer Commanding (GOC) British Troops in Egypt (BTE).
3. S. Sarkis was the official photographer BTE of Kasr el Nil Barracks.
4. It should be remembered that more than seventy years have now passed, and memories do not always remain clear. Not all the names of the officers were noted on the picture, but with the help of Ann Bayley, Tom Bird and those of the Royal Green Jackets Museum and Rifle Brigade Association and using the 16 May Officer Field Return I have been able to allocate names to most of those officers appearing in the photograph.
5. *Alamein* by C. E. Lucas Phillips, Lt Col. of 102nd (Northumberland Hussars) Anti-Tank Regiment.
6. *What did you do in the War, Auntie?: The BBC At War 1939-1945* by Tom Hickman.
7. *The Memoirs of Field Marshal The Viscount Montgomery of Alamein K.G.*
8. BBC TV programme *Sandhurst*, screened in 2011.
9. *Alamein* by Stephen Bungay.
10. *Double Cross* by Ben Macintyre.
11. *Ibid.*
12. The Royal Green Jackets website www.rgjmuseum.co.uk/
13. *Jackets of Green* by Arthur Bryant.
14. http://en.wikipedia.org/wiki/Top_(sailing_ship)
15. Later the 1st Duke of Wellington.
16. *The Rifle Brigade* by Basil Harvey.
17. Prince Albert Saxe-Coburg-Gotha, the Prince Consort of Queen Victoria.
18. *The Rifle Brigade* by Basil Harvey and The Rifle Brigade Association Journal, 2010.
19. The Rifle Brigade Association Journal, 2010.
20. Reproduced in the invitation to the Sounding the Retreat at the Guildhall on 23 July 2009, marking the 150th anniversary of the link between The Rifles and the City of London. The author had the honour of attending.
21. *Zulu Rising* by Ian Knight.
22. *Jackets of Green* by Arthur Bryant.
23. *Rifle Brigade Chronicle.*
24. The inventor of the Baker rifle wrote a book in 1803 on its use and training.
25. *Rifle Brigade Chronicle.*
26. Verbal history given by Rifleman Douglas Waller.
27. *Military History* magazine, May 2012 – 'A History of the British Army – Waterloo, 18 June 1815'.
28. Verbal history given by Rifleman Douglas Waller.

29. The Rifle Brigade Association Journal, 2002.
30. The Rifle Brigade Association Journal, 2010 and record sleeve of *High on a Hill – The Band & Bugles of The Royal Green Jackets*, copy held by Royal Green Jackets Museum.
31. Verbal history given by Rifleman Douglas Waller.
32. *The Rifle Brigade* by Basil Harvey.
33. *A Brilliant Little Operation* by Paddy Ashdown.
34. *The Rifle Brigade* by Basil Harvey.
35. Details of the War Establishment II/231/3 for a motor battalion.
36. *British Military Rifles* by Peter Duckers.
37. *Up Close and Personal* by David Lee.
38. It has been suggested that the height of the guardsmen of the King's Company, being in excess of six feet, made them unsuitable for the role.
39. *Pendulum of War: The Three Battles of El Alamein* by Niall Barr.
40. *Military Times*, February 2011 – 'Fading Glory' by Michael Prestwich.
41. The Royal Green Jackets website http://www.rgjmuseum.co.uk/
42. *El Alamein: The Battle that Turned the Tide of the Second World War* by Bryn Hammond.
43. *Alamein* by C. E. Lucas Phillips.
44. Details of the War Establishment II/231/3 for a motor battalion.
45. 2nd Battalion Rifle Brigade War Diaries 1942.
46. Montgomery was divisional commander of Jerusalem at the time.
47. *Jerusalem: The Biography* by Simon Sebag Montefiore.
48. *The Rifle Brigade* by Basil Harvey
49. The Middle East Command under General Wavell had approximately 30,000 troops stationed in Egypt to defend the Italian forces in Cyrenaica
50. *Finest Years: Churchill as Warlord 1940-45* by Max Hastings.
51. These initial troop convoys came to be known as 'Winston's Specials'; http://www.naval-history.net/xAH-WSConvoys03-1940.htm
52. *The Allied Convoy System 1939-1945* by Arnold Hague.
53. Rifleman W. F. W. Harding, personal archive.
54. 2nd Battalion Rifle Brigade War Diaries 1942.
55. *El Alamein* by John Sadler.
56. The 2-pounder gun had been designed for war in Europe where ranges were not expected to exceed 800 yards, whereas the African campaign was fought over longer distances.
57. *War Diaries 1939-1945: Field Marshal Lord Alanbrooke* edited by Alex Danchev and Daniel Todman.
58. The Rifle Brigade Association Journal, 2008 vol. 17, recounting the speech made at the El Alamein Dinner by Brig. Dunphie; citations provided by Maj. R. Cassidy MBE and Memorialisation of Sgt Swann Recollections by his son K. J. Swann. Further referred to as "Brig. Dunphie's El Alamein Dinner Speech."
59. *Desert Adversaries* by Chris Ellis and George Forty.
60. *Hellfire Tonight* – the diary of Albert Martin of 'S' Company 2nd Battalion The Rifle Brigade.
61. *Ibid.*
62. A type of lens manufactured by Carl Zeiss AG, founded in Jena, Germany, in 1846 and today renowned as one of the best and oldest manufacturers of optical systems.
63. *Up Close and Personal* by David Lee.
64. *Pendulum of War: The Three Battles of El Alamein* by Niall Barr.
65. *Ibid.*
66. *The Rifle Brigade in the Second World War 1939-1945* by Maj. R. H. W. S. Hastings.
67. Verbal history given by Rifleman Douglas Waller.
68. *The Crucible of War* by Barrie Pitt
69. Website of the Desert Rats Association, www.desertrats.org.uk, created and managed by Ian Paterson.
70. *El Alamein* by John Sadler.
71. *All Hell Let Loose* by Max Hastings.

72. *Military History* magazine, February 2012 – Codes and Ciphers.
73. *Ibid.*
74. *El Alamein* by John Sadler.
75. *Alamein* by Jon Latimer.
76. *El Alamein* by John Sadler.
77. *BBC History Magazine* – Q & A by Roger Moorhouse.
78. *Finest Years: Churchill as Warlord 1940-45* by Max Hastings.
79. *The Defence of the Realm: The Authorized History of MI5* by Christopher Andrew.
80. *Military History* magazine, February 2012 – Codes and Ciphers.
81. *El Alamein* by John Sadler.
82. *Alamein* by Stephen Bungay.
83. *El Alamein* by John Sadler.
84. Cyrenaica, named after the ancient city of Cyrene, is the historical name of the eastern region of Libya.
85. *Alamein* by Stephen Bungay.
86. *The Illustrated London News* for 6 December 1940
87. *El Alamein* by John Sadler.
88. War Cabinet Review 061142.
89. *A Brilliant Little Operation* by Paddy Ashdown.
90. *Operation Compass 1940* by Jon Latimer.
91. *Great Military Blunders: Politics by Other Means* – documentary by Darlow Smithson Productions.
92. *Ibid.*
93. *Hitler's War Directives 1939-1945* edited by H. R. Trevor-Roper
94. *The Chronicle of War* by Paul Brewer.
95. *Generals at War: Alamein* – Discovery Military documentary.
96. Adolf Hitler greatly admired Erwin Rommel's book *Infantry Attacks*; this brought him to the attention of the Nazi leadership and advanced his military career accordingly.
97. *Generals at War: Alamein* – Discovery Military documentary.
98. *El Alamein* by John Sadler.
99. *Ibid.*
100. http://www.ancientegypt.co.uk/geography/home.html
101. It is a misapprehension that the desert is covered in sand; it is in fact covered in a fine dust caused by the natural erosion of rocks. However, I will continue to refer to it as sand to avoid confusion.
102. http://www.ancientegypt.co.uk/geography/home.html
103. *All Hell Let Loose* by Max Hastings.
104. A road surface to which gravel has been applied, known as metalling.
105. *Desert Adversaries* by Chris Ellis and George Forty.
106. *Together We Stand* by James Holland.
107. *Alamein* by Stephen Bungay.
108. *El Alamein* by John Sadler.
109. *Alamein* by Stephen Bungay.
110. *Ibid.*
111. *El Alamein: The Battle that Turned the Tide of the Second World War* by Bryn Hammond.
112. *Alamein* by Stephen Bungay.
113. *Ibid.*
114. *El Alamein* by John Sadler.
115. Peter Whittingham recalled in *The Essex Family Historian* that the biscuits had been made by Peek Frean in 1918 and came in 7 lb tins.
116. *The Essex Family Historian*, September 2012 – 'One Man's War' by Betty Whittingham.
117. *Alamein* by Stephen Bungay.
118. *Images of War* – a Marshall Cavendish collection in association with the Imperial War Museum.
119. *Alamein* by Jon Latimer

120. *Operation Compass 1940* by Jon Latimer.
121. *Alamein* by Stephen Bungay.
122. *Alamein* by Jon Latimer.
123. *The Second World War* by Antony Beevor.
124. *Generals at War: Alamein* – Discovery Military documentary.
125. The blue cream was created by crushing a tablet of sulphapyridine in 2 oz of paraffin molle flavine – *War Surgery and Medicine* by T. Stout and M. Duncan.
126. Verbal history given by John Luxford of 1st KRRC and held at the Imperial War Museum.
127. *World War II: The Sharp End* by John Ellis.
128. Winston Leonard Spencer-Churchill served as the Prime Minister of the UK from 1940 onwards, and at the time of the photo was sixty-seven years of age.
129. Alan Francis Brooke served as CIGS – Chief of the Imperial General Staff – the professional head of the British Army from 1941, and as Chairman of the Chiefs of Staff Committee from 1942.
130. *War Diaries 1939-1945: Field Marshal Lord Alanbrooke* edited by Alex Danchev and Daniel Todman.
131. *El Alamein* by John Sadler.
132. *The Rifle Brigade* by Basil Harvey.
133. *Alamein* by Stephen Bungay.
134. In early 1942, just as Rommel was arriving in North Africa, military units were transferred to the Greek theatre.
135. *The Daily Telegraph World War II Eyewitness Experience* magazine collection.
136. *The Rommel Papers* edited by B. H. Liddell-Hart.
137. *Ibid.*
138. In November 1941, Auchinleck had replaced, originally on a temporary basis, Lt Gen. Alan Cunningham with Ritchie, who according to Montgomery had neither the experience nor qualifications for the job and was put in an impossible position when sent to command the Eighth Army. *The Memoirs of Field Marshal The Viscount Montgomery of Alamein K.G.*
139. *El Alamein* by John Sadler.
140. Malta, an island with a similar land mass to the Isle of Wight, is situated between Sicily and the Libyan coast; it had been under siege since June 1940, which resulted in regular operations against Axis shipping convoys.
141. *Ibid.*
142. *Ibid.*
143. *Ibid.*
144. *The Rommel Papers* edited by B. H. Liddell-Hart.
145. *El Alamein* by John Sadler.
146. *Ibid.*
147. The Retma box took its name from the area of Afhiret el Retma.
148. *2nd Battalion Rifle Brigade War Diaries 1942*
149. *Ibid.*
150. *Ibid.*
151. *2nd Battalion Rifle Brigade War Diaries 1942.*
152. This operation is described in *The Second World War* by Antony Beevor as being Operation Theseus.
153. *Auchinleck* by John Connell.
154. 90th Leichte-Afrika Division.
155. *Auchinleck* by John Connell.

Chapter 2

1. *The Crucible of War* by Barrie Pitt.
2. *Auchinleck* by John Connell.
3. *The Crucible of War* by Barrie Pitt.

4. The American-manufactured medium M3 tank was known to the British as the General Grant, whilst the version used by the Americans was known as the General Lee. The main armament was a 75-mm gun capable of firing a 14-pound shell at a muzzle velocity of 2,031 ft/sec., mounted in a side sponson, which was enough to penetrate the frontal armour of a Panzer III tank. A 37-mm gun was fitted in the top turret.

5. *2nd Battalion Rifle Brigade War Diaries 1942.*

6. *2nd Battalion Rifle Brigade War Diaries 1942*

7. Navy, Army and Air Force Institutes, established in 1921 to run recreational establishments.

8. *The Rifle Brigade in the Second World War, 1939-1945* by Maj. R. H. W. S. Hastings.

9. Messervy managed to escape shortly afterwards to rejoin his division.

10. *El Alamein* by John Sadler.

11. The RB had fought at Sidi Rezegh in November 1941

12. *The Second World War* by Antony Beevor.

13. Known as 'Smiling Albert', Kesselring had commanded Luftflotte 2 in the early air battles of the war and was initially responsible for the bombing of Southern England and London.

14. *The Crucible of War* by Barrie Pitt.

15. *The Rommel Papers* edited by B. H. Liddell-Hart.

16. *The Crucible of War* by Barrie Pitt.

17. *Auchinleck* by John Connell, 1959

18. *Ibid.*

. *The Daily Telegraph World War II Eyewitness Experience* magazine collection.

20. *Auchinleck* by John Connell.

21. *Ibid.*

22. *The Rifle Brigade in the Second World War, 1939-1945* by Maj. R. H. W. S. Hastings.

23. Part of the *Jagdgeschwader 27 Afrika*, the successful air formation deployed to support Rommel.

24. *The Rommel Papers* edited by B. H. Liddell-Hart.

25. His commendation states that for this and another later occasion when he was wounded while in the act of destroying an anti-tank gun and staff car, Calistan was awarded the Military Medal.

26. *Hellfire Tonight* – the diary of Albert Martin of 'S' Company 2nd Battalion The Rifle Brigade.

27. *Auchinleck* by John Connell.

28. *The Rommel Papers* edited by B. H. Liddell-Hart.

29. *2nd Battalion Rifle Brigade War Diaries 1942*

30. *The Rifle Brigade in the Second World War, 1939-1945* by Maj. R. H. W. S. Hastings.

31. *El Alamein: The Battle that Turned the Tide of the Second World War* by Bryn Hammond.

32. *The War Illustrated.*

33. *Hellfire Tonight* – the diary of Albert Martin of 'S' Company 2nd Battalion The Rifle Brigade.

34. *El Alamein* by John Sadler.

35. *The War Illustrated*

36. *The War Illustrated.*

37. There seems to be a disagreement as to whether they actually left the position on 11 or 12 June. Rommel and *The War Illustrated* state that the 90th Light Division occupied Bir Hacheim in the early morning of 11 June, whereas Alan Moorehead states that they left on the 12th.

38. There is a difference of opinion between texts; some state that the force was made up of the 4th and 2nd Armoured brigades and others that it was the 4th and 22nd Armoured brigades.

39. *The Rommel Papers* edited by B. H. Liddell-Hart.

40. *The Crucible of War* by Barrie Pitt.

41. *The Rommel Papers* edited by B. H. Liddell-Hart.

42. *The Rommel Papers* edited by B. H. Liddell-Hart.

43. The military term 'investment' is the tactic of surrounding an enemy position to prevent access or egress.

44. *The Rommel Papers* edited by B. H. Liddell-Hart.

45. *All Hell Let Loose* by Max Hastings.

46. *Auchinleck* by John Connell.

47. *Ibid.*

48. *The Rommel Papers* edited by B. H. Liddell-Hart.
49. *The Crucible of War* by Barrie Pitt.
50. 2nd Battalion Rifle Brigade War Diaries 1942.
51. Website of the Desert Rats Association, www.desertrats.org.uk, created and managed by Ian Paterson.
52. *The Crucible of War* by Barrie Pitt.
53. James Malcolm Leslie Renton, nicknamed 'Wingy' as he had only one arm (having lost his right arm during the First World War), was a Rifle Brigade man and had commanded the 2nd Battalion when it arrived in the desert in 1940.
54. *The Rifle Brigade in the Second World War, 1939-1945* by Maj. R. H. W. S. Hastings.
55. *Ibid.*
56. *Ibid.*
57. *The Rifle Brigade in the Second World War 1939–1945* by Maj. R. H. W. S. Hastings.
58. *The Crucible of War* by Barrie Pitt.
59. *The Rommel Papers* edited by B. H. Liddell-Hart.
60. *Auchinleck* by John Connell.
61. *The Rommel Papers* edited by B. H. Liddell-Hart.
62. *Ibid.*
63. *The Crucible of War* by Barrie Pitt.
64. *Auchinleck* by John Connell.
65. *The Crucible of War* by Barrie Pitt.
66. *Ibid.*
67. *Ibid.*
68. *Pendulum of War: The Three Battles of El Alamein* by Niall Barr.
69. *Military Illustrated* magazine, June 2002.
70. *Hellfire Tonight* – the diary of Albert Martin of 'S' Company 2nd Battalion The Rifle Brigade.
71. *The Rommel Papers* edited by B. H. Liddell-Hart.
72. *The Daily Telegraph World War II Eyewitness Experience* magazine collection.
73. *The Second World War* by Antony Beevor.
74. *Military Illustrated* magazine, June 2002.
75. *Ibid.*
76. *El Alamein* by John Sadler.
77. *The Crucible of War* by Barrie Pitt.
78. *Ibid.*
79. *The Rommel Papers* edited by B. H. Liddell-Hart.
80. *Alamein* by Stephen Bungay.
81. *The Daily Telegraph World War II Eyewitness Experience* magazine collection.
82. *Ibid.*
83. *El Alamein* by John Sadler.
84. *Ibid.*
85. *Operation Compass 1940* by Jon Latimer.
86. Rommel had also heard that the 7th and 10th Panzer divisions had been fitted out with tropical equipment in preparation for them going to Africa. This was to prove false.
87. In Rommel's book he states that he asked Il Duce (Mussolini) to lift the restrictions on the *Panzerarmee*'s freedom of operation and allow it to advance into Egypt, and that this permission was granted.
88. *Auchinleck* by John Connell.
89. *Ibid.*
90. *Ibid.*
91. Marmarica was the ancient name for the coast of the modern-day border region between Libya and Egypt, and included the towns of Bomba, Timimi, Tobruk, Acroma and Sidi Barrani.
92. *Masters and Commanders* by Andrew Roberts.
93. *Ibid.*
94. *Hellfire Tonight* – the diary of Albert Martin of 'S' Company 2nd Battalion The Rifle Brigade.

95. Capt. Crowder wrote to his sister Ann, informing her of the loss of their friend.
96. *End of the Beginning* by Tim Clayton & Phil Craig.
97. *Alamein* by Jon Latimer.
98. *End of the Beginning* by Tim Clayton & Phil Craig.
99. *The Rommel Papers* edited by B. H. Liddell-Hart.
100. In *The Second World War* by Antony Beevor he states that the acute shortage of competent and decisive commanders at the most senior levels in the British army clearly had a terrible influence on its performance. Brooke ascribed this to the deaths of the best young officers in the First World War.
101. *Auchinleck* by John Connell.
102. *The Second World War* by Antony Beevor.
103. *Auchinleck* by John Connell.
104. *Ibid.*
105. *Ibid.*
106. 2nd Battalion Rifle Brigade War Diaries 1942.
107. *Hellfire Tonight* – the diary of Albert Martin of 'S' Company 2nd Battalion The Rifle Brigade.
108. *Ibid.*
109. *The Crucible of War* by Barrie Pitt.
110. *Ibid.*
111. *Ibid.*
112. *Alamein* by Jon Latimer.
113. Verbal history given by Rifleman Douglas Waller.
114. *Forgotten Voices of the Second World War* by Max Arthur.
115. *Hellfire Tonight* – the diary of Albert Martin of 'S' Company 2nd Battalion The Rifle Brigade.
116. *The Rommel Papers* edited by B. H. Liddell-Hart.
117. 2nd Battalion Rifle Brigade War Diaries 1942.
118. *The Rifle Brigade* by Basil Harvey.
119. *Alamein* by Stephen Bungay.
120. *The Rommel Papers* edited by B. H. Liddell-Hart.
121. *Hellfire Tonight* – the diary of Albert Martin of 'S' Company 2nd Battalion The Rifle Brigade.
122. *The Crucible of War* by Barrie Pitt.
123. *Ibid.*
124. *The Rifle Brigade in the Second World War 1939–1945* by Maj. R. H. W. S. Hastings.
125. *Alamein* by C. E. Lucas Phillips.
126. *Ibid.*
127. Verbal history given by Tom Bird and held at the Imperial War Museum.
128. *Hellfire Tonight* – the diary of Albert Martin of 'S' Company 2nd Battalion The Rifle Brigade.
129. *Pendulum of War: The Three Battles of El Alamein* by Niall Barr.
130. Private correspondence of Mrs Ann Bayley.
131. *Auchinleck* by John Connell.
132. *Ibid.*
133. *Masters and Commanders* by Andrew Roberts.
134. *Auchinleck* by John Connell.
135. *Churchill* by Roy Jenkins.
136. *Masters and Commanders* by Andrew Roberts.

Chapter 3

1. *The Crucible of War* by Barrie Pitt.
2. *Auchinleck* by John Connell
3. *The Development of Armoured Warfare* by Lt Col. H. E. Pymann quoted in *The Pendulum of War* by Niall Barr.
4. *Auchinleck* by John Connell.
5. Famous as commanding the naval group which caused the *Graf Spee* to be scuttled at the Battle of the River Plate in December 1939, and the subject of the film of the same name.

6. The *Queen Elizabeth* was seriously damaged in an attack undertaken by Italians on 19 December 1941 using the new 'human torpedo'.
7. *Auchinleck* by John Connell.
8. *Alamein* by Stephen Bungay.
9. The Nazi German mobile killing squads formed as part of the 'Final Solution'.
10. *The Second World War* by Antony Beevor.
11. *Ibid.*
12. *The Rommel Papers* edited by B. H. Liddell-Hart.
13. Tom Bird wrote in *The Daily Telegraph* that he disagreed that the army was in any way demoralised.
14. *All Hell Let Loose* by Max Hastings.
15. *The Rommel Papers* edited by B. H. Liddell-Hart.
16. The Desert Air Force was also known as the Western Desert Air Force and was part of the RAF.
17. The riflemen's 6-pounder anti-tank gun was a larger calibre than that of the guns on either the Honey or Crusader tanks.
18. *El Alamein: The Battle that Turned the Tide of the Second World War* by Bryn Hammond.
19. *The Rommel Papers* edited by B. H. Liddell-Hart.
20. *Ibid.*
21. *Auchinleck* by John Connell.
22. *Alamein* by Jon Latimer.
23. *The Rommel Papers* edited by B. H. Liddell-Hart.
24. *The Rommel Papers* edited by B. H. Liddell-Hart.
25. W.M. (42) 85th Conclusions, Minute 3, Confidential Record (3 July 1942 – 12 noon), held in the National Archives.
26. *All Hell Let Loose* by Max Hastings.
27. Private correspondence of Mrs Ann Bayley.
28. *Hellfire Tonight* – the diary of Albert Martin of 'S' Company 2nd Battalion The Rifle Brigade.
29. *The Rommel Papers* edited by B. H. Liddell-Hart.
30. *Ibid.*
31. *The Crucible of War* by Barrie Pitt.
32. *The Crucible of War* by Barrie Pitt.
33. Private correspondence of Mrs Ann Bayley.
34. *Auchinleck* by John Connell.
35. *The Crucible of War* by Barrie Pitt.
36. *The Art of War* by Sun Tzu, edited by Samuel B. Griffith, detailing the treatise of the military strategist and tactician written in the 6th century BC.
37. Private correspondence of Mrs Ann Bayley.
38. Turner commanded No. 4 Company whilst at the motor depot to which Rifleman Harding had been assigned after completing his basic training in January 1940. Stephen Snelling wrote in his article 'Leading from the Front' in *Britain at War Magazine* for December 2012 that Turner was by nature an undemonstrative character whose modest demeanour masked a streak of defiant belligerence, a quietly determined man without a shred of brashness or bravado. Pearson is recorded in the article as saying, 'His personality was such that he rarely had to resort to military sanctions; it was sufficient for him to express his personal disapproval and emphasis that the delinquent was letting down the Regiment.' Marten recalled, 'His only real ambition, and it was the great ambition of his life, was to command a battalion,' and this was accomplished at this time.
39. Comment made by Maj. Hastings in *The Rifle Brigade in the Second World War, 1939-1945*.
40. *Ibid.*
41. *The Crucible of War* by Barrie Pitt.
42. Tel el Eisa means 'hill of the Lord' but is often incorrectly referred to as 'hill of Jesus' due to faulty reporting by war correspondents.
43. Private correspondence of Mrs Ann Bayley.
44. These being Col. Bonner Fellers and the Signals Intercept Company 621.

45. *Auchinleck* by John Connell.
46. 2nd Battalion Rifle Brigade War Diaries 1942.
47. *The Rommel Papers* edited by B. H. Liddell-Hart
48. Also known as the First Battle of Ruweisat Ridge.
49. *Alamein* by Jon Latimer
50. *Pendulum of War: The Three Battles of El Alamein* by Niall Barr.
51. *The Rommel Papers* edited by B. H. Liddell-Hart.
52. *The Rommel Papers* edited by B. H. Liddell-Hart and *The Crucible of War* by Barrie Pitt.
53. 2nd Battalion Rifle Brigade War Diaries 1942.
54. Private correspondence of Mrs Ann Bayley.
55. *Hellfire Tonight* – the diary of Albert Martin of 'S' Company 2nd Battalion The Rifle Brigade.
56. *Ibid.*
57. *Pendulum of War: The Three Battles of El Alamein* by Niall Barr.
58. *Alamein* by Stephen Bungay.
59. *Pendulum of War: The Three Battles of El Alamein* by Niall Barr.
60. *Ibid.*
61. *Alamein* by Jon Latimer.
62. *Ibid.*
63. *Auchinleck* by John Connell.
64. *The Rommel Papers* edited by B. H. Liddell-Hart.
65. Private correspondence of Mrs Ann Bayley.
66. *Pendulum of War: The Three Battles of El Alamein* by Niall Barr.
67. Patrol report of 23/24 July 1942, written by Capt. Whigham and contained in the War Diary of the 2nd RB.
68. *Ibid.*
69. 2nd Battalion Rifle Brigade War Diaries 1942 and *The Rifle Brigade in the Second World War, 1939-1945* by Maj. R. H. W. S. Hastings.
70. Patrol report of 24/25 July 1942, written by Maj. Bird and contained in the War Diary of the 2nd RB.
71. Patrol report of 24/25 July 1942, written by Maj. Bird and contained in the War Diary of the 2nd RB.
72. *The Rifle Brigade in the Second World War, 1939-1945* by Maj. R. H. W. S. Hastings.
73. *Pendulum of War: The Three Battles of El Alamein* by Niall Barr.
74. *Ibid.*
75. Rommel was under the impression that it was brigade strength.
76. *The Crucible of War* by Barrie Pitt.
77. *Auchinleck* by John Connell.
78. *Pendulum of War: The Three Battles of El Alamein* by Niall Barr.
79. Richard (Dick) Haywarden lost his father during the First World War and his mother shortly afterwards, when he was still young. He joined the regiment on 17 August 1940 after serving with the London Rifle Brigade in France. His name is on the remembrance wall of the El Alamein cemetery.
80. *Auchinleck* by John Connell.
81. *The Rommel Papers* edited by B. H. Liddell-Hart.
82. *Ibid.*
83. *Ibid.*
84. *Blood and Bullets* documentary on Royal Army Medical Corps.
85. *El Alamein: The Battle that Turned the Tide of the Second World War* by Bryn Hammond.
86. *The Crucible of War* by Barrie Pitt.
87. *Ibid.*
88. *Finest Years: Churchill as Warlord 1940-45* by Max Hastings.
89. *Masters and Commanders* by Andrew Roberts.
90. *Auchinleck* by John Connell.
91. Lt Gen. Tom Corbett was Chief of the General Staff in Cairo.

92. *War Diaries 1939-1945: Field Marshal Lord Alanbrooke* edited by Alex Danchev and Daniel Todman.
93. *War Diaries 1939-1945: Field Marshal Lord Alanbrooke* edited by Alex Danchev and Daniel Todman.
94. *Auchinleck* by John Connell.
95. *Images of War.*
96. *Auchinleck* by John Connell.
97. *Ibid.*
98. *Masters and Commanders* by Andrew Roberts
99. Jan Christiaan Smuts, the second and fourth Prime Minister of South Africa.
100. Richard Gavin Gardiner Casey moved to Cairo in 1942, when appointed Minister Resident in the Middle East.
101. *Masters and Commanders* by Andrew Roberts.
102. *Pendulum of War: The Three Battles of El Alamein* by Niall Barr.
103. *The Memoirs of Field Marshal The Viscount Montgomery of Alamein K.G.*
104. *War Diaries 1939-1945: Field Marshal Lord Alanbrooke* edited by Alex Danchev and Daniel Todman.
105. *Churchill* by Roy Jenkins.
106. *War Diaries 1939-1945: Field Marshal Lord Alanbrooke* edited by Alex Danchev and Daniel Todman.
107. *Ibid.*
108. Wilson was the 2nd RB Colonel-in-Chief, Gott had been with the KRRC, and Eden had been a captain with the 21st (Yeoman Rifle) part of KRRC during the First World War.
109. *Auchinleck* by John Connell.
110. Auchinleck took command of the Indian Army in June 1943.
111. 7th Motor Brigade War Diaries 1943.
112. *El Alamein: The Battle that Turned the Tide of the Second World War* by Bryn Hammond.
112. Stephen Bungay says in his book that the escape hatch was never opened and the passengers, including Gott, did not exit the plane before the enemy returned.
113. Gott's body was later removed and reburied in El Alamein cemetery.
114. *Finest Years: Churchill as Warlord 1940-45* by Max Hastings.
115. *Auchinleck* by John Connell.
116. *Finest Years: Churchill as Warlord 1940-45* by Max Hastings.
117. *The Memoirs of Field Marshal The Viscount Montgomery of Alamein K.G.* 205. *Alamein* by C. E. Lucas Phillips.
118. *Ibid.*
119. *El Alamein 1942* by Ken Ford.
120. *Generals at War: Alamein* – Discovery Military documentary.
121. The Memoirs of Field Marshal The Viscount Montgomery of Alamein K.G.
122. *What did you do in the War, Auntie?: The BBC At War 1939-1945* by Tom Hickman.
123. *Forgotten Voices* states that Sgt Longstaff was a member of the 2nd Battalion Rifle Brigade; however, reading further it appears that he may have been a member of the 2nd KRRC.
124. *Forgotten Voices of the Second World War* by Max Arthur.
125. *Rifle Brigade Chronicle.*
126. *The Diary of a Desert Rat* by R. L. Crimp.
127. Private correspondence of Mrs Ann Bayley.
128. *Forgotten Voices of the Second World War* by Max Arthur.
129. *The War Illustrated.*
130. *The Memoirs of Field Marshal The Viscount Montgomery of Alamein K.G.*
131. *Masters and Commanders* by Andrew Roberts.
132. *Ibid.*
133. *War Diaries 1939-1945: Field Marshal Lord Alanbrooke* edited by Alex Danchev and Daniel Todman.
134. *The Rommel Papers* edited by B. H. Liddell-Hart.

135. The Military General Staff for the Third Reich.
136. *The Rommel Papers* edited by B. H. Liddell-Hart.
137. *Rommel: Battles and Campaigns* by Kenneth Macksey.
138. *The Rommel Papers* edited by B. H. Liddell-Hart.
139. *Pendulum of War: The Three Battles of El Alamein* by Niall Barr.
140. *The Memoirs of Field Marshal The Viscount Montgomery of Alamein K.G.*
141. In intelligence jargon, the technique of planting misleading information by means of a faked accident was known as the 'haversack ruse' – *Operation Mincemeat.*
142. *The Art of War* by Sun Tzu, edited by Samuel B. Griffith, detailing the treatise of the military strategist and tactician written in the 6th century BC.
143. *The Rommel Papers* edited by B. H. Liddell-Hart.
143. *The Crucible of War* by Barrie Pitt.
144. *El Alamein: The Battle that Turned the Tide of the Second World War* by Bryn Hammond.
145. *Rommel: Battles and Campaigns* by Kenneth Macksey.

Chapter 4

1.   The Fairey Albacore was a British single-engine carrier-borne biplane flown by the Royal Navy's Fleet Air Arm and used for spotting and target-marking for heavier bombers.
2.   The Wellington was a two-engine British long-range medium bomber, designed by Barnes Wallis and built by Vickers, carrying 4,500 lb of bombs.
3.   Operational Order No. 29 issued to 7th Motor Brigade, dated 15 August 1942, held in the National Archives.
4.   *The Diary of a Desert Rat* by R. L. Crimp.
5.   *Ibid. The Rommel Papers* edited by B. H. Liddell-Hart.
6.   *El Alamein: The Battle that Turned the Tide of the Second World War* by Bryn Hammond.
7.   2nd Battalion Rifle Brigade War Diaries 1942.
8.   *The Rommel Papers* edited by B. H. Liddell-Hart.
9.   *Hellfire Tonight* – the diary of Albert Martin of 'S' Company 2nd Battalion The Rifle Brigade.
10. Operational Order No. 29 issued to 7th Motor Brigade, dated 15 August 1942, held in the National Archives.
11. *The Crucible of War* by Barrie Pitt and *The Rommel Papers* edited by B. H. Liddell-Hart.
12. *El Alamein* by Field Marshal Lord Carver.
13. *The Rifle Brigade in the Second World War, 1939-1945* by Maj. R. H. W. S. Hastings.
14. *The Crucible of War* by Barrie Pitt.
15. *El Alamein: The Battle that Turned the Tide of the Second World War* by Bryn Hammond.
16. The Greys were temporarily assigned to the 22nd Armoured Brigade, equipped with a mixture of Grant and Stuart tanks.
17. *El Alamein: The Battle that Turned the Tide of the Second World War* by Bryn Hammond.
18. *Images of War.*
19. *El Alamein: The Battle that Turned the Tide of the Second World War* by Bryn Hammond.
20. *El Alamein* by Field Marshal Lord Carver.
21. These were the remainder of the thirty panzers encountered by the 2nd RB earlier in the day, six of which were destroyed.
22. Referring to the formations performing a fly-past at the Nuremberg Party Rally celebrations.
23. *The Rommel Papers* edited by B. H. Liddell-Hart.
24. *Ibid.*
25. *Alamein* by Stephen Bungay.
26. United States Army Air Forces.
27. *The Rommel Papers* edited by B. H. Liddell-Hart.
28. *The Rommel Papers* edited by B. H. Liddell-Hart.
29. *Rommel: Battles and Campaigns* by Kenneth Macksey.
30. *El Alamein: The Battle that Turned the Tide of the Second World War* by Bryn Hammond.

31. Patrol report of 3/4 September written by Capt. Sturt, contained in the War Diary of the 2nd RB held in the National Archives.

32. *The Crucible of War* by Barrie Pitt.

33. *The Memoirs of Field Marshal The Viscount Montgomery of Alamein K.G.*

34. *Ibid.*

35. *Ibid.*

36. *Alamein* by Stephen Bungay.

37. *The Art of War* by Sun Tzu, edited by Samuel B. Griffith, detailing the treatise of the military strategist and tactician written in the 6th century BC.

38. *Images of War.*

39. Harding had been a student of Montgomery's at the Camberley Staff College.

40. The above is based on the description of the defences found in *Alamein* by Jon Latimer.

41. *Alamein* by Jon Latimer

42. *World War II Axis Booby Traps and Sabotage Tactics* by Gordon L. Rottman.

43. *El Alamein* by John Sadler.

44. *Alamein* by Jon Latimer.

45. *The Rommel Papers* edited by B. H. Liddell-Hart.

46. Codenames were generally provided by the Inter-Services Security Board, in relation to nations, cities, plans, etc., to disguise them under false names. In theory these codewords bore no resemblance to the actual operation but were taken from random lists. Churchill had given orders that frivolous names should not be used, but there were instances when commanders used names that had an operational meaning.

47. *Alamein* by C. E. Lucas Phillips.

48. *Alamein* by Stephen Bungay.

49. *Ibid.*

50. *Ibid.*

51. *El Alamein: The Battle that Turned the Tide of the Second World War* by Bryn Hammond.

52. *Hellfire Tonight* – the diary of Albert Martin of 'S' Company 2nd Battalion The Rifle Brigade.

53. In a memo contained in the 2nd Battalion Rifle Brigade War Diaries 1942.

54. *The Rifle Brigade in the Second World War, 1939-1945* by Maj. R. H. W. S. Hastings.

55. *War Diaries 1939-1945: Field Marshal Lord Alanbrooke* edited by Alex Danchev and Daniel Todman.

56. *El Alamein: The Battle that Turned the Tide of the Second World War* by Bryn Hammond.

57. *Generals at War: Alamein* – Discovery Military documentary.

58. *El Alamein* by John Sadler.

59. *Alamein* by Stephen Bungay.

60. *Ibid.*

61. *The Crucible of War* by Barrie Pitt.

62. *The Rommel Papers* edited by B. H. Liddell-Hart.

63. *Alamein* by Jon Latimer.

64. *The Second World War* by Antony Beevor.

65. *Alamein* by Jon Latimer.

66. *Ibid.*

67. 2nd Battalion Rifle Brigade War Diaries 1942.

68. One of the 'Hobart's Funnies', designed and constructed by Gen. Percy Hobart to overcome a variety of problems. Hobart was famous for forming and training the 7th Armoured Division (1939-40), the 11th Armoured Division (1941-42) and the 79th Armoured Division (1942-45).

69. *The Crucible of War* by Barrie Pitt.

70. *The Crucible of War* by Barrie Pitt.

71. *The Crucible of War* by Barrie Pitt.

72. 2nd Battalion Rifle Brigade War Diaries 1942.

73. *The Art of War* by Sun Tzu, edited by Samuel B. Griffith, detailing the treatise of the military strategist and tactician written in the 6th century BC. This principle was paraphrased by Mao Tse-tung.

74. *El Alamein* by John Sadler

75. Upon taking temporary command, Stumme had re-evaluated the situation and decided that an attack was more likely to take place during the full-moon period of 20-25 October. However, this expectation was ignored by *Oberst* Ulrich Liss, head of the Intelligence branch of the OKW, who thought that the British attack would not start before the beginning of November, and it was this opinion that was reported to Berlin and ultimately came to the attention of Montgomery via Ultra.

76. Brig. Dunphie's El Alamein Dinner Speech

77. *The Crucible of War* by Barrie Pitt.

78. *The Memoirs of Field Marshal The Viscount Montgomery of Alamein K.G.*

79. *Ibid.*

80. *Alamein* by C. E. Lucas Phillips.

81. *Ibid.*

82. *Alamein* by Jon Latimer.

83. A First World War term used for a faked or feint attack against the opposing trenches to either test the defensive ability of the enemy or their reaction times to repopulate positions. It was also used to convince the enemy of an infantry attack on that section of the line.

84. *El Alamein: The Battle that Turned the Tide of the Second World War* by Bryn Hammond.

85. *Ibid.*

86. *War Diaries 1939-1945: Field Marshal Lord Alanbrooke* edited by Alex Danchev and Daniel Todman.

87. *Ibid.*

88. *Alamein* by Jon Latimer

89. *Ibid.*

90. *All Hell Let Loose* by Max Hastings.

91. *Alamein* by Jon Latimer.

92. *Alamein* by C. E. Lucas Phillips.

93. *Forgotten Voices of the Second World War* by Max Arthur.

94. First draft of a book of Victor Gregg's life and the resultant book co-authored with Rick Stroud – *Rifleman: A Front Line Life*.

95. Private correspondence of Mrs Ann Bayley.

96. *Images of War*.

97. *Alamein* by C. E. Lucas Phillips

98. *End of the Beginning* by Tim Clayton & Phil Craig.

99. *Ibid.*

100. *What did you do in the War, Auntie?: The BBC At War 1939-1945* by Tom Hickman.

101. *End of the Beginning* by Tim Clayton & Phil Craig.

102. *The Diary of a Desert Rat* by R. L. Crimp.

103. *Alamein* by C. E. Lucas Phillips.

104. *Alamein* by Jon Latimer.

105. *War Diaries 1939-1945: Field Marshal Lord Alanbrooke* edited by Alex Danchev and Daniel Todman.

106. *The Rifle Brigade in the Second World War, 1939-1945* by Maj. R. H. W. S. Hastings.

Chapter 5

1. Egyptian Summer Time – one hour ahead of Greenwich Mean Time.

2. *Finest Years: Churchill as Warlord 1940-45* by Max Hastings.

3. It is difficult to set the exact number of guns used in this first barrage, as various texts quote different numbers. I have kept to the 882 stated in *The Crucible of War* and *Pendulum of War*.

4. Shells from different calibre and types of guns travel at different speeds; the firing pattern had therefore been calculated to allow for these differences in order that all the shells would land at the same time.

5. Report on conversations with von Thoma, held in the National Archives.

6. *The Crucible of War* by Barrie Pitt and *Pendulum of War: The Three Battles of El Alamein* by Niall Barr.
7. *Pendulum of War: The Three Battles of El Alamein* by Niall Barr.
8. *Forgotten Voices of the Second World War* by Max Arthur.
10. *El Alamein* by John Sadler.
11. *The War Illustrated.*
12. *The Crucible of War* by Barrie Pitt.
13. *Ibid.*
14. *The War Illustrated.*
15. *Pendulum of War: The Three Battles of El Alamein* by Niall Barr.
16. *Alamein* by C. E. Lucas Phillips.
17. *Ibid.*
18. *The War Illustrated.*
19. Light cotton or flax material.
20. *El Alamein 1942* by Ken Ford.
21. *Pendulum of War: The Three Battles of El Alamein* by Niall Barr.
22. This term describes a position taken by a tank or armoured vehicle where only the top of the body is visible, providing extra protection to the whole tank whilst still allowing the turret gun to fire at suitable targets.
23. *El Alamein 1942* by Ken Ford.
24. *The Rifle Brigade in the Second World War, 1939-1945* by Maj. R. H. W. S. Hastings.
25. *The War Illustrated.*
26. *The Rifle Brigade in the Second World War, 1939-1945* by Maj. R. H. W. S. Hastings.
27. *End of the Beginning* by Tim Clayton & Phil Craig.
28. *The Rifle Brigade in the Second World War, 1939-1945* by Maj. R. H. W. S. Hastings.
29. *The War Illustrated.*
30. 2nd Battalion Rifle Brigade War Diaries 1942.
31. The original plan called for gaps 40 yards wide, but due to delays the plan was changed, allowing for the gaps to be initially widened to 16 yards and then widened further after the gap had been completed.
32. *Ibid.*
33. *Alamein* by C. E. Lucas Phillips.
34. *El Alamein: The Battle that Turned the Tide of the Second World War* by Bryn Hammond.
35. *El Alamein* by John Sadler.
36. *Alamein* by C. E. Lucas Phillips.
37. 2nd Battalion Rifle Brigade War Diaries 1942.
38. *El Alamein: The Battle that Turned the Tide of the Second World War* by Bryn Hammond.
39. Kidney Ridge was in fact a depression and later became known as the Kidney feature. Despite this, I intend to continue to refer to the Kidney feature as a ridge so as to avoid confusion between texts.
40. *Alamein* by C. E. Lucas Phillips.
42. *The Crucible of War* by Barrie Pitt.
43. *Ibid.*
44. *Alamein* by C. E. Lucas Phillips.
45. *End of the Beginning* by Tim Clayton & Phil Craig.
46. *Afrika Korps at War* by George Forty.
47. *The Armies of Rommel* by George Forty.
48. *Pendulum of War: The Three Battles of El Alamein* by Niall Barr.
49. *El Alamein 1942* by Ken Ford.
50. *Pendulum of War: The Three Battles of El Alamein* by Niall Barr.
51. *Ibid.*
52. *The Crucible of War* by Barrie Pitt.
53. Roosevelt's offer to help Britain, made 149 days before and 5,668 miles to the west, was now solidified by Gen. Marshall when he sent 300 Sherman tanks to Egypt in six of America's fastest ships. Although one of them was torpedoed and sunk the day after leaving, the loss was

immediately made good and 252 of these tanks, codenamed Swallows for security, were available at the battle, having arrived on 3 September.

54. *The Crucible of War* by Barrie Pitt.
55. *Ibid.*
56. *End of the Beginning* by Tim Clayton & Phil Craig.
57. *Pendulum of War: The Three Battles of El Alamein* by Niall Barr.
58. *Ibid.*
59. The citation for CSM Jones' Military Cross – *The London Gazette*, 14 January 1943.
60. Reproduced in *El Alamein: The Battle that Turned the Tide of the Second World War* by Bryn Hammond.
61. *Ibid.*
62. *The Armies of Rommel* by George Forty.
63. *Pendulum of War: The Three Battles of El Alamein* by Niall Barr.
64. *Ibid.*
65. *Ibid.*
66. *Ibid.*
67. *El Alamein 1942* by Ken Ford.
68. *Alamein* by C. E. Lucas Phillips.
69. *Ibid.*
70. *Pendulum of War: The Three Battles of El Alamein* by Niall Barr.
71. *Ibid.*
72. *Pendulum of War: The Three Battles of El Alamein* by Niall Barr.
73. *Ibid.*
74. *Ibid.*
75. *Ibid.*
76. *Afrika Korps at War* by George Forty.

Chapter 6

1. This chapter was written using Maj. Hastings' book, the battalion report and the official report on the action as the main reference sources, with other elements included under separate reference notes.
2. Brig. Dunphie's El Alamein Dinner Speech
3. *Alamein* by C. E. Lucas Phillips.
4. Recording of a speech by Lt Col. Victor Buller Turner.
5. *Ibid.*
6. *Pendulum of War: The Three Battles of El Alamein* by Niall Barr.
7. *Pendulum of War: The Three Battles of El Alamein* by Niall Barr.
8. 2nd Battalion Rifle Brigade War Diaries 1942.
9. *Ibid.*
10. *Up Close and Personal* by David Lee.
11. *The Rifle Brigade in the Second World War, 1939-1945* by Maj. R. H. W. S. Hastings.
12. Recording of a speech by Lt Col. Victor Buller Turner.
13. *Ibid.*
14. David Lee in *Up Close and Personal* states that Parkes was killed.
15. War Diary of the 47th Royal Tank Regiment held in the National Archives.
16. Benzedrine is the trade name given to an amphetamine mixture used as a stimulant.
17. *El Alamein: The Battle that Turned the Tide of the Second World War* by Bryn Hammond.
18. *The Diary of a Desert Rat* by R. L. Crimp.
19. *Alamein* by C. E. Lucas Phillips.
20. *Ibid.*
21. *Up Close and Personal* by David Lee.
22. An address by Maj.-Gen. Raymond Briggs CB, DSO at the Empire Cinema, Brixton, 26 March 1944, during 'Salute the Soldier Week', reproduced in *Up Close and Personal* by David Lee.

23. Recording of a speech by Lt Col. Victor Buller Turner.
24. *El Alamein 1942* by Ken Ford.
25. Some texts put this bearing as 275°; however, reports based on battalion and 1st Armoured Division investigations note this as 270°.
26. *Up Close and Personal* by David Lee.
27. A wisp is a flock of birds, especially snipe, continuing the use of shooting terminology for the codewords.
28. Recording of a speech by Lt Col. Victor Buller Turner.
29. *Up Close and Personal* by David Lee.
30. *El Alamein: The Battle that Turned the Tide of the Second World War* by Bryn Hammond.
31. The jeep invented, developed and produced by the American Bantam Car Company; the 1940 model had four-wheel drive and 40 hp – known to the British as the Bantam jeep.
32. A code that called for an unciphered message to be sent in plain language but with certain words replaced with others previously agreed between the parties.
33. *Alamein* by C. E. Lucas Phillips.
34. Recording of a speech by Lt Col. Victor Buller Turner, and Tom Bird's speech to the Rifle Brigade Dinner.
35. *Up Close and Personal* by David Lee.
36. *The Diary of a Desert Rat* by R. L. Crimp.
37. Recording of a speech by Lt Col. Victor Buller Turner.
38. *Up Close and Personal* by David Lee.
39. Recording of a speech by Lt Col. Victor Buller Turner.
40. *Up Close and Personal* by David Lee.
41. *Alamein* by C. E. Lucas Phillips.
42. Some reports give this as two miles.
43. Despite Turner's position being 900 yards from the Snipe objective, I will continue to refer to it as the Snipe position to avoid confusion.
44. *Alamein* by C. E. Lucas Phillips.
45. *Up Close and Personal* by David Lee.
46. Personal recollections of Rifleman Moore – wireless operator.
47. *Ibid.*
48. *Up Close and Personal* by David Lee.
49. War Diary of the 239th Battery.
50. *Alamein* by C. E. Lucas Phillips.
51. Brig. Dunphie's El Alamein Dinner Speech
52. *Hellfire Tonight* – the diary of Albert Martin of 'S' Company 2nd Battalion The Rifle Brigade.
53. Flower gives this distance as 250 yards.
54. *Up Close and Personal* by David Lee.
55. Some records show the number of prisoners as between twenty and thirty-five. Flower writes that a dozen were taken prisoner, which would have been a reasonable 'fit' to have in the back of the carriers.
56. *Ibid.*
57. Flower states in *Up Close and Personal* that there were between fifty and sixty tanks.
58. *Alamein* by C. E. Lucas Phillips.
59. *El Alamein: The Battle that Turned the Tide of the Second World War* by Bryn Hammond.
60. *Up Close and Personal* by David Lee.
61. Situation report.
62. 7th Motor Brigade War Diaries 1943.
63. War Diary of the 239th Battery.
64. Recording of a speech by Lt Col. Victor Buller Turner.
65. War Diary of the 239th Battery.
66. Some reports state that it was the guns of 'S' Company that had this encounter; however, these had been divided up among the other companies prior to the operation. Turner spoke of the guns being part of 'A' Company.

67. *The Diary of a Desert Rat* by R. L. Crimp.
68. Turner eventually found out that he was wrong when, many years later, Noyle contacted Lucas Phillips after reading his book *Alamein*.
69. *Up Close and Personal* by David Lee.
70. Verbal history given by Sgt Swann and held at the Imperial War Museum.
71. 7th Motor Brigade War Diaries 1943.
72. *Up Close and Personal* by David Lee.
73. Ibid
74. *Ibid.*
75. *El Alamein 1942* by Ken Ford.
76. War Diary of the 47th Royal Tank Regiment held in the National Archives.
77. *El Alamein: The Battle that Turned the Tide of the Second World War* by Bryn   Hammond.
78. *Up Close and Personal* by David Lee.
79. *Ibid.*
80. *Ibid.*
81. *The War Illustrated.*
82. *El Alamein: The Battle that Turned the Tide of the Second World War* by Bryn Hammond.
83. *Up Close and Personal* by David Lee.
84. 'Leading from the Front' by Stephen Snelling in *Britain at War Magazine*, December 2012.
85. *The Rifle Brigade in the Second World War, 1939-1945* by Maj. R. H. W. S. Hastings.
86. Brig. Dunphie's El Alamein Dinner Speech and *Up Close and Personal* by David Lee.
87. First draft of a book of Victor Gregg's life and the resultant book co-authored with Rick Stroud – *Rifleman: A Front Line Life.*
88. *Hellfire Tonight* – the diary of Albert Martin of 'S' Company 2nd Battalion The Rifle Brigade.
89. Personal recollections of Rifleman Moore – wireless operator.
90. Blacker, an athletic six-footer with the nickname 'Muscles', was from the East End of London and had lied about his age when joining up. Whilst at Snipe, he was still two months short of his eighteenth birthday.
91. *Up Close and Personal* by David Lee.
92. Nelson had been commandeered by an officer for another duty.
93. *Up Close and Personal* by David Lee.
94. *Alamein* by C. E. Lucas Phillips.
95. *Ibid.*
96. *Up Close and Personal* by David Lee.
97. War Diary of the 41st Royal Tank Regiment held in the National Archives.
98. *Up Close and Personal* by David Lee.
99. Rifleman W. F. W. Harding personal archive.
100. *The Diary of a Desert Rat* by R. L. Crimp.
101. *Ibid.*
102. *Ibid.*
103. Personal recollections of Rifleman Moore – wireless operator.
104. *Up Close and Personal* by David Lee.
105. *Alamein* by C. E. Lucas Phillips.
106. *Ibid.*
107. *Ibid.*
108. *Hellfire Tonight* – the diary of Albert Martin of 'S' Company 2nd Battalion The Rifle Brigade.
109. *Ibid.*
110. *The Diary of a Desert Rat* by R. L. Crimp.
111. The naming of the tanks was a throwback to cavalry days when the horses were named by their riders and were often owned by the officers themselves. The first letter of the name corresponded to the designated alphabet letter of the squadron; therefore *Argenaute* was in 'A' Squadron, and *Badger* was part of 'B' Squadron.
112. *Sherman M4* published by Cassell.
113. *Pendulum of War: The Three Battles of El Alamein* by Niall Barr.

114. *Alamein* by Jon Latimer.
115. *El Alamein* by John Sadler.
116. *Alamein: War Without Hate* by John Bierman & Colin Smith.
117. *World War II: The Sharp End* by John Ellis.
118. War Diary of the 239th Battery.
119. *El Alamein: The Battle that Turned the Tide of the Second World War* by Bryn Hammond.
120. Brig. Dunphie's El Alamein Dinner Speech
121. *Ibid.*
122. First draft of a book of Victor Gregg's life and the resultant book co-authored with Rick Stroud – *Rifleman: A Front Line Life.*
123. *The Rifle Brigade in the Second World War, 1939-1945* by Maj. R. H. W. S. Hastings.
124. *Alamein* by C. E. Lucas Phillips.
125. *Ibid.*
126. There are conflicting opinions concerning the time because of the difference between Egyptian Summer Time and Italian Time, but as the battalion timings were set by R/T reports, they are considered correct.
127. Lt Salt had transferred over from 7th RB on 4 October 1942. He was the younger son of Mr and Mrs Salt of Purley and joined the regiment in February 1940, being promoted to lieutenant in August 1941, as written in his regimental obituary.
128. *Alamein* by Stephen Bungay.
129. *Ibid.*
130. *The Crucible of War* by Barrie Pitt.
131. However, after the battle it was found that no wrecks remained, the damaged tanks being towed away for repair after the battle.
132. Personal recollection of Eddie Blacker.
133. *Alamein* by C. E. Lucas Phillips.
134. *The Rommel Papers* edited by B. H. Liddell-Hart.
135. *Pendulum of War: The Three Battles of El Alamein* by Niall Barr.
136. *Up Close and Personal* by David Lee.
137. *Alamein* by C. E. Lucas Phillips.
138. *The War Illustrated.*
139. Verbal history given by Sgt Swann and held at the Imperial War Museum.
140. Brig. Dunphie's El Alamein Dinner Speech
141. *The Rifle Brigade in the Second World War, 1939-1945* by Maj. R. H. W. S. Hastings.
142. Brig. Dunphie's El Alamein Dinner Speech
143. *Alamein* by C. E. Lucas Phillips.
144. *Ibid.*
145. *Daily Mail*, 22 September 2011.
146. *The Diary of a Desert Rat* by R. L. Crimp.
147. *Ibid.*
148. There is some disagreement over the origin of this heavy barrage. The battalion report stated that it was the enemy firing, but Swann remembered that this was friendly fire, which was borne out by Pearson who, in response to Marten's request, attended the Royal Artillery Regimental HQ to ask that the shelling be stopped.
149. *The Diary of a Desert Rat* by R. L. Crimp.
150. *Up Close and Personal* by David Lee.
151. *Ibid.*
152. *Ibid.*
153. Rifleman W. F. W. Harding personal archive.
154. Private correspondence of Mrs Ann Bayley.
155. Rifleman W. F. W. Harding personal archive and private correspondence of Mrs Ann Bayley.
156. We do not have an exact time for Crowder's injury; however, if it had happened before 0900 hours then there is a good chance that as a seriously wounded casualty he would have been transported out by Shepherd-Cross. The first mention of Crowder is at 1400 hours in Hastings'

book. Therefore logically the incident happened between 0900 and 1400 hours, and as shells were hitting the position at midday, I have taken this as a likely time.

157. *Up Close and Personal* by David Lee.
158. Brig. Dunphie's El Alamein Dinner Speech
159. *Rommel: Battles and Campaigns* by Kenneth Macksey.
160. *Up Close and Personal* by David Lee.
161. Again there is a time difference in the account of operations of 12 Battalion 133rd Tank Regiment. As the timings of the battalion were set by R/T reports they are considered correct.
162. *Up Close and Personal* by David Lee and *Alamein* by C. E. Lucas Phillips.
163. *Up Close and Personal* by David Lee.
164. Brig. Dunphie's El Alamein Dinner Speech
165. Recording of a speech by Lt Col. Victor Buller Turner.
166. *Pendulum of War: The Three Battles of El Alamein* by Niall Barr.
167. 'Leading from the Front' by Stephen Snelling in *Britain at War Magazine*, December 2012.
168. Recording of a speech by Lt Col. Victor Buller Turner.
169. *Up Close and Personal* by David Lee.
170. *Ibid.*
171. Rifleman W. F. W. Harding personal archive.
172. Recording of a speech by Lt Col. Victor Buller Turner.
173. Recording of a speech by Lt Col. Victor Buller Turner.
174. *Ibid.*
175. 2nd Battalion Rifle Brigade War Diaries 1942.
176. *Up Close and Personal* by David Lee.
177. Recording of a speech by Lt Col. Victor Buller Turner.
178. *Alamein* by C. E. Lucas Phillips.
179. *Up Close and Personal* by David Lee.
180. First draft of a book of Victor Gregg's life and the resultant book co-authored with Rick Stroud – *Rifleman: A Front Line Life.*
181. *The Diary of a Desert Rat* by R. L. Crimp.
182. *Alamein* by C. E. Lucas Phillips.
183. *Up Close and Personal* by David Lee.
184. *Ibid.*
185. *Alamein* by C. E. Lucas Phillips.
186. *Up Close and Personal* by David Lee.
187. *Alamein* by C. E. Lucas Phillips.
188. *Ibid.*
189. Verbal history given by Tom Bird and held at the Imperial War Museum.
190. *Up Close and Personal* by David Lee.
191. *Alamein* by C. E. Lucas Phillips.
192. *Up Close and Personal* by David Lee.
193. Telephone conversation between Tim Marten and the author.
194. Some have reported that Turner said this, but he was very ill in the HQ dugout at this time; I have therefore attributed the quote to Marten.
195. *Pendulum of War: The Three Battles of El Alamein* by Niall Barr.
196. *Alamein* by C. E. Lucas Phillips.
197. *Pendulum of War: The Three Battles of El Alamein* by Niall Barr.
198. In *Pendulum of War* it notes that these were the 24th Armoured Brigade. I have stayed with the official report on Snipe.
199. German codename for Sherman and Grant tanks.
200. *Pendulum of War: The Three Battles of El Alamein* by Niall Barr.
201. Turner said that this was 200 yards.
202. *Alamein* by C. E. Lucas Phillips.
203. I think they mean Newman's, as Pearson's gun had been located to the south and by this time he was wounded.

204. War Diary of the 239th
205. *Rifle Brigade Chronicle*, various copies.
206. It should be noted that targets were hit by more than one gun and so the claims were often shared.
207. Many texts put this order down to Turner. However, by now he was delirious and not in a fit state to give such an order, and in a telephone conversation with Tim Marten I was told that it was he who had made the decision.
208. Telephone conversation between Tim Marten and the author.
209. Recording of a speech by Lt Col. Victor Buller Turner.
210. The battalion report states that a sergeant assisted Chard, and that this could have been Ayris. Brig. Dunphie's speech, however, said that it was Holt-Wilson who helped to turn the gun round. I have therefore included both men in the narrative.
211. *Ibid.*
212. Rifleman W. F. W. Harding personal archive.
213. *The Diary of a Desert Rat* by R. L. Crimp.
214. *Up Close and Personal* by David Lee.
215. Brig. Dunphie's El Alamein Dinner Speech
216. The official report stated that this was 200 yards. It is probably the case that he saw them at 200 yards and by the time he had crossed over and fired, the panzers were at 100 yards.
217. *Up Close and Personal* by David Lee.
218. *Alamein* by C. E. Lucas Phillips.
219. *Up Close and Personal* by David Lee.
220. *Pendulum of War: The Three Battles of El Alamein* by Niall Barr.
221. *Up Close and Personal* by David Lee.
222. *Alamein* by C. E. Lucas Phillips.
223. *Ibid.*
224. *Up Close and Personal* by David Lee.
225. *The Rifle Brigade in the Second World War, 1939-1945* by Maj. R. H. W. S. Hastings.
226. Recording of a speech by Lt Col. Victor Buller Turner.
227. *Ibid.*
228. *Up Close and Personal* by David Lee.
229. *Ibid.*
230. Brig. Dunphie's El Alamein Dinner Speech
231. Recording of a speech by Lt Col. Victor Buller Turner.
232. *Up Close and Personal* by David Lee.
233. *Sherman M4* published by Cassell.
234. *Up Close and Personal* by David Lee.
235. Tom Bird's speech to the Rifle Brigade Dinner.
236. The battalion diary states that they arrived at the 51st (Highland) dressing station.
237. Recording of a speech by Lt Col. Victor Buller Turner.
238. *Up Close and Personal* by David Lee.
239. Recording of a speech by Lt Col. Victor Buller Turner.
240. *Up Close and Personal* by David Lee.
241. *El Alamein: The Battle that Turned the Tide of the Second World War* by Bryn Hammond.
242. *The War Illustrated.*
243. *Up Close and Personal* by David Lee.
244. *Ibid.*
245. *Hellfire Tonight* – the diary of Albert Martin of 'S' Company 2nd Battalion The Rifle Brigade.
246. *Alamein* by C. E. Lucas Phillips.
247. Brig. Dunphie's El Alamein Dinner Speech
248. *The Diary of a Desert Rat* by R. L. Crimp.
249. *Up Close and Personal* by David Lee.
250. Rifleman W. F. W. Harding personal archive.
251. *Up Close and Personal* by David Lee.

252. Tom Bird's speech to the Rifle Brigade Dinner.
253. *The Diary of a Desert Rat* by R. L. Crimp.
254. *Hellfire Tonight* – the diary of Albert Martin of 'S' Company 2nd Battalion The Rifle Brigade.
255. *Pendulum of War: The Three Battles of El Alamein* by Niall Barr.
256. *Afrika Korps at War* by George Forty.

Chapter 7

1. Private correspondence of Mrs Ann Bayley.
2. At this time they did not know the fate of FOO Noyle or Lt Lightly, so I have shown the number of missing as two.
3. Report on Snipe included in 2nd Battalion Rifle Brigade War Diaries 1942.
4. 'Leading from the Front' by Stephen Snelling in *Britain at War Magazine*, December 2012.
5. *The Diary of a Desert Rat* by R. L. Crimp.
6. *El Alamein: The Battle that Turned the Tide of the Second World War* by Bryn Hammond.
7. *Rifle Brigade Chronicle*, various copies.
8. Ann Bayley has said that Penicillin was being used on Axis troops at the end of 1942, but that permission had not been granted to use the drug on Allied troops, which was a contributing factor to her brother's death.
9. *Blood and Bullets* documentary on Royal Army Medical Corps.
10. *Alamein* by Jon Latimer.
11. *Ibid.*
12. *Pendulum of War: The Three Battles of El Alamein* by Niall Barr.
13. *Ibid.*
14. *Ibid.*
15. *El Alamein* by John Sadler.
16. *Ibid.*
17. *Ibid.*
18. *Alamein* by C. E. Lucas Phillips.
19. *El Alamein* by Field Marshal Lord Carver.
20. 'Leading from the Front' by Stephen Snelling in *Britain at War Magazine*, December 2012.
21. Report on Snipe included in 2nd Battalion Rifle Brigade War Diaries 1942.
22. *The Rommel Papers* edited by B. H. Liddell-Hart.
23. 'Leading from the Front' by Stephen Snelling in *Britain at War Magazine*, December 2012.
24. Report on Snipe included in 2nd Battalion Rifle Brigade War Diaries 1942.
25. *Ibid.*
26. *Ibid.*
27. *The War Illustrated.*
28. Sgt Ayris is noted in Hastings' book to have been awarded the Military Cross, but unfortunately this is not supported by the official records – as advised to the author by Gary Ayris.
29. *Rifle Brigade Chronicle.*
30. 'Leading from the Front' by Stephen Snelling in *Britain at War Magazine*, December 2012.
31. In a letter to his girlfriend, later his wife, the text of which was given to the author by Ron Cassidy.
32. Calistan was later commissioned and was killed on 30 July 1944 while serving with the 7th RB.
33. *Rifle Brigade Chronicle*, various copies.
34. Recording of a speech by Lt Col. Victor Buller Turner.
35. Medal descriptions taken from http://www.stephen-stratford.co.uk/gallantry.htm
36. *Britain at War Magazine* interview by Tony Glenhill with Lord Ashcroft.
37. British Gallantry Awards – *Britain at War Magazine* supplement.
38. *Ibid.*
39. 'Posthumous VCs' section of the website of the National Army Museum, www.nam.ac.uk
40. British Gallantry Awards – *Britain at War Magazine* supplement.

41. DefenceNews / History and Honour / Victoria and George Cross Holders /The Worlds Most ExclusiveClub
42. British Gallantry Awards – *Britain at War Magazine* supplement.
43. *Focus on Courage* by Sir Christopher Wallace and Maj. Ron Cassidy.
44. *Ibid.*
45. British Gallantry Awards – *Britain at War Magazine* supplement.
46. *Focus on Courage* by Sir Christopher Wallace and Maj. Ron Cassidy.
47. British Gallantry Awards – *Britain at War Magazine* supplement.
48. *Ibid.*
49. *Ibid.*
50. Brig. Dunphie's El Alamein Dinner Speech

Chapter 8

1. *The Rommel Papers* edited by B. H. Liddell-Hart.
2. *Alamein* by Stephen Bungay.
3. *Ibid.*
4. *Pendulum of War: The Three Battles of El Alamein* by Niall Barr.
5. *Pendulum of War: The Three Battles of El Alamein* by Niall Barr.
6. *Afrika Korps at War* by George Forty.
7. *Pendulum of War: The Three Battles of El Alamein* by Niall Barr.
8. *Ibid.*
9. *End of the Beginning* by Tim Clayton & Phil Craig.
10. *War Diaries 1939-1945: Field Marshal Lord Alanbrooke* edited by Alex Danchev and Daniel Todman.
11. *Alamein* by Stephen Bungay.
12. *El Alamein* by John Sadler.
13. *End of the Beginning* by Tim Clayton & Phil Craig.
14. *Alamein* by Stephen Bungay.
15. *End of the Beginning* by Tim Clayton & Phil Craig.
16. *What did you do in the War, Auntie?: The BBC At War 1939-1945* by Tom Hickman.
17. *El Alamein* by John Sadler.
18. *War Diaries 1939-1945: Field Marshal Lord Alanbrooke* edited by Alex Danchev and Daniel Todman.
19. *Hellfire Tonight* – the diary of Albert Martin of 'S' Company 2nd Battalion The Rifle Brigade.
20. *The Diary of a Desert Rat* by R. L. Crimp.
21. 2nd Battalion Rifle Brigade War Diaries 1942.
22. *Afrika Korps at War* by George Forty.
23. *Alamein* by C. E. Lucas Phillips.
24. *Pendulum of War: The Three Battles of El Alamein* by Niall Barr.
25. *The Memoirs of Field Marshal The Viscount Montgomery of Alamein K.G.*
26. *Pendulum of War: The Three Battles of El Alamein* by Niall Barr.
27. *The Memoirs of Field Marshal The Viscount Montgomery of Alamein K.G.*
28. *The Rifle Brigade in the Second World War, 1939-1945* by Maj. R. H. W. S. Hastings.
29. There seems to be some confusion on the spelling of this vessel, between *Luisiano* and *Lousiano.*
30. *El Alamein: The Battle that Turned the Tide of the Second World War* by Bryn Hammond.
31. Some references state that the ship was sunk outside Tobruk harbour.
32. www.wrecksite.eu
33. Government casualty documents, 1942.
34. *Ibid.*
35. *Pendulum of War: The Three Battles of El Alamein* by Niall Barr.
36. *Alamein* by Stephen Bungay.
37. *Generals at War: Alamein* – Discovery Military documentary.
38. *The Memoirs of Field Marshal The Viscount Montgomery of Alamein K.G.*

39. *The Art of War* by Sun Tzu, edited by Samuel B. Griffith, detailing the treatise of the military strategist and tactician written in the 6th century BC.
40. *Pendulum of War: The Three Battles of El Alamein* by Niall Barr.
41. *Ibid.*
42. *Ibid.*
43. *El Alamein: The Battle that Turned the Tide of the Second World War* by Bryn Hammond.
44. *The Diary of a Desert Rat* by R. L. Crimp.
45. *Alamein* by C. E. Lucas Phillips.
46. *Pendulum of War: The Three Battles of El Alamein* by Niall Barr.
47. *El Alamein 1942* by Ken Ford.
48. *Pendulum of War: The Three Battles of El Alamein* by Niall Barr
49. *Alamein* by C. E. Lucas Phillips.
50. *Pendulum of War: The Three Battles of El Alamein* by Niall Barr.
51. *Images of War.*
52. *The War Illustrated.*
53. *Alamein* by C. E. Lucas Phillips.
54. *End of the Beginning* by Tim Clayton & Phil Craig.
55. *Alamein* by C. E. Lucas Phillips.
56. *Pendulum of War: The Three Battles of El Alamein* by Niall Barr.
57. *Ibid.*
58. *Alamein* by C. E. Lucas Phillips.
59. In their book *End of the Beginning*, Tim Clayton and Phil Craig put the figure as eighty-seven tanks destroyed.
60. *Alamein* by C. E. Lucas Phillips.
61. *El Alamein 1942* by Ken Ford.
62. *Hellfire Tonight* – the diary of Albert Martin of 'S' Company 2nd Battalion The Rifle Brigade.
63. *Pendulum of War: The Three Battles of El Alamein* by Niall Barr.
64. *Ibid.*
65. *Alamein: War Without Hate* by John Bierman & Colin Smith.
66. *Alamein* by C. E. Lucas Phillips.
67. *Pendulum of War: The Three Battles of El Alamein* by Niall Barr.
68. *Alamein* by C. E. Lucas Phillips.
69. 2nd Battalion Rifle Brigade War Diaries 1942.
70. *The Rifle Brigade in the Second World War, 1939-1945* by Maj. R. H. W. S. Hastings.
71. *Alamein* by C. E. Lucas Phillips.
72. There are a number of different estimates as to the actual number of Axis tanks; I have used the estimate provided by Lucas Phillips.
73. *Alamein* by C. E. Lucas Phillips.
74. *Pendulum of War: The Three Battles of El Alamein* by Niall Barr.
75. *Alamein* by C. E. Lucas Phillips.
76. *Ibid.*
77. *Ibid.*
78. *Ibid.*
79. *All Hell Let Loose* by Max Hastings.
80. *Pendulum of War: The Three Battles of El Alamein* by Niall Barr
81. *Ibid.*
82. 2nd RB also attacked without supporting barrage.
83. *El Alamein: The Battle that Turned the Tide of the Second World War* by Bryn Hammond.
84. *Ibid.*
85. *Ibid.*
86. They had been trying to find the Brigade HQ among the slit trenches and minefields full of 'S' mines. They never found the HQ, and needed the help of GOC 1st Armoured to find their way out of the maze.
87. *The Rifle Brigade in the Second World War, 1939-1945* by Maj. R. H. W. S. Hastings.

88. *Alamein* by C. E. Lucas Phillips and *The Rifle Brigade in the Second World War, 1939-1945* by Maj. R. H. W. S. Hastings.

89. Michael Henry Mosley was the son of the Bishop of Southwell, and was born in 1912 near Basingstoke. Originally intending to enter the church, he answered the call of war and joined the battalion in October 1940, receiving the MC for his actions during a night patrol at the Battle of Sidi Saleh. Following his death, his father presented a beautiful playing field to the village of Hannington as a lasting memorial to his son, who shares a grave with Rifleman Wade at the El Alamein cemetery. On 2 March 2010, Mosley's medals were presented to the Royal Green Jackets Museum.

90. Lucas Phillips states that they were killed by machine-gun fire.

91. RB Chronicle vol. 5, 1996.

92. *Hellfire Tonight* – the diary of Albert Martin of 'S' Company 2nd Battalion The Rifle Brigade.

93. *Ibid.*

94. *The Rifle Brigade in the Second World War, 1939-1945* by Maj. R. H. W. S. Hastings.

95. *El Alamein: The Battle that Turned the Tide of the Second World War* by Bryn Hammond.

96. *Hellfire Tonight* – the diary of Albert Martin of 'S' Company 2nd Battalion The Rifle Brigade.

97. *El Alamein* by John Sadler.

98. *Ibid.*

99. *Alamein* by C. E. Lucas Phillips.

100. *El Alamein* by John Sadler and *Pendulum of War: The Three Battles of El Alamein* by Niall Barr.

101. *Pendulum of War: The Three Battles of El Alamein* by Niall Barr.

102. *Pendulum of War: The Three Battles of El Alamein* by Niall Barr and *End of the Beginning* by Tim Clayton & Phil Craig.

103. *Pendulum of War: The Three Battles of El Alamein* by Niall Barr.

104. *The Rommel Papers* edited by B. H. Liddell-Hart.

105. *Alamein: War Without Hate* by John Bierman & Colin Smith.

106. *Pendulum of War: The Three Battles of El Alamein* by Niall Barr.

107. *Alamein* by C. E. Lucas Phillips.

108. *The Rommel Papers* edited by B. H. Liddell-Hart.

109. *Ibid.*

110. *Ibid.*

111. *Alamein* by C. E. Lucas Phillips.

112. *Alamein* by C. E. Lucas Phillips.

113. Rommel was still under the impression that the 7th had not moved north of the inter-corps line.

114. *Pendulum of War: The Three Battles of El Alamein* by Niall Barr.

115. *Alamein* by C. E. Lucas Phillips.

116. *Pendulum of War: The Three Battles of El Alamein* by Niall Barr.

117. *Alamein* by C. E. Lucas Phillips.

118. *El Alamein* by John Sadler.

119. *Alamein* by C. E. Lucas Phillips.

120. *Alamein* by Stephen Bungay.

121. *El Alamein: The Battle that Turned the Tide of the Second World War* by Bryn Hammond.

122. *Finest Years: Churchill as Warlord 1940-45* by Max Hastings.

123. Conversations with von Thoma – National Archives reference CAB/66/31/49.

124. *Alamein* by Stephen Bungay.

125. *El Alamein* by John Sadler.

126. *El Alamein: The Battle that Turned the Tide of the Second World War* by Bryn Hammond.

127. *Alamein* by Stephen Bungay.

128. *Alamein* by C. E. Lucas Phillips.

129. *All Hell Let Loose* by Max Hastings.

130. *The Rommel Papers* edited by B. H. Liddell-Hart.

131. *Finest Years: Churchill as Warlord 1940-45* by Max Hastings.

132. *End of the Beginning* by Tim Clayton & Phil Craig.
133. *Ibid.*
134. *War Diaries 1939-1945: Field Marshal Lord Alanbrooke* edited by Alex Danchev and Daniel Todman.
135. Apart from a false alarm in September 1940.
136. *Rifles* by Mark Urban.
137. *End of the Beginning* by Tim Clayton & Phil Craig.
138. *Pendulum of War: The Three Battles of El Alamein* by Niall Barr
139. *Ibid.*
140. *Auchinleck* by John Connell.
141. *End of the Beginning* by Tim Clayton & Phil Craig.
142. *Alamein* by Stephen Bungay.
143. *What did you do in the War, Auntie?: The BBC At War 1939-1945* by Tom Hickman.
144. *Never Give In!: The Best of Winston Churchill's Speeches* selected by Winston S. Churchill.
145. *What did you do in the War, Auntie?: The BBC At War 1939-1945* by Tom Hickman.
146. *Pendulum of War: The Three Battles of El Alamein* by Niall Barr.
147. *El Alamein* by John Sadler.
148. *Pendulum of War: The Three Battles of El Alamein* by Niall Barr.
149. *End of the Beginning* by Tim Clayton & Phil Craig.
150. In *Pendulum of War* it states that this was five miles.
151. *Pendulum of War: The Three Battles of El Alamein* by Niall Barr.
152. *Pendulum of War: The Three Battles of El Alamein* by Niall Barr.
153. *A Noble Crusade: The History of Eighth Army 1941-45* by Richard Doherty.
154. *Images of War*.
155. 7th Motor Brigade War Diaries 1943.
156. *The Rifle Brigade in the Second World War, 1939-1945* by Maj. R. H. W. S. Hastings.
157. 2nd Battalion Rifle Brigade War Diaries 1942.
158. *Hellfire Tonight* – the diary of Albert Martin of 'S' Company 2nd Battalion The Rifle Brigade.
159. *Military Illustrated* magazine, June 2002.
160. 2nd Battalion Rifle Brigade War Diaries 1942.
161. *Afrika Korps at War* by George Forty.
162. 2nd Battalion Rifle Brigade War Diaries 1942.
163. *The Rommel Papers* edited by B. H. Liddell-Hart.
164. *Alamein* by Stephen Bungay.
165. *Images of War*.
166. *Alamein: War Without Hate* by John Bierman & Colin Smith.
167. *The Rifle Brigade in the Second World War, 1939-1945* by Maj. R. H. W. S. Hastings.
168. The initial attacks by the First Army, after Operation Torch, had been successful, against an enemy taken by surprise. This was soon corrected when Hitler reinforced them, but the comment clearly shows the stress Rommel was under.
169. *The Rommel Papers* edited by B. H. Liddell-Hart.
170. *Hellfire Tonight* – the diary of Albert Martin of 'S' Company 2nd Battalion The Rifle Brigade.
171. *The Rommel Papers* edited by B. H. Liddell-Hart.
172. *Ibid.*
173. *Ibid.*
174. 2nd Battalion Rifle Brigade War Diaries 1942.
175. *Ibid.*
176. *Alamein: War Without Hate* by John Bierman & Colin Smith.
177. *The Times* newspaper, 19 November 1942.
178. *El Alamein* by John Sadler.
179. 'The Army Medical Services during the 1939-1945 War' held at the Wellcome Foundation.
180. *Alamein* by Stephen Bungay.
181. *Forgotten Voices of the Second World War* by Max Arthur.
182. *Images of War*.

183. *The Daily Telegraph World War II Eyewitness Experience* magazine collection.
184. *Generals at War: Alamein* – Discovery Military documentary.
185. *Forgotten Voices of the Second World War* by Max Arthur.
186. *Alamein* by Stephen Bungay.
187. *Ibid.*
188. *The Armies of Rommel* by George Forty.
189. *Finest Years: Churchill as Warlord 1940-45* by Max Hastings.
190. *Alamein* by Stephen Bungay.

Chapter 9

1. *Pendulum of War: The Three Battles of El Alamein* by Niall Barr.
2. *The Memoirs of Field Marshal The Viscount Montgomery of Alamein K.G.*
3. *The Times* newspaper, Wednesday 16th December 1942.4. *The Rommel Papers* edited by B. H. Liddell-Hart.
4. *Afrika Korps at War* by George Forty.
5. *War Diaries 1939-1945: Field Marshal Lord Alanbrooke* edited by Alex Danchev and Daniel Todman.
6. *Ibid.*
7. *The Rommel Papers* edited by B. H. Liddell-Hart.
8. *Alamein* by Jon Latimer.
9. *Afrika Korps at War* by George Forty.
10. *The Rommel Papers* edited by B. H. Liddell-Hart.
11. *Afrika Korps at War* by George Forty.
12. *The Rommel Papers* edited by B. H. Liddell-Hart.
13. *The War Illustrated.*
14. *A Noble Crusade: The History of Eighth Army 1941-45* by Richard Doherty.
15. Also known as Wadi Zemzem.
16. *The Rommel Papers* edited by B. H. Liddell-Hart.
17. *Ibid.*
17. 5th *Panzerarmee* and the *Deutsch-Italienische Panzerarmee.*
18. *The Rommel Papers* edited by B. H. Liddell-Hart.
19. 7th Motor Brigade War Diaries 1943.
20. *A Noble Crusade: The History of Eighth Army 1941-45* by Richard Doherty.
21. *The Rommel Papers* edited by B. H. Liddell-Hart.
22. *Alamein: War Without Hate* by John Bierman & Colin Smith.
21. *The War Illustrated*
22. *The Memoirs of Field Marshal The Viscount Montgomery of Alamein K.G.*
23. *A Noble Cruade: The History of Eighth Army 1941-45* by Richard Doherty.
24. 7th Motor Brigade War Diaries 1943.
25. *Ibid.*
26. *Images of War.*
27. *Double Cross* by Ben Macintyre.
28. *Operation Mincemeat* by Ben Macintyre.
29. *The Chronicle of War* by Paul Brewer.
30. *A Brilliant Little Operation* by Paddy Ashdown.
31. *The Second World War* by Antony Beevor.
32. *Hitler's Mediterranean Gamble* by Douglas Porch.
33. *Battlefield* – Discovery History programme.
34. *Hitler's Mediterranean Gamble* by Douglas Porch.
35. *Masters and Commanders* by Andrew Roberts.
36. *Never Give In!: The Best of Winston Churchill's Speeches* selected by Winston S. Churchill (abridged version of the speech).
37. *Desert Rats at War* by George Forty.

38. *Churchill: The Victorian Man of Action* by David Jablonsky.
39. *Never Give In!: The Best of Winston Churchill's Speeches* selected by Winston S. Churchill.
40. *The Desert War* by George Forty.
41. *Hitler's Mediterranean Gamble* by Douglas Porch.
42. *Alamein* by Stephen Bungay.
43. *Hitler's Mediterranean Gamble* by Douglas Porch.
44. *The Rommel Papers* edited by B. H. Liddell-Hart.
45. The new versatile Panzer Mk V Panther incorporated several of the features of the Russian T-34, including sloped armour, 75-mm gun, wide tracks and a powerful V12 engine – a welcome addition to the Axis armament but not in sufficient numbers to make a difference.
46. The eleven 60-ton Panzer VI Tigers, which Hitler assured Kesselring would be decisive in Tunisia, were nicknamed 'furniture vans' by the troops. Proving unreliable, they guzzled precious petrol at the rate of just under a gallon a mile, making the Sherman tank appear almost fuel-efficient, and chewed up tarmac, collapsed bridges and, despite their size, were still vulnerable to the 6-pounder anti-tank guns.
47. *Hitler's Mediterranean Gamble* by Douglas Porch.
48. As Rommel feared in the letter to his wife of 13 November.
49. *The Rommel Papers* edited by B. H. Liddell-Hart.
50. *Alamein: War Without Hate* by John Bierman & Colin Smith.
51. *Masters and Commanders* by Andrew Roberts.
52. *The Rommel Papers* edited by B. H. Liddell-Hart.
53. *The Illustrated London News.*
54. *Ibid.*
55. *The Memoirs of Field Marshal The Viscount Montgomery of Alamein K.G.*
56. *The Rommel Papers* edited by B. H. Liddell-Hart.
57. *Ibid.*
58. *Churchill's Desert Rats 2* by Patrick Delaforce.
59. *Tigers in Combat* Vol. 1 by Wolfgang Schneider.
60. *Turning the Tide* by Nigel Cawthorne.
61. *Churchill's Desert Rats 2* by Patrick Delaforce.
62. *Ibid.*
63. *Ibid.*
64. *Ibid.*
65. *Hitler's Mediterranean Gamble* by Douglas Porch.
66. *The Memoirs of Field Marshal The Viscount Montgomery of Alamein K.G.*
67. *Hitler's Mediterranean Gamble* by Douglas Porch.
68. *The Rommel Papers* edited by B. H. Liddell-Hart.
69. *The Rifle Brigade in the Second World War, 1939-1945* by Maj. R. H. W. S. Hastings.
70. *Hellfire Tonight* – the diary of Albert Martin of 'S' Company 2nd Battalion The Rifle Brigade.
71. *Hellfire Tonight* – the diary of Albert Martin of 'S' Company 2nd Battalion The Rifle Brigade.
72. *Hellfire Tonight* – the diary of Albert Martin of 'S' Company 2nd Battalion The Rifle Brigade.
73. 7th Motor Brigade War Diaries 1943.
74. 2nd Battalion Rifle Brigade War Diaries 1942
75. *Ibid.*
76. *Hellfire Tonight* – the diary of Albert Martin of 'S' Company 2nd Battalion The Rifle Brigade.
77. The riflemen rode in trucks, but the War Diaries record these as 'marches'.
78. *The Diary of a Desert Rat* by R. L. Crimp.
79. *A Noble Crusade: The History of Eighth Army 1941-45* by Richard Doherty.
80. *Kasserine Pass 1943* by Steven J. Zaloga.
81. *Hitler's Mediterranean Gamble* by Douglas Porch.
82. *Hitler's Mediterranean Gamble* by Douglas Porch.
83. *Turning the Tide* by Nigel Cawthorne.
84. *The Rifle Brigade in the Second World War, 1939-1945* by Maj. R. H. W. S. Hastings.
85. *Churchill's Desert Rats 2* by Patrick Delaforce.

86. Antony Beevor states that the Desert Air Force harried the retreating German forces, one of the casualties being *Oberst* Claus Schenk Graf von Stauffenberg, who lost a hand and an eye, and was later involved in the 'Valkyrie' plot to assassinate Hitler.

87. *The Rifle Brigade in the Second World War, 1939-1945* by Maj. R. H. W. S. Hastings.

88. *Ibid.*

89. *Ibid.*

90. *Alamein* by C. E. Lucas Phillips.

91. *The Rifle Brigade in the Second World War, 1939-1945* by Maj. R. H. W. S. Hastings.

92. *Churchill's Desert Rats 2* by Patrick Delaforce.

93. A butterfly bomb was a German anti-personnel bomb, so called because of the thin metal outer shell which hinged open when the bomb was deployed. It was dropped from containers holding between two and 108 individual units.

94. *The Rifle Brigade in the Second World War, 1939-1945* by Maj. R. H. W. S. Hastings.

95. *The War Illustrated.*

96. *Kasserine Pass 1943* by Steven J. Zaloga.

97. *The Rifle Brigade in the Second World War, 1939-1945* by Maj. R. H. W. S. Hastings.

98. *Ibid.*

99. *The Rifle Brigade in the Second World War, 1939-1945* by Maj. R. H. W. S. Hastings.

100. 7th Motor Brigade War Diaries 1943.

101. *The Rifle Brigade in the Second World War 1939–1945* by Maj. R. H. W. S. Hastings.

102. Patton had been moved in preparation for Operation Husky.

103. *Alamein: War Without Hate* by John Bierman & Colin Smith.

104. After serving under Eisenhower for Operation Torch, Cunningham returned to his role as C-in-C Mediterranean Fleet in February 1943.

105. *Alamein: War Without Hate* by John Bierman & Colin Smith.

106. John Beksa in the *Daily Mail*, 11 February 2013.

107. *Hitler's Mediterranean Gamble* by Douglas Porch.

108. Antony Beevor also records that on Sunday 18 April, four American fighter squadrons and a squadron of Spitfires jumped a group of sixty-five transports escorted by twenty fighters, in what was to become known as the 'Palm Sunday Turkey Shoot'. The Allied fighters shot down seventy-four aircraft.

109. *The Second World War* by Antony Beevor.

110. *Hitler's Mediterranean Gamble* by Douglas Porch.

111. *The Southern Front* – Time-Life Books.

112. *Churchill's Desert Rats 2* by Patrick Delaforce.

113. 7th Motor Brigade War Diaries 1943.

114. Alexander had originally planned only a minor role for the Americans, but Bradley put pressure on Eisenhower who persuaded Alexander to include the US II Corps taking Bizerta.

115. Djebel Bou Kournine is situated within the Zaghouan area.

116. 2nd Battalion Rifle Brigade War Diaries 1942.

117. Personal recollections of Rifleman Moore – wireless operator.

118. Moore was returned to Britain where he was treated at East Grinstead Cottage Hospital by Sir Archibald McIndoe who was known as a pioneer of plastic surgery techniques, his patients being referred to as the 'Guinea Pigs'.

119. *Hellfire Tonight* – the diary of Albert Martin of 'S' Company 2nd Battalion The Rifle Brigade.

120. *The Rifle Brigade in the Second World War, 1939-1945* by Maj. R. H. W. S. Hastings.

121. *Alamein* by C. E. Lucas Phillips.

122. *The Diary of a Desert Rat* by R. L. Crimp

123. *Hellfire Tonight* – the diary of Albert Martin of 'S' Company 2nd Battalion The Rifle Brigade.

124. *Alamein* by C. E. Lucas Phillips.

125. *The Diary of a Desert Rat* by R. L. Crimp.

126. *Ibid.*

127. *The Rifle Brigade in the Second World War, 1939-1945* by Maj. R. H. W. S. Hastings.

128. *Hellfire Tonight* – the diary of Albert Martin of 'S' Company 2nd Battalion The Rifle Brigade.
129. *Alamein* by C. E. Lucas Phillips.
130. *Hellfire Tonight* – the diary of Albert Martin of 'S' Company 2nd Battalion The Rifle Brigade.
131. *The Diary of a Desert Rat* by R. L. Crimp.
132. 2nd Battalion Rifle Brigade War Diaries 1942.
133. *The Diary of a Desert Rat* by R. L. Crimp.
134. *Hitler's Mediterranean Gamble* by Douglas Porch.
135. *The Rifle Brigade in the Second World War, 1939-1945* by Maj. R. H. W. S. Hastings.
136. *Hitler's Mediterranean Gamble* by Douglas Porch.
137. *Hitler's Mediterranean Gamble* by Douglas Porch.
138. *The Desert War* by George Forty.
139. *The Rifle Brigade in the Second World War, 1939-1945* by Maj. R. H. W. S. Hastings.
140. *The Rifle Brigade in the Second World War, 1939-1945* by Maj. R. H. W. S. Hastings.
141. *Churchill's Desert Rats 2* by Patrick Delaforce.
142. *Alamein* by C. E. Lucas Phillips.
143. *Hitler's Mediterranean Gamble* by Douglas Porch.
144. *The Rifle Brigade in the Second World War, 1939-1945* by Maj. R. H. W. S. Hastings.
145. *Hitler's Mediterranean Gamble* by Douglas Porch.
146. *Turning the Tide* by Nigel Cawthorne.
147. *Churchill's Desert Rats 2* by Patrick Delaforce.
148. *The Diary of a Desert Rat* by R. L. Crimp.
149. *The Rifle Brigade in the Second World War, 1939-1945* by Maj. R. H. W. S. Hastings.
150. *Hitler's Mediterranean Gamble* by Douglas Porch.
151. *The Diary of a Desert Rat* by R. L. Crimp.
152. *The Rifle Brigade in the Second World War, 1939-1945* by Maj. R. H. W. S. Hastings.
153. 2nd Battalion Rifle Brigade War Diaries 1942
154. *Ibid.*
155. Capt. Marten spoke fluent German and would therefore prove an even more valuable asset in these circumstances.
156. Royal Artillery Observation Officer.
157. *The Diary of a Desert Rat* by R. L. Crimp.
158. 2nd Battalion Rifle Brigade War Diaries 1942
159. *Ibid.*
160. *The Diary of a Desert Rat* by R. L. Crimp.
161. Rifleman W. F. W. Harding personal archive.
162. 7th Motor Brigade War Diaries 1943.
163. *The Diary of a Desert Rat* by R. L. Crimp.
164. 2nd Battalion Rifle Brigade War Diaries 1942.
165. *The Rifle Brigade in the Second World War, 1939-1945* by Maj. R. H. W. S. Hastings.
166. 2nd Battalion Rifle Brigade War Diaries 1942.
167. It should be noted that Pearson as a captain in February 1941 accepted the surrender of the Italian Gen. Bergonzoli at Sidi Saleh.
168. It was the 10th Panzer Division that had fought against the 1st RB at Calais, so there was some irony when they surrendered to the 2nd RB in Tunisia.
169. *The Diary of a Desert Rat* by R. L. Crimp.
170. *The Rifle Brigade in the Second World War, 1939-1945* by Maj. R. H. W. S. Hastings.
171. *Afrika Korps at War* by George Forty.
172. *Hitler's Mediterranean Gamble* by Douglas Porch.
173. *The Rommel Papers* edited by B. H. Liddell-Hart.
174. *Rommel: Battles and Campaigns* by Kenneth Macksey.
175. *El Alamein* by John Sadler.
176. *War Diaries 1939-1945: Field Marshal Lord Alanbrooke* edited by Alex Danchev and Daniel Todman.
177. *The Rifle Brigade in the Second World War, 1939-1945* by Maj. R. H. W. S. Hastings.

178. *Images of War.*
179. *The War Illustrated.*
180. *El Alamein* by John Sadler.

Chapter 10

1. *The Memoirs of Field Marshal The Viscount Montgomery of Alamein K.G.*
2. Worth about £3.24 in 2005, as calculated by the National Archives currency converter.
3. *The Rifle Brigade* by Basil Harvey.
4. Private correspondence of Mrs Ann Bayley.
5. *Rifle Brigade Chronicle.*
6. Private correspondence of Mrs Ann Bayley.
7. Ibid
8. *Ibid.*
9. *Ibid.*
10. *Ibid.*
11. *Ibid.*
12. *Ibid.*
13. MP for Oxford, later Lord Hailsham.
14. *Rifle Brigade Chronicle.*
15. Private correspondence of Mrs Ann Bayley.
16. *Up Close and Personal* by David Lee.
17. Obituary held at the Royal Green Jackets Museum.
18. *Rifle Brigade Chronicle*, various copies.
19. Obituary held at the Royal Green Jackets Museum.
20. Taken from the obituaries recorded in the *Rifle Brigade Journal.*
21. Obituary held at the Royal Green Jackets Museum.
22. *Rifles* by Mark Urban.
23. *Images of War.*
24. *Hellfire Tonight* – the diary of Albert Martin of 'S' Company 2nd Battalion The Rifle Brigade.
25. *Rifle Brigade Chronicle*, various copies.
26. 7th Motor Brigade War Diaries 1943.
27. Tom Bird's letter of the 23 August 2006 to the author.
28. Private correspondence of Mrs Ann Bayley.
29. *Ibid.*
30. *The Independent* newspaper – obituaries, 3 May 2004.
31. *The Rifle Brigade in the Second World War, 1939-1945* by Maj. R. H. W. S. Hastings.
32. *Alamein* by Stephen Bungay.
33. *Ibid.*
34. Naval & Military Press
35. *Ibid.*
36. 'The Remembrance Poppy' by Dr Nick Saunders in *Military History* magazine, November 2011.
37. *Ibid.*
38. *Family History Monthly.*
39. *The Weekend Trippers* by Carole McEntee-Taylor.
40. *War Diaries 1939-1945: Field Marshal Lord Alanbrooke* edited by Alex Danchev and Daniel Todman.
41. *The Weekend Trippers* by Carole McEntee-Taylor.
42. *Memorial Bulletin Magazine*, Spring 2008.
43. *Ibid.*

Bibliography

A Brilliant Little Operation by Paddy Ashdown, ISBN 9781845137014.
A Noble Crusade: The History of Eighth Army 1941-45 by Richard Doherty, ISBN 9781885119636.
Afrika Korps at War by George Forty, ISBN 0711025797.
Alamein by C. E. Lucas Phillips.
Alamein by Jon Latimer, ISBN 9780719562136.
Alamein by Stephen Bungay, ISBN 1854109294.
Alamein: War Without Hate by John Bierman & Colin Smith, ISBN 9780141004679.
All Hell Let Loose by Max Hastings, ISBN 9780007450725.
Auchinleck by John Connell.
Battlefields of the Second World War by Richard Holmes, ISBN 0563537825.
Battles with Panzers by Patrick Delaforce, ISBN 0750932449.
British Army Handbook 1939-1945 by George Forty, ISBN 9780750914031.
British Military Rifles by Peter Duckers, ISBN 9780747806332.
Churchill by Roy Jenkins, ISBN 0330488058.
Churchill: The Victorian Man of Action by David Jablonsky.
Churchill's Desert Rats 2 by Patrick Delaforce, ISBN 0750929294.
Churchill's Wizards: The British Genius for Deception 1914-1945 by Nicholas Rankin,
    ISBN 9780571221967.
Desert Adversaries by Chris Ellis and George Forty, ISBN 9781840138290.
Desert Rats at War by George Forty, ISBN 071100661X.
Double Cross by Ben Macintyre, ISBN 9781408819906.
El Alamein by Field Marshal Lord Carver, ISBN 1840222204.
El Alamein by John Sadler, ISBN 9781848681019.
El Alamein 1942 by Ken Ford, ISBN 1841768677.
El Alamein: The Battle that Turned the Tide of the Second World War by Bryn Hammond,
    ISBN 9781849086400.
End of the Beginning by Tim Clayton & Phil Craig, ISBN 0340766808.
Finest Years: Churchill as Warlord 1940-45 by Max Hastings, ISBN 9780007263677.
Focus on Courage by Sir Christopher Wallace and Maj. Ron Cassidy, ISBN 0954937015.
Forgotten Voices of the Second World War by Max Arthur, ISBN 9780091917746.
Hellfire Tonight by Albert Martin, ISBN 1857760514.
Hitler's Mediterranean Gamble by Douglas Porch, ISBN 0297846329.
Hitler's War Directives 1939-1945 edited by H.R. Trevor-Roper.
Jackets of Green by Arthur Bryant, ISBN 0002117231.
Jerusalem: The Biography by Simon Sebag Montefiore, ISBN 9780753828793.
Kasserine Pass 1943 by Steven J. Zaloga, ISBN 9781841769141.
Libya Geographical Map published by Gizi Map, ISBN 9638680806.
Masters and Commanders by Andrew Roberts, ISBN 9780141029269.
Monuments to Courage by David Harvey, ISBN 9781847348098.
Never Give In!: The Best of Winston Churchill's Speeches selected by Winston S. Churchill,
    ISBN 0712667210.

Officers of the Rifle Brigade 1800-1965 by Maj. R. D. Cassidy MBE.
Operation Compass 1940 by Jon Latimer, ISBN 1855329670.
Operation Mincemeat by Ben Macintyre, ISBN 9781408809211.
Pendulum of War: The Three Battles of El Alamein by Niall Barr, ISBN 022406195X.
Rifleman: A Front Line Life by Victor Gregg with Rick Stroud, ISBN 9781408813966.
Rifles by Mark Urban, ISBN 0571216803.
Rommel: Battles and Campaigns by Kenneth Macksey.
Sherman M4 published by Cassell.
The Allied Convoy System 1939-1945 by Arnold Hague. ISBN 1861761473.
The Armies of Rommel by George Forty, ISBN 9781854093790.
The Army at War published by the Ministry of Information.
The Art of War by Sun Tzu, edited by Samuel B. Griffith, ISBN 0195014766.
The Battle of Egypt published by the Ministry of Information.
The Chronicle of War by Paul Brewer, ISBN 9781844422029.
The Crucible of War by Barrie Pitt, ISBN 0304359513.
The Defence of the Realm: The Authorized History of MI5 by Christopher Andrew, ISBN 9780713998856.
The Desert War by George Forty, ISBN 0750928107.
The Desert War: The North African Campaign 1940-43 by Alan Moorehead, ISBN 9780140275148.
The Diary of a Desert Rat by R. L. Crimp, ISBN 0850520398.
The Eighth Army published by the Ministry of Information.
The Man Who Broke into Auschwitz by Denis Avey, ISBN 9781444714197.
The Memoirs of Field Marshal The Viscount Montgomery of Alamein K.G.
The Rifle Brigade by Basil Harvey – 'Famous Regiments' series.
The Rifle Brigade in the Second World War, 1939-1945 by Maj. R. H. W. S. Hastings.
The Rommel Papers edited by B. H. Liddell-Hart.
The Rough Guide to Egypt, ISBN 9781843532101.
The Rough Guide to Tunisia, ISBN 9781843534877.
The Second World War by Antony Beevor, ISBN 9780297844976.
The Southern Front published by Time-Life Books, ISBN 0809470160.
The Weekend Trippers by Carole McEntee-Taylor, ISBN 9781904408277.
Tigers in Combat Vol. 1 by Wolfgang Schneider, ISBN 9780811731713.
Together We Stand by James Holland, ISBN 9780007176472.
Turning the Tide by Nigel Cawthorne, ISBN 0572028415.
Ultra Goes to War by Ronald Lewis, ISBN 9780141390420.
Up Close and Personal by David Lee, ISBN 139781853676680.
War Diaries 1939-1945: Field Marshal Lord Alanbrooke edited by Alex Danchev and Daniel Todman, ISBN 0297607316.
War Surgery and Medicine by T. Stout and M. Duncan.
What did you do in the War, Auntie?: The BBC At War 1939-1945 by Tom Hickman, ISBN 0563371161.
World War II Axis Booby Traps and Sabotage Tactics by Gordon L. Rottman, ISBN 9781846034503.
World War II: The Sharp End by John Ellis, ISBN 9781845134594.
Zulu Rising by Ian Knight, ISBN 9781405091855.

Daily Mail, 22 September 2011 and 11 February 2013.
The Independent, 3 May 2004.
The London Gazette, 14 January 1943.
The Times, 19 November 1942 and 1 December 2000.

BBC History Magazine, Q & A by Roger Moorhouse.
Britain at War Magazine, 'Leading from the Front' by Stephen Snelling, December 2012.
Britain at War Magazine, 'UXB Malta' by S. A. M. Hudson, December 2012.
Britain at War Magazine, interview by Tony Glenhill with Lord Ashcroft.
Britain at War Magazine supplement – British Gallantry Awards.
Family History Monthly

Illustrated London News
Images of War
Memorial Bulletin Magazine, Spring 2008.
Military History magazine, 'Codes and Ciphers', February 2012.
Military History magazine, 'History of the British Army – Waterloo, 18 June 1815', May 2012.
Military History magazine, 'Invasion of the Third Reich' by Patrick Delaforce, July 2011.
Military History magazine, 'The Remembrance Poppy' by Dr Nick Saunders, November 2011.
Military History magazine, 'Victorian Army', December 2011.
Military Illustrated magazine, March 2000 and June 2002.
Military Times magazine, 'Fading Glory' by Michael Prestwich, February 2011.
Military Times magazine, December 2010.
The Daily Telegraph World War II Eyewitness Experience magazine collection.
The Essex Family Historian, 'One Man's War' by Betty Whittingham, September 2012.
The War Illustrated – various volumes.

http://en.academic.ru/dic.nsf/enwiki/598267
http://en.wikipedia.org/wiki/Top_(sailing_ship)
http://samilitaryhistory.org/vol132jj.html
http://ww2talk.com/forums/page/index.html
https://maps.google.co.uk
www.2-15battalionaif.net.au/index.php/battalion-history/introduction-a-overview/173-overview
www.ancientegypt.co.uk/geography/home.html
www.atsremembered.org.uk/templetonsheetpdf.pdf – memories of Sgt Betty Cory.
www.bbc.co.uk/ww2peopleswar/stories/86/a6951486.shtml – 'A Disaster of WW2?' by John Constant.
www.bbcattic.org/ww2peopleswar/stories/43/a3203443.shtml – 'Journey into the Unknown' by William Ledbury
www.cgsc.edu/carl/resources/csi/hart/hart.asp
www.convoyweb.org.uk
www.desertrats.org.uk
www.distancecalculator.com
www.Firstworldwar.com
www.google.co.uk/ig/directory?type=gadgets&url=www.google.com/ig/modules/builtin_weather.xml
www.nationalarchives.gov.uk/currency/default0.asp
www.naval-history.net/xAH-WSConvoys03-1940.htm
www.naval-military-press.com
www.nzetc.org/tm/scholarly/tei-WH2-2Epi-c3-WH2-2Epi-i.html – 'The Official History of New Zealand in the Second World War 1939-1945: Ruweisat Ridge' by R. Walker
www.rgjmuseum.co.uk
www.riflebrigadehistory.info
www.stephen-stratford.co.uk/gallantry.htm
www.timeanddate.com/date/duration.html
www.victoriacross.org.uk
www.websters-online-dictionary.org
www.what-if-you.com/ww2memorial/wwii__chapter_16.htm
www.wikipedia.org
www.wrecksite.eu

Battlefield – Discovery History television programme.
Battlefield: El Alamein – DVD Ref. No. 5022802210079.
Blood and Bullets documentary on Royal Army Medical Corps.
Britain's Greatest Codebreaker – television programme for Channel 4.
British Campaigns: Western Desert – DVD Ref. No. 5019322062783.
Desert Battles of World War II – DVD Ref. No. 5023093051488.
Generals at War: Alamein – Discovery Military documentary.

Gladiator – starring Russell Crowe, directed by Ridley Scott.
Great Military Blunders: Politics by Other Means – Darlow Smithson Productions documentary.
Ice Cold in Alex – starring John Mills, imdb.com/title/tt0053935.
Sandhurst – television programme for the BBC.
The Desert Rats – starring Richard Burton, imdb.com/title/tt0045679.

1st Battalion Rifle Brigade War Diaries 1942 – WO 169/5054, held in the National Archives.
2nd Battalion Rifle Brigade War Diaries 1942 – WO 169/5055, held in the National Archives.
7th Motor Brigade War Diaries 1943 – WO 169/8869, held in the National Archives.
41st Royal Tank Regiment War Diary, held in the National Archives.
47th Royal Tank Regiment War Diary, held in the National Archives.
Bishopsgate Museum.
Cabinet document held in the National Archives, ref. CAB/66/11/42.
Churchill Museum and Cabinet War Rooms.
Conversations with von Thoma held in the National Archives, ref. CAB/66/31/49.
Details of the War Establishment II/231/3 for a Motor Battalion.
Enemy attack report contained in the 2nd Battalion Rifle Brigade War Diary, July 1942.
Government casualty documents, 1942.
Imperial War Museum.
Movement Order contained in the 2nd Battalion Rifle Brigade War Diaries, held in the National
    Archives.
National Army Museum.
Official Snipe report contained in the 2nd Battalion Rifle Brigade War Diaries 1942 – WO 169/5055.
Operation Order No. 2, dated 12 April 1942, held in the National Archives.
Operational Order No. 27, dated 2 August 1942, held in the National Archives.
Operational Order No. 29, dated 15 August 1942, held in the National Archives.
Patrol report of 23/24 July 1942 written by Capt. Whigham, contained in the War Diary of the 2nd RB,
    held in the National Archives.
Patrol report of 24/25 July 1942 written by Capt. Sturt, contained in the War Diary of the 2nd RB, held
    in the National Archives.
Patrol report of 24/25 July 1942 written by Maj. Bird, contained in the War Diary of the 2nd RB, held in
    the National Archives.
Patrol report of 3/4 September 1942 written by Capt. Sturt, contained in the War Diary of the 2nd RB,
    held in the National Archives.
Personal narrative written by Maj. Trappes-Lomax.
Personal recollection of Eddie Blacker.
Personal recollection of Rifleman Moore.
Photograph of the officers of The 2nd Battalion The Rifle Brigade, provided by the Royal Green Jackets
    Museum and Mrs Ann Bayley.
Private correspondence of Mrs Ann Bayley.
Recording of a speech by Lt Col. Victor Buller Turner given to the author by Eddie Blacker.
Report on Calais by Maj. R. D. Cassidy.
Rifle Brigade Association Journal, 2002, 2008, 2009 and 2010.
Rifle Brigade Association Journal, 2008 vol. 17, recounting the speech made at the El Alamein Dinner
    by Brig. Dunphie; citations provided by Maj. R. Cassidy MBE and Memorialisation of Sgt Swann
    Recollections by his son K. J. Swann. Referred to in the Endnotes as "Brig. Dunphie's El Alamein
    Dinner Speech."
Rifle Brigade Chronicle, various copies.
Rifleman W. F. W. Harding personal archive.
Royal Artillery Museum.
Royal Green Jackets Museum.
'The Army Medical Services during the 1939-1945 War' held at the Wellcome Foundation.
Tom Bird's letter of 23 August 2006 to the author.
Tom Bird's speech to the Rifle Brigade Dinner.

Verbal history given by Douglas Waller and held at the Imperial War Museum – ref. 23447.
Verbal history given by Frederick Jones and held at the Imperial War Museum – ref. 10689/3.
Verbal history given by John Luxford and held at the Imperial War Museum – ref. 10485/4.
Verbal history given by Sgt Swann and held at the Imperial War Museum – ref. 27437.
Verbal history given by Tom Bird and held at the Imperial War Museum – ref. 16303.

Index

Eighth Army Forces

Corps

Divisions

Brigades

Regiments